I0065109

DATA RESOURCE INTEGRATION

UNDERSTANDING AND RESOLVING
A DISPARATE DATA RESOURCE

MICHAEL H. BRACKETT

Published by:
Technics Publications, LLC
Post Office Box 161
Bradley Beach, NJ 07720 U.S.A.
www.technicspub.com

Edited by Carol Lehn
Cover design by Mark Brye

All rights reserved. No part of this book may be reproduced or transmitted in any form or by any means, electronic or mechanical, including photocopying, recording or by any information storage and retrieval system, without written permission from the publisher, except for the inclusion of brief quotations in a review.

The author and publisher have taken care in the preparation of this book, but make no expressed or implied warranty of any kind and assume no responsibility for errors or omissions. No liability is assumed for incidental or consequential damages in connection with or arising out of the use of the information or programs contained herein.

All trade and product names are trademarks, registered trademarks, or service marks of their respective companies, and are the property of their respective holders and should be treated as such.

This book is printed on acid-free paper.

Copyright © 2012 by Michael Brackett

ISBN, print ed.   978-1-9355042-3-8

First Printing 2012
Library of Congress Control Number: 2011943081

ATTENTION SCHOOLS AND BUSINESSES: Technics Publications books are available at quantity discounts with bulk purchase for educational, business, or sales promotional use. For information, please write to Technics Publications, PO Box 161, Bradley Beach, NJ 07090, or email Steve Hoberman, President of Technics Publications, at me@stevehoberman.com.

Dedicated to all of the
business professionals and data management professionals
who want to make a difference!

CONTENTS AT A GLANCE

CONTENTS

FIGURES

PREFACE

Organizations have a choice! They can choose how they perceive the business environment and how they operate in that environment. They can choose how to build and maintain a data resource that supports their operation in the business environment. The data resource is not destined! An organization has the free will to choose whether their data resource is formally developed, or just allowed to develop.

Never Cease To Be Amazed

I never cease to be amazed at the ingenious ways that organizations can screw up their data resource. Just when I think I've seen it all, I go into another organization and look at their disparate data resource. My first thought is *What the (you fill in the phrase) is this*? Usually someone will start into a lengthy explanation about how things evolved over the years. About five minutes into the explanation I get a real splitting headache.

What organizations do to their data resource is totally unnecessary and unreasonable. Organizations seem to lack the basic concepts, principles, and techniques for building and maintaining a high quality data resource, or even a high quality database. They allow brute-force-physical approaches that mush the data around to meet current needs and deadlines.

I've been in the data management business nearly 50 years, yet I haven't seen it all yet. I still encounter disasters of monumental proportions. I often wonder *What were people thinking when they built these databases.* It reminds me of the popular television show What Were You Thinking?

I frequently ask people where they got their knowledge and skills for building a data resource, or even a database. I get answers like *I took a vendor class once, I found a book in the library, or It just seemed to be the right thing to do.* The best I've heard was *We were in a hurry so I just did what needed to be done.*

Experiences

Before I retired from the State of Washington, I used to be concerned that all of the data resource problems would be solved before I had a chance to work on data resource integration. To my surprise, and horror, they hadn't been resolved by the time I retired or even today, some 15 years after I retired. Actually, the situation has gotten worse—much worse. It seems that the hype is driving the data resource further into disparity.

I heard an interesting comment about *turning data into useful answers.* I thought that would be a good theme for resolving disparate data. The theme is turning disparate data into comparate data and comparate data into information that is useful to the business. After all, the basic objective of data resource management is to manage a set of raw material (data) that can be used to prepare useful answers to the business (information).

I was on a panel at an international conference several years ago with three other prominent industry leaders. A question was asked if any of the panel members had found, seen, or even heard of any organization, public or private, that had an organization-wide integrated data resource. The normally outspoken panel members looked at each other in silence and shook their heads. None of them, including me, had been involved with, seen, or heard of any organization with an organization-wide integrated data resource, or even a complete model of their existing data resource.

The question was turned back to the audience—did any audience member know of any organization with an organization-wide integrated data resource or complete data resource model. Did any audience member know of a major segment of an organizations data resource being integrated or modeled? Silence. That's discouraging news indeed.

I was approached by an organization that wanted help with understanding and integrating their disparate data resource. During an initial interview they emphasized that their data were a corporate asset and very critical to the continued success of the organization. After expounding on the critical nature of a valuable resource, which caused me to wonder if they were trying to convince me or themselves, they finally got to the project at hand. The first task they wanted me to perform was to convince executive management that resolving the data disparity and developing an integrated data resource was necessary, and worth the effort and expense they had outlined in their proposal. Needless to say, the project was flawed from the beginning and I chose not to continue.

I recently gave a presentation to a professional group based on *Data Resource Simplexity*. One person asked me what they should do if only a one-percent chance existed that the organization would follow what I had just explained. First, I pointed out that the organization had a choice about improving the quality of their data resource. Then I asked if his organization was satisfied with the quality of their data resource. Could they meet the business information demand? Were there any concerns over the quality of the information received? Did business professionals fully understand the data? He received the message.

After another presentation I gave on *Data Resource Simplexity,* a prominent person stated that he agreed with everything I said, but stated that no organization would do all those things. Did I really expect an organization to perform all those tasks and follow all those principles?

I gave him two reasons why they should. First, those concepts, principles, and techniques are the detail of a data management profession. If a person wants to be a data management professional, they need to follow those concepts, principles, and techniques. Second, would he want to ride on an airplane, boat, or train, where the builder didn't have the time for all of the detail and simply cut corners because they didn't want to do something? Probably not. Further, a data resource supports many disciplines and professions. If those disciplines and professions are to do things right, then the data resource must provide the right data. He received the message, but had no idea how he would implement the concepts, principles, and techniques in his organization.

The excuse that I often get is that it's just too expensive to resolve the data disparity. Resolving data disparity is not worth the expense. My response is along the lines of what's the cost of wrong business decisions, inappropriate business actions, missed opportunities, and so on? What's the impact on public sector citizens and private sector customers?

A Knotted Jump Rope

I was working in my garage one summer day with the door open for fresh air. One of the girls in the neighborhood came by with a long jump rope that was all in knots. She came up to me and asked if I could help her. I said I could and asked her what was the problem. She said "My jump rope is all tangled up and I can't get it untangled."

I sat down with her and said it's very simple. You have to find one end, find where it comes from, and pull it back through. Then you do the same thing over and over until it's all untangled. I showed her how to do it and she said, "Oh, I can do that." She took the bundle and kept going one knot at a time. It wasn't long until she had the jump rope all untangled, thanked me, and went running down the street to her friends.

I got to thinking that her jump rope is an excellent analogy about what we do to untangle disparate data. We take the disparate data, one piece at a time, and figure out what it is within the context of a common data architecture. When we understand the data, we can begin building a new data resource. The process itself is very simple, it's just very detailed and takes some time to get through all of the *knots*.

I've done considerable reading outside data management about how people face and resolve problems. I learn all I can about how they face the unknown and seemingly insurmountable problems, find a breakthrough, and come to an equitable resolution. I then apply those approaches to data resource management and untangling a disparate data resource.

Critical Resources

The quality of the data resource in most public and private sector organizations today is really bad. The sad news is that the quality is not getting any better: it is getting worse over time. In spite of many new techniques and the continued hyperbole about data resource quality improvement, the quality of the data resource in most organizations is deteriorating.

Every organization has four critical resources that it must properly manage to become and remain a high-quality, fully-successful organization. Those four resources are the human resource, the financial resource, real property, and the data resource. Generally, the first three of those resources are properly managed. However, the data resource is seldom properly managed, which leads to low quality data and to a less than fully successful organization.

One can ask the question what would happen if the first three resources were managed the way that the data resource is currently managed. The answer should be quite clear. Civil and criminal actions are taken for not properly managing the human resource. Civil and criminal actions are also taken for not properly managing the financial resource. The same is true for not properly managing real property, such as the violation of environmental codes, building codes, and so on.

However, the same is not true when the data resource is not properly managed. The data resource can be mismanaged, often to the detriment of the organization, yet few civil or criminal actions are taken. In many situations the reverse is often true. Organizations often require extensive justification for proper management of the data resource, which is implicit approval for the ongoing mismanagement.

I am repeatedly asked why such a situation might be true. The best answer I've found over the years is that the data resource is intangible and inexhaustible. The data resource is not tangible like people, money, or real property. Data cannot be *held in your hand* the same as people, money, and real property. Further, the data resource is inexhaustible because the data can be used over and over again without being depleted. The same is not true for people, money, or real property. They can be exhausted.

The intangible and inexhaustible nature of the data resource seems to be the underlying reason why the data resource is not properly managed as a critical resource of an organization. The lack of proper data resource management has, over the years, led to the existence of large quantities of disparate data. These disparate data are not contributing to a high-quality, fully-successful organization. Further, they will not contribute to such an organization until the current disparity is resolved and future disparity is prevented.

The Answer Is Known

We know why the data resource goes disparate. We know why people don't share disparate data. We know how to understand and resolve existing disparate data. We know how to prevent disparate data from happening. We know how to build a high-quality, sharable data resource within a single enterprise-wide data architecture. We know how to develop a data resource that supports a high-quality, fully-successful organization. So, why don't we use that knowledge?

The answer lies partly in the intangible and inexhaustible nature of the data resource. It lies partly in the hyperbole of quick fixes, silver bullets, and magic wands. It lies partly in the attitude of accepting the routine creation of disparate data while requiring justification to create a high-quality, sharable data resource within a single enterprise-wide data architecture.

The real answer is in the recognition and formal management of data as a critical resource for the organization. Given the current state of the data resource in most organizations, a two-pronged approach is needed. First, the further creation of disparate data must be stopped. Second, the existing disparate data must be resolved. The creation of disparate data must be prevented with good data resource management techniques, and the existing disparate data must be resolved so the data are fully useful to the organization.

Formal data resource management is hard, but it is not impossible. It has never really achieved its promises, and investment in data resource management has been cyclic. It has swung between hyperbole and promise to failure and discouragement. It has not delivered consistently in a reasonable time frame. Data resource management has been a collection of disciplines rather than a formal profession. The only hope is to create a formal, certified, recognized, and respected data management profession that delivers on a high quality data resource that supports current and future business information needs.

Bruno Walter, an orchestral conductor, says that in order to achieve precision, we must concentrate on precision. The same approach is true for data resource quality. In order to achieve quality, you must concentrate on quality. In order to improve understanding, you must concentrate on understanding. In order to achieve data resource integration, you must concentrate on data resource integration.

A Demon Haunted World

I read Carl Sagan's book *The Demon Haunted World: Science as a Candle in the Dark*. The book describes much of the hyperbole and mysticism prominent in the world, both historically and today. Science is emphasized as the discipline for approaching and either substantiating or disproving things, sorting out the facts, and separating the truth from all of the fiction.

Information technology, including data resource management, is characterized by considerable hype and mysticism, much the same as Carl Sagan explains. Architecture is the discipline for approaching the disparity of information technology. The common data architecture that has been developed over the last 20 years is the discipline for approaching the disparate data problem and developing a high quality, sharable data resource. It is the science for data resource management: the candle in the dark for untangling disparate data.

The concept of a common data architecture evolved through the late 1980's and early 1990's and was first presented in *Data Sharing Using a Common Data Architecture* (Brackett, 1994). The concept was developed to resolve the huge quantities of disparate data that exist in the public sector, and to meet the urgent need to identify, understand, and share those data. The book presented the vision, concepts, and techniques for developing a common data architecture.

The concept was excellent and was used on many projects, resulting in considerable input and enhancements. These enhancements, along with the evolution of data warehouse concepts and techniques, led to *The Data Warehouse Challenge: Taming Data Chaos* (Brackett, 1996). The term *data warehouse* was used in the sense of a fully integrated data resource within a common data architecture. The book presented enhancements to the common data architecture and techniques to apply the common data architecture concept to many of the data problems that exist in both public and private sector organizations.

Data Resource Quality: Turning Bad Habits Into Good Practices (Brackett, 2000) put the initial concepts, principles, and techniques in place for properly managing a data resource. After ten years of applying those concepts, principles, and techniques, and getting considerable feedback, revisions were made in *Data Resource Simplexity: How Organizations Choose Data Resource Success Or Failure* (Brackett, 2011). The primary emphasis was on how to stop any further disparity in the data resource.

The Current Book

The current book deals with how to resolve the rampant disparity that currently exists in the data resource of most public and private sector organizations. It builds on *Data Resource Simplexity*, and presents the concepts, principles, and techniques necessary for fully understanding and resolving disparate data and creating a comparate data resource. It describes a sound approach for resolving disparate data that does not rely on hype, silver bullets, or magic wands. The approach has been used in many organizations and has proven to be successful.

After many years of working with disparate data, writing about disparate data, and giving presentations about disparate data, I've amassed considerable material on how to understand and resolve disparate data. That material, along with all of the nitty-gritty detail, is presented in the current book. I may not have covered every single situation that may exist in every organization, but I covered most of the detail. In addition, I've provided the process for understanding and resolving disparate data so that people can use that process to handle any specific situation they may encounter.

At one conference, I gave a tutorial on the Common Data Architecture and data resource integration. After the presentation, one attendee stated that the presentation was very good, but I didn't cover all of the detail that one might encounter when trying to understand and resolve disparate data. His statement was correct, but limited time was available in a tutorial.

The current book describes all of the concepts, principles, and techniques for understanding and resolving disparate data. It provides the detail that couldn't be presented in a conference presentation or even a tutorial. It provides a phased approach that produces results that can be done on-the-fly as an organization continues its business activities. It's based on over 25 years of experience gained as I worked with many public and private sector organizations to build a common data architecture and resolve disparate data.

The current book is not about data integration to temporarily bring data together from different sources and platforms for operational processing. It's about formally and permanently integrating a disparate data resource within a common data architecture, and developing a comparate data resource that meets the business information demand. It's about formally integrating not only the disparate data resource itself, but the disparate data culture managing that data resource. Solving one without the other will not resolve the disparate data problem.

The current book is a paradigm shift that not only changes the future, but also changes the past. How does it change the past? After understanding and resolving disparate data, people will never be able to look at an old data resource in the same way. They will see how the data resource happened and the impacts it caused. They will see a new way to manage data as a critical resource that provides quality information to support the business. People who have been through the process tell me they will never, ever manage data the way they did in the past.

The current book shatters past and present hype about how data should be managed. It shatters terms creating the lexical challenge in data resource management, and presents terms with comprehensive and denotative meanings. As Bruno Walter said about orchestras—to achieve quality, you must concentrate on quality.

Another common saying is that by concentrating on precision one arrives at techniques, but by concentrating on techniques, one does not arrive at precision. The key concept for formal data resource integration is to concentrate on precision, and use techniques that achieve that precision.

Comparison To *Data Resource Simplexity*

I've been asked how the material in *Data Resource Integration* relates to the material in *Data Resource Simplexity*, and whether a person should buy one or the other. Generally, *Data Resource Simplexity* describes how to stop rampant data disparity and *Data Resource Integration* describes how to resolve the existing data disparity. The diagram below shows a more detailed relationship between the two books.

Data Resource Simplexity	Data Resource Integration
1. Rampant Data Disparity	1. Toward A Comparate Data Resource
2. Planned Data Comparity	2. Data Resource Integration Concept
3. Common Data Architecture	3. Integrating The Data Resource
4. Formal Data Names	4. Data Variability
5. Comprehensive Data Definitions	5. Data Inventory Concept
6. Proper Data Structure	6. Data Inventory Process
7. Precise Data Integrity Rules	7. Data Cross-Reference Concept
8. Robust Data Documentation	8. Data Cross-Reference Process
9. Reasonable Data Orientation	9. Preferred Data Concept
10. Acceptable Data Availability	10. Preferred Data Process
11. Adequate Data Responsibility	11. Data Transformation Concept
12. Expanded Data Vision	12. Data Transformation Process
13. Appropriate Data Recognition	13. Integrating The Data Culture
14. A Cultural Choice	14. Managing The Data Resource

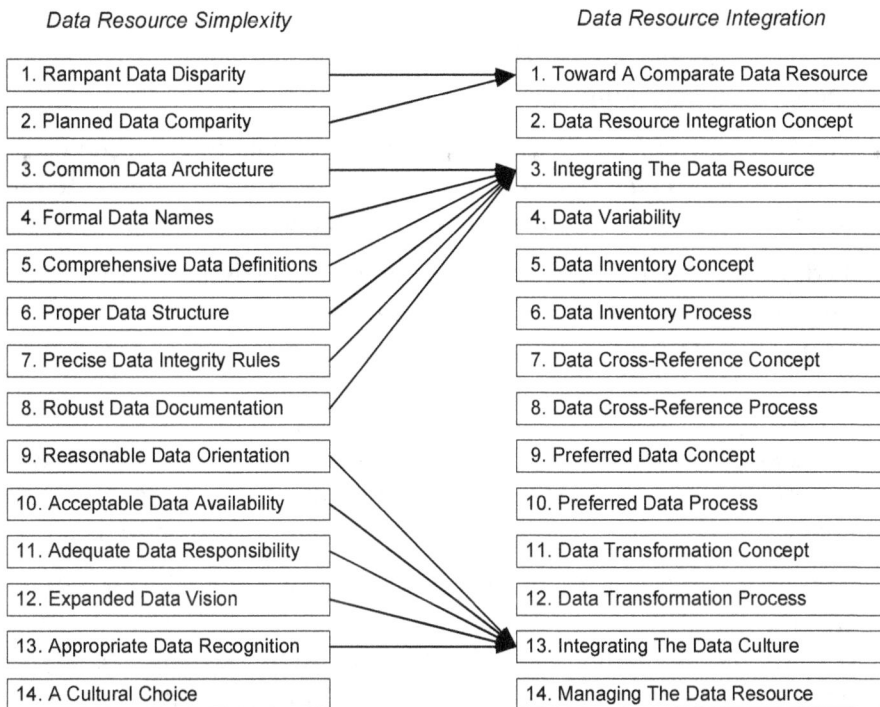

Chapters 1 and 2 of *Data Resource Simplexity* are briefly summarized in Chapter 1 of *Data Resource Integration*, and some new material has been added. Chapter 2 of *Data Resource Integration* provides an overview of data resource integration. Together, Chapters 1 and 2 of *Data Resource Integration* provide the problems leading to disparate data and the concept for resolving that disparity.

Chapters 3 through 8 of *Data Resource Simplexity* have been summarized in Chapter 3 of *Data Resource Integration*, and some new material has been added. Chapters 4 through 12 in *Data Resource Integration* are new material describing the concepts and processes for integrating a disparate data resource. Chapter 4 describes the extent of data variability. Chapters 5 and 6 describe the data inventory concept and process. Chapters 7 and 8 describe the data cross-reference concept and process. Chapters 9 and 10 describe the concept and process for designating a preferred data architecture. Chapters 11 and 12 describe the concept of and process for transforming data. Together, Chapters 4 through 12 of *Data Resource Integration* described the phased approach to integrating a disparate data resource.

Chapters 9 through 12 of *Data Resource Simplexity* have been summarized in Chapter 13 of *Data Resource Integration*, and considerable new material has been added about integrating the data culture. Chapter 14 of *Data Resource Integration* summarizes the effort to manage data as a critical resource of the organization. Together, Chapters 13 and 14 of *Data Resource Integration* provide a cultural approach to managing data as a critical resource.

The Glossary in *Data Resource Integration* includes all of the items from the Glossary in *Data Resource Simplexity* to provide a complete Glossary that helps resolve the lexical challenge in data resource management.

Today, the quality of the data resource is an issue of ever-increasing importance. The quality of the entire data resource, from operational data stores, to true data warehouses, to true data mining is mandatory for a business to be fully successful. That's what the current book is about: improving the quality of data as a critical resource of the organization. It's about understanding the problems and attacking those problems with proven techniques and knowledgeable people to stop the continued creation of disparate data and resolve the existing disparate data.

You won't find little quips and puns in the current book, nor will you find specific problems and disaster stories. You won't find much humor, because the disparate data problem is not humorous—it's deadly serious. You won't find much about sampling, statistics, project management, or justifying the existence of disparate data. You won't find much about charters and job descriptions.

You will find a meat and potatoes approach to improving the quality of the data resource with sound data resource management techniques. You will find techniques to improve data resource quality, techniques to build an integrated data resource within a common data architecture, and techniques to provide sharable data that support business strategies and goals. You will find a definitive description of data architecture and data culture integration.

Audience

Data Resource Integration is a reference book intended for two broad audiences. The first audience is the experienced data management and business professionals who will use the material for resolving the existing data resource disparity rather than living with the disparity and performing repetitive data integration. The second audience is the data management instructors or trainers who will teach the material to those interested in resolving data resource disparity. The book is not intended for general audiences interested in data resource management, nor is it intended for casual reading from cover to cover.

I have been dealing with data in many different public and private sector organizations, large and small, new and old, for nearly 50 years. I've learned how disparate data are created and how a disparate data resource evolved. I have learned how to prevent the creation of disparate data and how to resolve existing disparate data. I have learned how to create a high quality, sharable data resource within an organization-wide common data architecture. The primary purpose of the current book is to pass some of the knowledge and skills I've acquired on to the reader.

If you or your organization have no disparate data and do not ever foresee having disparate data, *Data Resource Integration* is not for you. However, if you do have disparate data in your organization and the situation is getting worse, or you foresee having disparate data in the future, you really need to read *Data Resource Integration* and apply the concepts, principles, and techniques to create a high quality, sharable data resource. I suspect the latter is true.

> Michael Brackett
> Olympic Mountains, Washington
> January, 2012

ACKNOWLEDGEMENTS

I thank all of the business professionals and data management professionals that have contributed their insights about data resource management. Those providing positive insight confirm that I'm on the right track. Those providing negative insight push me to find better approaches to managing data as a critical resource and to presenting those approaches.

I thank my publisher, Steve Hoberman, for all his thought, encouragement, and comments about publishing technical material. He has become a good professional friend as well as a skilled publisher.

Finally, I thank Sandy Hostetter and Eva Smith, who have been long term professional and personal friends. Each has provided tremendous insight into the work I've done and the material I've prepared for managing data as a critical resource of the organization. It's through their support and input that I've made professional achievements.

ABOUT THE AUTHOR

Mr. Brackett retired from the State of Washington in June, 1996, where he was the State's Data Resource Coordinator. He was responsible for developing the State's common data architecture that spans multiple jurisdictions, such as state agencies, local jurisdictions, Indian tribes, public utilities, and Federal agencies, and includes multiple disciplines, such as water resource, growth management, and criminal justice. He is the founder of Data Resource Design and Remodeling and is a Consulting Data Architect specializing in developing integrated data resources.

Mr. Brackett has been in the data management field for nearly 50 years, during which time he developed many innovative concepts and techniques for designing applications and managing data resources. He is the originator of the Common Data Architecture concept, the Data Resource Management Framework, the data naming taxonomy and data naming vocabulary, the Five-Tier Five-Schema concept, the data rule concept, the Business Intelligence Value Chain, the data resource data concept, the architecture-driven data model concept, and many new techniques for understanding and integrating disparate data.

Mr. Brackett has written seven books on the topics of application design, data design, and common data architectures. His books *Data Sharing Using a Common Data Architecture* and *The Data Warehouse Challenge: Taming Data Chaos* describe the concept and uses of a common data architecture for developing an integrated data resource. His book on *Data Resource Quality: Turning Bad Habits into Good Practices* describes how to stop the creation of disparate data. His latest book on *Data Resource Simplexity: How Organizations Choose Data Resource Success Or Failure* describes the approach to data resource management that avoids the creation of disparate data, and sets the stage for the current book. He has written numerous articles and is a well-known international author, speaker, and trainer on data resource management topics.

Mr. Brackett has a BS in Forestry (Forest Management) and a MS in Forestry (Botany) from the University of Washington, and a MS in Soils (Geology) from Washington State University. He was a charter member and is an active member of DAMA-PS, the Seattle Chapter of DAMA International established in 1985. He saw the formation of DAMA National in 1986 and DAMA International in 1988. He served as Vice President of Conferences for DAMA International; as the President of DAMA International from 2000 through 2003; and as Past President of DAMA International for 2004 and 2005. He was the founder and first President of the DAMA International Foundation, an organization established for developing a formal data management profession, and is currently Past President of the DAMA International Foundation. He was the Production Editor of the DAMA-DMBOK released in April, 2009.

Mr. Brackett received DAMA International's Lifetime Achievement Award in 2006 for his work in data resource management, the second person in the history of DAMA International to receive that award (Mr. Brackett presented the first award to John Zachman in 2003). He taught Data Design and Modeling in the Data Resource Management Certificate Program at the University of Washington, and has been a member of the adjunct faculty at Washington State University and The Evergreen State College. He is listed in *Who's Who in the West*, *Who's Who in Education*, and *International Who's Who*.

Mr. Brackett is semi-retired and enjoys a variety of activities, including back country hiking, cross-country skiing, snowshoeing, roller blading, biking, dancing, and writing. He lives in a log home he built in the Olympic Mountains near Lilliwaup, Washington. He can be reached through the publisher.

Chapter 1

TOWARD A COMPARATE DATA RESOURCE

Only a comparate data resource fully supports the business.

The discussion of data resource integration must begin with an explanation of the existing disparate data resource in an organization and what's needed to develop a comparate data resource. Chapter 1 briefly summarizes Chapters 1, and 2 from *Data Resource Simplexity*. Chapter 1 is a review only, and if more detail is needed, the reader should consult *Data Resource Simplexity*. Some additional material has been added based on comments received, and additional terms have been defined. A common approach to resolving disparity is presented, which includes a Common Data Architecture and a Common Data Culture.

RAMPANT DATA DISPARITY

The data resource in most public and private sector organizations is in a state of complete disarray. The data resource does not conform to any consistent organization-wide data architecture. It is seldom maintained by any formal set of concepts, principles, and techniques. It is seldom managed with the same intensity as other critical organization resources.

The Business Information Demand

An *organization* represents any administrative and functional structure for conducting some form of business, such as a public sector organization, quasi-public sector organization, private sector organization, association, society, foundation, and so on, however large or small, whether for profit or not for profit, and for however long it has been operating. The term *organization* will be used throughout the book. The term *enterprise* will not be used because of its private sector and profit centric meaning.

Every organization has a dynamic demand for information to support the business. The *business information demand* is an organization's continuously increasing, constantly changing, need for current, accurate,

1

integrated information, often on short notice or very short notice, to support its business activities. It is a very dynamic demand for information to support a business that constantly changes.

I've received several questions about what is meant by *business*. What about science, or recreation, or other areas that are not viewed as a true business? The *business* is in the eyes of the beholder, and is not necessarily just a for-profit business in the private sector. The *business* is what an organization is accomplishing, regardless of the organizational objectives.

The problem in most public and private sector organizations today is that the business information demand is not being supported by the data resource, or is not being fully supported to the organization's satisfaction.

What seems to have happened is that people forgot the basic principles of data resource management and are forging ahead without a solid foundation. The basic theories relevant to data resource management are set theory, graph theory, normalization theory, relational theory, dependency theory, communication theory, semiotic theory, and so on. Specific concepts and principles for data resource management are based on these theories. The specific concepts and principles would have led to development of a data resource that fully supported an organization's business information demand had they been followed.

Data processing as we know it today began back in the mid-20th Century. It evolved from hand-kept records, to punch cards, to magnetic tape, to larger and more powerful computers, to the information technology that we have today. While considerable discussion abounds about whether that evolution has been beneficial and cost effective to the business, that evolution has occurred and organizations are living with the results.

Prominent people, such as Claude Shannon, Edgar F. 'Ted' Codd, Peter Chen, John Zachman, and others, have contributed substantially to the basic principles for properly managing data as a critical resource of the organization. James Martin and others promoted canonical synthesis in the 1960's and 1970's. If organizations had followed the canons of data management, the resulting individual data models would readily connect to form a seamless data architecture for the organization. However, the canons were not complete and, even if enhanced by an organization, were seldom followed. The result is a major contribution to the creation of disparate data.

Several years ago I gave a seminar to a class of university students completing their Master's program in information management. They were astounded to hear many of the topics I presented. I asked for a show of hands from the students that were well versed in the basic theories, concepts, and principles I presented. No hands went up—and they are at the end of a Master's program! The students immediately turned on the professor wanting to know why these basic theories, concepts, and principles were not being taught.

The Y2K panic of the late 1990s should have been an alert to the pending problems with data resource management. However, the panic ended, very few problems occurred, and organizations moved on to their traditional data resource management feeling they successfully averted a major crisis, confirming that their data resource management practices were acceptable.

The millennium date problem is not the end. What about other monetary units, such as the European monetary unit? What if phone numbers added digits to become a 3-4-4 or a 4-4-4 number, or became alpha-numeric? What if the metric conversion were enforced? What if the Social Security Number added a digit? Can any of these situations be successfully handled?

Lexical Challenge

Information technology in general, and data resource management in particular, have a major lexical challenge. Words and terms are created, often used interchangeably, misused, abused, corrupted, and discarded without regard for the real meaning or any impact on the business. Words and terms often have no definitions, minimal definitions, poor definitions, conflicting definitions, unclear definitions, or multiple definitions. Many words and terms have been defined and redefined to the point they are meaningless. Many synonyms and homonyms have been created, adding to the problem. As a result, the data management profession today is lexically weak.

I recently heard an interesting statement when I was at an event. The promoter of a business was extolling the features of their business. In his pitch he said that their business operated 24–7–365. I thought about that for a minute and wondered if he really meant their business would be around for seven years. I'm sure he meant either 24–365 or 24–7–52. I was going to question him, but he was so into pumping words that I decided not to interrupt.

The lexical challenge is not unique to data management. I do considerable outside reading and watch numerous documentary programs. I heard one program discuss the geology of the Moon and another program discuss the geology of Mars. I thought that interesting because geology comes from *geo logos*, meaning *Earth study*. In other words, geology is a study of the Earth. Therefore, the term *geology of the Moon* would literally mean *study of the Earth of the Moon*, which doesn't make much sense. The true words would be *lunology* for study of the Moon and *aerology* for the study of Mars.

To help resolve the lexical challenge and promote a lexically rich data management profession, proper words and terms are presented, comprehensively defined to provide a denotative meaning, and used consistently throughout the book.

Data

Data are the individual facts that are out of context, have no meaning, and are difficult to understand. They are often referred to as *raw data*, such as 123.45. Data have historically been defined as plural.

Data in context are individual facts that have meaning and can be readily understood. They are the raw facts wrapped with meaning, such as 123.45 is the checking account balance at a point in time. However, data in context are not yet information.

A *resource* is a source of supply or support; an available means; a natural source of wealth or revenue; a source of information or expertise; something to which one has recourse in difficulty; a possibility of relief or recovery; or an ability to meet and handle a situation.

A *data resource* is a collection of data (facts), within a specific scope, that are of importance to the organization. It is one of the four critical resources in an organization, equivalent to the financial resource, the human resource, and real property. The term is singular, such as the *organization data resource*, the *student data resource*, or the *environmental data resource*. The data resource must be managed equivalent to the other three critical resources.

Data resource management is the formal management of the entire data resource at an organization's disposal, as a critical resource of the organization, equivalent to the human resource, financial resource, and real property, based on established concepts, principles, and techniques, leading to a comparate data resource that supports the current and future business information demand.

Information

Information is a set of data in context, with relevance to one or more people at a point in time or for a period of time. Information is more than data in context—it must have relevance and a time frame. Information has historically been defined as singular.

Information management is coordinating the need for information across the organization to ensure adequate support for the current and future business information demand. It should not be confused with data resource management.

Knowledge

Knowledge is cognizance, cognition, the fact or condition of knowing something with familiarity gained through experience or association. It's the acquaintance with or the understanding of something, the fact or condition of being aware of something, or apprehending truth or fact. Knowledge is information that has been retained with an understanding about the significance of that information. Knowledge includes something gained by experience, study, familiarity, association, awareness, and/or comprehension.

Tacit knowledge, also known as *implicit knowledge*, is the knowledge that a person retains in their mind. It's relatively hard to transfer to others and to disseminate widely. ***Explicit knowledge***, also known as *formal knowledge*, is knowledge that has been codified and stored in various media, such as books, magazines, tapes, presentations, and so on, and is held for mankind, such as in a reference library or on the web. It is readily transferable to other media and capable of being disseminated.

Organizational knowledge is information that is of significance to the organization, is combined with experience and understanding, and is retained by the organization. It's information in context with respect to understanding what is relevant and significant to a business issue or business topic—what is meaningful to the business. It's analysis, reflection, and synthesis about what information means to the business and how it can be used. It's a rational interpretation of information that leads to business intelligence.

Knowledge management is the management of an environment where people generate tacit knowledge, render it into explicit knowledge, and feed it back to the organization. The cycle forms a base for more tacit knowledge, which keeps the cycle going in an intelligent learning organization. It's an emerging set of policies, organizational structures, procedures, applications, and technology aimed toward increased innovation and improved decisions. It's an integrated approach to identifying, sharing, and evaluating an organization's information. It's a culture for learning where people are encouraged to share information and best practices to solve business problems.

5

Disparate Data

Disparate means fundamentally distinct or different in kind; entirely dissimilar. *Disparate data* are data that are essentially not alike, or are distinctly different in kind, quality, or character. They are unequal and cannot be readily integrated to meet the business information demand. They are low quality, defective, discordant, ambiguous, heterogeneous data. *Massively disparate data* is the existence of large quantities of disparate data within a large organization, or across many organizations involved in similar business activities.

A *disparate data resource* is a data resource that is substantially composed of disparate data that are dis-integrated and not subject-oriented. It is in a state of disarray, where the low quality does not, and cannot, adequately support an organization's business information demand.

I've encountered some naysayers since *Data Resource Simplexity* was published. One complained that *comparate* was not a recognized word, and by creating it, I was adding to the lexical challenge. Well, I did find *comparate* in one of those large dictionaries sitting on a pedestal in a library, so it is a recognized word. Also, *comparate* helps resolve the lexical challenge because it doesn't carry any connotative meanings. I define it and use it consistently to help resolve the lexical challenge.

Another naysayer said that *simplexity* was not a real word and added to the lexical challenge. Again, *Simplexity* is the title of an excellent book by Jeffrey Kluger. The concept he presented was so powerful that I decided to adopt that concept and apply it to data resource management. Like *comparate*, *simplexity* carries no connotative meanings. I define it and use it consistently to help resolve the lexical challenge.

Structured Data

Structured means something arranged in a definite pattern of organization; manner of construction; the arrangement of particles or parts in a substrate or body, arrangement or interrelation of parts as dominated by the general character of the whole; the aggregate of elements of an entity in their relationships to each other; the composition of conscious experience with its elements and their composition.

Structured data are data that are structured according to traditional database management systems with tables, rows, and columns that are readily accessible with a structured query language. Structured data are considered tabular data.

Unstructured means not structured, having few formal requirements, or

6

not having a patterned organization; without structure, having no structure, or structureless. **Unstructured data** are data that are not structured, have few formal requirements, or do not have a patterned organization. Use of the term *unstructured data* is most inappropriate, and will not be used.

In *Data Resource Simplexity* I established the term *super-structured data* to replace *unstructured data*, and justified the change. The comments I received were very positive, because people realized that *unstructured data* was the wrong term and another more accurate term was needed. However, the comments were negative because the term *super-structured* was easily confused with the term *superstructure*. *Superstructure* means a vertical extension of something above a base, such as the superstructure of a battleship, and has no meaning with respect to the data resource.

After looking at a variety of terms that represent an intricate interweaving of multiple structures, I've settled on a better term. **Complex** means composed of two or more parts; having a bound form; hard to separate, analyze, or solve; a whole made up of complicated or interrelated parts; a composite made up of distinct parts; intricate as having many complexly interrelating parts or elements.

Complex structured data are any data that are composed of two or more intricate, complicated, and interrelated parts that cannot be easily interpreted by structured query languages and tools. The complex structure needs to be broken down into the individual component structures to be more easily analyzed. Complex structured data include text, voice, video, images, spatial data, and so on. Therefore, I now use the sequence unstructured data, structured data, highly structured data, and complex structured data.

I've recently run across the terms *poly-structured data* and *multi-structured data*. However, those terms are used in reference to database management systems. They are not used in reference to an organization's entire data resource, including data within and without a database management system.

The terms represent complex structured data that have been broken down into simpler structures that can be handled in database management system. Hence, the complex structure of the data is managed as various sub-structures that comprise that complex structure. However, used in that context, the terms do not adequately represent the very intricate structure that can be found in an organization's data resource, both within and without database management systems.

People ask me what is perpetuating the lexical challenge in data resource management. People are simply pumping the words without realizing what they are saying, or what the words really mean. Data management professionals need to stop pumping words and terms without understanding their true meaning. They need to start using words and terms that are well defined and are used consistently. That's the only way to resolve the lexical challenge.

More on Information

Information was defined above. However, some people have different perceptions of information. One perception is that information is the same as *data in context*. Whenever raw data are wrapped with meaning, those data become information.

However, if *information* is considered to be *data in context*, then what is the term for information that is relevant and timely? That might lead to *relevant information* and *non-relevant information*. Now two hierarchies exist, as shown below.

Data – Data in context – Information – Knowledge

Data – Relevant information / Non-relevant information – Knowledge

The problem with the second hierarchy is that non-relevant information does not contribute to knowledge. The result is that the lexical challenge is not resolved. Therefore, the first hierarchy is the proper definition, and the one that will be used throughout the book.

Another perception is that information is any summary data or derived data. The perception is not valid because whether data are primitive or derived, they are still data. They have not yet become relevant or timely and are not yet information. The distinction will become clear as a disparate data resource is understood and resolved.

If data in context are not relevant or timely, then they are not information. However, the data may not be relevant to a specific individual at the current time, but could be relevant to someone at some time. Tide tables are a good example. If you are going sailing in Puget Sound and someone gives you tide tables for Nantucket, you would say that's not information because it's not relevant. However, those tide tables could be relevant to someone going sailing on the East Coast.

Therefore, the definition of *information* can be expanded. **Specific information** is a set of data in context that is relevant to a person at a point in time or for a period of time. **General information** is a set of data in context that could be relevant to one or more people at a point in time or for a period of time.

Information overload is a misused term and is part of the lexical challenge. The term will not be used in the current book. Several terms can be used to replace *information overload.*

Information assimilation overload occurs when information is coming too fast for a person to take in and understand. A certain amount of time is needed for information to be assimilated, and the delivery needs to match that assimilation.

Disparate information is any information that is disparate with respect to the recipient. It could result from information acquired from different sources that are organized differently, or it could result from information created from disparate data that provide conflicting information. In other words, disparate information could be disorganized information or it could be conflicting information.

Sorting through disparate information to organize that information or find the correct information is not information assimilation overload. It's a processing overload to organize the disparate information into a form appropriate to the recipient.

Information paranoia is the fear of not knowing everything that is relevant or could be relevant at some point in time. It's a situation where a person is obsessed with gaining information for information's sake.

Non-information is a set of data in context that is not relevant or timely to the recipient. It is neither specific information nor general information.

Information sharing is the sharing of information between people and organizations according to the definition of information. For example, several jurisdictions may create a task force for a major criminal activity. The task force meets and shares the information each jurisdiction has about the criminal activity. The material shared is timely and relevant, and qualifies as information sharing.

Data overload is a deluge of data or data in context coming at a recipient, but it is not relevant and timely. It's a deluge of non-information that is not wanted by the recipient. It's not information assimilation overload.

Data Are Plural

I made a strong case in *Data Resource Simplexity* that the term *data* is plural. Since then, I've received many comments about whether *data* should be singular or plural. Traditionally, *data* has been plural equivalent to *facts*, and *datum* has been singular equivalent to *a fact*. However, current usage seems to accept *data* as singular, although I've seen no good, denotative definition of *data* in the singular form.

The most common comment I hear is *'data are' just doesn't sound right*. That's a poor excuse for considering *data* as singular. Saying *a data is easy to manage* is like saying *people is easy to manage*. Other phrases using data in the singular are equally confusing.

One approach to resolving the problem is to consider *data* an irregular noun like *deer* or *sheep* where the meaning is in the context. In other words, *data* can be used in either the singular or plural form depending on the context. In the singular form, *data* represents an individual fact similar to the traditional *datum*. In the plural form, *data* represents a collection of facts and *datum* is the singular form. However, the data management profession has enough confusion without treating *data* as an irregular noun.

I often ask people to provide a comprehensive, denotative definition of data in the singular by completing the phrase *Data is …* I have very few responses, and the responses I do receive are really definitions of the data resource rather than data. Therefore, *data* will be used as plural throughout the book to emphasize that the data resource contains many data (facts) about the business that are important to the operation and evaluation of the business. *Datum* will be used as the singular of *data*.

Data Are a Resource

I made a strong case in *Data Resource Simplexity* that data are managed as a resource of the organization, and not as an asset of the organization. I've had a number of discussions with data management professionals who claim, some rather adamantly, that data are an asset. The reason seems to be that if data are considered an asset, then somehow, almost automatically, they will be managed properly. That reason alone implies, or is even an admission, that data are not properly managed, and will only be properly managed if they are considered an asset.

Any item or resource is only considered an asset or a durable asset when it appears on the General Ledger or Chart of Accounts for an organization. CFOs place things on the General Ledger or Chart of Accounts when they consider those things to be an asset of the organization. The determination is made by a CFO, not by data management professionals.

When a data management professional declares or demands that data are an asset, then one should ask the organization's CFO if data are listed on the General Ledger or Chart of Accounts. In the vast majority of organizations, data are not listed. Hence, data are not viewed by the CFO as an asset of the organization. Many executives and managers actually consider the data resource to be a liability rather than an asset because of the disparity.

The attitude that if *they* (CFOs) consider the data as an asset, then *we* (data management professionals) will properly manage those data just has to cease. Data management professionals have a very long way to go to stop the burgeoning data disparity and resolve the existing data disparity before the data resource can be considered properly managed. Data management professionals have to earn the right for data to be considered an asset of the organization.

The best approach in most organizations, and the approach I use, is to consider data as a critical resource of the organization. Then properly manage that critical data resource so well that it fully supports the current and future business information demand and is considered to be a real asset to the organization by the CFO.

Information and Knowledge Storage

When specific or general information is stored, it becomes part of the data resource, it is treated as data, and is managed like any other data. Those data will only become information again when they become relevant and timely. The same is true for knowledge. Stored knowledge becomes data and is managed like any other data. Those data will only become knowledge again when they are extracted as information, combined with experience, and retained.

A book on a shelf, a document on a server, raw data, a stored form or document, a stored report, and so on, are all considered data and managed as part of the organization's data resource. The documentation of information or knowledge is still data to other people, and may become information or knowledge to those people.

Looking at the situation the other way around, all information and knowledge were data at one time. By becoming relevant and timely, those data became information. By being combined with business experience and retained, that information became knowledge. Therefore, no information resource or knowledge resource exists with respect to stored information and knowledge.

The *data-information-knowledge cycle* is the cycle from data, to data in context, to specific or general information, to knowledge, and back to data when stored, as shown in Figure 1.1.

I don't want to belabor the issue, but when information and knowledge are stored, they become part of the organization's data resource and are managed according to formal data resource management concepts, principles, and techniques. Whether those data were once raw data, specific or general information, or knowledge makes no difference. Everything stored is part of the data resource, is considered data, and is formally managed as data.

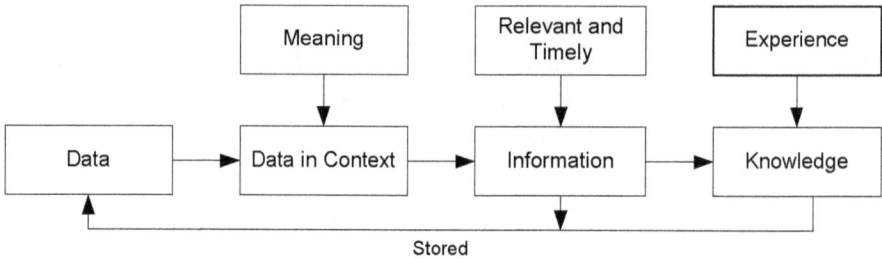

Figure 1.1. The data–information–knowledge cycle.

As the process of data resource integration is unfolded, the reason for considering stored information and knowledge as data in the organization's data resource will become clear.

Basic Problems

A disparate data resource exists for many specific reasons. A whole book could be written about the specific reasons for disparate data. I never cease to be amazed at how ingenious people can be at screwing up a data resource. Just when I think I've seen it all, I run across yet another way that people have used to create disparate data.

The multitude of reasons for the creation of disparate data can be grouped into four basic problems. These are the basic problems that need to be prevented to stop further creation of disparate data, and resolved to integrate existing disparate data into a comparate data resource.

Lack of Awareness

The first basic problem is that the organization at large is not aware of all the data, within or without the organization, that are at their disposal. Organizations seldom have a complete inventory of all data within the organization, and are less likely to have an inventory of data available from outside the organization. Individuals within the organization often know the data that are available for their business activities, but are not aware of all the data available to the organization.

The lack of a formal data inventory leads to a huge *hidden data resource* that could be available to the organization. That hidden data resource contains *dormant data* that could be used by the organization. Not being able to use those dormant data leads to *hidden information* about the business, which leads to *hidden knowledge*. The result is a failure to fully support the business information demand.

Lack of Understanding

The second basic problem is that organizations have a general lack of thorough understanding about the data available in their data resource. Even if a complete, current, detailed inventory of all data available to the organization were maintained, the organization at large still lacks a thorough understanding of those data. A few individuals may thoroughly understand a small subset of the data they routinely use, but the organization lacks a widespread, common understanding of all the data in their data resource.

Some people claim that it's not necessary for everyone in the organization to understand all of the data. But, that's not the point. The point is that people need to understand the existing data well enough to not create additional disparate data. All data need to be documented to the extent that anyone in the organization can readily understand those data when the need arises.

High Data Redundancy

The third basic problem is that data in the existing data resource are highly redundant. The same business fact has been independently captured and stored in multiple locations in the organization's data resource. *Data redundancy* is the unknown and unmanaged duplication of business facts in a disparate data resource. The *data redundancy factor* is the number of sources for a single business fact in an organization's data resource.

Data redundancy should not be confused with data replication. *Data replication* is the consistent copying of data from one primary data site to one or more secondary data sites. The copied data are kept in synch with the primary data on a regular basis.

High Data Variability

The fourth basic problem is a high variability in the format and content of disparate data. The format can vary across databases, reports, screens, documents, and forms. The format and content may change from one data file to another and from one data record to another within the same data file.

Data variability is the variation in format and content of a redundant fact stored in a disparate data resource. The *data variability factor* is the number of variations in format or content for a single business fact.

Disparate Data Trends

Several prominent trends contribute to development of a disparate data resource, including the disparate data cycle, the natural data resource drift of the data resource toward disparity, the data resource spiral, data deluge, Malthusian Principle, the data dilemma that organizations face, and disparate data shock. Each of these trends is summarized below. A more detailed description can be found in *Data Resource Simplexity*.

Disparate Data Cycle

The *disparate data cycle* is a self-perpetuating cycle where disparate data continue to be produced at an ever-increasing rate because people do not know about existing data or do not want to use existing data. People come to the data resource, but can't find the data they need, don't trust the data, or can't access the data. These people create their own data, which perpetuates the disparate data cycle. The next people that come to the data resource find the same situation, and the cycle keeps going.

Data Resource Drift

Data resource drift is the natural, steady drift of a data resource towards disparity if its development is not properly managed and controlled. The natural drift is toward a disparate, low quality, complex data resource. The longer the drift is allowed to continue, the more difficult it will be to achieve a comparate data resource. The natural drift is continuing unchecked in most public and private sector organizations today, and will continue until organizations consciously alter that natural drift.

Disparate Data Spiral

The evolution of data disparity from traditional operational data into new technologies, such as spatial data, data analytics, complex structured data, and so on, creates a situation where the disparate data cycle is spiraling out of control with no foreseeable end in sight. The evolution is increasing by orders of magnitude and is creating disparate data faster than ever before.

The *disparate data spiral* is the spiraling increase in data disparity from existing technologies into new technologies. Both the volume of disparate data and the complexity of those disparate data are increasing. The spiraling disparity severely impacts the business activities of the organization.

Data Deluge

The *data deluge* is the situation where massive quantities of data are being captured and stored at an alarming rate. These data are being captured by traditional means, by scanning, by imaging, by remote sensing, by machine generation, and by derivation. Those data are being stored on personal computers, networks, departmental computers, and mainframe computers. The quantity of data in many organizations is increasing exponentially. If the data proliferation continues, the data deluge of the 1990s and early 2000s will appear trivial.

Malthusian Principle

The *Malthusian principle* deals with the power of populations to overwhelm their means of subsistence, causing misery, suffering, and eventually leading to extinction of that population if no corrective action is taken. Populations tend to grow geometrically, while their means of subsistence tend to grow arithmetically. At some point in time, the population growth exceeds the means of subsistence.

In *Data Resource Simplexity* I (loosely) applied the Malthusian Principle to an organization's data resource. The volume of disparate data is growing geometrically, while the organization's ability to understand and manage those data is only growing arithmetically. At some point in time the volume of disparate data will overwhelm an organization and could result in that organization failing to be fully successful.

I also (loosely) applied the Malthusian Principle to the organization's growing volume of comparate data. The volume of comparate data is growing geometrically, according to Moore's Law. The ability of an organization to thoroughly understand and use those comparate data to support the business information demand is only growing arithmetically. At some point in time the sheer volume of comparate data will overwhelm the organization.

Since I wrote *Data Resource Simplexity*, several people have pointed out that the Malthusian Principle is wrong. Technology comes along just in time to save a population from starving. As a population steadily grows, technology takes incremental jumps to keep up with the demand for food. Several people claim that my application of the Malthusian Principle to the data resource is wrong because technology steadily improves to manage larger volumes of data, provide faster processing, and provide faster transfer rates.

However, that's only one aspect of the Malthusian Principle as applied to the data resource. The other aspect is the progressive loss of understanding with the increased volume of disparate data. Eventually the loss of understanding of the growing volume of data will limit an organization's ability to effectively and efficiently use the data, unless some means are taken to capture and retain that understanding. Technology can help retain the understanding, but technology cannot understand the data.

Data resource integration lowers data disparity and helps organizations better manage the data through better understanding of the less disparate data. That may be technology coming to the aid of data resource management, but it's a different type of technology than the technology of speed storage capacity and data transfer. It's an understanding technology that is sorely lacking today.

Data Dilemma

The *data dilemma* is the situation where the ability to meet the business information demand is being compromised by the continued development of large quantities of disparate data. The dilemma exists in most organizations facing a growing disparate data resource. It arises from the conflict between building and maintaining a high-quality data resource, within a formal data architecture, for long term stability, to meet the high demand for integrated data to support the business; and the need to strive for early deliverables, inexpensive implementations, and quick fixes to current problems.

Disparate Data Shock

Disparate data shock is the sudden realization that a data dilemma exists in an organization and that it is severely impacting an organization's ability to be responsive to changes in the business environment. It's the panic that an organization has about the poor state of its data resource. It's the realization that disparate data are not adequately supporting the current and future business information demand. It's the panic that sets in about the low quality of the data resource, that the quality is deteriorating, and very little is being done to improve the situation.

Data Disparity Factors

The creation of disparate data is more than the natural drift of the data resource, the natural occurrence of events, or a few things not being done correctly. Specific factors contributing to the burgeoning data disparity are constant change, hype-cycles, and attitudes. Each of these factors is summarized below.

Constant Change

Data resource management is facing two major types of change. First, is the constant change in the business environment, which requires constant change in the management of data to support the business environment. Second, is the constant change in the technology of data resource management. Managing these two changes is often overwhelming.

The rate and magnitude of change has been increasing, and continues to increase. Change is relentless and persistent. Nothing stays constant for very long with today's business and technology. The only thing constant today is the increasing rate and magnitude of change. Organizations must learn to move at the speed of change, or move at the speed of the business.

The business in most public and private sector organizations is very dynamic. Technology is evolving rapidly, employee turnover is higher, skills are in high demand, resources are down in a tight economy, the demand for integrated data is up, lead times are shorter, and quicker turnaround for critical situations is needed. Organizations cannot properly handle constant change with massive quantities of disparate data.

Hype-Cycles

A *hype-cycle* is a major initiative that is promoted in an attempt to properly manage an organization's data resource, but often ends up making that data resource more disparate and impacting the business. A hype-cycle runs its course when the income from conferences, books, consulting, training, and software declines. Then a new hype-cycle begins and the process starts all over. Several major hype-cycles are prominent in data resource management today.

Data Governance. The first is data governance. It's the latest in a string of hype-cycles from database management, through data administration, to data governance. The previous hype-cycles failed, and data governance is failing. The basic problem with data governance is that you can't govern the data, any more than you could administer data.

I explained in *Data Resource Simplexity* that you can't govern data or any other object; you can only govern people. I made the case that any management of the data as a resource to an organization is really data resource management—managing the data resource; not administering or governing the data resource.

Data governance includes a whole shopping list of topics and individual techniques. Some are unique to data resource management and some

17

apply to all disciplines and professions. I have yet to see a basic set of concepts, principles, and techniques for data governance. What I see is a collection of topics without a foundation.

I recently ran across a new theme for data governance—business driven data governance. My first thought was if that is a new theme, then what was the former theme? Was the former theme non-business driven data governance? If so, why would any initiative regarding something as important as managing a critical data resource not be driven by the business?

I also saw two other new themes—data governance for meta-data and data governance for master data. Again, if those themes are really new, then traditional data governance did not include meta-data or master data, both of which are components of an organization's data resource. Why were they initially excluded?

The answer to these questions, I believe, is that data governance is a hype-cycle and these new themes are needed just to keep the hype-cycle going. New themes will continue to be added until a hype-cycle eventually dies, just like database management and data administration died.

I recently saw an article on extending governance to information— information governance. I wondered what that term really meant, because you can't govern information any more than you can govern data. How would you govern the relevance and timeliness of something that a person needs? How could you even govern what information a person needs? Like data, you might have information management that coordinates the need for information within an organization, but I fail to see how you could have information governance.

The article provided nothing to clarify what information governance really meant. It was the same old hype as data governance, but with a new title for information governance. Actually, the article confused, yet again, the difference between data and information. The hype-cycles continue.

Master Data Management . The second is master data management. It has become so broad and undefined (or multi-defined) that one does not know the real meaning of master data management. Does it mean there are slave data? Does it mean data reference sets? Does it mean core business data? Does it mean business critical data? Does it mean the highest in a series of skill levels? Does it mean the record of reference? Does it mean the same as data governance? Master data management is failing because it is ill-defined and is not supported by a sound set of concepts, principles, and techniques.

If master data management is about the management of reference data, then the term should be *reference data management*. If it is about core business data or data critical to the business, then the terms should be *core business data* and *business critical data*. I recently heard a new theme that master data management was really about meta-data. If that's true, then the term should be *meta-data management*. Other perceptions of master data management should have specific terms within data resource management.

I see articles about how master data management and data governance are maturing. I went through exactly the same cycle with database management and data administration from when they started, through their maturity, to their decline and replacement by data governance and master data management. Wouldn't it be nice to establish formal data resource management and make it persistent?

Other Hype-Cycles. A multitude of other hype-cycles have come and some have gone, such as service oriented architecture, canonical synthesis, the object-oriented paradigm, XML, cloud computing, federated databases, client-server, RPG, enterprise architecture, NoSQL, ERPs, and so on. I can remember when client-server first came along and would solve all of the existing data disparity problems. I heard the same for federated databases and with a variety of design tools. Yet, the data disparity got worse.

I recently saw online discussions stating data modeling is dead and relational technology is dead. The general theme over time has been *Oh, now that (fill in the blank) is here, (fill in the blank) is no longer needed.* That theme is simply an attempt to put the final coup-de-grace on an old hype-cycle and promote a new hype-cycle.

Comments About Hype-Cycles. I've received many comments about data governance and master data management being hype-cycles. People claim they are substantive, they are real, they are not hype, and so on. So, the question becomes what are master data management, data governance, and similar terms?

Data governance, master data management, and other hype-cycles are not formal data resource management. At best, they are initiatives or campaigns within an organization to manage the data resource. Most likely, they are hype-cycles, driven by personal or financial incentives, that will eventually run their course and be replaced by other hype-cycles. The name may change, but the hype-cycles live on.

Hype-cycles usually lead to increased disparate data, either directly or indirectly. Usually, the intention is to resolve data disparity and formalize data resource management. However, the end result is often an increase in data disparity. A good rhetorical question is Who's at fault— the perpetuators or the adopters of hype-cycles?

Knowledge Areas. Data resource management contains knowledge areas that are persistent and transcend initiatives. Initiatives are often labeled with catchy terms that catch people's eyes according to the mood of the time. Initiatives come and go while the basic knowledge areas remain persistent.

What if terms were created for documenting disparate data, mapping all public works, organizing health care data, and so on? Do these terms become knowledge areas within data resource management, or do they simply become initiatives that use appropriate knowledge areas. Data resource management will never stabilize, and a data management profession will never be created, if every hype-cycle and initiative that is established becomes a data resource management knowledge area.

Attitude

Attitude includes the attitudes of business professionals, data management professionals, consultants and trainers, conference providers, software vendors, and so on. It includes ego, arrogance, a need for control, a lack of teamwork, limited cooperation, limited scope, individual independence, personal agendas, conflicts of interest, atypical behavior, the not-invented-here syndrome, change for change sake, my model versus your model, my tool versus your tools, my perception versus your perception, and so on. All of these attitudes lead to a disparate data resource.

The prominent attitudes are lack of a business perspective, being private sector centric, paralysis-by-analysis, a brute-force-physical approach, and concentrating on the T of IT. Each of these is summarized below.

Lack of Business Perspective. Many data professionals lack a real business perspective. They are fixated on how things should be according to their perception and experience with databases, rather than how the business perceives the world in which they operate. The data resource must represent how the organization perceives the business world from their perspective, based on the way they operate in that business world.

Private Sector Centric. Many data management professionals are private sector centric. They think primarily of the private sector with respect to data resource management and largely ignore the public sector. Data resource management is extremely important in the public sector with their broad range of business activities, broad time frame, monumental projects requiring sustained efforts, relatively permanent lines of business, different funding structure with legislative mandates, a relatively fixed citizen set, short terms for executives, emotionally charged situations, readily shared data, and so on.

Related to the public sector focus is the term *CRM*, which usually means *customer relationship management*. However, in the public sector it means *citizen relationship management*. Relations with citizens in the public sector are considerably different than relations with customers in the private sector.

Paralysis-By-Analysis. Many projects are paralyzed by ongoing analysis. *Paralysis-by-analysis* is a process of ongoing analysis and modeling to make sure everything is complete and correct. Data analysts and data modelers are well known for analyzing a situation and working the problem forever before moving ahead. They often want to build more into the data resource than the organization really wants or needs. The worst, and most prevalent, complaint about data resource management is its tendency to paralyze the development process by exacerbating the analysis process. Prolonging analysis delays the project and forces the business to proceed with development, often at the expense of creating disparate data.

Brute Force Physical Approach. The opposite of paralysis-by-analysis is a brute-force-physical approach for developing and maintaining a data resource. The **brute-force-physical** approach goes directly to the task of developing the physical database. It skips all of the formal analysis and modeling activities, and often skips the involvement of business professionals and domain experts. People taking such an approach consider that developing the physical database is the real task at hand. The result is the creation of more disparate data.

A related situation is cutting the database code without any formal analysis. The primary purpose of most data modeling tools, in spite of how they are advertised and marketed, is to cut the code for the physical database. Physical data models are often developed, maybe reviewed superficially by the business professionals, and the database is developed. The result is usually increased data disparity.

Another related situation is conceptual modeling, which is often used as an excuse to get something in place quickly to keep the business happy, and then forge ahead with developing the physical database. Formal data normalization and even data denormalization are often ignored in the process.

Concentrating on the T of IT. Many people concentrate on the T of Information Technology rather than the I of Information Technology. People have been concerned with what new technology can do, rather than what it can do for the business.

The *new technology syndrome* is a repeating cycle of events that occurs with new technology. New technology appears as a new way of doing things. People play with the new technology, in a physical sense, to see what it can do or is capable of doing, like a child plays with a new toy. Then people use the new technology in some aspect of the business, or base major segments of the business on the new technology. It's like a new tool looking for a place to be useful. Disparity begins to creep in because of the physical implementation. When people finally decide to formalize the technology, the disparity already exists.

Other Attitudes. Other attitudes that lead to a disparate data resource are data standards, which are often physical oriented and often conflict; data registries, which create a perception that if the data model is documented in a registry, it becomes official; universal data models and generic data architectures, which are an attempt to get every organization to manage their data the same way; and purchased applications, which often require the organization to warp their business to fit the application.

Result of Disparate Data Factors

The result of the constant change, hype-cycles, and attitudes described above lead to an organization sacrificing its future for the present and the creation of a Borgesian Nightmare.

Sacrificing the Future for the Present. Organizations have been sacrificing the future for the present. They have concentrated on developing applications, building databases, and using technology that will meet the current business information demand, but not the future business information demand. The emphasis is on short term deliverables, rather than long term viability of the data resource.

Most organizations are now *in the future* and are suffering from emphasis on the *present of yesteryear*. They are suffering from an orientation toward technology, not toward information. The historical orientation to the present and to technology has finally caught up with them and the disparity is severely hampering the organization's business activities. Organizations are literally facing the neglects of the past.

Organizations must concentrate on both the short term and the long term use of information technology. They must meet the short term demands while considering the long term demands for good information. They need to concentrate on long term support of the business as well as short term support. To do otherwise simply perpetuates disparity.

Borgesian Nightmare. The increasing data resource disparity results in a Borgesian nightmare. A *Borgesian nightmare* is a labyrinth that is impossible to navigate, which causes people to have nightmares. The disparate data resource in many organizations is becoming a Borgesian nightmare. Organizations are drowning in a labyrinth of disparate data and people have nightmares about how to effectively and efficiently manage the data resource to fully meet an organization's current and future business information demand.

No Quick Solutions

Preventing and resolving data resource disparity has no quick fix. Quick fixes are simply another hype that doesn't provide any solutions. A *silver bullet* is an attempt to achieve some gain without any pain. The *silver bullet syndrome* is the on-going syndrome that organizations go through searching for quick fixes to their data problems. A *tarnished silver bullet* is the result of attempting to find a silver bullet—considerable pain with minimal gain, and maybe considerable loss.

Plausible deniability is the ability of an organization to deny the fact that their data resource is disparate and live with the illusion of high quality data. Most public and private sector organizations have enough plausible deniability about the state of their data resource to last the rest of their organizational lives.

What an organization believes about the quality of their data resource and the real quality of their data resource are often quite different. Most people are aware of the disparate nature of the organization's data resource, but don't want to believe (deny) that the data resource quality is low. Many are ashamed or embarrassed to admit that the data resource is disparate.

The result of silver bullets and plausible deniability lead to a self-defeating fallacy. The *self-defeating fallacy* states that no matter how much you believe that something can happen, if it is not possible, it will not happen. The *self-fulfilling prophecy* states that if you really believe in something that can happen, and it is possible, it will happen.

A status quo does not work. The natural drift of the data resource toward disparity will continue and the data resource will become more disparate. A status quo simply leads to organizational failure by reason of information deprivation.

Data resource disparity has no quick fixes or magic cures. Tools won't stop or resolve data disparity, because tools can't understand the data. Only people can understand data, and tools document that understanding. Scanners are good for an inventory, but can't understand the data. They often create a false confidence in the data resource by providing a complete inventory.

Standards can't resolve data disparity, and often don't help prevent data disparity. Standards themselves are often disparate and actively add to the data disparity. The same situation exists with generic data architectures and universal data models, data registries, data repositories, and so on.

Beware of high-tech solutions that appear to resolve data disparity. Technology won't solve the disparate data problem. The real solution is hard work—the real hard-thinking kind of work. The real solution comes from people who can understand the disparate data resource and develop a comparate data resource.

Data Risk and Hazard

The constant change, hype-cycles, and attitudes create both a hazard and a risk for the organization. *Hazard* is a possible source of danger or a circumstance that creates a dangerous situation. *Risk* is the possibility of suffering harm or loss from some event; a chance that something will happen.

Data resource hazard is the existence of disparate data. A greater volume and a greater degree of disparity make the hazard greater. *Data resource risk* is the chance that use of the disparate data will adversely impact the business. Both the data resource hazard and data resource risk are large in most public and private sector organizations.

Probability neglect is overestimating the odds of things we most dread happening and underestimating the odds of things we least dread happening. Probability neglect for the data resource is happening in most public and private sector organizations. *Data resource probability neglect* is overestimating the odds of not meeting the current business information demand and underestimating the odds of not meeting the future business information demand.

The *availability heuristic* states that the better you can imagine a dangerous event, the likelier you are to be afraid of that event. The reverse is actually true for the data resource in most organizations.

Organizations are not imagining the danger of failing to meet the future business information demand and are not afraid of that failure. Looking deeper into a disparate data resource makes the availability heuristic quite obvious. One comment I heard from a client after realizing their data resource was disparate was *How did we ever manage to do this to our data resource?*

COMPARATE DATA RESOURCE

Comparate is the opposite of disparate and means fundamentally similar in kind. *Comparate data* are data that are alike in kind, quality, and character, and are without defect. They are concordant, homogeneous, nearly flawless, nearly perfect, high-quality data that are easily understood and readily integrated.

A *comparate data resource* is a data resource composed of comparate data that adequately support the current and future business information demand. The data are easily identified and understood, readily accessed and shared, and utilized to their fullest potential. A comparate data resource is an integrated, subject oriented, business driven data resource that is the official record of reference for the organization's business.

The discussion of a comparate data resource includes data resource quality, data resource management concepts, supporting theories and principles, the Data Resource Management Framework, a comparate data resource vision, and how to achieve that vision. Each of these is described below.

Data Resource Quality

The second law of thermo dynamics can be applied to the data resource. *Entropy* is the state or degree of disorderliness. It is a loss of order, which is increasing disorderliness. Entropy increases over time, meaning that things become more disorderly over time, as shown by the natural drift of the data resource toward disorder. Disorderliness means low quality, which is a disparate data resource.

The data resource is an open system and follows the laws of increasing entropy, virtually without limit. However, the entropy can be reversed to restore orderliness, but only with the input of energy. Work must be done to restore orderliness. Orderliness means high quality, which is a comparate data resource.

Quality is a peculiar and essential character, the degree of excellence, being superior in kind. Quality is defined through four virtues—clarity, elegance, simplicity, and value.

Data resource quality is a measure of how well the data resource supports the current and future business information demand. Ideally, the data resource should fully support the current and future business information demand of the organization to be considered a high quality data resource. *Data quality* is a subset of data resource quality dealing with data values. *Ultimate data resource quality* is a data resource that is stable across changing business and changing technology, so it continues to support the current and future business information demand.

Proactive data resource quality is the process of establishing the desired quality criteria and ensuring that the data resource meets those criteria from this point forward. It's oriented toward preventing defects from entering the data resource. *Retroactive data resource quality* is the process of understanding the existing quality of the data resource and improving the quality to the extent that is reasonably possible. It's oriented toward correcting the existing low quality data resource by removing defects.

Data Resource Simplexity was oriented toward proactive data resource quality. The current book on *Data Resource Integration* is oriented toward retroactive data resource quality.

Information quality is how well the business information demand is met. It includes both the data used to produce the information and the information engineering process. The information engineering process includes everything from determining the information need to the method of presenting the information.

Information engineering is the discipline for identifying information needs and developing information systems to meet those needs. It's a manufacturing process that uses data from the data resource as the raw material to construct and transmit information.

The *information engineering objective* is to get the right data, to the right people, in the right place, at the right time, in the right form, at the right cost, so they can make the right decisions, and take the right actions. The operative term in the definition is *the right data*, meaning high quality data. The information quality can be no better than the data used to produce that information.

Data engineering is the discipline that designs, builds, and maintains the organization's data resource and makes the data available to information engineering. It's a formal process for developing a comparate data resource. Data engineering is also responsible for maintaining the disparate data resource and for transforming that disparate data resource to a comparate data resource. Data resource management includes data engineering, plus all of the architectural and cultural components of data resource management.

Quality is not free, as some people claim. Quality is less expensive if built in from the beginning, compared to being built in later, but it is not free. The second law of thermodynamics substantiates that quality is not free, and the data resource will not correct itself. The sooner that a comparate data resource is developed, the less costly it will be.

Data Resource Management Concepts

Developing a comparate data resource begins with the description of a few basic concepts about data resource management. These concepts include understanding the data resource, developing an independent data architecture, the Business Intelligence Value Chain, and the comparate data cycle. Each of these topics is summarized below. More detailed descriptions can be found in *Data Resource Simplexity*.

Uncertainty and Understanding

The disparate data cycle is perpetuated by uncertainty, both uncertainty about the business and uncertainty about the organization's disparate data resource. Uncertainty about the organization's data resource is the primary concern for data resource integration. Resolving uncertainty about the data resource helps people face the uncertainty about the business.

Uncertainty is resolved through understanding. The ***thorough understanding principle*** states that a thorough understanding of the data with respect to the business resolves uncertainty and puts the brakes on data disparity. It's the understanding of data with respect to the business that's important. Thoroughly understanding the organization's data resource is a major step towards lowering uncertainty and preventing further disparity.

Data de-coherence is an interference in the coherent understanding of the true meaning of data with respect to the business. It is due to the variability in the meaning, structure, and integrity of the data. The variability is large in a disparate data resource leading to a large data de-coherence.

Independent Data Architecture

The data resource is one component of an information technology infrastructure that also contains the platform resource, the business activities, and information system. Disparity exists in all four components of the infrastructure. Resolving disparity in the data resource helps resolve disparity in the other components.

However, the architectures of the four components must be kept separate. The *principle of independent architectures* states that each primary component of the information technology infrastructure has its own architecture independent of the other architectures. That principle must be kept in mind when developing a comparate data resource.

Business Intelligence Value Chain

Intelligence is the ability to learn or understand or deal with new or trying situations; the skilled use of reason; the ability to apply knowledge to manipulate one's environment or to think abstractly. *Business Intelligence* is a set of concepts, methods, and processes to improve business decision making using any information from multiple sources that could affect the business, and applying experiences and assumptions to deliver accurate perspectives of business dynamics.

The *Business Intelligence Value Chain* is a sequence of events where value is added from the data resource, through each step, to the support of business goals. The data resource is the foundation that supports the development of information. Information supports the knowledge worker in a knowledge environment. The knowledge worker provides business intelligence to an intelligent, learning organization. Business intelligence supports the business strategies, which support the business goals of the organization.

Any level in the Business Intelligence Value Chain has no better quality than its supporting level. Since the data resource is the foundation, the quality of any higher level, such as information, can be no better than the quality of the data resource. Therefore, the degree to which business goals are met can be no better than the quality of the data resource.

Comparate Data Cycle

The *comparate data cycle* is a self-perpetuating cycle where the use of comparate data is continually reinforced because people understand and trust the data. It is the flip side of the disparate data cycle. When people come to the data resource, they can usually find the data they need, can trust those data, and can readily access those data. The result is a shared data resource. Similarly, people who can't find the data they need formally add their data to the data resource, and the enhanced data resource is readily available to anyone looking for data to meet their business need.

Supporting Theories and Principles

Several theories and principles from outside data resource management support the resolution of data disparity and the creation of a comparate data resource. Each of these theories and principles is summarized below. More detailed descriptions can be found in *Data Resource Simplexity*.

Basic Definitions

A *theory* is a plausible or scientifically acceptable general principle or body of principles offered to explain phenomena; a body of theorems presenting a concise systematic view of a subject.

A *concept* is something conceived in the mind, a thought, or a notion; an abstract or generic idea generalized from particular instances; a generic or generalized ideal from specific instances. A concept can be basic, applying to data resource management in general, or it can be specific, applying to one aspect of data resource management.

A *principle* is a comprehensive and fundamental law, doctrine, or assumption; a rule of conduct. A principle can be basic, applying to data resource management in general, or it can be specific, applying to one aspect of data resource management.

A *technique* is a body of technical methods; a method of accomplishing a desired aim. Technique, as used here, represents how to accomplish a principle; the principle is the *what* and the technique is the *how*.

Basic Principles

Several basic principles support development of a comparate data resource, including think globally—act locally, the precautionary principle, the principles of unintended consequences and intended consequences, the data resource comparity principle, the data resource iatrogenesis principle, cognitive dissonance, and the principles of gradual change and delayed change. Each of these principles is summarized below.

People need to stop thinking locally and acting locally with respect to the organization's data resource. The *think globally – act locally principle* provides a broad orientation for developing a comparate data resource. People need to think globally about the comparate data resource, but act locally to ensure that data resource contains their data and those data are readily available.

The *precautionary principle* states that if an action or policy has a suspected risk of causing harm to the public or the environment, in the absence of scientific consensus that the action is not harmful, the burden of proof that it is not harmful falls on those who advocate taking the action. The *data resource precautionary principle* states that if an action or policy has a suspected risk of causing harm to the data resource, in the absence of scientific consensus that the action or policy is not harmful, the burden of proof that it is not harmful falls on those who advocate taking the action.

The *principle of unintended consequences* states that any intervention in a complex system may or may not have the intended result, but will inevitably create unintended and often undesirable outcomes. The *principle of intended consequences* states that any intervention in a complex system, such as a data resource, should be guaranteed to have the intended result. If that guarantee cannot be made, then the intervention should not be taken.

The *anthropic principle* is the law of human existence. Our existence in the universe depends on numerous constants and parameters whose values fall within a very narrow range. If a single variable is slightly different we would not exist. The *data resource anthropic principle* states that if the data resource management rules are followed, a comparate data resource will be developed. The rules create the right conditions for development of a comparate data resource. If the rules are not followed, a disparate data resource will be developed.

Iatrogenesis refers to the inadvertent adverse effects or complications caused by or resulting from medical treatment or advice. The term originated in medicine and is generally referred to as harm caused by the healer. The *data resource iatrogenesis principle* states that the disparate data resource was caused by or resulted from the actions of the data management professionals and/or business professionals in an effort to create data to meet the business information demand. Unlike medicine, the actions may have been intentional or unintentional.

Cognitive dissonance is the disharmony that is created when an individual's personal reality does not fit the actual reality of the situation. When a person perceives that the state of the data resource is pretty good and receives information that the actual state of the data resource is bad, a tremendous disharmony is created. That person usually reacts in some way, such as ignoring the situation, denying that the situation exists, laying blame for the situation, or setting about correcting the situation.

The *principle of gradual change* states that the disparate data resource evolved slowly and almost unnoticed until it was too late to correct. The *principle of delayed change* states that nothing will change to prevent a situation from getting worse until it's too late. When the situation is finally discovered, such as a disparate data resource, it becomes a monumental task to resolve the problem.

Supporting Theories

Several theories from outside data resource management support development of a comparate data resource, including communication theory, semiotic theory, set theory, graph theory, and relational theory. Each of these theories is summarized below.

Communication theory states that information is the opposite of entropy, where entropy is disorderliness or noise. A message contains information that must be relevant and timely to the recipient. If the message does not contain relevant and timely information, it is simply noise (non-information). *Syntactic information* is raw data. It is arranged according to certain rules. Syntactic information alone is meaningless—it's just raw data. *Semantic information* has context and meaning. It is relevant and timely. It is also arranged according to certain rules.

Note that *syntactic information* from communication theory has been defined as *data*, and *semantic information* has been split into *data in context* and *information*. The distinctions were made to lay a better foundation for understanding and resolving disparate data.

Semiotics is a general theory of signs and symbols and their use in expression and communication. *Semiotic theory* deals with the relation between signs and symbols, and their interpretation. It consists of syntax, semantics, and pragmatics. *Syntax* deals with the relation between signs and symbols, and their interpretation. Specifically, it deals with the rules of syntax for using signs and symbols. *Semantics* deals with the relation between signs and symbols, and what they represent. Specifically, it deals with their meaning. *Pragmatics* deals with the relation between signs and symbols, and their users. Specifically, it deals with their usefulness.

Set theory is a branch of mathematics or of symbolic logic that deals with the nature and relations of sets. The traditional form has been slightly modified to be useful for managing data.

Graph theory is a branch of discrete mathematics that deals with the study of graphs as mathematical structures used to model relations between objects from a certain collection. A graph consists of a collection of vertices (or nodes), and a collection of edges (or arcs) that connect pairs of vertices. The edges may be directed from one vertex to another, or undirected, meaning no distinction between the two vertices.

Relational theory was developed by Dr. Edgar F. (Ted) Codd to describe how data are designed and managed. The theory represents data and their interrelations through a set of rules for structuring and manipulating data, while maintaining their integrity. It is based on mathematical principles and is the base for design and use of relational database management systems.

Data Resource Management Framework

The ***Data Resource Management Framework*** is a framework that represents the discipline for complete management of a comparate data resource. It represents the cooperative management of an organization-wide data resource that supports the current and future business information demand. The segments and components of the Data Resource Management Framework are shown in Figure 1.2.

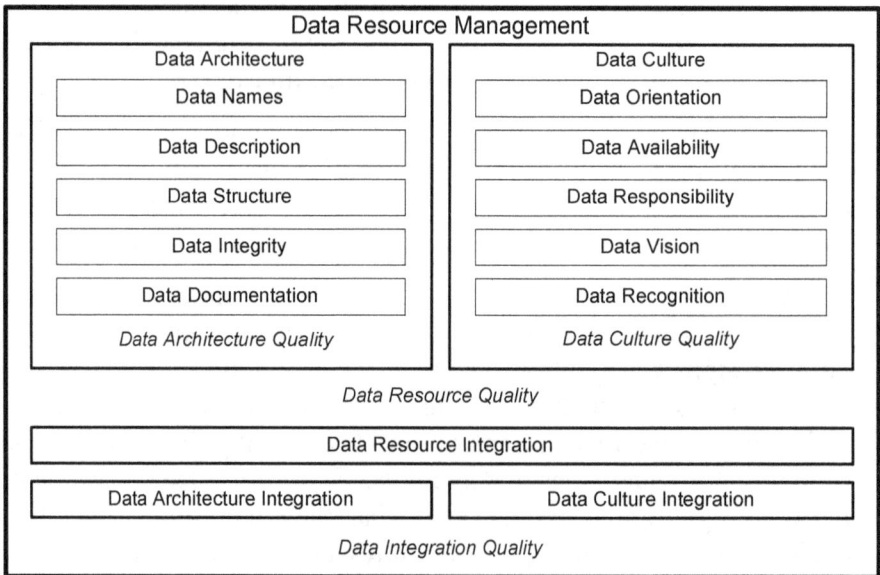

Figure 1.2. The Data Resource Management Framework.

The Data Resource Management Framework contains two main segments, data architecture and data culture, commonly referred to as the *data architecture segment* and the *data culture segment*. Each of these two segments has a quality aspect, specifically *data architecture quality* and *data culture quality*. Together, these two quality aspects provide the overall data resource quality.

The data architecture segment contains components for data names, data definitions, data structure, data rules, and data documentation. The data culture segment contains components for data orientation, data availability, data responsibility, data vision, and data recognition.

The Data Resource Management Framework has been enhanced to include data resource integration, consisting of data architecture integration and data culture integration. These two topics are described in the next chapter on Data Resource Integration. The details of data architecture integration are described in Chapter 3 on Data Architecture Integration, and the details of data culture integration are described in Chapter 13 on Data Culture Integration.

The Data Resource Management Framework has been formally merged into the Data Column of the Zachman Framework as the complete discipline for managing an organization's data resource. The initial merger was done in 2005, before the enhancement of the Data Resource Management Framework that included data resource integration. However, the enhancement for data resource integration is included in the merger by extension to provide an enhanced discipline for managing an organization's data resource.

Data architecture quality is how well the data architecture components contribute to overall data management quality. ***Data culture quality*** is how well the data culture components contribute to the overall data management quality.

Data Architecture Segment

Architecture (general) is the art, science, or profession of designing and building structures. It's the structure or structures as a whole, such as the frame, heating, plumbing, wiring, and so on, in a building. It's the style of structures and method of design and construction, such as Roman or Colonial architecture. It's the design or system perceived by people, such as the architecture of the Solar System

Architecture (data) is the art, science, or profession of designing and building a data resource. It's the structure of the data resource as a whole. It's the style or type of design and construction of the data resource. It's a system, conceived by people, that represents the business world.

Data architecture (1) is the method of design and construction of an integrated data resource that is business driven, based on real-world subjects as perceived by the organization, and implemented into appropriate operating environments. It consists of components that provide a consistent foundation across organizational boundaries to provide easily identifiable, readily available, high-quality data to support the current and future business information demand.

Data architecture (2) is the component of the Data Resource Management Framework that contains all of the activities, and the products of those activities, related to the identification, naming, definition, structuring, integrity, accuracy, effectiveness, and documentation of the data resource.

The architectural segment consists of five components, data names, data definitions, data structure, data integrity, and data documentation, that define the architecture of the data resource The first four components deal with understanding the organization's perception of the business world and the activities they perform in that business world. The fifth component is documentation of that single, robust understanding for all to view.

Data Culture Segment

The cultural segment contains five components, data orientation, data availability, data responsibility, data vision, and data recognition It represents the cultural aspects of building, managing, and using the data resource to support the business information demand. It deals with people's ability to build, maintain, and use the common single understanding for business success.

Culture is the act of developing the intellectual and moral faculties; expert care and training; enlightenment and excellence of taste acquired by intellectual and aesthetic training; acquaintance with and taste in fine arts, humanities, and broad aspects of science; the integrated pattern of human knowledge, belief, and behavior that depends upon man's capacity for learning and transmitting knowledge to succeeding generations; the customary beliefs, social forms, and material traits of a racial, religious, or social group.

Data culture (1) is the function of managing the data resource as a critical resource of the organization equivalent to managing the financial resource, the human resource, and real property. It consists of directing and controlling the development, administering policies and procedures, influencing the actions and conduct of anyone maintaining or using the data resource, and exerting a guiding influence over the data resource to support the current and future business information demand.

Data culture (2) is the component of the Data Resource Management Framework that contains all of the activities, and the products of those activities, related to orientation, availability, responsibility, vision, and recognition of the data resource.

Comparate Data Resource Vision

The *comparate data resource vision* is the disparate data resource thoroughly understood and integrated into a comparate data resource, supported by a Data Resource Guide, to fully support the current and future business information demand. The comparate data resource vision is shown in Figure 1.3. The existing data and any new data are integrated into a comparate data resource. The comparate data resource is supported by a comprehensive Data Resource Guide that fully documents the data resource. People can go to that Data Resource Guide, find the data they need to perform their business activities, and extract those data to appropriate information systems to meet the business information demand.

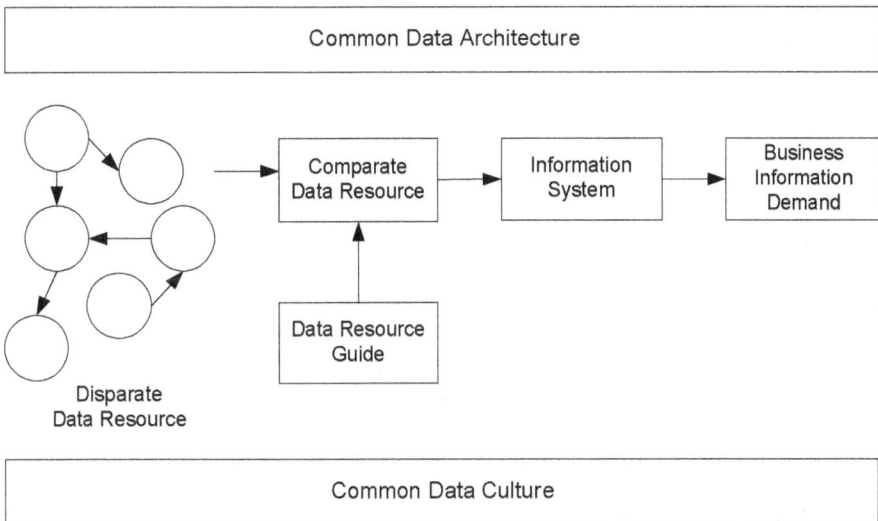

Figure 1.3. Comparate data resource vision.

Data engineering has the responsibility to understand the disparate data resource and build the comparate data resource and the Data Resource Guide. That responsibility is driven by the need to support the current and future business information demand. Information engineering has the responsibility to use the comparate data resource to meet the business information demand.

A common data architecture and a common data culture are the two contexts for resolving data disparity and developing a comparate data resource. Together they help the organization move from the complexity of disparate data to the simplicity of a comparate data resource. They help the organization break the disparate data cycle and begin a comparate data cycle. The Common Data Architecture is described in Chapter 3, and the Common Data Culture is described in Chapter 13.

Disparity is a common and persistent problem in all aspects of information technology. Disparity has been happening since data processing first began, and has continued without interruption as data processing evolved into information technology. It is continuing at an ever-increasing rate, with no end in sight. Disparity is impacting the business of both public sector and private sector organizations in ways that are obvious and in ways that are not so obvious.

The only real end to the existing disparity is when an organization goes out of business and ceases to exist. At that point the disparity disappears, unless, of course, another organization inherits the disparity. Although going out of business may be an option for some private sector organizations, it is generally not an option for public sector organizations. Public sector organizations need to keep operating regardless of the level of disparity.

Another option to resolving disparity is to close down the business for six months to a year, resolve the disparity, set a new higher quality foundation, and then restart the business. Such action is not possible for any business that I know about. In today's business world, closing shop for even a few weeks or months is tantamount to going out of business.

The only option left is to resolve disparity on-the-fly, if an organization is to stay in business and remain successful in that business. However, an organization must first stop the ever-increasing disparity before they can begin resolving the existing disparity. It has been shown over and over that trying to resolve the existing disparity without first stopping the increasing disparity will not produce meaningful results. Disparate data are produced faster than they can be understood and resolved.

Development of a comparate data resource is driven by three basic rules. First, any data that are known to be false, or are not known to be true, will not be promoted. Second, the truth about the quality of the data in a disparate data resource will never be concealed or altered. Third, the organization should have no suspicion about the work, the intentions, or the integrity of the data.

Achieving a Comparate Data Resource

Achieving a comparate data resource requires a change in attitudes and an organizational orientation toward developing a comparate data resource. Each of these topics is described below.

Attitudes

Since I wrote *Data Resource Simplexity,* I've talked with a number of people about the problems with data resource management today. Many agree with what I stated, but felt that too many problems existed to be addressed at one time, or the problems were outside their particular span of control. They asked what I'd recommend as the top three things to address in their organization to reduce the data hazard and data risk.

I explained my choice of the three things I'd address, not necessarily in order of severity. Other things certainly need to be addressed, but these are my top three.

First, is the attitude of database managers and technicians who feel they don't need no stinking data architect to tell them how to build their databases. Note the attitude toward personalizing the database, which inevitably leads to brute-force-physical development and further data disparity.

Second, is the attitude of some data modelers who don't listen to the business, have their own perception of the business, or have their own modeling notation. A good data modeler must listen to the business and develop a data model that represents the business as the business professionals describe it, in a manner that those business professionals readily understand.

Third, is the attitude of some vendors who want to warp the business to fit their particular software product. Not all vendors have such an attitude, but beware of those that do. The result will only be detrimental to the business, will likely go over budget and beyond the due date, and will likely not meet the objectives as originally defined. Find a vendor that will work with the organization to provide a solution that represents business the way the organization does business.

Organizational Orientation

I've been asked several times what I would do to help an organization get started on the path toward building a comparate data resource. My response has been that organizations need to recognize that disparate data exist and adopt an orientation toward resolving those disparate data and creating a comparate data resource. My emphasis on a new orientation is described below.

Organizations have the opportunity to accept or reject the concepts, principles, and techniques that lead to a comparate data resource. Organizations can choose between a disparate and a comparate data resource, and between success or failure of the data resource to adequately support the current and future business information demand.

Organizations need to recognize and avoid patterns of failure and choose to adopt patterns of success. A pattern of failure is a sequence of events that lead toward a disparate data resource and its failure to support the current and future business information demand. It's a pattern of thought or behavior that is often profit or attitude driven. A pattern of success is a sequence of events that lead toward a comparate data resource and full support for the current and future business information demand.

Organizations have the opportunity to choose to adjust their attitudes about how the data resource is developed and managed. Attitude, behavior, ego, arrogance, and so on, are patterns of failure that lead to a disparate data resource.

Organizations need to embrace formal data resource management concepts, principles, and techniques, and use them consistently to develop a comparate data resource. The concepts, principles, and techniques are well known, have been around for years, and have been proven successful.

Organizations can, and must, choose to mitigate the risks and hazards of a disparate data resource. They need to put the brakes on the disparate data cycle and the natural drift of the data resource toward disparity. They need to start a comparate data cycle that leads to a comparate data resource. To do otherwise may be hazardous to the organization's health.

Organizations need to consider establishing a chief data architect, because it's obvious that the chief information officer is not interested in the data resource. One person who is primarily responsible for development of a comparate data resource needs to be designated.

The orientation almost sounds too simple in principle, but it can and has been achieved. The concepts, principles, and techniques described in the current book are simple, yet they are elegant in resolving disparate data and developing a comparate data resource; detailed, yes, but simple and elegant in their orientation.

SUMMARY

The data resource in most public and private sector organizations today is really bad. Data resource quality in many organizations is at an all-time low, and is getting worse. Some evidence shows that people are actively making the data quality worse, knowingly or unknowingly.

Tackling data resource disparity is not easy, but it is far from impossible. It takes real tough thinking and hard work to understand and resolve disparate data and create a comparate data resource. The tough thinking is understanding the existing disparate data. The hard work is getting people to change their attitudes about developing a comparate data resource. Architectural issues are relatively easy, but the cultural issues are relatively difficult.

Organizations must choose to understand the disparate data resource and develop a comparate data resource. They must accept that theories, concepts, principles, and techniques are available for understanding disparate data and developing a comparate data resource. They must remove the past barriers and allow people to see things in a very elegant and simple way, and use the technology available to develop a comparate data resource that fully supports the current and future business information demand of the organization.

QUESTIONS

The following questions are provided as a review of existing disparate data and development of a comparate data resource, and to stimulate thought about evolving from a disparate data resource to a comparate data resource.

1. What are the basic theories that support data resource management?

2. What are the components of relational theory, and which of those support development of a comparate data resource within a common data architecture?

3. What does the Data Resource Management Framework represent?

4. Why does a lexical challenge exist in data resource management?

5. What are the basic problems with a disparate data resource?

6. Why do hype-cycles lead to a disparate data resource?

7. Why do attitudes lead to a disparate data resource?

8. Why are there no quick solutions to resolving disparate data and creating a comparate data resource?

9. Why are both a common data architecture and a common data culture needed to achieve a comparate data resource?

10. Why should data be considered a critical resource of the organization?

Chapter 2

DATA RESOURCE INTEGRATION CONCEPT

Integration includes both the data resource and data culture.

The Data Resource Management Framework contains two segments for Data Architecture and Data Culture. The Data Architecture segment represents the data resource, and the Data Culture segment represents the business of managing the data resource. Each of these components must be formally integrated to achieve a comparate data resource that supports the current and future business information demand.

Organizations often emphasize integration of the data resource without considering integration of the organizational culture managing that data resource. Chapter 2 provides an overview of the integration process for the data resource and the data culture. The integration concepts and principles are described for overall data resource management integration, data resource integration, and data culture integration. The various states of the data resource and data culture are described.

Integration of the data resource within a Common Data Architecture is described in more detail in Chapters 3 through 12. Integration of the organization's data culture into a Common Data Culture is described in more detail in Chapter 13.

INTEGRATING DATA RESOURCE MANAGEMENT

Most public and private sector organizations are not formally integrating their disparate data resource or the fragmented management of their data resource. Most integration efforts that are initiated are usually incomplete or inconsistent, and seldom go to any meaningful conclusion. By meaningful conclusion, I mean resolving a substantial portion of their disparate data resource and fragmented data culture, and making that integration persistent over time. By substantial, I mean eighty percent or more of their disparate data resource, and ninety percent or more of their fragmented data culture.

Many public and privates sector organizations have started some type of data resource integration initiative, but have not been as successful as expected. In some situations, the result has been worse than expected, with the data resource becoming more disparate and the data culture becoming more fragmented. The basic reason for the failure is that the organization didn't have a robust strategy for approaching integration.

Concept

An organization's data resource management, including the data resource and the data culture, must be substantially integrated within the Data Resource Management Framework. The Data Resource Management Framework provides the overall construct for understanding and resolving a disparate data resource and a fragmented data culture.

How does an organization go about resolving their disparate data resource? How does an organization create a comparate data resource? How does an organization proceed from the current state of low quality data to the ideal state of high quality data? How does an organization go about integrating their data culture? How does an organization go from a state of fragmented data culture to a state of cohesive data culture? These valid questions are answered in the current and subsequent chapters.

The disparate data resource and the fragmented data culture must each be integrated to have formal data resource management. If only the disparate data resource is integrated, the fragmented data culture leads to continued data disparity. If only the fragmented data culture is integrated, the disparate data resource continues to be a problem.

The primary reason for integrating the disparate data resource and the fragmented data culture is to be able to meet the organization's current and future business information demand. That demand has historically not been met through the disparate data resource, the fragmented data culture, or both. Therefore, both the disparate data resource and the fragmented data culture must be integrated.

The lexical challenge in data resource management is a monumental problem, as described in *Data Resource Simplexity* and Chapter 1 of the current book. That lexical challenge is pervasive through all aspects of data resource management. To make any real progress toward data resource management integration, the lexical challenge must be resolved right up front.

The following terms apply to data resource management integration and are used consistently throughout the book. Additional, more detailed, terms are presented throughout the book as the integration process is described in more detail. Some of these terms may be mainstream terms to which a specific meaning has been applied, while other terms may be contrary to mainstream terms. In either case, the terms are specifically defined and used consistently throughout the book.

Data Resource Management Integration

Discordant is being at variance; disagreeing; quarrelsome; relating to disagreement or clashing. ***Discordant data resource management*** is the situation where the overall management of an organization's data resource, including the data resource itself and the data culture, has a high variance and disagreement.

Concordant means agreeing; in a state of agreement; a harmonious combination. ***Concordant data resource management*** is the situation where the overall management of an organization's data resource, including the data resource itself and the data culture, is in agreement and harmony.

Integrate means to form or blend into a whole; to unite with something else; to incorporate into a larger unit; to bring into common organization. *Integration* is the act or process of integrating.

Data resource management integration is the overall integration of the management of an organization's data resource, including integration of the data resource itself and integration of the data culture. It is the process of moving from discordant data resource management to concordant data resource management. It includes all components of the Data Resource Management Framework. Both the data resource itself and the data culture must be integrated to fully support the current and future business information demand.

Data Resource Management Transition

Transition is the passage from one state, stage, or place to another; a movement, development, or evolution from one form, stage, or style to another. It is moving in a consistent direction toward a desired goal. It implies permanence of the passage or evolution without a return to the former state.

Data resource management transition is the transition from a state of discordant data resource management to a state of concordant data resource management. It includes both data resource transition and data culture transition. The transition has a direction and purpose, and permanence to the extent that a return is not made to discordant data resource management.

Traditionally, organizations have been concentrating on the *how* of data integration—the physical integration of the data. That's where the industry emphasis is placed, and most organizations follow that trend. Organizations need to concentrate on the *what* of data resource management integration with the objective of sharing of comparate data. That's not where the industry emphasis is being placed.

The *what* of data resource management integration needs to be the first step, followed by the *how* of data resource integration and the *how* of data culture integration. Therefore, organizations need to move systematically from the *what* of data resource management integration through the *how* of data resource integration and the *how* of data culture integration. That's the only way that the business information demand will be met.

Basic Principles

Several basic principles apply to data resource management integration, including contrarian thinking, integration is not a migration, descriptive and prescriptive aspects, retrospective and prospective aspects, probabilistic and deterministic aspects, the need to be value added, effectiveness and efficiency, integration is a discovery process, the point of diminishing returns, understanding and uncertainty, and the need for prevention before resolution. Each of these principles is described below.

Contrarian Thinking

Data resource management transition follows the principle of contrarian thinking. **Contrarian thinking** is not following the herd and thinking outside the box. Current wisdom is not simply accepted without question. Current practices are always scrutinized for better ways. The questions *Why?* or *Why not?* are frequently asked. Wanting to know what others are doing, and why, is persistent. Multiple voices are encouraged to speak on issues. Risk taking and innovations are valued and leveraged for maximum benefit. Thinking gray is common, without group think or crowd mentality. Synergy and teamwork are encouraged.

Contrarian thinking was used for developing the current concepts, principles, and techniques for data resource management integration. It's also used for getting people involved to resolve a disparate data resource and a fragmented data culture.

Not a Migration

Data resource management integration is a transition, not a migration. **Migration** is a movement to change location periodically, especially by moving seasonally from one region or country to another. It's wandering without a long term purpose, or wandering with only current objectives in mind, like nomadic wandering or bird migration. It's a lack of a permanent settlement, especially resulting from seasonal or periodic movement.

Data management today places considerable emphasis on data migration, and that's the problem! Too much short term wandering without any long term purpose has already been done. Too much creating additional disparate data without understanding what already exists has already been done. Too much emphasis on the data resource and not the data culture. Formal data resource management integration must be done to resolve the existing disparate data and fragmented data culture.

The term *data migration* is a major part of the lexical challenge. Again, people are pumping the words without really understanding what they are saying. Therefore, the term is inappropriate and is not used within the context of data resource management integration.

Descriptive and Prescriptive

Descriptive is to describe; referring to, consulting, or grounded in matters of observation or experience; expressing the quality, kind, or condition of what is denoted by a modified term. It is finding out what currently exists and describing it. *Prescriptive* is serving to prescribe; acquired by, founded on, or determined by prescription or long-standing custom. It's describing how to get from an existing situation to a desired situation.

Data resource management integration is both descriptive and prescriptive. The descriptive aspect is determining what currently exists in the data resource and within the data culture, and describing them in enough detail that integration can proceed to a meaningful conclusion. It includes thoroughly understanding the current state of the data resource and the data culture. The data resource is described within the context of a Common Data Architecture and the data culture is described within the context of a Common Data Culture.

The prescriptive aspect is describing how to get from a disparate data resource state to a comparate data resource state, and from a fragmented data culture to a cohesive data culture state. It includes both describing the desired state (to-be) and how to get from the current state (as-is) to the desired state.

Retrospective and Prospective

Retrospective is the act or process of surveying the past; based on memory; affecting things past; looking back, contemplating, or directing to the past. It is looking at what has happened in the past to reach what currently exists. *Prospective* is likely to come about; likely to be or become; expected to happen; looking to the future. It is looking ahead at what's needed.

Data resource management integration is both retrospective and prospective. The retrospective aspect is looking at what has happened to the data resource and the data culture in the past and how they arrived at their current state. It's how the organization arrived at the current disparate data resource state and the fragmented data culture state. The prospective aspect is looking ahead at what is needed for a comparate data resource and a cohesive data culture. It's what the organization desires for it's the management of a critical resource.

The retrospective aspect is descriptive in nature—describing what currently exists and how the organization arrived at that current state. The prospective aspect is prescriptive in nature—prescribing what needs to be done and how to achieve that end state.

Deterministic and Probabilistic

Probabilistic is of, referring to, based on, or affected by probability, randomness, or chance. *Deterministic* is the quality or state of being determined; every event, act, and decision is the consequence of some previous event, act, and decision.

In the past and in the present day, data resource management has been a mixture of probabilistic and deterministic. Many of the problems seen today resulted from a probabilistic approach to data resource management. The data resource and the data culture seem to have just happened. To correct these problems, and ensure that data resource management leads to a comparate data resource and a cohesive data culture, the approach must be deterministic, based on sound concepts, principles, and techniques.

Value Added

The value added concept has been around for many years. Basically, every step in a process must be value added, meaning that the step adds value to any previous step or steps. Every step in a process must add value. Any step in a process that does not add value, must be removed.

The problem with data resource management to date is that many process steps are not value added. Many steps are redundant or virtually useless. A good example of redundant steps is repeatedly modeling the same set of data many times over. A good example of useless steps is esoteric or very abstract modeling that does not add any understanding and often adds confusion. The result is a fragmented data culture and the creation of a disparate data resource. The problems can only be corrected by ensuring that any process in data resource management is a fully value added process.

Effectiveness and Efficiency

In simple terms, effectiveness is doing the right thing. It's performing the right processes for properly managing data as a critical resource. Any process or process step that is not needed to achieve the end objective are considered to be ineffective.

In simple terms, efficiency is doing the thing right. It's performing a process as expeditiously as possible. Any process that is not performed in the most expeditious manner is inefficient, wastes resources, and could produce undesirable results. Whether a process is effective or not, it can be performed efficiently or inefficiently.

Both effectiveness and efficiency are closely related to the value added concept. Value added means that the right processes are performed, that they are performed efficiently, and that they add value.

Past data resource management has been both ineffective and inefficient, resulting in a fragmented data culture, a loss of productivity, and creation of a disparate data resource. Data resource management must be both effective and efficient.

A Discovery Process

Data resource management integration is a discovery process that requires thought, analysis, intuition, perception, and a bit of luck. It's an evolutionary process due to the uncertainty with the disparate data resource. Anyone involved in data resource management transition must be an explorer, detective, investigator, archeologist, and so on, to find and understand the existing data resource and data culture. It's an evolutionary process due to the uncertainty that is faced with a disparate data resource and a fragmented data culture.

Point of Diminishing Returns

Data resource management integration has a point of diminishing returns. It is not feasible for most organizations to achieve one hundred percent integration of the data resource and the data culture. The cost is too prohibitive to achieve perfect quality in either the data resource or the data culture.

Quality is endless, and perfect quality is seldom necessary to operate the business successfully. Each organization must determine the level of quality they need based on the cost to achieve that quality. Data resource management integration is then performed until that level of quality is achieved. Going beyond that level becomes too costly for the organization.

Data resource management integration must be just good enough for business success. Where is the biggest bang for the buck? What is the return on investment? What is the benefit / cost ratio? What is the benefit to the business? All of these questions must be answered to establish a point of diminishing returns before data resource management integration begins.

The level of quality improvement is what's good for the organization prospectively. The past quality can be reviewed retrospectively to determine problems that need to be resolved. However, the improvement in quality is from the current situation forward.

Understanding and Uncertainty

Albert Einstein once said if he had only one hour to save the world he would spend fifty-five minutes defining the problem and only five minutes finding the solution. The statement shows that thoroughly understanding the problem is absolutely necessary before that problem can be solved. Thoroughly understanding disparate data is absolutely necessary before those disparate data can be resolved and a comparate data resource built.

Too many people charge ahead with resolving disparate data before understanding those disparate data, which is a brute-force-physical approach. The result is often failure or a result that is less than desirable. The result is often the creation of additional disparate data. Therefore, it's most important to thoroughly understand the disparate data before any attempt is made to resolve those disparate data.

The basic principle is that the quality of any solution to a problem is proportional to the quality of the understanding of that problem. The better the understanding of the problem, the better the solution to that problem will be. In addition, a better understanding of the problem often leads to an easier solution to that problem.

Some people involved in data resource integration concentrate on budgets, organizational structures, project management, commitment, interpersonal communication, and so on. These items are certainly important as support, but are not primary to data resource management integration.

The primary emphasis is on data resource management, not on ancillary items. The primary emphasis is thoroughly understanding the data with respect to the business and the culture to manage those data. Understanding the data resource and the culture, and documenting that understanding is the key. With a thorough understanding, the organization can agree on how to integrate the data resource and the data culture. When an agreement is reached, the actual data resource management integration becomes relatively routine.

Preventing Discordance Before Resolving Discordance

I made the point in *Data Resource Simplexity* that the creation of disparate data must be stopped before the existing disparate data can be resolved. The creation of disparate data progresses much faster than those disparate data can be resolved. If the creation of disparate data is not stopped before an attempt is made to resolve those disparate data, the disparate data resolution process will never be completed.

The process of stopping the creation of disparate data before resolving existing disparate data may be done for the organization at large or for a major data subject area. That choice is up to the organization. The point to be made is that the continued creation of disparate data in any specific data subject area must be stopped before an attempt is made to resolve the existing disparate data in that data subject area.

A similar situation exists with a fragmented data culture. The proliferation of a fragmented data culture must be stopped before the existing data culture can be resolved. Little good comes from resolving the fragmented data culture in one part of the organization while the fragmented data culture runs rampant in another part of the organization.

Unlike resolving disparate data, which can be done one data subject area at a time, resolving a fragmented data culture must be done on an organization wide basis. The reason is that data and business processes are orthogonal to each other. In other words, many different business processes across the organization use the same set of data. Therefore, the fragmented data culture must be resolved before any attempt to resolve disparate data is made.

Data Resource Simplexity is about stopping the creation of disparate data by developing data within a Common Data Architecture, and about stopping the creation of a fragmented data culture by managing the data resource within a Common Data Culture. It presented the concepts, principles, and techniques for stopping the development of disparate data and a fragmented data culture. The current book is about resolving the existing disparate data resource and fragmented data culture.

The problem faced by most organizations is that they seldom see the benefits of prevention until it's too late. Prevention is often perceived as not being beneficial and as impacting business operations. However, the future impact of non-prevention can result in a devastating loss to the organization.

The reason that organizations don't see the benefits of prevention is that the distinction between memory and imagination is often blurred. What an organization believes about the quality of their data resource is often quite different from the actual quality of their data resource. When an organization believes that their data resource quality is high, they fail to see the benefits of preventing further disparity, or even the need to resolve existing disparity.

The often discouraging news is that organizations only see the benefits of prevention after going through data resource management integration. Only after realizing the impacts of non-prevention, after the fact, can an organization begin to see the benefits of prevention. One of my biggest hopes, which I may never see, is for organizations that have seen the benefits of prevention after data resource integration to somehow pass that information on to other organizations. The data resource management profession would be much more respected if they could make organizations aware of the benefits of prevention.

INTEGRATING THE DATA RESOURCE

Data resource integration is one segment of data resource management, as shown in the Data Resource Management Framework and described above. An overview of data resource integration sets the stage for the following chapters that describe the data resource integration process in detail. The overview includes the concepts, the lexical challenge, basic principles, and the data resource states.

Concept

The *data resource integration concept* is to resolve the disparate data and produce a comparate data resource that meets the current and future business information demand. An awareness of the data resource and a thorough understanding of it lead to the resolution of the disparate data. The result is an integrated data resource that is readily shared across the organization.

Many data integration approaches today concentrate on specific sets of data for a specific purpose. They are often uncoordinated and seldom substantially resolve the disparate data. Data resource integration applies to the entire data resource and emphasizes the substantial resolution of disparate data.

Data resource integration is like archeology. Archeology looks at the bones and skeletons, makes assumptions about climate and geology, and tries to figure out the life cycle of ancient species. Data resource integration looks at the exiting disparate data, makes assumptions about the environment at the time the data were captured and stored, and tries to figure out the intent and meaning of those data.

The data resource integration concept is often ignored in many data integration initiatives. After looking at many different data resource integration initiatives in many different public and private sector organizations, it appears that the only thing standard about data resource integration is a non-standard approach to data integration. That situation needs to be changed to a formal approach to data resource integration.

Common Data Architecture

The formal integration of anything must be done within some common context. Integration cannot be done successfully unless it is done within some overarching construct within which the integration is performed. Many people have tried to integrate data without an overarching construct, but the effort either completely fails or is less than fully successful.

I had a memorable experience with one state that was attempting to understand their data before integration by cross-referencing the data in each database of each agency to databases in every other agency. The project was encountering some difficulty, as can be imagined. After some analysis, we determined that the process would never go to completion, and if it did go to completion, the state didn't have enough computer capacity to store the results. Further, the results would have little meaning for integrating those data.

The *Common Data Architecture* is a single, formal, comprehensive, organization-wide, data architecture that provides a common context within which all data are understood, documented, integrated, and managed. It transcends all data at the organization's disposal, includes primitive and derived data; elemental and combined data; fundamental and specific data, structured and complex structured data; automated and non-automated data; current and historical data; data within and without the organization; high level and low level data; and disparate and

51

comparate data. It includes data in purchased software, custom-built application databases, programs, screens, reports, and documents. It includes all data used by traditional information systems, expert systems, executive information systems, geographic information systems, data warehouses, object oriented systems, and so on. It includes centralized and decentralized data, regardless of where they reside, who uses them, or how they are used.

The Common Data Architecture is a paradigm, an archetype, a construct for an organization to use for developing a comparate data resource that adequately supports the current and future business information demand. It's an elegant and simple solution that provides a higher level of technology to understand and resolve a disparate data resource and create a comparate data resource.

A *common data architecture* (not capitalized) represents the actual common data architecture built by an organization for their data resource, based on concepts, principles, and techniques of the Common Data Architecture. The common data architecture contains all of the data used by the organization, as defined by the Common Data Architecture.

A common data architecture provides the overarching construct for providing a common view of all data. All variations in data names, meanings, formats, structures, integrity, and so on, are understood within the context of a common data architecture. All preferred data for developing the comparate data resource are designated within the context of a common data architecture. All data transformation rules are developed within the context of a common data architecture.

Formal Data Resource Integration

Formal data resource integration is any data resource integration done within the context of a common data architecture. It's more than a simple extract – transform – load. It's more than minor data cleansing. It's more than physically merging databases. Data resource integration is moving steadily through a series of very formal, but relatively simple, steps that go from a disparate data resource to a comparate data resource.

Informal data resource integration is any data resource integration done outside the context of a common data architecture. It usually does not result in a comparate data resource or any substantial resolution to the disparate data. It may result in increased data disparity. The term *data resource de-integration* is sometimes used to describe the results of informal data resource integration.

The Lexical Challenge

A formal approach to data resource integration requires that the lexical challenge be resolved. The definitions below set the stage for formal data resource integration.

The term *integration* is used often in many different contexts, but is largely undefined. It could mean integration of disparate data, integration of current and historical data, integration across platforms, integration for analysis to support business intelligence, and so on. I've seldom seen the term used properly for the integration of disparate data and never seen it used for the integration of a disparate data culture.

Many people use the term *information integration, data integration,* and *data resource integration* interchangeably. Yet again, interchanging these terms is most inappropriate and contributes to the lexical challenge in data resource management. All three terms have valid meanings, and the terms should be formally defined and used appropriately.

I've seen a variety of other terms, such as data purification, data cleansing, data scrubbing, data reconciliation, data conditioning, data filtering, data washing, data rinsing, data hygiene, data health, data decontamination, and so on. All of these terms are slang terms that are used without any formal definition and contribute to the lexical challenge. People are again pumping the words without any denotative meaning about what those words represent.

The terms below are formally defined to provide a denotative meaning and are used consistently throughout the book to resolve the lexical challenge.

Data Resource Integration and Transition

Data resource integration is the thorough understanding of existing disparate data within a common data architecture, the designation of preferred data, and the development of a comparate data resource based on those preferred data. It is the act or process to form, coordinate, or blend disparate data into a comparate data resource. It resolves the existing data disparity.

Data resource integration is not a simple union of data records from multiple databases or a simple join of existing databases. Nor is it a combination of existing databases. The process is much more detailed and requires thoroughly understanding the disparate data within a common context, then making informed decisions about how to create a comparate data resource.

An *integrated data resource* is a data resource where all data are integrated within a common context and are appropriately deployed for maximum use supporting the current and future business information demand. Data awareness and data understanding are increased. Data variability is at a minimum and data redundancy is reduced to a known and manageable level. Data integrity is known and at the desired level. The data are as current as the organization needs to conduct its business.

Data resource transition is the transition of an organization's data resource from a disparate data resource state, through an interim data resource state and a virtual data resource state, to a comparate data resource state. It's the pathway that is followed from a disparate data resource to a comparate data resource. It's unique to each organization depending on their current situation and future needs.

Data resource transition is a consistent movement toward the long term objective of a comparate data resource that provides one version of truth about the business. Ultimately, the comparate data resource contains only one source for each business fact. The comparate data resource may be replicated for operational efficiency, but the replications must be kept in synch with the primary source on a regular basis.

Data Integration

Merge means to blend or combine together, to become combined or united. *Data integration* is the merging of data from multiple, often disparate, sources, usually based on some record of reference, to provide a single output, such as an interim database or report. It does not resolve any existing data disparity, and may further increase data disparity. It is seldom done within the context of a common data architecture.

Data integration usually means combining two or more sets of data, often from different databases or operating environments, together in the same physical location for operational processing, which is not the concept of data resource integration. The initial databases remain unchanged and the disparity still exists. Simply merging disparate data into a single location will not resolve data disparity.

Data Migration and Consolidation

Data migration is the movement of data to change location periodically from one database or platform to another depending on the physical environment and the needs of the organization. The migration seldom includes a thorough understanding of the data and is usually done outside of any context. The term *migration* is acceptable because periodic movements can be made depending on the conditions.

Data consolidation is the process of merging existing data from different sources into one location. The data may be restructured slightly, but nothing is done to thoroughly understand the data or to resolve data disparity.

Database merge is the process of merging separate compatible databases together into one single database. The data are not altered in any way. Data records are simply merged into one database. For example, middle school and high school student databases are merged together into one combined database for middle school and high school students.

Data conversion is the process of changing the same physical data schema from one database management system to another database management system. The data values are not altered in any way. They are simply moved from one database management system to another.

Database conversion is the process of changing a database management system from one operating environment to another operating environment. The data are not altered in any way. The database management system is simply moved from one operating platform to another.

Information Integration

Information integration is the integration of information, using the formal definition of information, from multiple sources into an understandable set of information for a specific use. It's the process of taking disparate information and developing comparate information for some business activity.

For example, a person may be doing a web search for the medical treatment of some illness. The information that person gains from each web site is relevant and timely, according to the formal definition of *information*. However, the different sets of information gained from all of the web sites is disparate in the sense that the information is not in the same format, the same construct, the same sequence, and so on. The disparate information is difficult for a person to assimilate.

The person needs to integrate that information in some meaningful and cohesive manner that makes the information interpretable and comprehensible to the individual for treatment of the illness. How that disparate information is integrated is beyond the scope of the current book, and depends on the individual and the subject matter. The point to be made is that the integration of information is different from the integration of a disparate data resource.

Data Transformation

Data transformation deals with actually changing the structure, meaning, integrity, and sometimes the values, of the data. It will not be defined or described here. It will be defined and described in great detail in Chapter 11 on Data Transformation Concept, and in Chapter 12 on Data Transformation Process.

Basic Principles

Several basic principles support data resource integration, including integrating at the data level, semantic and structural integration, a detailed process, not reengineering, no single record of reference, no physical approaches, not scrap and rework, no lack of technical talent, and supporting tools. Each of these principles is described below.

Note that these basic principles for data resource integration are in addition to the basic principles described above for data resource management integration.

Integration at the Data Level

Data resource integration must be done at the data level. It cannot be done at the information level, the knowledge level, or the intelligence level. In fact, as will be described in detail through the following chapters, the integration must be done at the data variation level. The disparate data must be thoroughly done at the data variation level so those data can be successfully integrated.

Thoroughly understanding data at the variation level requires mentally separating the data from the product or database where those data are used or stored. Mentally separating the data from the product or database allows the data to be understood within the context of a common data architecture. Therefore, all data must be logically separated from the product or database to be thoroughly understood within a common data architecture and properly integrated.

Semantic and Structural Integration

The typical approaches to data resource integration have been either semantic or structural. Considerable discussion and conflict surround whether the semantics or the structure should drive data resource integration.

Formal data resource integration includes both semantic data integration and structural data integration. A choice between semantics or structure does not need to be made. Within the concept of a common data architecture, both semantics and structure are treated equally. In other words, a true understanding of the data is based on both semantics and structure.

Semantics is the meaning of the data with respect to the business, based on how they perceive the business world and operate in that business world. Structure is the arrangement of the data with respect to the business, based on formal data normalization and denormalization techniques. The structure is determined somewhat by the semantics, but largely by normalization and denormalization techniques.

Therefore, both the semantics and the structure must be thoroughly understood with respect to the business to resolve disparate data and develop a comparate data resource. Both are driven by the organization's perception of the business world. Neither is more important than the other.

A Detailed Process

Data resource integration is a very detailed process: however, it is not impossible if a few simple concepts, principles, and techniques are followed. Many people believe that data resource integration is a very difficult process, meaning complex or complicated, which is why many people look for quicker physical options and software tools. However, the process is not complex or complicated, it's just very detailed.

Data resource integration is not a major, one-time, one-pass, total resolution of the organization's disparate data. The resources required, the time involved, and the impacts on the business prevent tackling the entire disparate data resource in one pass. A more reasonable approach is a slow, steady, very detailed, evolutionary transition from a disparate data resource to a comparate data resource one major data subject at a time. The most successful approach is a slow change of disparate data to comparate data that produces benefits along the way. A known, planned, well-managed transition with short term benefits that promote success motivation is the only reasonable approach.

Not Reengineering

I initially referred to *data reengineering*, but abandoned that term because for something to be reengineered it must have been engineered in the first place. The disparate data resource in most organizations was obviously not engineered—it was just created. Hence, there can be no reengineering.

I then introduced *data refining* and defined it as refining disparate data within a common context to increase the awareness and understanding of data, remove data variability and redundancy, and develop an integrated data resource. The analogy was similar to oil refining that takes crude oil, refines it into useful products, stores those products for future use, and discards waster products.

However, oil refining only separates the products that already exist in crude oil. It cannot create products that don't already exist in the crude oil and has very little waste that is discarded. Resolving disparate data may well create new products and has considerable waste that is ultimately discarded.

Similarly, *re-architecting the data* does not apply. Most data were never really architected in the first place, hence re-architecting those data cannot occur. *Architecting the data* could be used, since the disparate data are being brought together within a common data architecture. However, data resource integration is more than just bringing the data together within a common data architecture. Therefore, the term *data resource integration* will be used throughout the book.

No Single System of Reference

I frequently run across the terms *system of reference, record of reference*, or *system of record*. These terms mean that, out of all the disparate data, a single system of reference should be found and that system of reference should become the comparate data resource. All other systems are then discarded. Miraculously, data resource integration is complete.

However, I've never seen any public or private sector organization where the system of reference approach worked. An organization's disparate data resource is usually so entangled with databases, applications, bridges, feeds, and so on, that it's nearly impossible to find a single system of reference. Further, if a single system of reference were designated, it's nearly impossible to simply abandon all other data and use the single system of reference. The applications tied to the other data would not be able to operate.

I've heard a variation of the same theme, which I refer to as the *big behemoth*. The largest database in the organization that connects to the most applications is designated as the system of reference. It becomes, almost automatically, the comparate data resource. All other applications either convert to that database or are abandoned. I like to use the term *the law of gross tonnage* when referring to the big behemoth.

The problem with the big behemoth approach is that it may be the biggest, but not necessarily the best. It likely contains redundant and variable data and still exhibits all of the features of disparate data. As such, it cannot ever be considered as the comparate data resource.

The best approach is to put all data through the data resource integration process and, at the very least, thoroughly understand those data and determine their disparity. Then an informed decision can be made about developing a comparate data resource. In nearly every situation where I've been involved, no single system of reference exists and some degree of data resource integration always occurs.

No Physical Approaches

I've described two physical approaches above and in *Data Resource Simplexity* that are essentially forbidden in data resource integration. The first is the *brute-force-physical approach* where people jump right into the physical changes to the databases. Adjustments are made to the databases and to the applications in an attempt to resolve data disparity. However, little progress is made toward data resource integration, and the result is often worse than the initial situation.

The second is the *suck-and-squirt approach* where data, usually from a system of reference, are sucked out of one database, pushed through some superficial data cleansing tool, and squirted into another database under the assumption that the result is comparate data. Again, little progress is made toward data resource integration, and the result is often worse than the initial situation.

The problem with these physical approaches is that people presume to thoroughly understand the data, and forge ahead to physically change those data. These people avoid the formal process to thoroughly understand the disparate data and formally plan the transformation to comparate data. By avoiding the formal process, the result is usually a more disparate data resource and wasted productivity. Therefore, it's best to go through the formal process, thoroughly understand the disparate data, plan the comparate data resource, and then transform the data according to that plan.

Not Scrap and Rework

I've heard *scrap and rework* used many times in reference to data resource integration. The term might be good for manufacturing, but it does not apply to data resource integration. No organization can afford to scrap their existing data resource and then build a comparate data resource from scratch. It just won't happen.

The data resource is the raw material for developing information to meet the business information demand and that raw material has tremendous intrinsic value. Scrapping that raw material leaves nothing for developing information, and without information, the organization virtually ceases to operate. *Scrap and rework* may apply where the product is scrapped and raw material is used to build a new product. It may even apply to scrapping the raw material when that raw material has no intrinsic value and can be easily replaced. However, no organization can afford to scrap their valuable data resource and then rebuild it again.

No Lack of Technical Talent

Once we figure out what needs to be done, there is no want for technical talent about how to get it done. *How will we ever accomplish all this? Who will do the work? How will it get done?* All are monumental questions I've heard many times. I've found that once the existing disparate data situation has been described, the preferred data architecture has been prescribed, and the data transformation rules have been defined, technical talent is readily available, generally enthusiastic, and very willing to tackle the task of creating a comparate data resource.

Supporting Tools

Generally, software tools cannot be purchased that can perform the entire data integration process for an organization. Software tools are available for scanning, inventorying, data quality improvement (such as addresses), data documentation, and so on. However, software tools are not available to understand the disparate data and transform those data to a comparate data resource. Improved software tools to support various aspects of data resource integration may come in the future, once the data resource integration process is formally defined. However, the difficulty of understanding disparate data and the uniqueness of each organization makes a complete data integration tool virtually impossible.

Beware of software tools that will completely resolve disparate data. Look carefully at the product to determine what it can do for the organization's disparate data resource and how it can support a data resource integration initiative. Usually, those software tools will perform far less than is claimed by the vendor.

Another reason that software tools for data resource integration don't exist is that those tools will work themselves out of existence. Once the disparate data are gone, the tools have no further use, hence vendors hesitate to invest in those tools. To some extent, vendors may have a vested interest in keeping disparate data around, because they can continue to sell software, books, consulting, and so on.

Organizations have two basic scenarios they can follow. First, they can look for software tools that perform the data resource integration process with minimum human intervention. Second, they can establish a formal approach for understanding and resolving disparate data, and look for software tools to support various aspects of that approach. The first approach has a high probability of failure and likely creates more disparate data. The second has a high probability of success and likely results in creation of a comparate data resource.

One organization that engaged me had purchased all of the books and software tools, and took many classes about integrating data. However, they could not get started, even with understanding the data. The basic problem is that tools can't understand the data or decide how to integrate those data. Only people can understand data and determine how to resolve those data—tools only support and document that understanding. One phrase I frequently use is *Tools won't solve the sins of disparate data. Only people working within the context of a common data architecture can resolve the sins of disparate data.*

A better approach for an organization is to develop their own custom data resource integration tools to match their unique environment. As mentioned above, I've found no lack of technical talent in an organization once the disparate data have been described and the comparate data resource has been prescribed. Most technical people are more than willing to resolve the disparate data mess.

Data Resource States

Data resource transition consists of four states, progressing from a low quality disparate data resource, through a formal data resource and a virtual data resource, to a high quality comparate data resource, as shown in Figure 2.1. All four states are part of the organization's data resource. The disparate data resource state is outside the common data architecture. The formal data resource state, virtual data resource state, and comparate data resource state are managed within a common data architecture.

An organization's data resource matures as it moves through the transition states. The existing disparate data resource is immature. The maturity improves as the data are understood, and the variability and redundancy are reduced. The comparate data resource is the mature state. Each of these states is described below.

Disparate Data Resource State

The ***disparate data resource state*** is the current state of a disparate data resource in an organization and is outside the context of a common data architecture. The data exhibit the four characteristics of disparate data: unknown existence, unknown meaning, high redundancy, and high variability. The disparate data cycle is in full swing and the natural drift of the data resource is toward disparity. It's the least desirable state of the data resource and is the initial state for the data resource transition process.

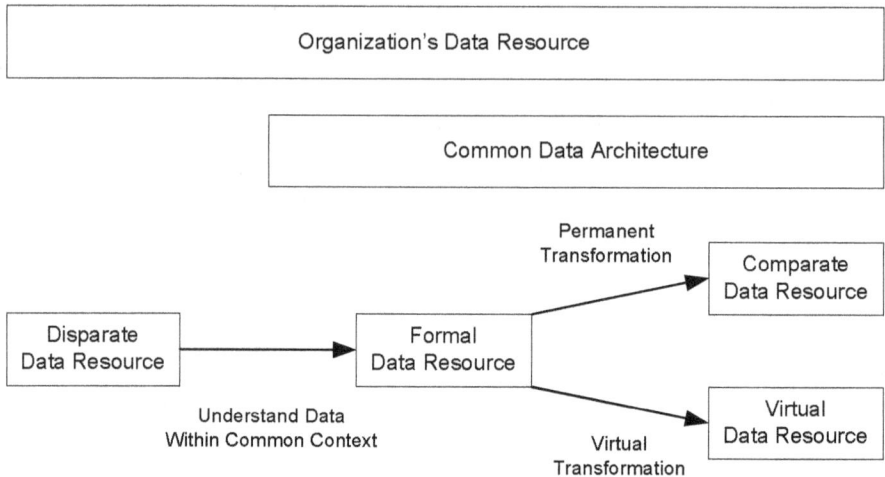

Figure 2.1. Data resource transition states.

Formal Data Resource State

The *formal data resource state* is a necessary state where the disparate data are readily understood within the context of a common data architecture. It's the first step in the data resource transition process where disparate data are put in context using a common data architecture. It's not a separate data resource since the data are only understood within a formal context.

The disparate data are inventoried and cross-referenced to the common data architecture. The data awareness problem and the understanding problem common with disparate data are resolved. Preferred data are designated and data translation rules are developed between the non-preferred and preferred data variations. These processes set the stage for reducing or resolving data redundancy and data variability. The integrity is known but has not been adjusted to the desired level.

The formal data resource state is an interim, non-destructive state where the existing data are not altered in any manner or moved from their present location. One of the problems with many techniques today is their destructive approach, which mandates the alteration or movement of existing data to improve understanding, often outside any formal construct. Such an approach is enough to turn most people against any effort to develop a comparate data resource.

Virtual Data Resource State

The *virtual data resource state* is an interim state between the formal data resource and a comparate data resource where real-time data transformation is performed to produce interim comparate data. The data are transformed in real time, according to formal data transformation rules, in either direction between disparate data and comparate data. Disparate data may be transformed to comparate data to support new applications or databases. Comparate data may be transformed to disparate data to support disparate applications or databases.

The data transformation is usually transparent to the recipient and is usually done through a formal data broker. The data transformation is non-persistent because the disparate data have not been resolved. Virtual data transformation is sometimes referred to as *just in time data transformation*, or *just in time comparate data*.

The virtual data resource state helps support the business operations while the comparate data resource is being developed and applications are being adjusted to access comparate data. It changes the natural drift of the data resource from disparate toward comparate data. Data bridges are resolved and applications are changed from using disparate data to using comparate data. It's the interim state of virtual data sharing as organizations strive to achieve the ideal state of a comparate data resource.

Comparate Data Resource State

The *comparate data resource state* is the desired state where disparate data have been substantially and permanently transformed to comparate data and the disparate data are substantially gone from the organization's data resource. It's a persistent data transformation where the data are subject oriented according to the organization's perception of the business world and are integrated within the common data architecture. The disparate data cycle is broken and the natural drift of the data resource is toward comparate data.

The comparate data resource is the ideal, mature situation for an organization's data resource. The disparate data are formally transformed one final time to a comparate data resource, usually through a data broker. The majority of data bridges are gone and the majority of applications have been transformed to directly use and maintain comparate data.

Some disparate data may still exist, but they are beyond the point of diminishing returns where it is not feasible to transform the data. A few applications may still use or maintain disparate data, but they are usually minor applications and it's not feasible to transform them.

The comparate data resource resolves most of the problems that perpetuate the disparate data cycle. The formal data resource state started breaking the disparate data cycle by raising the awareness and increasing the understanding of disparate data. The virtual data resource state further breaks the disparate data cycle by allowing access to those disparate data and real-time transformation to and from comparate data. The comparate data resource state has completely broken the disparate data cycle and the predominant drift of the data resource is toward comparity.

The comparate data resource state may not be achieved for ten years or more in most public and private sector organizations. However, progress toward a comparate data resource can be made within six months of beginning data resource integration, and substantial progress can be made in the first few years of a data resource integration initiative.

INTEGRATING THE DATA CULTURE

Data culture integration is one segment of data resource management, as shown in the Data Resource Management Framework. An overview of data culture integration sets the stage for Chapter 13, which describes data culture integration in detail. The overview includes the concept, the basic principles, and the data culture states.

Concept

The *data culture integration concept* is to resolve the fragmented data culture and create a cohesive data culture for the management of a critical data resource. A thorough understanding of the current fragmented data culture leads to its resolution and the creation of a cohesive data culture. That cohesive data culture, along with a comparate data resource, supports formal data resource management.

Fragmented is broken apart, detached, or incomplete; consisting of separate pieces. A *fragmented data culture* is a data culture that is broken apart into separate pieces that are unrelated, incomplete, and inconsistent. It is similar to a disparate data resource, and leads to the creation of a disparate data resource. A fragmented data culture cannot effectively or efficiently manage an organization's data resource.

Cohesive is sticking together tightly, a union between similar parts. A *cohesive data culture* is a data culture composed of business processes that are integrated to effectively and efficiently manage an organization's data resource. The business processes are seamless, consistent, and work together in a coordinated manner to develop and maintain a comparate data resource.

Common Data Culture

The ***Common Data Culture*** is a single, formal, comprehensive, organization-wide data culture that provides a common context within which the organization's data culture is understood, documented, and integrated. It includes all components in the Data Culture Segment of the Data Resource Management Framework for a reasonable data orientation, acceptable data availability, adequate data responsibility, expanded data vision, and appropriate data recognition.

The Common Data Culture is a paradigm, an archetype, a construct for an organization to use for understanding their fragmented data culture and developing a cohesive data culture. It transcends all data resource management functions, the fragmented and cohesive data culture, and all data in the organization's data resource as defined for the Common Data Architecture.

It's an elegant and simple approach that pulls all of the fragmented data resource management functions and processes together to provide consistent management of the organization's data resource, in an efficient and effective manner, so the data resource fully supports the current and future business information demand. It is based on formal concepts, principles, and techniques, similar to the Common Data Architecture, for coordinating data resource management.

A ***common data culture*** (lower case) is the actual data culture built by an organization for the proper management of their data resource. It's based on the concepts, principles, and techniques of the Common Data Culture. It provides the overarching construct for a common view of the organization's data culture. All variations in the data culture are understood within the context of a common data culture. The preferred data culture is defined within the context of a common data culture. Data culture integration is done within the context of a common data culture.

Formal Data Culture Integration

Data culture integration is the thorough understanding of the existing fragmented data culture within a common data culture, the designation of a preferred data culture, and the transition toward that preferred data culture. It's the act or process of integrating and coordinating the organization's data management function and processes into a cohesive data culture. It resolves a fragmented data culture by getting people to work together to build and maintain a comparate data resource.

Data culture integration is not a simple union of existing data management processes. It's not simply understanding and documenting the existing data culture. It's more detailed and requires thoroughly understanding the fragmented data culture within a common context, determining the preferred data culture, and transitioning to that preferred data culture.

Formal data culture integration is any data culture integration done within the context of a common data culture. *Informal data culture integration* is any data culture integration done outside the context of a common data culture. It usually does not resolve variability in the data culture and seldom leads to development and maintenance of a comparate data resource.

An *integrated data culture* is a data culture where all of the data management functions and processes in an organization are integrated within a common context, and are oriented toward developing and maintaining a comparate data resource. Data culture variability has been resolved and data resource management is performed consistently across the organization.

Data culture transition is the transition of an organization's data culture from a fragmented data culture state, through a formal data culture state, to a cohesive data culture state. It's a pathway that is followed from a fragmented data culture to a cohesive data culture. It's unique to each organization depending on their existing data culture and desired data culture.

Data culture transition is separate from data resource transition. However, it must be done in parallel with data resource integration and with equal emphasis as data resource integration so that the data resource is managed consistently across the organization. Data resource integration without data culture integration will not resolve the disparate data situation.

Data culture transformation is actually changing the data culture in an organization and will not be described here. It will be described in detail in Chapter 13 on Data Culture Integration.

Basic Principles

Several basic principles support data culture integration, including being done in concert with data resource integration, integrating the complete data culture, integrating the data culture organization-wide, being simple yet difficult, must be persistent, not data governance, and must be both internal and external. Each of these principles is described below.

Note that these basic principles for data culture integration are in addition to the basic principles described for data resource management integration.

In Concert with Data Resource Integration

Data culture integration must be done in concert with data resource integration. Ideally, data culture integration should be done before data resource integration. However, that approach is seldom feasible because it's difficult to implement a new data culture, then wait before applying that new data culture to management of the data resource. Therefore, it's best to implement both data resource integration and data culture integration together.

Integrate the Complete Data Culture

All components of the cohesive data culture, including data orientation, data availability, data responsibility, data vision, and data recognition, must be implemented at the same time. Implementing only a subset of those components does not fully resolve the fragmented data culture. If the fragmented data culture is not fully resolved, disparate data could still be produced.

Organization-Wide

Data culture integration must be performed organization-wide. Little good comes from implementing the cohesive data culture to only part of the organization. Other parts of the organization simply continue creating disparate data. Since the data are usually orthogonal to the organization structure, the disparate data cannot be resolved as long as some of the business units have not been included in data culture integration. Therefore, data culture integration must be organization-wide.

Simple But Difficult

Data culture integration is simpler than data resource integration in many respects, yet it is more difficult to implement. It is simpler in the sense that it is not as detailed as data resource integration, fewer steps are involved, the steps are relatively straight forward, the variability is lower than the data resource, the understanding process is easier, and the documentation is easier. The variability in the data culture is relatively easy to identify, whether or not the data culture is formally documented.

Data culture integration is more difficult than data resource integration in the sense that changing the culture is more difficult than changing the architecture. Having the culture change the architecture is difficult enough, but having the culture change the culture can be quite difficult. People may show some resistance to change when integrating the data resource, but usually see the need. However, people often show great resistance to change when changing the way they manage the data resource. It's often very difficult to convince people that changing the data culture is mandatory for creating and maintaining a comparate data resource.

Must Be Persistent

Implementing a cohesive data culture must be persistent. If the data culture transition is not persistent, people will drift back to their old ways of managing data and data disparity will increase. Therefore, a considerable effort must be made to understand the resistance to change that people have, and address that resistance. A considerable effort must be made to show people how a cohesive data culture develops a comparate data resource and how reversion to the fragmented data culture creates disparate data, and convince them that data culture integration is important.

Not Data Governance

I've talked with many people about data culture integration. Most of those people make some comment like *Oh, that's data governance.* They proceed to tell me how they perceive that data governance addresses the data culture issue. However, I haven't seen anything in data governance that specifically addresses the data culture to the level addressed with a Common Data Culture. I haven't seen any formal set of concepts, principles, and techniques related to transitioning from a fragmented data culture to a cohesive data culture. Therefore, I don't believe that data governance adequately addresses the data culture issue. The Common Data Culture approach is much more robust.

Both Internal and External

Data culture integration must be done both within and without the organization. The internal aspect is with the employees in the organization. The employees must buy into data culture integration and commit to making data resource management work if a comparate data resource is to be developed and maintained.

The external aspect includes the consultants, vendors, trainers, and so on, that the organization utilizes to support their data resource management effort. These external people often have their own thoughts, ideas, and agendas, which are frequently not in synch with the organization. Allowing these thoughts, ideas, and agendas to alter the data culture integration or the cohesive data culture is only to the detriment of the organization.

An organization should accept thoughts and ideas, where appropriate, to support their data culture integration effort. But, they should also reject any thoughts and ideas that are contrary to their data culture integration effort. The best approach is to select consultants, vendors, trainers, and so on, that agree with and support the organization's cohesive data culture, and put appropriate statements in formal agreements.

Data Culture States

Data culture transition consists of three states, progressing from the fragmented data culture state, through a formal data culture state, to a cohesive data culture state, as shown in Figure 2.2. All three states are part of the organization's data culture. The fragmented data culture state is outside the common data culture. The formal data culture state and cohesive data culture state are within the common data culture.

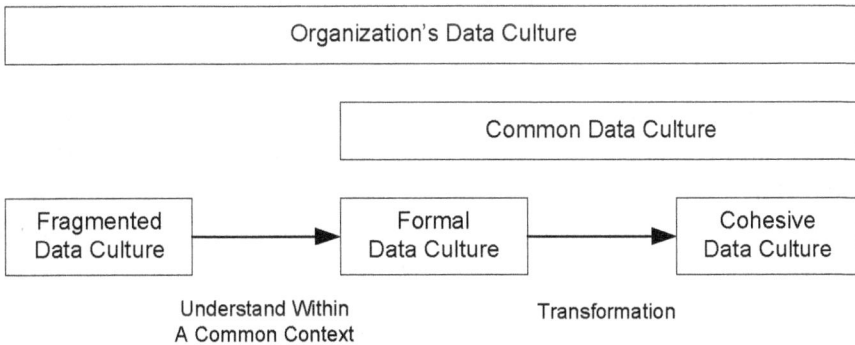

Figure 2.2. Data culture transition states.

An organization's data culture matures as it moves through the data culture transition states. The existing fragmented data culture is immature. The maturity improves as the existing data culture is understood, the data culture variability is identified, and the preferred data culture is defined. A cohesive data culture is the mature state. Each of these data culture states is described below.

Fragmented Data Culture

The *fragmented data culture state* is the situation where every organizational unit, and possibly every person, is managing data in their own way, with their own orientation, vision, processes, and software tools. The data culture is highly variable and exhibits all of the characteristics of a fragmented data culture. The management is informal and seldom documented, and the fragmentation is not known. It is the least desirable state and is the initial state for data culture integration.

Formal Data Culture

The *formal data culture state* is a necessary state where the data culture is readily understood within the context of a common data culture. The variability of the fragmented data culture is understood and documented, the preferred data culture is designated, and the data culture integration is prescribed. No changes to the data culture have yet been made, pending review and approval by the organization.

Cohesive Data Culture

The *cohesive data culture state* is the desired state where the fragmented data culture has been substantially and permanently transformed to a cohesive data culture. It's a persistent integration according to the preferred data culture prescription. A single set of processes has been established across the organization. It's the ideal, mature state for management of the organization's data resource.

SUMMARY

The following outline is provided as a summary of the data resource integration concept. Organizations can choose whether they want to develop a comparate data resource and a cohesive data culture. If they choose to develop them, then the following topics are of paramount importance and set the stage for understanding all of the detailed concepts, principles, and techniques related to developing a comparate data resource and a cohesive data culture.

Data Resource Management Integration
  Concept is to create concordant data resource management
  Basic Principles
    Contrarian Thinking
    Not a Migration
    Descriptive and Prescriptive
    Retrospective and Prospective
    Deterministic and Probabilistic
    Value Added
    Effectiveness and Efficiency

A Discovery Process
Point of Diminishing Returns
Prevent Discordance before Resolving Discordance

Data Resource Integration
  Concept is to create a comparate data resource
  Basic Principles
    Integration at the Data Level
    Semantic and Structural Integration
    A Detailed Process
    Not Reengineering
    No Single System of Reference
    No Physical Approaches
    Not Scrap and Rework
    No Lack of Technical Talent
    Supporting Tools
  Data Resource States
    Disparate Data Resource State
    Formal Data Resource State
    Virtual Data Resource State
    Comparate Data Resource State

Data Culture Integration
  Concept is to create a cohesive data culture
  Basic Principles
    In Concert with Data Resource Integration
    Integrate the Complete Data Culture
    Organization-Wide
    Simple but Difficult
    Must Be Persistent
    Not Data Governance
    Both Internal and External
  Data Culture States
    Fragmented Data Culture
    Formal Data Culture
    Cohesive Data Culture

QUESTIONS

The following questions are provided as a review of the data resource integration concept, and to stimulate thought about data resource integration.

1. What is the difference between integration and transition?

2. Why is transition not a migration?

3. What is a Common Data Architecture?

4. What is the difference between semantic integration and structural integration?

5. Why does a system of reference seldom exist?

6. What is the purpose of each of the data resource states.

7. What is a Common Data Culture?

8. Why does data culture integration and data resource integration need to be in concert?

9. What is the purpose of each of the data culture states?

10. Why does an organization need to consider data resource integration and data culture integration?

Chapter 3

INTEGRATING THE DATA RESOURCE

The approach to understanding and integrating disparate data.

Integrating the data resource is the first of two components for fully integrating data resource management. The chapter begins with a summary of the Common Data Architecture concepts, principles, and techniques for preventing data disparity, described in detail in *Data Resource Simplexity*. Those concepts, principles, and techniques will be used extensively during the data resource transition process.

Next, the chapter provides an overview of the concepts and principles for understanding and integrating disparate data within the context of a common data architecture. The following nine chapters (Chapters 4 through Chapter 12) describe the specific concepts, principles, and techniques for understanding the existing disparate data, designating a preferred data architecture, and performing data transformation to create a comparate data resource.

The second component for fully integrating data resource management is described in detail in Chapter 13 on Integrating the Data Culture.

CONCEPTS

I've had many experiences over the years dealing with disparate data in a wide variety of public and private sector organizations. I've used many different techniques to understand and resolve disparate data, and have published many of those techniques. All those techniques had good and bad features, and I learned from each experience. The concepts, principles, and techniques described here are the best I've found (so far) for understanding and resolving disparate data and creating a comparate data resource.

The most important single thing I've learned through all of these experiences, as described in *Data Resource Simplexity*, is that the creation of disparate data must cease before any attempt is made to understand and resolve those disparate data. Disparate data are created much faster than they can ever be resolved. If the creation of disparate data is not stopped before attempting to resolve those disparate data, the resolution effort will be for naught.

Lest you missed that message—*The creation of disparate data must be stopped before any effort is made to understand and resolve those disparate data!*

The following concepts are summarized from *Data Resource Simplexity* to set the stage for integrating the data resource. *Data Resource Simplexity* described in detail what went wrong that resulted in disparate data and what needs to be done to stop the creation of disparate data. That's the starting point for effective and efficient data resource integration.

Data Sharing Concept

The ***data sharing concept*** states that shared data are transmitted over the data sharing medium as preferred data. Any organization, whether source or target, that does not have or use data in the preferred form is responsible for translating the data.

The Common Data Architecture provides a construct for readily sharing data, whether disparate or comparate, as shown in Figure 3.1. When the source data are in the preferred form, they can be readily shared over the data sharing medium. When the data are not in the preferred form, the source organization must translate those non-preferred data to the preferred form before they are shared over the data sharing medium.

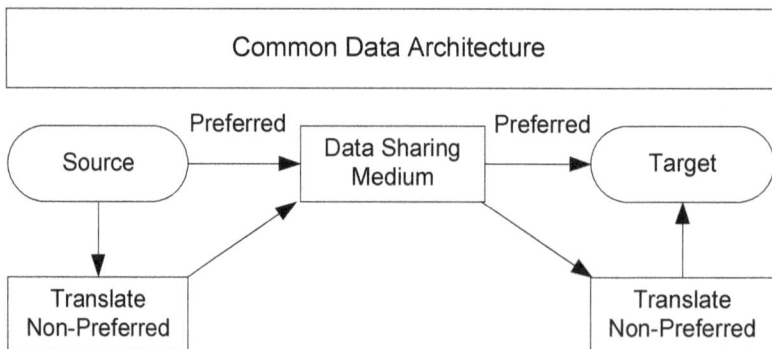

Figure 3.1. Data sharing concept.

Similarly, when the target organization uses the preferred data, those data can be readily received from the data sharing medium. When the target organization does not use preferred data, they must translate the preferred data to their organization's non-preferred form.

The data sharing concept allows source and target organizations to independently change their data resource from disparate to comparate without impacting other organizations. It avoids the constant changes to data transfer files that is common in many organizations, which eases data sharing and improves productivity.

The data sharing concept has been used with great success in many public sector organizations that readily share data between public agencies, and in some large private sector organizations. Organizations that want to begin a data resource integration initiative can start by establishing a data sharing initiative, where all data are defined within a common context so they can be thoroughly understood and readily shared in the preferred form to meet the current and future business information demand.

Common Data Architecture Concept

The Common Data Architecture is the common context for inventorying and documenting all data, understanding the content and meaning of data, improving data quality, understanding and integrating disparate data, defining new data, managing dynamic data deployment, and managing change, regardless of where the data reside, who uses them, how they are used, or how they are structured.

The Common Data Architecture ensures that data are integrated within the organization, and often across organizations in the public sector. It enables a shift from reactive data resource management to proactive data resource management. It promotes development of a comparate data resource that can be readily shared.

The Common Data Architecture is a principle-based paradigm based on sound theory, concepts, and principles that have been known for a long time. It provides a set of techniques that supports the concepts and principles. It is not hypothetical, esoteric, or academic. It is a simple and elegant, practical, and proven way to develop a comparate data resource.

I began in the 1970s developing the concept, although I didn't know at the time that it would become the Common Data Architecture concept. At that time, the concept of a single organization-wide data architecture did not exist. In fact, the concept of any type of data architecture seldom existed. Data modeling was becoming prominent, and emphasis on logical data modeling based on the business was just emerging.

Data models were often developed independently, with little coordination between data models. The scope of data models varied with the scope of the development project. Canonical synthesis emerged, but had little effect on developing a single data architecture for the organization. The result was the beginning of a trend of disparate data models and disparate data resources.

The concept evolved through the 1980s, as experience was gained in understanding how to design a data resource that could be readily shared. The evolution was driven by problems found with data management in a wide variety of public and private sector organizations. I defined disparate data in the late 1980s and comparate data in the early 1990s.

The concept of a formal Common Data Architecture emerged in the early 1990s. The concept has been continually refined until today, where it is now the definitive approach for understanding all data in a common context, designating a preferred data architecture, and developing a comparate data resource. Although minor enhancements may be made based on problems encountered, the concept is substantially complete.

Basic Principles

The Common Data Architecture contains four basic principles: subject oriented, integrated, business driven, and supported by a comprehensive Data Resource Guide.

A *subject-oriented data resource* is a data resource that is built from data subjects that represent business objects and events in the business world that are of interest to the organization. The basic structure of a comparate data resource is based on data subjects and the relations between those data subjects. All characteristics of a data subject are stored with that data subject.

Architected data are any data that are formally understood and managed within a common data architecture, including both disparate and comparate data. *Non-architected data* are any data that are not formally managed within a common data architecture. *Partially architected data* is the situation where some data are managed within a common data architecture and some data are not managed within a common data architecture.

A *business driven data resource* is a data resource where the design, development, and maintenance are driven by business needs, as defined by the business information demand. The data resource is about the business, by the business, and for the business. The Common Data architecture provides the construct for an orientation towards business needs.

The *organization perception principle* states that the comparate data resource developed to support an organization's business must be based on the organization's perception of the business world. If a comparate data resource is to support an organization's business activities, that comparate data resource must be based primarily on the organization's perception of the business world and how the organization chooses to operate in that business world.

A ***Data Resource Guide*** provides a complete, comprehensive, integrated index to the organization's data resource. It provides a thorough understanding of the data resource, and is readily available to everyone in the organization so they can use the data resource to support their business needs. It provides one version of truth about the data resource, in the same manner that a comparate data resource provides one version of truth about the business.

Common Data Architecture Scope

The scope of the Common Data Architecture is shown in Figure 3.2. The disparate data, as well as any new data, are integrated into a comparate data resource. The comparate data resource is supported by a comprehensive Data Resource Guide that fully documents the data resource. People can go to that Data Resource Guide, find the data they need to perform their business activities, and extract those data to the appropriate information systems that meet the business information demand. All of those tasks are performed within the context of a Common Data Architecture.

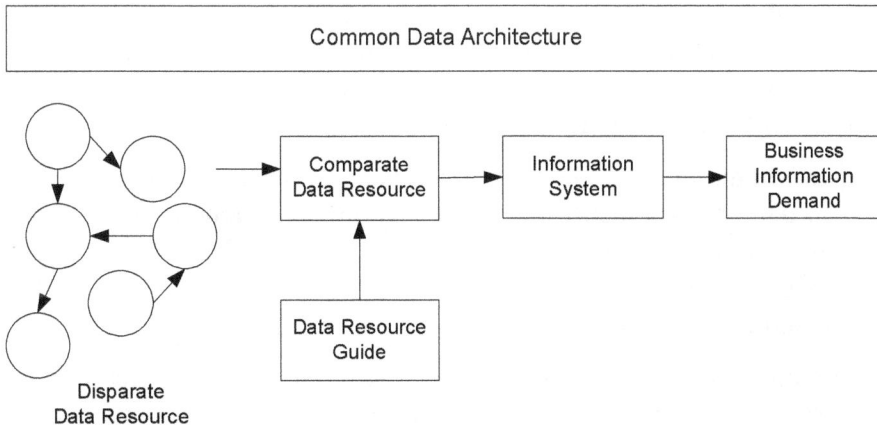

Figure 3.2. Common Data Architecture Scope.

Common Data Architecture Size

The common data architecture continues to increase in size during the data resource integration process. First, the common data architecture grows for each project until all of the disparate data have been inventoried and cross-referenced. It grows very rapidly, particularly during the initial projects, and often looks complex, insurmountable, overwhelming, and discouraging.

Second, a common data architecture grows as derived data are identified and defined. Primitive data generally grow to a plateau and then remain relatively constant or grow slowly. Derived data continue to grow steadily, often at an exponential rate, with development of evaluational data.

Third, a common data architecture grows as the preferred data are defined. As definitions, structure, and integrity rules are defined for the preferred data architecture, the size of the common data architecture continues to grow.

The growth of the common data architecture tapers off as the disparate data are transformed to comparate data. Ideally, the preferred data architecture becomes the only component remaining within the common data architecture. However, organizations may want to keep the understanding of those disparate data around for reference, even though the disparate themselves have been transformed and no longer exist.

The size of an organization's data resource is measured both in the breadth and depth of the data. *Data volume breadth* is how many data entities and data attributes are in the data resource and data models, and how many data files and data items are in the databases. It depends on the number of business facts and how those business facts are grouped into data entities and stored in data files. *Data volume depth* is how many data occurrences exist for the data entities and how many data records are stored in the data files.

The common data architecture size is based on the data volume breadth. The data volume depth has relatively little influence on the size of the common data architecture. The more data entities, data attributes, and data occurrences, and the more data files and data records, the larger the common data architecture.

Organizations should plan on the common data architecture growing during data resource integration. They should not plan on any reduction in the size of the common data architecture until disparate data have been removed from the data resource, and little possibility exists for disparate data to be found in applications, reports, documents, and so on.

Simple Approach

The Common Data Architecture ensures that a comparate data resource is an elegant and simple approach to facing the complexity of a disparate data resource and building a comparate data resource. It follows Albert

Einstein's *simplicity principle* that states everything should be a simple as possible … but not simpler. The Common Data Architecture follows that principle. It's the simplest approach to both developing a comparate data resource and to integrating a disparate data resource.

The Common Data Architecture also follows Occam's Razor. As initially translated, it means *Entities should not be multiplied more than necessary. That is, the fewer assumptions an explanation of a phenomenon depends on, the better it is.* It essentially means keep it simple.

Higher Level of Technology

The Common Data Architecture follows another of Albert Einstein's principles that a problem cannot be resolved with the same technology that was used to create the problem. The resolution requires a higher level of technology.

Einstein's principle provides a new direction for creating a higher level of technology to solve the problems of an ever-growing disparate data resource. The Common Data Architecture is that higher level of technology.

Includes Data Integrity

The Common Data Architecture supports both semantic and structural integration, as described in the last chapter. It does not favor one over the other and resolves the ongoing discussion about whether data resource integration should be driven by the semantics of the data or the structure of the data.

The only missing component from formal data resource integration is the data integrity. The Common Data Architecture ensures that data resource integration includes data integrity. Data resource integration is not driven by data integrity, as it is by semantics and structure, but it must include data integrity to understand the quality of existing disparate data and ensure the quality of the comparate data.

Customized Approach

The Common Data Architecture is not a one-size-fits-all approach. It contains the concepts, principles, and techniques for building and maintaining a comparate data resource, and for resolving disparate data. These concepts, principles, and techniques are combined with an organization's problems, needs, and operating environment to provide a customized approach for understanding disparate data and building a comparate data resource.

Emphasizes Understanding

The common data architecture does not integrate the data—it provides a base for understanding the data so they can be integrated. People need to understand the data with respect to the business before those data can be integrated. Data resource integration is primarily an understanding issue, and secondarily a data issue. A common data architecture provides the context for thoroughly understanding the data with respect to the business.

Aldous Huxley said that *facts do not cease to exist because they are ignored.* Similarly, the meaning of the data does not change because people don't thoroughly understand that meaning. Also, the true meaning of the data does not change based on people's understanding of the meaning. Only the business changes based on the understanding of the data.

Understanding the data includes semantic understanding, structural understanding, and integrity understanding. It includes understanding the data and how those data support the business. When people understand both the data and how the data support the business, the stage is set for data resource integration.

As understanding goes up, uncertainty goes down. When people are uncertain about the data, they are uncertain about the business. When people understand the data, they understand the business, and the business has a better chance of being successful. Therefore, the data must be thoroughly understood to have a successful business.

Understanding data within a common context avoids the elephant syndrome by focusing on the whole picture. The *elephant syndrome* is the situation where a blindfolded person feels one portion of an elephant, such as trunk, leg, tail, ear, and so on, and tries to describe the object they feel, usually incorrectly. Trying to understand data without a common context is like trying to describe the elephant while blindfolded.

It should become clear why the category of *data in context* was inserted into the scheme of data, information, and knowledge. Data in context requires a thorough understanding of the data, both for understanding the business and for data resource integration. Without data in context, only raw data exist and there can be no real understanding of the business or successful data resource integration.

Data resource integration is not a precise process because of the uncertainty in disparate data, it's a cyclic and evolutionary process that discovers meaning and enhances understanding. Sometimes the process deals with vagueness, but it's vagueness at the business level, not at the data level. Resolving vagueness at the data level helps resolve vagueness at the business level.

Remodeling Analogy

Integrating disparate data is much like remodeling a house. When people start remodeling a house, they have no idea where the plumbing, electrical, phone, and heating ducts are located. They can only observe electrical outlets, phone jacks, light fixtures, heat registers, and so on. However, those terminations don't identify where things are routed within the walls and floors. People can crawl under the house or in the attic to get a better idea of where things are located. They can pull circuit breakers and turn off water valves, but they still are not sure where everything is located until they tear out the walls, usually with surprises.

The same situation is true for integrating disparate data. People can observe documents, screens, and reports. They can look at the database definitions. They can run automated documentation tools. They still have very little idea about the true content and meaning of the disparate data until they begin to tear those data apart, usually with surprises.

Wouldn't it be nice to know all of the things about a house, like its structure, plumbing, wiring, heating, lumber quality, roofing, paint, anomalies, and so on? Wouldn't it be nice to have a comprehensive architecture for a house that contained the description of all components, the structure of those components, and the integrity of those components? Wouldn't that blueprint make use and maintenance of the house much easier?

The same applies to disparate data. Wouldn't it be nice to know all of the things about data, their structure, their meaning, and their anomalies? Wouldn't it be nice to have a comprehensive blueprint so that people do not have to make assumptions about the data? Wouldn't it be nice to be able to readily identify, locate, and access the data needed to support business activities, and know those data are accurate and current?

A house is remodeled by making an initial model of what exists, based on perceptions, assumptions, and available documentation. As the remodeling process continues, things are discovered, perceptions change, and assumptions are proven or changed. The initial model is enhanced to represent the current state of knowledge. When the remodeling is completed, an accurate model of the house is available.

That's exactly what data resource integration accomplishes. It starts with an initial common data architecture based on an organization's perception of the business world. As the process continues, new things are discovered, perceptions change, and assumptions are proven or changed. The initial common data architecture is enhanced to represent the current understanding about the disparate data, and it continues to evolve until all disparate data are integrated. The data resource integration process provides one accurate model of all disparate data.

Building Code Analogy

Every data resource is different, just like every house is different. Data resources, like houses, were built to serve a particular purpose and do not fit a specific, universal, or generic design constraint. However, houses do need to follow a certain set of building codes to ensure the house is structurally sound and safe for the occupants.

The Common Data Architecture contains the concepts, principles, and techniques for building and maintaining a comparate data resource. It's the building codes for an organization's data resource. It helps ensure that the data resource is built according to the building codes, while still adequately representing the organization's perception of the business world where it operates.

In other words, the building codes for a comparate data resource are consistent across all organizations, but the comparate data resource that is actually developed represents the unique needs of the organization.

Leaping Broad Chasms

I saw a diagram many years ago where a man on a pogo-stick was bouncing along across a stretch of flat land. However, he was approaching a broad chasm and the length of each pogo-stick bounce was far less than the width of the chasm. He had a very startled look on his face. Many organizations are in the same situation with their disparate data resource.

The near side of the chasm is a disparate data resource and the far side of the chasm is a comparate data resource. Understanding and integrating the disparate data is the chasm. Bridging that chasm seems daunting, if not impossible. The Common Data Architecture provides the bridge necessary to span broad data resource integration chasms incrementally.

Data Architectnology

Data architectnology is the technology for producing comparate data within a common data architecture. It's the formal technology for building a common data architecture within an organization and managing data within that architecture. It consists of specific concepts, principles, and techniques for developing a comparate data resource. It's very formal and detailed, yet results are very elegant and simple.

Data architectnology uses the least energy to develop and maintain a comparate data resource. It minimizes the energy to incorporate business and technology change—to keep the data resource current. It minimizes the energy to ensure integrity and accuracy. It minimizes the energy to understand and resolve disparate data.

Data Model Concept

A *data model* includes formal data names, comprehensive data definitions, proper data structures, and precise data integrity rules. A complete data model must include all four of these components.

The *data model concept* is the development of a data model, for a specific audience, representing a particular business activity, using appropriate data modeling techniques, based on data contained in the Data Resource Guide. The data model is an expression of knowledge about the data resource that is presented in an appropriate form for a specific audience. It is best to use the appropriate form consistently across the organization.

The data model concept is shown in Figure 3.3. On the left, the business information demand drives an analysis of that demand within the context of a common data architecture, which is documented in the Data Resource Guide. On the right, disparate data go through an understanding process within the context of a common data architecture, which is documented in the Data Resource Guide.

The appropriate data are taken from the Data Resource Guide, for a particular business activity, to produce a data model, using appropriate data modeling techniques, for a specific audience. All data models are developed within the context of a common data architecture. The concept changes the orientation from a model driven data architecture to architecture driven data models.

Five-Tier Five-Schema Concept

The *Five-Tier Five-Schema concept* represents all of the schemas involved in data resource management within the context of a common data architecture, as shown in Figure 3.4. The five tiers are strategic logical, tactical logical, operational, analytical, and predictive. The five schemas in the operational, analytical, and predictive tiers are business schema, data view schema, logical schema, deployment schema, and physical schema.

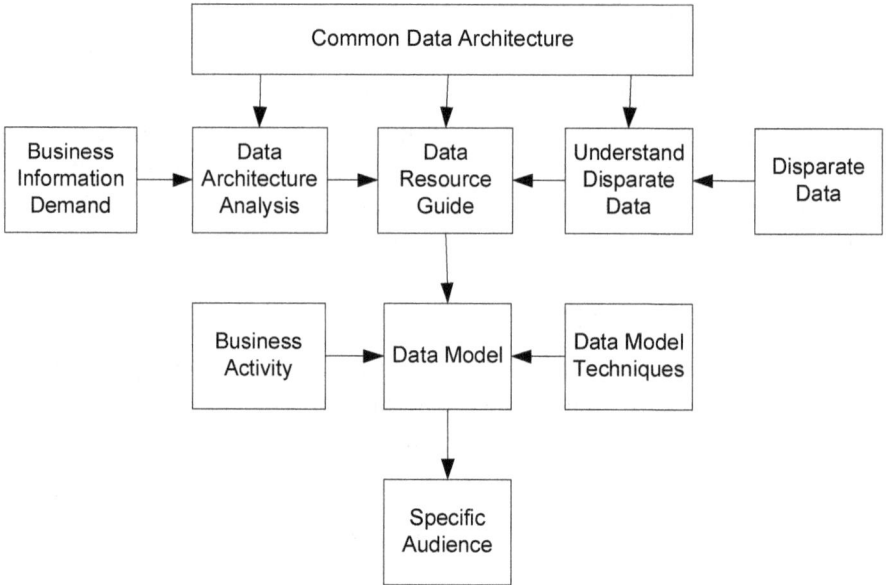

Figure 3.3. Data model concept.

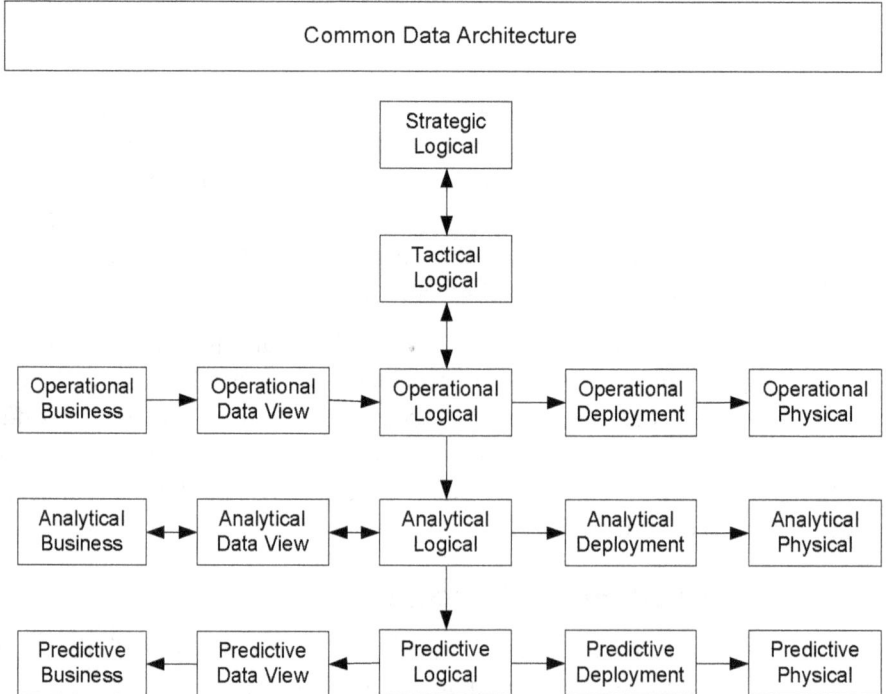

Figure 3.4. Five-Tier Five-Schema Concept.

Data resource integration deals with understanding the existing disparate schemas and developing comparate schemas within the Five-Tier Five-Schema concept. Disparate business schemas, data view schemas, logical schemas, deployment schemas, and physical schemas are all understood and resolved within the context of a common data architecture.

Data Rule Concept

The concept of data rules is briefly summarized below. *Data Resource Simplexity* provides a more detailed description of the data integrity rules, and Appendix A contains examples of data integrity rules.

A *rule* is an authoritative, prescribed direction for conduct, or a usual, customary, or generalized course of action or behavior; a statement that describes what is true in most or all cases; a standard method or procedure for solving problems. A *data rule* is a subset of business rules that deals with the data column of the Zachman Framework. They specify the criteria for maintaining the quality of the data resource.

Data rules are further classified data integrity rules, data source rules, data extraction rules, data translation rules, and data transformation rules. *Data integrity rules* specify the criteria that need to be met to insure that the data resource contains the highest quality necessary to support the current and future business information demand. The other data rules are described in subsequent chapters.

Data integrity rules are further classified as described below.

A *data value rule* is a data integrity rule that specifies the unconditional data domain for a data attribute that applies under all conditions. It specifies the rule with respect to the business, not with respect to the database management system. No exceptions are allowed to a data value rule.

A *conditional data value rule* is a data integrity rule that specifies the domain of allowable values for a data attribute when conditions or exceptions apply. It specifies both the conditions for optionality and the condition for a relationship between data values in other data attributes. It specifies the rule with respect to the business, not with respect to the database management system.

A *data structure rule* is a data integrity rule that specifies the data cardinality for a data relation between two data entities that applies under all conditions. No exceptions are allowed to a data structure rule.

A *conditional data structure rule* is a data integrity rule that specifies the data cardinality for a data relation between two data entities where conditions or exceptions apply. It specifies both the conditions and exceptions with respect to the business, not with respect to the database management system.

A *data derivation rule* is a data integrity rule that specifies the contributors to a derived data value, the algorithm for deriving the data value, and the conditions for deriving a data value. A *data rederivation rule* is a data integrity rule that specifies when any rederivation is done after the initial derivation. A derived data value may be rederived when the conditions change or the contributors change, which often occurs in a dynamic business environment. The derivation algorithm and the contributors are usually the same, but timing of the rederivation needs to be specified.

A *data retention rule* is a data integrity rule that specifies how long data values are retained and what is done with those data values when their usefulness is over. It specifies the criteria for preventing the loss of critical data through updates or deletion, such as when the operational usefulness is over, but the evaluational usefulness is not over.

A *data selection rule* is a data integrity rule that specifies the selection of data occurrences based on selection criteria. The selection notation in the data naming taxonomy is used to document the selected set of data occurrences.

A *data translation rule* is a data rule that defines the translation of a data value from one unit to another unit. It represents the translation of the values of a single fact to different units, and is not considered to be a data derivation rule.

A *data deployment rule* specifies how the data are deployed from the primary data site to secondary data sites, and how those deployed data are kept in synch with the primary data site.

A *data integrity violation action* specifies the action to be taken with the data when the data violate a data integrity rule. That action may be to override the error with meaningful data, to suspend the data pending further correction, to apply a default data value, to accept the data, or to delete the data. Overriding the error could include implementing an algorithm to correct the data, such as reformatting a phone number. The new data are again passed through the data integrity rules to ensure they pass.

A *data integrity notification action* specifies the action to be taken for notifying someone that data have failed the data integrity rules and a violation action was taken. The action may alert someone who is responsible for taking action, or place an appropriate entry in an error log that will be reviewed by someone at a later date. The notification action includes the implementation of an algorithm to correct the data.

Data integrity rules use *When* rather than *If* because it is more meaningful to the business, and it indicates a logical condition rather than a mathematical condition. Also, a *When* condition does not have a corresponding *Else* clause like the *If* condition. An *Else* clause often leads to poor data integrity because everything else does not always fall into the *Else* clause. A much better approach is to specify *When* for every possible condition that could exist.

Data Resource Data Concept

One of the major lexical challenges in data resource management is the term *meta-data*. It has been used, misused, and abused to the point that the meaning is totally unclear. The traditional definition of *data about data* is a tautology and provides no denotative meaning. The term needs to be abandoned. The cause is lost!

A much better term is *data resource data*. **Data resource data** are any data necessary for thoroughly understanding, formally managing, and fully utilizing the data resource to support the business information demand. Similarly, **data resource information** is any set of data resource data in context, with relevance to one or more people at a point in time or for a period of time. The **data resource information demand** is the organization's continuously increasing, constantly changing, need for current, accurate, integrated information about the data resource that is necessary for formally managing the data resource.

The data resource data are stored and maintained in the Data Resource Guide. Data resource data are retrieved from the Data Resource Guide to support formal data resource management, including understanding existing disparate data and developing a comparate data resource.

Good data resource data are necessary to understand the data resource. Understanding the data resource is necessary to understand the business. Understanding the business is necessary to have good business intelligence and meet business goals. Therefore, the term data resource data will be used throughout the book.

Terminology

The lexical challenge in data resource management is only resolved with specific terms that have a denotative meaning. The matrix in Figure 3.5 shows the specific terms used for managing data, including the business, the Common Data Architecture, mathematics, logical data models, and physical databases, and the relationship between the terms. The matrix has been enhanced since *Data Resource Simplexity*, based on comments received. A column was added for the terms as used in mathematics so they could be compared to the terms used in data modeling. A row was added for the grouping of data from the business to the physical database. The result is a complete set of terms that have denotative meaning and can be used by anyone from business professional to database technician.

Business	Common Data Architecture	Mathematics	Logical Data Model	Physical Database
Business Object Business Event	Data Subject	Entity Set	Data Entity	Data File
Business Feature	Data Characteristic			
	Data Characteristic Variation		Data Attribute	Data Item
Business Object Existence	Data Occurrence	Entity	Data Occurrence	
Business Event Happening	Data Instance		Data Instance	Data Record
Business Object Group Business Event Group	Data Occurrence Group	Set of Entities	Data Occurrence Group	Data Record Group

Figure 3.5. Matrix of terms and relationships.

Business Terms

A *business object* is a person, place, thing, or concept in the real world, such as a customer, river, city, account, and so on. A *business event* is any happening in the real world, such as a sale, purchase, fire, flood, accident, and so on. A *business feature* is a trait or characteristic of a business object or event, such as a customer's name, a city's population, a fire date, and so on. A *business object existence* is the actual existence of a business object, such as a specific person, river, vehicle, account, and so on.

A *business event happening* is the actual happening of a business event, such as a specific sale, purchase, a fire, a flood, an accident, and so on. A *business object group* is a subset of business objects based on specific selection criteria. A *business event group* is a subset of business events based on specific selection criteria.

Common Data Architecture Terms

A *data subject* is a person, place, thing, concept, or event that is of interest to the organization and about which data are captured and maintained in the organization's data resource. Data subjects are defined from business objects and business events, making the data resource subject oriented based on the business.

A *data characteristic* is an individual fact that describes or characterizes a data subject. It represents a business feature and contains a single fact, or closely related facts, about a data subject, such as the make of a vehicle, or a person's height. Each data subject is described by a set of data characteristics.

A *data characteristic variation* is a variation in the content or format of a data characteristic. It represents a variant of a data characteristic, such as different units of measurement, different monetary units, different sequences in a person's name, and so on. Each data characteristic usually has multiple variations, particularly in a disparate data resource.

A *data occurrence* is a logical record that represents the existence of a business object or the happening of a business event in the business world, such as an employee, a vehicle, and so on. It represents a business object existence or a business event happening.

A *data instance* is a specific set of data values for the characteristics in a data occurrence that are valid at a point in time or for a period of time. Many data instances can exist for each data occurrence, particularly when historical data are maintained. One data instance is the current data instance and the others are historical data instances.

A *data occurrence group* is a subset of data occurrences within a specific data subject based on specific criteria, such as all the employees that have pilot licenses form a pilot certified employee data occurrence group. A data occurrence group represents a business object group or a business event group.

Mathematic Terms

An *entity* in mathematics is a single existent, such as an employee John. J Smith. It's equivalent to a data subject. An *entity set* in mathematics is a group of like entities, such as Employees. It's equivalent to a data

89

occurrence. A *set of entities* in mathematics is a subgroup of an entity set, such as Retirement Eligible Employees. It's equivalent to a data occurrence group.

Logical Data Model Terms

An *entity* is a being, existence; independent, separate, or self-informed existence, the existence of a thing compared to its attributes; something that has separate and distinct existence and object or conceptual reality. A *data entity* is a person, place, thing, event, or concept about which an organization collects and manages data. The name is singular since it represents single data occurrences. It represents a data subject in a logical data model.

An *attribute* is an inherent characteristic, an accidental quality, an object closely associated with or belonging to a specific person, place, or office; a word describing a quality. A *data attribute* is the variation of an individual fact that describes or characterizes a data entity. It represents a data characteristic variation in a logical data model. Even in a logical data model, a data attribute usually has specific content or format, such as measurement units, or a normal or abbreviated name sequence. Therefore, it is equivalent to a data characteristic variation, not a data characteristic.

Database Terms

A *data file* is a physical file of data that exists in a database management system, such as a computer file, or outside a database management system, such as a manual file. It is referred to as a table in a relational database. A data file generally represents a data entity, subject to adjustments made during formal data denormalization. A *data item* is an individual field in a data record and is referred to as a column in a relational database. A data item represents a data attribute, subject to adjustments made during formal data denormalization. A *data record* is a physical grouping of data items that are stored in or retrieved from a data file. It is referred to as a row or tuple in a relational database. A data record represents a data instance in a data file. A *data record group* is a subset of data records based on specific selection criteria. A data record group represents a data occurrence group in a data file.

Rationale

I've been asked many times why I created new terms for use within the Common Data Architecture. After all, the terms data entity and data attribute are quite acceptable. What benefit do the new terms provide, other than creating more terms to remember?

The reason is that data entity and data attribute are used within logical data models. Those logical data models are often quite disparate with the development of your model – my model, your technique – my technique, and so on. Therefore, the data entities and data attributes in those data models are disparate. Something that is disparate itself cannot be used as an overarching construct to understand and resolve disparity.

In addition, the data attributes typically used in logical data models are already some variation of the business feature, such as a date format or sequence of a person's name. Therefore, the term *data attribute* cannot be used to represent a variation in the format or content of itself. Another term is needed, which is the data characteristic variation.

People have suggested I just use the terms *common data entity*, *common data attribute*, and *common data attribute variation*. The suggestion has merit, and has been tried. The problem is in the meaning when those terms are used to understand and resolve disparate data. For example, the phrase *a data attribute is cross-referenced to a common data attribute variation* could be quite confusing, even with denotative definitions of the terms. Therefore, a totally new set of terms were created to form the overarching construct for understanding and resolving disparate data.

The reader should begin to see the relationship between the terms and the reason for specifying different terms. The reason will become even clearer as the process of data resource integration is described.

Additional Terms

Several additional terms apply to understanding and resolving a disparate data resource.

Primitive data are data that are obtained by measurement or observation of an object or event in the business world. *Derived data* are data that are obtained from other data, not by the measurement or observation of an object or event.

Elemental data are individual facts that cannot be subdivided and retain any meaning. *Combined data* are a concatenation of individual facts.

Fundamental data are data that are not stored in databases and are not used in applications, but support the definition of specific data. *Specific data* are data that are stored in databases and are used in applications. Data inheritance is the process of using fundamental data to support consistent definitions of specific data.

DATA ARCHITECTURE COMPONENTS

The problems and principles for the five components of the Data Architecture Segment of the Data Resource Management Framework are summarized below. *Data Resource Simplexity* should be consulted for a more detailed description.

Data Names

Data names is the first component of the Data Architecture Segment. A *data name* is a label for a fact or a set of related facts contained in the data resource, appearing on a data model, or displayed on screens, reports, or documents. *Informal* means casual, not in accord with prescribed forms, unofficial, or inappropriate for the intended use. An *informal data name* is any data name that is casual and inappropriate for the intended purpose of readily and uniquely identifying each fact, or set of related facts, in an organization's data resource. It has no formality, structure, nomenclature, or taxonomy.

J.C. Fabricius, a student of Carl Linneaus, stated in Philosophia Entomologica that if the names are lost, the knowledge also disappears. That statement is of profound importance to data resource management, including data resource integration. Formal data names are mandatory for understanding and resolving disparate data, and building a comparate data resource.

Informal Data Names

The problems with informal data names are summarized below.

A *meaningless data name* is any data name that has no formal meaning with respect to the business.

A *non-unique data name* is any data name, whether abbreviated or unabbreviated, that is not unique across the organization or across multiple organizations engaged in the same business activity.

A *data name synonym* is the same business fact with different data names. A *data name homonym* is different business facts with the same data name.

A *structureless data name* is any data name that has no formal structure to the words composing the data name.

An *incorrect data name* is any data name that does not correctly represent the contents of the data component. Incorrect data names are just flat wrong.

A *multiple fact data field* is any data field that contains multiple unrelated business facts. Multiple unrelated facts lead to incorrect data names.

An *informal data name abbreviation* is any abbreviated data name that has no formality to the abbreviation.

Disparate data names usually contain many data name synonyms and homonyms.

Data names may be physically or process oriented, indicating how the data are captured, how they are stored, or how they are used.

Many components of the data resource, such as data sites, data versions, data reference sets, coded data values, data occurrence groups, and so on, are seldom formally named.

Formal Data Names

Formal means having an outward form or structure, being in accord with accepted conventions, consistent and methodical, or being done in a regular form. A *formal data name* readily and uniquely identifies a fact or group of related facts in the data resource, based on the business, and using formal data naming criteria.

The formal data naming criteria are summarized below.

Every component of the data resource must have one and only one primary data name

The primary data name must be based on the data naming taxonomy.

The primary data name must be the real-world, fully spelled out data name that is not codified or abbreviated in any way, and is not subject to any length restrictions.

The primary data name must be unique across the organization's data resource.

The primary data name must provide consistency across the organization's data resource.

The primary data name must be fully qualified, meaningful, understandable, and unambiguous to everyone in the organization.

The primary data name must indicate the content and meaning of the data with respect to the business, not how the data are collected, stored, or used. It might not provide the complete business meaning, but it must indicate the business meaning.

The primary data name must identify variations in the format and content.

The primary data name must indicate the logical structure of the data. It might not provide the complete structure, but it must indicate the structure.

The primary data name words must progress from general to specific.

All other data names are alias data names and are cross-referenced to the primary data name.

The formal data name principles are summarized below.

Taxonomy is the science of classification, a system for arranging things into natural, related groups based on common features. The *data naming taxonomy* provides a primary name for all existing and new data, and all components of the data resource. It provides a way to uniquely identify all components of the data resource as well as all of the disparate data. It meets all of the data naming criteria and complies with the three components of semiotic theory.

The data naming taxonomy is a structural taxonomy that is based on data structure not on data use. Any data naming taxonomy based on data use is unstable and eventually leads to data synonyms and homonyms. The structural approach is stable over time because the structure of the data is relatively stable over time.

A *common word* is a word that has consistent meaning whenever it is used in a data name. A *data name vocabulary* is the collection of all twelve sets of common words representing the twelve components of the data naming taxonomy.

The *primary data name principle* states that each business fact, or set of closely related business facts, in the data resource must have one and only one primary data name. All other data names are aliases of the primary data name.

A *primary data name* is the formal data name that is the fully spelled out, real world, unabbreviated, un-truncated, business name of the data that has no special characters or length limitations. An *alias data name* is any data name, other than the formal data name, for a fact or group of related facts in the data resource.

The *primary data name abbreviation principle* states that data name word abbreviations, data name abbreviation algorithms, and data name abbreviation schemes be developed to consistently provide formal data name abbreviations. A *data name abbreviation* is the shortening of a primary data name to meet some length restriction. A *formal data name abbreviation* is the formal shortening of a primary data name to meet a length restriction according to formal data name word abbreviations and a formal data name abbreviation algorithm.

A *data name abbreviation algorithm* is a formal procedure for abbreviating the primary data name using an established set of data name word abbreviations. A *data name abbreviation scheme* is a combination of a set of data name word abbreviations and a data name abbreviation algorithm.

Data Definitions

Data definitions are the second component of the Data Architecture Segment. A *definition* is a statement conveying a fundamental character or the meaning of a word, phrase, or term. It is a clear, distinct, detailed statement of the precise meaning or significance of something.

Vague Data Definitions

Vague means not clearly expressed; stated in indefinite terms; not having a precise meaning; not clearly grasped, defined or understood. A *vague data definition* is any data definition that does not thoroughly explain in simple, understandable terms, the real content and meaning of the data with respect to the business.

The problems with vague data definitions are summarized below.

Non-existent data definitions have never been developed, or were developed at one time and have since been misplaced or lost. Whatever the reason, there exists considerable data in the data resource that have no data definition.

Unavailable data definitions are data definitions that are not readily available. The best data definitions may have been written, but if they are not readily available, it's the same as being non-existent.

Short data definitions are data definitions that are short, truncated phrases, or incomplete sentences that provide little meaning.

Meaningless data definitions are data definitions that are meaningless to the business. The English and grammar may be acceptable, but the explanation of the content and meaning of the data with respect to the business is useless.

Outdated data definitions are data definitions that are not current with the business. The business of most organizations constantly changes over time, and the data values representing the business also change to reflect the business change. However, the data definitions are not kept current with the changes in the business or the data.

Incorrect data definitions are data definitions that are incorrect or inaccurate with respect to the business. The definitions are not in synch with the data name, the data structure, the data integrity rules, or the business.

Unrelated data definitions are data definitions that are unrelated to the content and meaning of the data with respect to the business. The data definition may be useful in another context, but it is not useful for understanding the data with respect to the business.

Comprehensive Data Definitions

Comprehensive means covering completely or broadly. A ***comprehensive data definition*** is a data definition that provides a complete, meaningful, easily read, readily understood definition that thoroughly explains the content and meaning of the data with respect to the business. It helps people thoroughly understand the data and use the data resource efficiently and effectively to meet the current and future business information demand.

I've received a few comments that *comprehensive* is not the opposite of *vague*, because a definition could be comprehensive yet still vague. *Specific* is the opposite of *vague*, while *partial, fragmentary, incomplete,* and *limited* are the opposite of *comprehensive*. The comments are valid, but not substantial enough to change the existing terms.

I've also received comments that a comprehensive data definition should include the purpose of the data. Those comments depend on the meaning of *purpose*. If *purpose* means the use of the data, then the purpose should not be included in the definition because it will never be complete, and may inhibit people from seeing other purposes for the data. If *purpose* means meaning with respect to the business, then the purpose must be included in the definition because it increases understanding of the data from a business perspective.

The comprehensive data definition criteria are summarized below.

The data definition must be meaningful with respect to the business.

The data definition must not include data entry instructions, source of the data, or use of the data.

The data definition must be understandable by anyone using the data resource to support their business needs.

The data definition must be denotative and not lead to any connotative meaning.

The data definition must provide a complete definition without any length limitation.

The data definition must accurately represent the business.

The data definition must be kept current with the business.

The data definition must be in synch with the formal data name.

The comprehensive data definition principles are summarized below.

The *denotative meaning principle* states that a comprehensive data definition must have a strong denotative meaning that limits any individual connotative meanings. The denotative meaning principle supports semiotic theory and the development of comprehensive data definitions.

A *denotative meaning* is the direct, explicit meaning provided by a data definition. A *connotative meaning* is the idea or notion suggested by the data definition, that a person interprets in addition to what is explicitly stated.

The *meaningful data definition principle* states that a comprehensive data definition must define the real content and meaning of the data with respect to the business. It is not based on the use of the data, how or where the data are used, how they were captured or processed, the privacy or security issues, or where they were stored.

The *thorough data definition principle* states that a comprehensive data definition must be thorough to be fully meaningful to the business. To be thorough, a data definition must not have any length limitation. The data definition must be long enough to fully explain the data in business terms.

The *accurate data definition principle* states that a comprehensive data definition must accurately represent the business. The data definition could be meaningful, and it could be thorough, but it may not be accurate.

The *current data definition principle* states that a comprehensive data definition must be kept current with the business.

The *data name - definition synchronization principle* states that a comprehensive data definition and a formal data name must be kept in synch. Formal data names help guide development of comprehensive data definitions, and comprehensive data definitions help verify formal data names. Synchronization is a two-way, value-added approach ensuring that formal data names match comprehensive data definitions.

Fundamental data definitions are the comprehensive data definitions for fundamental data. *Specific data definition*s are the comprehensive data definitions for specific data.

The *data definition inheritance principle* states that specific data definitions can inherit fundamental data definitions or other specific data definitions to minimize the size and increase the consistency of specific data definitions. The *define once and inherit many times* approach results in maximum meaning and consistency with minimum wording.

Fundamental data definition inheritance is the process of comprehensively defining fundamental data and allowing specific data definitions to inherit those fundamental data definitions. *Specific data definition inheritance* is the process of specific data definitions inheriting other specific data definitions.

Data Structure

Data structure is the third component of the Data Architecture Segment. A *data structure* is a representation of the arrangement, relationships, and contents of data subjects, data entities, and data files in the organization's data resource. The term is often used in a physical sense, meaning the physical structure of the data for implementation. Although physical structure is one aspect of a data structure, it is not the only aspect. A data structure must also represent the logical structure of the data, independent of the physical operating environment.

Improper means not suited to the circumstances or needs. An *improper data structure* is a data structure that does not provide an adequate representation of the data supporting the business for the intended audience.

The problems with improper data structures are summarized below.

A detail overload with semantic statements, data cardinality, data attributes, and primary and foreign keys.

The wrong audience focus with the wrong detail, poor presentation format, and audiences not covered.

Inadequate business representation with incomplete business detail, incomplete business coverage, and redundant business coverage.

Poor structuring techniques for data normalization and denormalization, primary key designations, data definition inclusion, and incorrect data structure.

Proper Data Structure

Proper means marked by suitability, rightness, or appropriateness; very good, excellent; strictly accurate, correct; complete. A *proper data structure* is a data structure that provides a suitable representation of the business, and the data supporting the business, that is relevant to the intended audience.

The proper data structure criteria are summarized below.

Proper data structures must represent the structure of the data with respect to the business.

Proper data structures must contain a diagram of the data entities and the relations between data entities.

Proper data structures must contain the structure and roles of the data attributes.

Proper data structures must contain formal data names.

Proper data structures must not contain data definitions.

Proper data structures must cover the entire data resource for an organization.

Proper data structures must be developed by appropriate data structuring techniques.

The presentation of proper data structures must be oriented toward the intended audiences.

The presentation of proper data structures must include only relevant materials that are presented in an understandable manner.

Proper data structures must be developed for all appropriate audiences.

The proper data structure principles are summarized below.

Follow established theories, concepts, and principles from outside data resource management and within data resource management.

Follow formal data normalization and data denormalization techniques.

The *data structure components principle* states that a proper data structure must integrate data entity-relation diagrams, data relations, semantic statements, data cardinalities, and data attribute structures. All of these components must be developed to have a complete proper data structure.

The *technically correct – culturally acceptable principle* states that a proper data structure must be both technically correct in representing the data and culturally acceptable for the intended audience. A proper data structure must integrate all of the technical detail about the data resource and present it in a manner that is acceptable to the recipients.

The *data structure uniformity principle* states that all proper data structures in an organization must have a uniform format.

The *structurally stable – business flexible principle* states that a proper data structure must remain structurally stable across changing technology and changing business needs, yet adequately represent the current and future business as it changes. Being structurally stable and business flexible encourages business process improvement, which is extremely difficult, if not impossible, without a stable, comparate data resource.

The *appropriate detail principle* states that a proper data structure must contain all the detail needed for all audiences, but only provide the detail desired by a specific audience. The principle allows a wide variety of audiences to become involved in developing and maintaining a comparate data resource.

The *data structure integration principle* states that each component of proper data structures must be stored once and only once within the organization's data resource, and then integrated as necessary when data structures are presented to specific audiences.

Proper sequence principle states that proper design proceeds from development of logical data structures that represent the business and how the data support the business, to the development of physical data structures for implementing databases.

The proper data structure can be easily read to any audience.

The *application alignment principle* states that purchased applications must be selected that align with the business and prevent or minimize warping the business into the application.

The *generic data structure principle* states that universal data models and generic data architectures can be used to guide an understanding of the organization's data, but should not be used in lieu of thoroughly understanding the organization's business.

Data Integrity Rules

Data integrity rules is the fourth component of the Data Architecture Segment. *Integrity* is the state of being unimpaired, the condition of being whole or complete, or the steadfast adherence to strict rules. *Data integrity* is a measure of how well the data are maintained in the data resource after they are captured or created. It indicates the degree to which the data are unimpaired and complete according to a precise set of rules.

Data integrity rules specify the criteria that need to be met to ensure the data resource contains the highest quality necessary to support the current and future business information demand. Examples of data integrity rules are shown in Appendix A.

Imprecise Data Integrity Rules

Imprecise means not precise, not clearly expressed, indefinite, inaccurate, incorrect, or not conforming to a proper form. *Imprecise data integrity rules* are data integrity rules that do not provide adequate criteria to ensure high quality data. Low data integrity results from the poor specification of data integrity rules, poor enforcement of data integrity rules, or both.

The problems with imprecise data integrity rules are summarized below.

Ignoring a high data frequency of data errors.

Incomplete data integrity rules.

Delayed data error identification.

Default data values.

Non-specific data domains.

Non-specific data optionality.

Undefined data derivation and data rederivation.

Uncontrolled data deletion.

Precise Data Integrity Rules

Precise means clearly expressed, definite, accurate, correct, and conforming to proper form. *Data integrity* was defined above. A *precise data integrity rule* is a data integrity rule that precisely specifies the criteria for high quality data values and reduces or eliminates data errors.

A data definition is not a data rule. Data definitions comprehensively define the meaning of the data. Data rules specify the criteria for maintaining data integrity.

Accuracy is freedom from mistakes or error, conformity to truth or to a standard, exactness, the degree of conformity of a measure to a standard or true value. *Data accuracy* is a measure of how well the data values represent the business world at a point in time or for a period of time.

Data accuracy includes the method used to identify objects in the business world and the method of collecting data about those objects. It describes how an object was identified and the means by which the data were collected.

Data completeness is a measure of how well the scope of the data resource meets the scope of the business information demand. It ensures that all the data necessary to meet the current and future business information demand are available in the organization's data resource.

Data currentness is a measure of how well the data values remain current with the business. The term *data currentness* is used rather than *currency* to prevent any confusion with the management of money (another lexical challenge). Data currentness ensures that data volatility and the collection frequency are appropriate to support the business information demand.

The precise data integrity rule criteria are summarized below.

Data integrity rules must be formally named according to the data naming taxonomy and vocabulary.

Data integrity rules must be normalized to match the normalized data.

Data integrity rules must be comprehensively defined.

Data integrity rules must have a formal notation that is easy to understand and use.

Specific data integrity rules must be defined for each type of situation encountered in the data resource.

Data integrity rules may inherit other data integrity rules, the same as data definitions are inherited.

Data integrity rule lockout must be identified and prevented.

Data integrity rule versions must be properly documented.

Data integrity rules must be stated explicitly.

Data integrity rules may be adjusted by combining and splitting rules.

Data integrity rules must be properly documented and be readily available to all audiences.

Data integrity rules must be denormalized and implemented as data edits as close to the data source as possible.

Data integrity rules must be uniformly enforced across all data.

Actions must be specified when data fail a data integrity rule.

Appropriate people must be notified of data integrity rule violations.

Default actions must be specified and documented.

Data quality improvement must be proactive to prevent data errors before they happen.

The precise data integrity rule principles are summarized below.

The *data integrity rule name principle* states that every data integrity rule must be formally and uniquely named according to the data naming taxonomy and supporting vocabulary.

The *data integrity rule normalization principle* states that data integrity rules are normalized to the data resource component which they represent or on which they take action.

The *data integrity rule definition principle* states that each data integrity rule must be comprehensively defined, just like data entities and data attributes are comprehensively defined. The definition must explain the purpose of the data integrity rule and the action that is taken.

The *data integrity rule notation principle* states that each data integrity rule must be specified in a notation that is acceptable and understandable to business and data management professionals, must be based on mathematical and logic notation where practical, and must use symbols readily available on a standard keyboard.

The *data integrity rule type principle* states that nine different types of data integrity rules must be identified and defined. The nine types are data value rules, conditional data value rules, data structure rules, conditional data structure rules, data derivation rules, data rederivation rules, data retention rules, data selection rules, and data translation rules.

Data integrity rules can be developed and inherited in the same way as fundamental data definitions. A *fundamental data integrity rule* is a data integrity rule that can be developed for and used by many specific data attributes. The data integrity rule is defined once and is applied to many different situations. A *specific data integrity rule* is a data integrity rule that is developed and applied to the data.

The *data rule version principle* states that data rule versions are designated by the version notation in the data naming taxonomy. The business constantly changes and the understanding of the business by data management and business professionals increases. Both of these situations lead to a modification of data integrity rules to ensure the data adequately support the business.

An *implicit data integrity rule* is a data integrity rule that is implied in a proper data structure. The *explicit data integrity rule principle* states that any implicit data integrity rule shown on a proper data structure must be shown explicitly in a precise data integrity rule. All data integrity rules must be stated explicitly so they can be enforced.

The *data integrity rule lockout principle* states that the precise data integrity rules must be reviewed to ensure that the rules do not result in a lockout, where data are prevented from entering the data resource.

The *data integrity rule edit principle* states that precise data integrity rules must be denormalized as the proper data structure is denormalized, and be implemented as physical data edits. Data integrity rules are the logical specification and must match the logical data structure, while data edits are the physical specification and must match the physical data structure.

The *data integrity failure principle* states that a violation action and a notification action must be taken on any data that fail precise data integrity rules. The violation and notification actions to be taken must be specified and followed.

The *data integrity rule management principle* states that the management of data integrity rules must be proactive to make optimum use of resources and minimize impacts to the business.

Data Documentation

Data documentation is the fifth component of the Data Architecture Segment. Data documentation applies to all components of the Data Architecture Segment, including data names, data definitions, data structure, and data integrity rules.

Limited Data Documentation

Limited data documentation is any documentation about the data resource that is sparse, incomplete, out of date, incorrect, inaccessible, unknown, poorly presented, poorly understood, and so on.

The problems with limited data documentation are summarized below.

Documentation not complete.

Documentation not current.

Documentation not understandable.

Documentation is redundant.

Documentation not readily available.

Documentation existence unknown.

Robust Data Documentation

Robust means having or exhibiting strength or vigorous health; firm in purpose or outlook; strongly formed or constructed; sturdy. *Robust data documentation* is documentation about the data resource that is complete, current, understandable, non-redundant, readily available, and known to exist.

The criteria for robust data documentation are summarized below.

The data documentation must be complete for the entire scope of the data resource and for all aspects of the data resource.

The data documentation must be formally designed, the same as business data.

Historical data documentation must be saved to adequately understand the historical data.

The data documentation must be formally documented to prevent a loss of institutional memory.

The data documentation must be current with the business so that it adequately represents the business.

The data documentation must be meaningful and understandable to all audiences.

The data documentation must not be redundant. It must represent one version of the truth about the organization's data resource.

The data documentation must be readily available to all audiences.

The data documentation must be known to exist.

The data documentation must promote development of a comparate data resource that is readily shared.

The principles for robust data documentation are summarized below.

The *data resource data aspect principle* states that data documentation must include both the technical aspect and the semantic aspect of the data resource. Both are needed for all audiences to fully understand, manage, and utilize the organization's data resource.

The *complete data documentation principle* states that data documentation must cover the entire scope of the data resource, and must include both the technical and the semantic aspects of the data resource.

The *data documentation design principle* states that all data resource data must be formally designed the same as business data. Data resource data are part of the data resource, the same as business data, and need to be designed the same as business data.

The *current data documentation principle* states that the data resource data must be kept current with the business. They must represent the current state of the data resource for both business and data management professionals.

The *understandable data documentation principle* states that the data resource data must be understandable to all audiences. The appropriate data resource data must be selected and presented to the intended audience in a manner appropriate for that audience.

The *non-redundant data documentation principle* states that the data resource data must represent a single version of truth about the data resource. The data resource data needs to include documentation about the existing disparate data as well as the new compare data, and the transformation of disparate data to compare data.

The *readily available data documentation principle* states that all data resource data must be readily available to all audiences. Both technical and semantic data must be available.

The *documentation known to exist principle* states that the data resource data must be known to exist so data management and business professionals can take advantage of those data.

The *Data Resource Guide principle* states that the data resource data must be placed in a comprehensive Data Resource Guide which serves as the primary repository for all data resource data. It contains data resource data about disparate data, compare data, and the transformation of disparate data to compare data. The Data Resource Guide contains the single version of truth about the data resource.

DATA RESOURCE INTEGRATION OVERVIEW

Data resource integration is a very detailed, but relatively straight forward, process. It's based on all of the theory, concepts, and principles described in the last chapter and the current chapter. An overview of the data resource integration process is presented below. The details of the process are presented in the following chapters.

John Zachman often makes the statement *It makes one wonder if there actually is a technical solution to the problem.* My answer is *Yes, there is, and it has been around for many years.* The technical solution is in all of the theory, concepts, and principles for managing a data resource described in *Data Resource Simplexity*. If they had been followed, the data resource would not have become disparate.

The technical solution to integrating a disparate data resource has also been around for a number of years, and is described in the current book. The technical solution exists in the form of concepts, principles, and techniques for understanding and resolving disparate data.

All that data resource managers need to do is understand and apply the theory, concepts, principles, and techniques for preventing disparate data and resolving disparate data. They already exist and just need to be followed.

Discovery Principle

Disparate data integration is a discovery process that requires knowledge, analysis, evaluation, thought, interpretation, reasoning, intuition, vision, an open mind, and some luck. It's a people oriented process that takes the knowledge and synergy of people to find the true content and meaning of the disparate data. It's the people who understand the data and the business, and make the discovery.

The real knowledge about disparate data is in people, not in documents, programs, or dictionaries. The discovery process captures that knowledge and documents it as data resource data. The process cannot be performed by tools or automated applications. Tools can only support the discovery process. Knowledgeable people must be involved.

The *data resource discovery principle* states that data resource integration is a discovery process where any insights about the data resource are captured, understood, and documented. The process is performed by people, who may be supported by automated tools.

Building a comparate data resource is not a precise process because of the uncertainty involved with disparate data. It's an evolutionary process based on discovery and enhancement that can only be done by people. The process cannot be automated because automated techniques cannot understand the true content and meaning of data. It's just not possible to run a program that scans data files or applications and dumps a thorough understanding into a data dictionary. The result will be meaningless, and may be worse in some situations. However, tools can support the people who perform data resource integration.

Critical Mass Principle

People analyze disparate data piece by piece to determine the true content and meaning of those disparate data. The analysis requires a real understanding and awareness of the common data architecture, the business activities of the organization, and the data that support those business activities. Just when it appears that the entire process is getting out of hand, the true content and meaning of disparate data will never be determined, and cross-references will never be made, everything collapses into a meaningful understanding. Just when it appears that the task is insurmountable, the critical mass of insight is achieved and disparate data fall into place within the common data architecture.

The **critical mass principle** states that when the understanding of disparate data appears insurmountable, a critical mass of information is reached and collapses into a meaningful understanding of the disparate data.

My first integration project, many years ago in a county EAM shop, introduced me to both the data resource discovery principle and the critical mass principle. The task was to take a large storage room with rows of filing cabinets containing punched cards and convert them to magnetic tape. The task sounded easy at first. Just take the cards and load them onto magnetic tape. What could be easier?

However, the punched cards had an implied meaning in the rows of cabinets, the cabinets themselves, and the drawers in a cabinet, and the color of the cards. The cards were in a specific sequence and contained considerable redundant data. My task was to understand the punched cards and get them loaded onto magnetic tape in a meaningful and useful manner. The task was not trivial, but I succeeded in getting the magnetic tapes built into what today would be called an integrated data resource.

Incidentally, database disasters are not unique to the electronic age. In the days of punched cards, which often did not have a sequence number of any kind, a real database disaster was to spill a tray of cards. Many hours have been spent rebuilding the database by looking through the punches in the cards and determining how they should be sequenced when put back into the tray.

Approach Overview

An overview of the approach to data resource integration is shown in Figure 3.6. The top row represents the organization's entire data resource. That data resource may be either the existing disparate data resource or the desired comparate, as shown in the second row. The data resource is understood within a common data architecture, as shown in the third row.

Organization Data Resource			
Disparate Data		Comparate Data	
	Common Data Architecture		
Disparate State Current	Formal State Necessary	Virtual State Desired	Comparate State Ideal
Not Understood	Understood	Transformed	
Probabilistic		Deterministic	
Retrospective		Prospective	
Descriptive		Prescriptive	

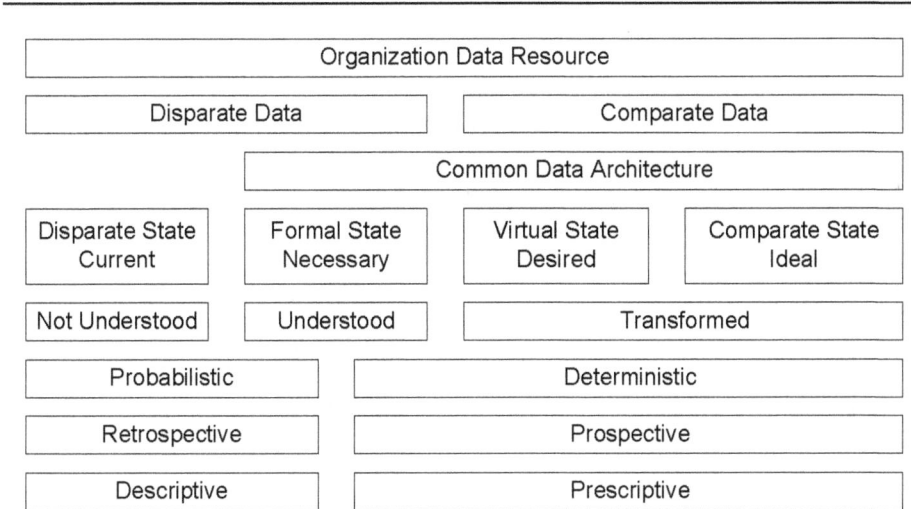

Figure 3.6. Data resource integration overview.

The disparate state is the current state of the data resource that is not well understood. The formal state is a necessary state where the disparate data are understood within a common context. The virtual state is the desired state where data are transformed temporarily to meet operational needs. The comparate state is the ideal state where the data have been permanently transformed.

The data resource is not well understood in the disparate state. It is understood within the context of a common data architecture in the formal state. It is transformed within a common data architecture in the virtual state and comparate state.

The disparate data were likely developed probabilistically, but the comparate data resource is developed deterministically. The change from probabilistic to deterministic is made in the formal state. The understanding of the disparate data is done retrospectively in the formal state. The comparate data are determined prospectively in the formal state, which is carried through the virtual and comparate states. The understanding of the disparate data is documented descriptively in the formal state. The comparate data are determined prescriptively in the formal state, which is carried through the virtual and comparate states.

Process Flow Overview

The general flow of the data resource integration process is shown in Figure 3.7. The disparate data are in the upper left and the comparate data are in the lower right. First, the existing disparate data are inventoried and documented as data resource data. Second, the inventoried data are cross-referenced to a common data architecture so they can be thoroughly understood in a common context. The cross-referencing is documented as data resource data. Third, the preferred data designations are made based on understanding the data in a common context, and are documented as data resource data.

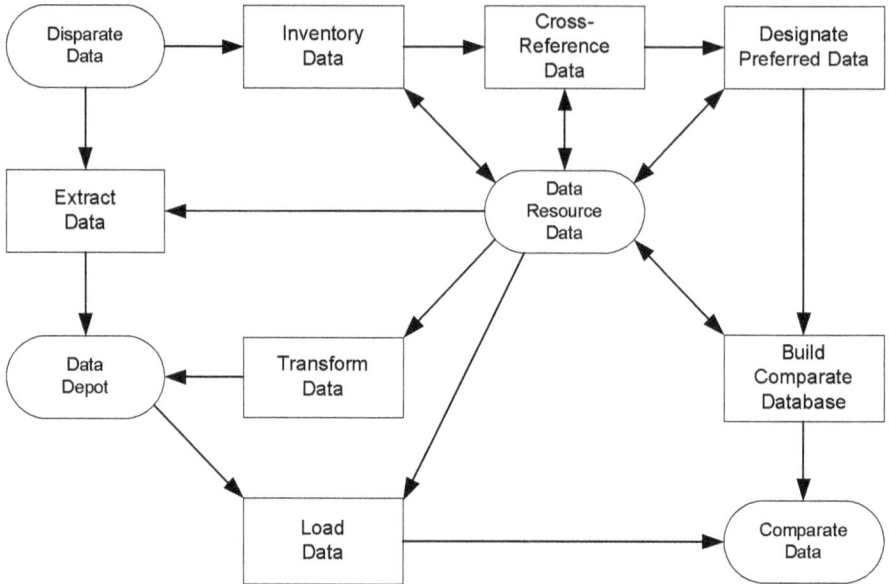

Figure 3.7. Data resource integration process flow.

Fourth, the compare databases are developed based on the documented preferred data designations. Fifth, the appropriate disparate data are extracted to a data depot in preparation for data transformation based on the preferred data designations. Sixth, the disparate data are transformed to comparate data within the data depot based on the data transformation rules. Seventh, the comparate data are loaded from the data depot into the comparate database based on the data resource data.

Integrating disparate data within a common data architecture is a real change for most people, and it causes them to procrastinate. However, the problem is not whether to integrate the disparate data, but how to start integrating disparate data. The problem is understanding how to build a common data architecture and integrate disparate data within that common data architecture.

SUMMARY

Integrating the data resource is the first of two components for the total integration of data resource management. The second is integrating the data culture. The current chapter described integrating the data resource by presenting concepts, principles, and analogies for understanding and resolving a disparate data resource, and terms related to integrating the data resource.

The five components of the Data Architecture segment of the Data Resource Management Framework were summarized from *Data Resource Simplexity*. These problems and principles of these components are used to both stop any further data disparity, and to understand and resolve existing data disparity. The point was strongly emphasized that the creation of data disparity must be stopped before the existing data disparity can be resolved.

Two overviews were provided for integrating the data resource. The first was an approach overview that described the relationships between the data resource states, the common data architecture, and the approaches to understanding disparate data and creating comparate data. The second was a flow overview that showed the seven basic steps for understanding and resolving disparate data.

The data resource integration process is not easy, but it's far from impossible. It's very detailed and often seems overwhelming, but if one persists, the process will lead to an understanding of the disparate data and the creation of comparate data that meet the current and future business information demand.

QUESTIONS

The following questions are provided as a review of data resource integration, and to stimulate thought about the integration of a data resource.

1. What is the data sharing concept?

2. How does data resource integration support the data sharing concept?

3. How does the Common Data Architecture concept support data resource integration?

4 Why is the Common Data Architecture a higher level of technology?

5. Why are both semantics and structure important in data resource integration?

6. How does the data model concept support data resource integration?

7. What does the data rule concept emphasize?

8. Why is the data resource data concept important?

9. Why are new terms needed for the Common Data Architecture?

10. What is the overall process for data resource integration?

Chapter 4

DISPARATE DATA VARIABILITY

All aspects of a disparate data resource are highly variable.

The naming, definition, structure, integrity, and documentation of disparate data are highly variable. The result of high variability in disparate data is a poor understanding about how well the data actually represent the business. That poor understanding increases the uncertainty about how the organization operates in the business world.

Thoroughly understanding disparate data is a primary objective of data resource integration. That thorough understanding begins with an understanding of the different types of variability that may be encountered in a disparate data resource. When the types of variability can be readily recognized, the stage is set for thoroughly understanding the disparate data and building a comparate data resource to adequately support an organization's business information demand.

Chapter 4 describes the different types of variability that may be encountered in a disparate data resource. It does not include how to document that variability or how to resolve that variability. Those topics are described in the following chapters. The chapter does provide an overview of the wide range of variability that can be encountered in a disparate data resource.

CONCEPTS AND PRINCIPLES

The discussion of disparate data variability begins with an overview of the concepts and principles regarding the wide range of variability in a disparate data resource. The overview includes a definition of data resource variability, the acceptable and unacceptable levels of variability, the need to expect anything when understanding a disparate data resource, the use of a common data architecture as a reference, the need to thoroughly understand disparate data, and the types of data variability that can be expected.

Data Resource Variability

A *disparate data resource*, as defined earlier, is a data resource that is substantially composed of disparate data that are dis-integrated and not subject oriented. It is in a state of disarray, where the low quality does not, and cannot, adequately support an organization's business information demand.

Variability is the quality, state, or degree of being variable or changeable; apt or liable to vary or change; changeable; inconsistent; characterized by variations; having much diversity; or not true to type. *Variation* is the act or process of varying; the state or fact of being varied; the existent to which a thing varies; or an instance of varying. *Data variation* is the variation in the data meaning, data structure, data integrity, data domain, data content and format, and so on.

Disparate data resource variability is a state where all aspects of a disparate data resource are inconsistent, characterized by data variations, and are not true to the concepts and principles of a comparate data resource. The data are highly variable in their names, definitions, structure, integrity, and documentation. The variability is pervasive throughout the disparate data resource.

The more disparate data that an organization has, the greater the data variability. The more geographically or functionally diverse an organization is, the greater the data variability. The longer an organization has been in business and the larger the organization, the greater the data variability. The more mergers and acquisitions an organization has, the greater the data variability.

Greater data variability makes the task of gaining control of the data and developing a comparate data resource more difficult. Greater data variability causes greater uncertainty about the disparate data. Most of the other problems managing a data resource are relatively minor compared to the problems associated with data variability and uncertainty.

The disparate data resource variability may be explicit or implicit. *Explicit disparate data resource variability* is the variability that can be readily seen or identified in the data names, definitions, structure, integrity, and documentation of a disparate data resource. *Implicit disparate data resource variability* is the variability that is not readily seen or identified in the data names, definitions, structure, integrity, and documentation of a disparate data resource. Implicit disparate data resource variability is either implied by existing documentation or exists in people's minds.

Disparate data resource variability is like different languages or dialects of a language. The variability is different in each organization and needs to be thoroughly understood before the data can be integrated into a comparate data resource. Anyone who is seriously interested in integrating a data resource must be able to readily understand the *language* of disparate data variability.

The *presumed data resource variability principle* states that disparate data are highly variable in their names, definitions, structure, integrity, and documentation. Data resource variability should be considered as the norm in most public and private sector organizations. Seldom does one find an existing data resource that does not have some degree of variability.

Acceptable Variability

Acceptable variability is the situation where a normal range of variability is acceptable. Variability exists in all aspects of a business and a normal level of variability must be accepted to perform business successfully. *Unacceptable variability* is the situation where the variability exceeds the normal range and becomes unacceptable. Most organizations seek to resolve the unacceptable variability.

Acceptable data resource variability is the acceptable level of variability for an organization's data resource. Acceptable data resource variability can be either temporal or cultural. *Temporal variability* is the normal change in the data resource due to changes in the business over time. Organizations add or drop lines of business, reorient their focus, establish new initiatives, and so on. The data resource must reflect these changes. *Cultural variability* is the normal differences due to culture, geography, politics, and so on, such as different names, addresses, monetary units, and so on. The data resource must reflect these cultural differences.

Unacceptable data resource variability is any temporal or cultural variability in the data resource that is beyond the acceptable level. Any data resource variability that is unacceptable and impacts the business must be resolved. A comparate data resource must be developed that fully supports the current and future business information demand.

The *data resource variability principle* states that every data resource has a level of variability that must be accepted and clarified, and that any variability above that acceptable level must be resolved. Data resource integration seeks to resolve the unacceptable data resource variability and to clarify the acceptable level of variability.

Expect Variability

Both acceptable and unacceptable data resource variability must be expected when integrating a disparate data resource. The *expect anything principle* states that when seeking to understand and resolve disparate data, anything should be expected. One should expect any situation, even if it seems irrational. One thing I learned in years of law enforcement was to expect the irrational, look for the irrational, learn to understand the irrational, and then deal with it appropriately. When I explain some of the situations I encounter with disparate data, people often respond with *That's irrational.* I simply say *My point exactly.*

An old saying states that *Anything which is not expressly forbidden is guaranteed to occur.* That saying is quite true. However, with a disparate data resource, even things that are expressly forbidden do occur. A better statement, with respect to a disparate data resource, is *Anything that can occur, will occur.* Therefore, expect anything when attempting to understand and resolve a disparate data resource, no matter how irrational it might seem.

Common Data Architecture Reference

The Common Data Architecture will be used as the reference point for understanding and resolving disparate data. The terms *data subject* and *data characteristic* will be used rather than *data entity* and *data attribute* for two reasons. First, data entities and data attributes are used in data models, and those data models are often disparate. Anything that is itself disparate cannot be used to understand and resolve disparity. Second, the Common Data Architecture will be the base for designating preferred data to build a comparate data resource. Therefore, it is best to use the Common Data Architecture throughout the entire data resource integration process.

The *common data architecture reference principle* states that the thorough understanding and resolution of a disparate data resource, and the development of a comparate data resource, are done within the construct of a common data architecture. The Common Data Architecture is the common construct for understanding and resolving a disparate data resource and developing a comparate data resource that fully supports the business information demand.

Disparate Data Understanding

A disparate data resource needs to be thoroughly understood before any attempt can be made to resolve that disparity. The *disparate data understanding principle* states that all disparate data variability, including data names, definitions, structure, integrity, and existing documentation will be understood and formally documented at a detailed level within the context of a common data architecture. Any attempt to resolve data disparity and integrate a disparate data resource without thoroughly understanding the disparate data will likely end in failure or a result that is less than fully successful.

Data Variability Types

Even after many years of working with disparate data in a wide variety of public and private sector organizations, I'm still amazed at the number of ingenious ways that people can screw up the data resource. Just when I think I've seen it all, I run across yet another way that data are managed improperly. I'll probably continue to encounter new ways of messing with the data as long as I'm involved in data resource management.

The five types of data variability correspond to the five components of a data architecture: data names, data definitions, data structure, data integrity, and data documentation. Data name and definition variability pertain to the meaning of the data—the semantics—and will be presented together. Data structure variability pertains to the arrangement and relationships of the data—the structure. Data integrity variability pertains to the rules for maintaining the data resource—the quality. Data documentation variability pertains to the formal documentation of the semantics, structure, and quality of the data resource.

The following sections describe each type of data variability with examples. The basic types of data variability are described, but the manifestation of all the basic types are not described—that would take a book unto itself. A table is presented in the Summary that shows the possible combinations of the basic types of data variability. I've attempted to cover all of the different types of variability, but there may be types I've never seen.

Any person interested in understanding and resolving a disparate data resource must be aware of these types of data variability and be able to readily recognize them when attempting to thoroughly understand a disparate data resource.

DATA NAME AND DEFINITION VARIABILITY

Data resource integration includes the integration of the semantics, structure, quality, and documentation of the data resource. The semantic component includes data names and data definitions. The last chapter on

Data Architecture Integration summarized the data name and data definition problems leading to informal data names and vague data definitions that could be expected with a disparate data resource. Those problems are the root cause of the variability in data names and data definitions.

Data name variability is the situation where data names are informal and have a wide range of variability that contributes little to understanding the data resource. The informal data names often detract from thoroughly understanding the data resource.

Data definition variability is the situation where data definitions are vague and have a wide range of variability that contributes little to understanding the data resource. The vague data definitions often detract from thoroughly understanding the data resource.

Informal data names and vague data definitions are prevalent throughout operational and evaluational data, structured and complex structured data, electronic and non-electronic data, logical and physical data models, and forms, screens, and reports. Anyone attempting to understand and resolve disparate data must learn to recognize the existence of informal data names and vague data definitions, and learn to develop formal data names and comprehensive data definitions to provide a strong semantic understanding about the data resource.

DATA STRUCTURE VARIABILITY

Disparate data do have a structure, but that structure is improper for a comparate data resource that fully meets the business information demand. The last chapter on Integrating the Data Resource summarized the data structure problems leading to improper data structures. The current section describes the data structure variability that exists in a disparate data resource. Knowing the different ways that disparate data are improperly structured helps develop the proper structure for a comparate data resource.

Each new data integration project brings new insights into how physical data can be designed without the benefit of formal logical and physical data modeling. Data files have been developed in every imaginable way, and even some unimaginable ways. Just when I think I've seen it all, I encounter yet another way that disparate data are structured.

The primary cause of improper data structures is a lack of proper data normalization and denormalization at all levels, including the data files, data occurrences, data instances, data items, and data codes. Ideally, all data go through a formal data design process that includes data normalization and data denormalization. However, most disparate data never went through formal data modeling, data normalization, or data denormalization. Any structure that does exist is usually a physical structure of the data files developed to meet a specific database or application needs. The result is a disparate data resource that is substantially un-normalized.

Data structure variability is the variability that exists in the improper structure of data in a disparate data resource. Data structure variability can occur with data files, data records, data items, data codes, and data relations, and usually occurs with all five. One major task of data resource integration is identifying the data structure variability and resolving that data variability. Knowing the data structure variability makes it easier to perform data inventory, make the data cross-references, make preferred designations, and develop a comparate data resource.

The current section describes the prominent structural abnormalities that could exist in a disparate data resource. These structural abnormalities apply to all aspects of a data resource, including operational and evaluational data, structured and complex structured data, electronic and non-electronic data, logical and physical data models, and forms, screens, and reports. The basic types of abnormalities and brief examples are provided.

Data File Variability

Data file variability is the variability that exists within and across data files in a disparate data resource. Data file variability can exist at the data file level, the data record level, and the data instance level. Each of these types of data file variability are described below, followed by a description of the data redundancy that results from data file variability.

Data Files

A *data file*, as defined earlier, is a physical file of data that exists in a database management system, such as a computer file, or outside a database management system, such as a manual file.

A *data subject*, as defined earlier, is a person, place, thing, concept, or event that is of interest to the organization and about which data are captured and maintained in the organization's data resource.

Ideally, a data file represents a data subject that has gone through formal data normalization and denormalization. However, most data files containing disparate data never went through that process, as described above. They were usually built to meet a specific database or application need. In many situations, the data from one data subject is split across many data files, and multiple data subjects are often combined into one data file.

A *disparate data file* is a data file that did not go through formal data normalization and data denormalization, and does not represent a single, complete data subject, or related data subjects resulting from formal data denormalization. Disparate data files often represent multiple data subjects, partial data subjects, or a combination of multiple and partial data subjects.

For example, a training data file contains data about employees, training courses, training classes, and training facilities. However, all of the employee data may be spread across multiple data files for training, payroll, affirmative action, project involvement, and so on.

Similarly, an equipment data file contains data about equipment, equipment breakdowns, equipment maintenance, and mechanics working on the equipment. Other data files may contain additional data about where the equipment was purchased, equipment maintenance schedules, mechanic certifications, and so on.

Disparate data files can contain single data subjects or multiple data subjects. A *single subject data file* is a data file that contains all of the data items, or a subset of the data items, representing the data characteristics for a single data subject. A *multiple subject data file* is a data file that contains all of the data items, or a subset of the data items, representing the data characteristics for multiple data subjects.

Disparate data files can contain complete data subjects or partial data subjects. A *complete subject data file* is a data file that contains all of the data items representing all of the data characteristics for a single data subject or for multiple data subjects. A *partial subject data file* is a data file that contains a subset of the data items representing the data characteristics for a single data subject or for multiple data subjects.

These categories of disparate data files can be combined into four basic data file types that could exist in a disparate data resource.

A *single complete subject data file* is relatively rare because it is very difficult to determine if all of the data characteristics have even been identified for a data subject. For example, a timber stand data file is reviewed and appears to contain all of the data items representing timber stands, such as species, slope, aspect, form class, and so on, and may be considered to represent a complete data subject for timber stands. However, data files may be encountered later that contain additional data items representing timber stands.

A *multiple complete subject data file* is also relatively rare for the same reason. For example, a class data file contains data items representing data characteristics for the student, for the class, for the course, and for the school data subjects. However, the data file does not contain all of the data items for a student, class, course, or school. Additional data items for those data subjects are contained in other data files.

A *single partial subject data file* is relatively common. For example, stream segment data, such as volume, flow rate, length, width, depth, gradient, sediment load, and so on, are often spread across multiple data files. However, each of those data files contains only data items about stream segments.

A *multiple partial subject data file* is very common. For example, a data file contains data items representing the data characteristics for a building data subject, such as structure, construction material, rooms, and so on, and for the land parcel where the residence is located, such as size, slope, aspect, and so on. However, it does not contain all of the data items for a resident or land parcel.

Partial subject data files, whether single subject or multiple subject, usually means that the data characteristics for a single data subject are scattered across many different data files. These scattered data characteristics are often redundant and out of synch with each other, which contributes to the variability found in a disparate data resource.

Similarly, complete subject data files do not guarantee that redundant data characteristics don't exist for that data subject in other data files. One should not assume that when a complete subject data file is encountered, whether single or multiple, that other data files don't exist containing redundant data items.

Looking at the data file disparity the other way around shows single file data subjects and multiple file data subjects. A **single file data subject** is a complete data subject that is contained in a single data file. The situation almost never exists in a disparate data resource. A **multiple file data subject** is a data subject that exists in multiple data files. The situation is common in a disparate data resource.

Data Records

A *data record,* as defined earlier, is a physical grouping of data items that are stored in or retrieved from a data file. It is the basic component of a data file. A *data occurrence*, as defined earlier, is a logical record that represents the existence of a business object or the happening of a business event in the business world.

Ideally, a data record represents a single data occurrence for a single data subject. For example, data occurrences in the Employee data subject for John J. Jones, Sally S. Smith, Marilyn M. McDonald, and so on, have corresponding data records in the Employee data file. However, data records in a disparate data resource do not always represent a single data occurrence for a single data subject. They may represent a partial data occurrence, a single data occurrence, or multiple data occurrences from the same data subject or from a subordinate data subject.

A *disparate data record* is data record that did not go through formal data normalization and denormalization, and does not represent a single data occurrence, or multiple data occurrences resulting from formal data denormalization. Disparate data records often represent partial data occurrences or multiple data occurrences.

A *complete occurrence data record* is a data record that contains all of the data items for a data occurrence. A *partial occurrence data record* is a data record that contains only part of the data items for a data occurrence. The complete data occurrence is split across multiple data records, usually due to some length limitation.

The practice of splitting data occurrences across multiple data records was common with punched cards, where the record length was limited to 80 columns, and continued into formal database management systems. A complete data occurrence often needed two or more punched cards to store all the data. For example, an employee's personal data might be placed in one record type and professional data in another record type. A partial occurrence data record is relatively common, particularly in an older disparate data resource.

The data record types may be explicitly identified with a name or number, such as 1, 2, 3, and so on. However, in some situations, the data record type may be implicitly identified by its sequence in the data file. The later situation was common with punched card data files, where room did not exist on the punched card for a record identifier, so the sequence implied the data record type. One of the major problems that was encountered in EAM days was someone dropping a tray of punched cards that had no record type identification.

A *single occurrence data record* is a data record that represents a single data occurrence. For example, all of the data about a stream segment is contained in one data record, or all of the data about a timber stand is contained in one data record. A single occurrence data record is relatively common in a disparate data resource.

A *multiple occurrence data record* is a data record that represents multiple data occurrences in a single data record. A multiple occurrence data record may contain subordinate data occurrences or parallel data occurrences.

A *subordinate data occurrence* is a data occurrence from a data subject that is subordinate to the data subject represented by the data file. For example, a single data record contains the data occurrence for the annual profits of the organization, but also contains the quarterly profits for that year. The quarterly profits represent a subordinate data subject to the annual profits. A subordinate data occurrence is relatively common and could be the result of formal data denormalization.

A *parallel data occurrence* is a data occurrence from the same data subject represented by the data file. For example, several short data occurrences for periodic stream flow data might be placed in the same data record. A parallel data occurrence is relatively rare, but does exist with some punch card data files and may have migrated to database management systems.

Data Instances

A *data instance*, as defined earlier, is a specific set of data values for the characteristics in a data occurrence that are valid at a point in time or for a period of time. Many data instances can exist for each data occurrence, particularly when historical data are maintained.

A *current data instance* is the most recent data instance that represents the most recent values of the data items in the data occurrence. An *historical data instance* is any data instance, other than the current data instance, that represents previous data values of the data items in the data occurrence.

A *complete historical data instance* contains a complete set of data items in the data occurrence, whether or not the data values changed. A *partial historical data instance* contains a subset of data items in the data occurrence, usually the data items whose data values changed and appropriate identifiers. Both complete and partial historical data instances exist in a disparate data resource.

Note that the complete and partial designations for data instances only applies to the set of data items contained in the data record, not to the full set of data items that may exist for a data subject across multiple data files. For example, if a data file is a partial subject data file and all of those data items are stored as a historical data instance, then the historical data instance is a complete data instance. However, if only the data items whose data value changed are stored, then the historical data instance is a partial data instance.

Self-contained historical data is the situation where historical data instances are retained in the same data file along with the current data instance. *Separate historical data* is the situation where historical data instances are retained in a separate data file. Both self-contained and separate historical data exist in a disparate data resource.

Historical data instances can be extremely variable in a disparate data resource. Looking at all the possible situations described above with data files, data records, and data instances, it should be quite obvious that the retention of historical data instances can lead to very disparate data. *Disparate data instances* is the situation where the retention of historical data instances across disparate data files and disparate data records can easily result in large quantities of disparate data.

Data Redundancy

Redundant means exceeding what is necessary or normal; superfluous; characterized by or containing an excess; characterized by similarity or repetition; profuse; or lavish. *Redundant data* are inconsistently maintained on different data sites, by different methods, and are seldom kept in synch. *Data redundancy* is the unknown and unmanaged duplication of business facts in a disparate data resource. It's the same facts, for the same data occurrence, for the same time period. It's the situation where a single business fact is stored in more than one location, and the locations may not be in synch. It's the unnecessary duplication of data that is a major contributor to data disparity.

Replication is a copy or reproduction; the action or process of replicating or reproducing; or creating a replica. *Data replication* is the consistent copying of data from one primary data site to one or more secondary data sites. The copied data are kept in synch with the primary data on a regular basis. Data replication is usually performed for operational efficiency.

A strong distinction is made between data redundancy and data replication during data resource integration. Data redundancy is unnecessary and confusing, and needs to be resolved during data resource integration. Data replication is necessary for operational efficiency and the data are kept in synch with the source. The replicated data certainly have redundancy, since they are copied from a primary data source that has redundancy. However, the emphasis is on resolving the data redundancy in the primary data source. When that data redundancy is resolved, the redundancy of the replicated data will be resolved.

A distinction also needs to be made about data redundancy. Data items with the same name in different data files do not always mean that data redundancy exists. For example, two student data files with the same set of data items may actually contain different data occurrences. One data file may be for middle school students and the other data file may be for high school students. Clearly, these are not redundant data. Another example is two data files for students, where one is high school students and the other is middle school and high school students. One of the sets of high school students is redundant. A third example is two data files for middle school students, but on close examination, one is for students from 1971 through 1990, and the other is for students from 1991 through 2010. These data are not redundant. Data redundancy only occurs with the same data characteristics for the same data occurrence for the same time frame.

Redundant data items is the situation where a data item representing the same data characteristic exists in different data files or different data records, whether that data item has the same data name or a different data name. Redundant data items do not necessarily mean that redundant data exist.

Disparate data files, disparate data records, and disparate data instances create two levels of data redundancy. The ***first level of data redundancy*** is created when disparate data files and disparate data records contain redundant data. The data redundancy can be quite large, particularly in organizations that have been in business for many years and have a large data resource.

The ***second level of data redundancy*** is created when disparate data instances contain redundant data. The data redundancy greatly magnifies the data redundancy created in the first level of data redundancy, leading to massive quantities of redundant data.

Four situations lead to the second level of data redundancy. The first situation is when complete historical data instances are maintained. Complete historical data instances make it easy to extract data for evaluational processing because the complete records are available and don't need to be rebuilt. However, massive data redundancy is created by saving data values that did not change.

The second situation is when data items representing the same data characteristic exist in multiple data files, and each of those data files maintains complete data instances. Massive data redundancy can be created.

The third situation is when partial historical data instances are maintained, but they contain more than the data values that changed and the necessary identifiers. The data values retained that did not change contribute to the data redundancy.

The fourth situation is when redundant data exist and the data history is out of synch. One data file received the change and created a historical data instance, yet another data file did not receive the change and did not create a historical data instance. The same thing happens when the data files received the change at different times and created historical data instances with different times. The same thing also happens when one data file received the change and created a historical data instance, while the other file received the change but not create a historical data instance.

Data redundancy is a major problem in a disparate data resource and requires considerable effort to understand and resolve.

Data Item Variability

A *data item*, as defined earlier, is an individual field in a data record. It represents a data attribute, subject to adjustments made during formal data denormalization. Ideally, a data item represents an elemental or combined data characteristic. However, data items in disparate data files do not always represent an elemental or combined data characteristic.

A *data characteristic*, as defined earlier, is an individual fact that describes or characterizes a data subject. It represents a business feature and contains a single fact, or closely related facts, about a data subject.

Data item variability is the variability in the format or content of data items representing the same business fact. It's a measure of how many different formats or contents exist for a particular data item across data files, and on screens, reports, and forms. However, many disparate data items represent multiple data characteristics that may or may not be closely related, partial data characteristics, or complex data characteristics. Each of these situations is described below.

An *elemental data characteristic* is a single elemental fact that cannot be further divided and retain its meaning, such as a month number or a day number within a month.

A *combined data characteristic* is the combination of two or more closely related elemental data characteristics into a group that is managed as a single unit. Note that the elemental data characteristic must be closely related. For example, the elemental data characteristics for century, year, month, and day are closely related and may be combined into a data characteristic for date. Similarly, the data characteristics for a person's individual name, middle name, and family name are closely related and may be combined into a data characteristic for the person's complete name.

A *multiple data characteristic* is two or more single or combined data characteristics that are not closely related and should not be stored together or managed as a single unit. The data characteristics may be from the same data subject or from different data subjects. For example, the combination of a project name and project initiation date would be a multiple data characteristic.

A *disparate data item* is a data item that contains other than an elemental or combined data characteristic. Disparate data items may contain multiple data characteristics, partial data characteristics, or complex data characteristics.

Single Characteristic Data Items

A *single characteristic data item* is a data item that contains only one elemental or combined data characteristic. For example, vegetation scientific name is an elemental data characteristic, and a project leader's name is a combined data characteristic.

A *consistent characteristic data item* is a data item that always contains an elemental or combined data characteristic. For example, a data item consistently contains a vehicle's model name, or a data item always contains a driver's name.

A *variable characteristic data item* is a data item that could contain several different data characteristics, but only one of those data characteristics appears in any data record. In other words, the data characteristics are mutually exclusive. The data characteristic that is contained in the data item is usually determined by the data value in another data item or by the data value itself. For example, a land parcel owner's birth date data item could contain the actual birth date or the reason for no birth date.

A *data item format* is the physical format of the data value contained in the data item. A *fixed format data item* is a data item whose data value is always in the same format. For example, a student's name is always in the normal sequence and right justified, or an applicant's name is always in the inverted sequence and left justified. A *variable format data item* is a data item whose data value could be one of a variety of different formats. For example, a shipping date could be in any of a wide variety of date formats, such as MDY, M/D/Y, YMD, Y/M/D, and so on.

Variable format data items may have an identifier for the format, although the practice is not common. For example, variable format codes might be D1, D2, D3, and so on, for MDY, M/D/Y, YMD, and so on, and could appear before the data item or at the beginning of the data record.

Data item content is the physical variation in the data values contained in a data item. For example, a data item may represent a street segment length. However, the data value may be in feet, meters, miles, and so on.

Data item length is the physical length of the data value contained in the data item. A *fixed length data item* is a data item whose length is fixed. For example, a vehicle manufacturer's name is always 50 characters long. A *variable length data item* is a data item whose length is variable. For example, the length of a textual description or accident explanation might vary.

The length of a variable length data item is usually determined by a length value or by a delimiter. The length value typically precedes the data value, as shown below.

12John R Smith

However, the length value may be stored in a variety of other locations, such as all of the data item lengths at the beginning of a data record.

A delimiter is a special character, such as a comma, ampersand, or colon that appears after each data item. The example below shows a comma as the data item delimiter.

John R Smith,12345 Jackson Highway S,Apartment 6,

Variable Sequence Data Items

Variable sequence data item is the situation where the data items can be in any sequence in a data record. The specific data item is identified by a keyword or mnemonic, followed by the data value. The example below shows mnemonics for tree measurements where SN is the species name, DM is the diameter, HT is the height, and AG is the age. The example shows a variable length with delimiters. However, the length could be fixed.

SNDouglas Fir,DM14.2,HT125,AG50

Multiple Characteristic Data Items

A ***multiple characteristic data item*** is a data item that contains a more than one data characteristic. For example, a data item contains both a plant's common name and its scientific name, such as Red Alder,Alnus

Rubra.

Like single characteristic data items, a multiple characteristic data item can contain consistent or variable data characteristics with a fixed or variable format and a fixed or variable length. The variable lengths of multiple characteristics within a data item are delineated similar to the way the variable lengths of single characteristic data items are delineated in a data record.

Partial Characteristic Data Items

A *partial characteristic data item* is a data item that contains part of a data characteristic. Other parts of the data characteristic are contained in one or more other data items. For example, an accident description may exceed the allowed length of a textual data item, resulting in the description running to multiple data items. The sequence of the multiple data items may be indicated by a number, or may be implied by the sequence of the data items in the data record.

A partial characteristic data item is usually a consistent characteristic with a fixed format, although it may have a fixed or variable length. However, since anything is possible in a disparate data resource, a partial characteristic data item could have a variable composition and a variable format.

More on Delimiters

Multiple data item length delimiters may appear in rare situations. For example, a comma could be used as a length delimiter for data items in a string of data items, such as between each project team member in a string of team member names, as shown below.

John Jones,Jack Smith,Sue Wilson,Bill Arnold

In addition, an ampersand could be used between groups of related data items, such as between a string of project team member names and a string of project team members' responsibility on the team, as shown below. Note that the team member responsibilities belong to a different data subject than the project team member names.

John,Jack,Sue,Bill&ProjectLead,Secretary,Analyst,Analyst

The groups of related data items could belong to the same data subject, such as the project team member names and their birth dates, as shown below.

John,Jack,Sue,Bill&3/12/78,4/16/82,9/9/88,12/1/72

The team responsibility could be implied by the position of the team member name. In the example below, the first position is project lead, the second position is secretary, the third position is analyst, and the fourth position is designer.

John,Jack,Sue,Bill

Successive delimiters would indicate a missing position on the team. In the example below, the secretary and analyst are missing from the team, as shown by the successive delimiters.

Jack,,,Jason

Any person interested in understanding and resolving disparate data must be aware of these possible situations with data items and be able to readily identify them.

Data Code Variability

Data code variability is the variability in the coded data values, names, definitions, and domain of codes in a set of data codes. It's a measure of how many variations exist for a particular set of data codes across data files. Ideally, a data code represents a single property of a data subject, and a data code set represents a single data subject. However, many variations of the ideal occur in a disparate data resource.

Data code variability is one of the most confusing things about disparate data, and one of the most difficult to understand and resolve. Data codes can have the same name with different codes, the same codes with different names, the same definitions with different names and/or codes, the same meaning with different definitions, the same codes and names with different meanings, and so on. People have found many ways to invent data code structures that are very difficult to use and to understand.

A *data property* is a single feature, trait, or quality within a grouping or classification of features, traits, or qualities belonging to a data characteristic. For example, gender has data properties for male, female, and unknown. Management level has data properties for executive, manager, supervisor, and lead worker.

A *data code* is any data item whose data value has been encoded or shortened in some manner. For example, the gender data properties might be coded as M, F, and U, and the management level data properties might be encoded as E, M, S, and L. A data code is also known as a *coded data value*.

A *data code set* is a complete group of data codes that represent all of the data properties for a single data subject. For example, data code sets are defined for the data properties of gender or management level, which are

130

data subjects.

A *set of data codes* is a subset of a data codes representing only part of the data properties for a complete data code set, or a mixture of properties from different data code sets. For example, a set of data codes for management level might include only E for Executive and M for Manager, or a set of data codes might include a mixture of hair color and eye color.

Data Code Properties

Ideally, each data code represents a single data property. However, data codes may be multiple property or partial property. Each of these situations is described below.

A *single property data code* is a data code that represents one specific data property of a single data subject. For example, Br represents brown hair and Bl represents blond hair in the data subject for hair color. Another example is management level codes E for Executive, M for Manager, S for Supervisor, and L for Lead Worker. Single property data codes are very common in a disparate data resource.

A *multiple property data code* is a data code that represents two or more data properties of the same data subject. For example, 1 represents blond and gray hair, 2 represents black and brown hair, and so on. Another example is management level codes E for executive and manager, S for supervisor, and L for lead worker. The executive and manager data properties have been combined into one data code. Multiple property data codes are relatively common in a disparate data resource.

Note that a complex property data code doesn't exist. A data code represents either a single data property, multiple data properties, or a partial data property. A data code cannot represent any combination of a single data property, multiple data properties, or partial data properties.

Data Code Subjects

The examples above were data codes that represented data properties for a single data subject, such as hair color, gender, management level, and so on. Data codes can also represent multiple data subjects.

A *single subject data code* is a data code that represents a single data subject, such as the ones shown above for gender, management level, and hair color. Single subject data codes are very common in a disparate data resource.

A *multiple subject data code* is a data code that represents two or more different data subjects. For example, gender, hair color, and eye color might be combined so that 1 is male, blond hair, blue eyes; 2 is female, blond hair, blue eyes; 3 is male brown hair, blue eyes; and so on. Multiple subject data codes are relatively common in disparate data. Multiple subject data codes are relatively common in a disparate data resource.

Note that complex subject data codes don't exist. A data code represents either a single data subject or multiple data subjects. A data code can't represent both a single data subject and a multiple data subject. Also, partial subject data codes don't exist.

Sets of Data Codes

The examples above were data codes that represented single, multiple, or partial data properties, and single or multiple data subjects. A set of data codes can be complete or partial, and can represent a single data subject or multiple data subjects.

A *complete set of data codes* contains all of the data properties for a single data subject. For example, engine type codes are defined for gasoline, diesel, propane, and electric. Complete sets of data codes are very common in a disparate data resource.

A *partial set of data codes* contains a subset of the data properties for a single data subject. For example, the engine type codes above would be a partial data code set if wind, wood, coal, and human power were considered as engine types. Partial sets of data codes are relatively rare in a disparate data resource, but do exist when the entire data resource is considered.

A *single subject set of data codes* is a set of data codes that represent one data subject. Single subject sets of data codes are relatively common in a disparate data resource.

A *multiple subject set of data codes* is a set of data codes that represent more than one data subject. For example, a set of county codes has data codes 1 through 41, yet the state has only thirty-nine counties. Code 40 means outside of the state but within the United States, and code 41 means outside of the United States. Although the data codes are mutually exclusive, they obviously represent more than one data subject. Multiple subject sets of data codes are relatively rare in a disparate data resource, but do exist.

Note that a complex subject set of data codes doesn't exist. A set of data codes represents either a single data subject or multiple data subjects. Similarly, a partial subject set of data codes doesn't exist.

Disparate data codes is the situation where data codes can represent single, multiple, or partial data properties; where data codes can represent single or multiple data subjects; where sets of data codes can represent single or multiple data subjects; and where sets of data codes can be complete or partial.

Coded Data Codes

Coded data codes is the situation where single property data codes are combined into a multiple property data code. For example, gender, eye color, and hair color data codes might be combined so that 1 is M Br Bl (male, brown eyes, blond hair), 2 is F Br Bl, and so on. Coded data codes are very rare in a disparate data resource, but do occur.

Hidden Hierarchies

A *hidden data code hierarchy* is the situation where a single set of data codes represents a hierarchy of data codes. For example, the Census Race Code is a three-digit number. However, buried in the three-digit number is a hidden three-level hierarchy of codes. These three levels were defined as Census Race Category, Census Race Group, and Census Race. Census Race Category is identified by a range of three-digit numbers, such as 653 through 699 is Pacific Islander. Census Race Group is identified by another range of three-digit numbers within Census Race Category, such as 653 through 659 is Polynesian. Census Race is identified by a single three-digit number within Census Race Group, such as 653 for Hawaiian.

Another form of a hidden data hierarchy is a single set of data codes that represents a hierarchy of codes, but the distinction is sequential through the data value. For example, a customer identification number might be a seven-digit number. However, the first two digits represent the sales region, the next two digits represent the sales district within the sales region, and the next three digits represent the customer number within the sales district.

Hidden hierarchies are relatively common in a disparate data resource. Anyone working with a disparate data resource must be able to recognize the existence of hidden hierarchies.

Data Relation Variability

Data relation variability is the variability that exists with the data relations, the names and cardinalities for those data relations, primary keys, and foreign keys. Ideally, data relations with their names and cardinalities, primary keys, and foreign keys are formally designed. However, that is far from the norm in a disparate data resource. The different types of data relation variability are described below.

Data Relations

A *data relation* is an association between data occurrences in different data subjects or data entities, or within a data subject or data entity, or between data records in different data files or within a data file. It provides the connections between data subjects for building the proper data structure, and between data files for navigating in the database.

A *Logical data relation* is an association between data occurrences in different data subjects or data entities, or within a data subject or data entity. It is defined during data normalization and has a name or short phrase describing the data relation.

A *Physical data relation* is an association between data records in different data files or within a data file. It is typically defined during formal data denormalization and has now name.

Data Cardinality

Data cardinality is a specification of the number of data occurrences that are allowed or required in each data subject or data entity that are involved in a data relation, or the number of data records that are allowed or required for each data file that are involved in the data relation.

General data cardinality is the data cardinality specified by the data relation or by a semantic statement for the data relation. A semantic statement is a textual statement of the relationship between data entities. General data cardinality indicates one-to-one, one-to-many, and many-to-many data relations. General data cardinality typically appears for logical data relations, but not for physical data relations.

Specific data cardinality is the data cardinality specified by a notation at the end of a data relation and is more specific than the general data cardinality. General data cardinality indicates 0, 1, M, 0/M, or 1/M data occurrences or data records. Specific data cardinality may appear on logical data relations, but typically does not appear on physical data relations.

Primary Keys

Data relations are based on primary and foreign keys, or simply on the same data characteristics, regardless of the data item names, that exist in different data files.

Primary key is a set of one or more data attributes whose values uniquely identify each data occurrence in a data entity in a logical data model. In a database, a primary key is a set of one or more data items whose values uniquely identify each data record in a data file.

Ideally, primary keys are formally identified during logical and physical data modeling and then incorporated into the data files. However, the primary keys in most disparate data files were defined as they were needed, frequently without any formal data normalization or denormalization. That practice resulted in disparate primary keys.

A *disparate primary key* is any primary key defined in a disparate data resource that does not meet the formal criteria for a true primary key. The specific situations are described below.

Primary keys often contain data items that are not necessary for the unique identification of each data record in the data file. For example, the primary key for a vehicle might contain the vehicle's license number and the manufacture date. The situation is relatively common in a disparate data resource.

Primary keys may exist in a data file, but may not be readily identifiable. The situation is very common in a disparate data resource.

Primary keys may never have been defined, particularly if no attempt was made to uniquely identify each data record in a data file. The situation is rare in a disparate data resource, but it does exist with data files that are not part of a formal database management system.

Primary keys may be defined and maintained without any valid need. Many disparate data files have primary keys that are maintained but never used. The situation is relatively rare in a disparate data resource.

Primary keys may be defined and maintained, but do not uniquely identify each data record in the data file; additional data items are needed for unique identification of each data record. The situation is relatively rare in a disparate data resource, but does exist in data files that are not part of a database management system.

Different data files may contain the same primary key, even though the data item names may be different, and may represent the same data subject or different data subjects. The situation is relatively common in a disparate data resource.

System identifiers or counters are often used as the primary key, but they make it difficult to identify which data item or set of data items uniquely identify a data record. In addition, some system identifiers and counters are often reused when a data record has been deleted. The situation is relatively common in a disparate data resource.

Data files representing the same data subject could have different primary keys. For example, a vehicle purchase data file could have a primary key for vehicle identification number and purchase date, a vehicle surplus data file could have a primary key for vehicle license number and sale date, and a vehicle inventory data file cold have a primary key for the vehicle license number. The situation is relatively common in a disparate data resource.

In addition to the variability described above, primary keys could also contain the variability mentioned earlier for data items. The combined variability often results in extreme difficulty identifying primary keys in a disparate data resource.

Foreign Keys

A *foreign key* in logical data models is the primary key of a data occurrence in a parent data entity that is placed in each data occurrence of a subordinate data entity to identify the parent data occurrence in that parent data entity. In data files, a foreign key is the primary key of a data record in a parent data file that is placed in each data record of a subordinate data file to identify the parent data record in that parent data file.

A *disparate foreign key* is any foreign key defined in a disparate data resource that does not meet the formal criteria for a true foreign key. The specific situations are described below.

Foreign keys may not be readily identifiable and are often difficult to identify. The situation is very common in a disparate data resource.

A foreign key may be readily identified, but have no corresponding primary key in any data file. The situation is relatively rare in a disparate data resource.

A foreign key may go, or at least appear to go, to many different parent data files based on the data item names. The situation is very common in a disparate data resource.

A foreign key may be a subset of the primary key in a parent data file, particularly when the primary key contains data items that are not necessary for uniqueness. The situation is relatively common in a disparate data resource.

A foreign key may have different data item names than the primary key, even though it represents the same data characteristics. The situation is relatively common in a disparate data resource.

A foreign key may have the same data item names as a primary key, but those data items do not represent the same data characteristics. Therefore, the foreign key is not valid for that parent data file. This situation is relatively common in a disparate data resource.

A foreign key may contain data items that uniquely identify a data record in a parent data file, even though those data items are not designated as a primary key. This situation is relatively rare in a disparate data resource.

Data files subordinate to the same parent data file may have different foreign keys to that parent data file. This situation is relatively rare in a disparate data resource.

The same data files in different databases may have different foreign keys to the same parent data file. This situation is relatively common in a disparate data resource.

A subordinate data file in different databases may have different parents. In other words, the foreign keys to all possible parent data files across databases may not exist in a data file in a particular database. The situation is relatively common in a disparate data resource.

In addition to the variability described above for foreign keys, foreign keys can also contain the variability mentioned earlier for primary keys and for data items. The combined variability often results in extreme difficulty identifying foreign keys in a disparate data resource.

DATA INTEGRITY VARIABILITY

Disparate data do have some level of data integrity, usually in the form of data edits and constraints that are applied through database management systems or applications. However, most of those data edits and constraints are imprecise for a comparate data resource that fully meets the business information demand. The primary reason for the imprecise data edits is that people just didn't take the time to formally specify the data integrity criteria and ensure those criteria were properly implemented.

Like data structures, I never cease to be amazed at the low integrity in a disparate data resource. The more I look at disparate data in various public and private sector organizations, the more I'm appalled at the lack of formal data edits that are consistently applied to the data resource. The result is a low quality data resource that leads to low quality information.

137

The last chapter on Integrating the Data Resource summarized the problems leading to imprecise data integrity. The current section describes the types of data integrity variability that can be expected in a disparate data resource. Knowing the variability in data edits helps develop precise data edits for a comparate data resource.

Data integrity variability is the variability that exists with data edits in a disparate data resource. Ideally, data integrity rules are defined during logical data modeling and are transformed to data edits during physical data modeling. However, that is not true for most disparate data resources. Data integrity rules were seldom defined during logical data modeling, and data edits that were often superficial and incomplete were prepared during physical implementation of the data.

Data integrity variability applies to operational and evaluational data, structured and complex structured data, electronic and non-electronic data, logical and physical data models, and forms, reports, and screens. Anyone attempting to understand and resolve disparate data must learn to recognize imprecise data integrity rules, and learn to prepare precise data integrity rules that ensure quality in a comparate data resource.

Data accuracy, as defined earlier, is a measure of how well the data values represent the business world at a point in time or for a period of time. Data accuracy includes the method used to identify objects in the business world and the method of collecting data about those objects. It describes how an object was identified and the means by which the data were collected.

Disparate data have widely varying degrees of accuracy, although the accuracy is frequently unknown and not readily apparent. The accuracy cannot be changed or improved during the data integration process. It can only be identified and documented to increase understanding of the data.

DATA DOCUMENTATION VARIABILITY

Disparate data are frequently documented to some extent. However, the documentation is largely incomplete and inadequate. The last chapter on Integrating the Data Resource summarized the problems leading to limited data documentation. The current section describes the types of data documentation variability that can be expected in a disparate data resource. Knowing the variability in data documentation helps develop robust data documentation for a comparate data resource.

I'm astounded at the lack of formal documentation that exists for the data resource in most public and private sector organizations. It seems to me that any resource that is critical to an organization should be thoroughly documented. However, the critical data resource is not documented to the same extent that other critical resources are documented.

Data documentation variability is the variability that exists with the documentation about a disparate data resource. Ideally, all components of the organization's data resource are formally documented and readily available. However, that is not true for most disparate data resources. The documentation is sparse, inconsistent, and widely scattered through the organization, in people's minds, in database management systems, in data models, and in applications.

Data documentation variability applies to operational and evaluational data, structured and complex structured data, electronic and non-electronic data, logical and physical data models, and forms, reports, and screens. Anyone attempting to understand and resolve disparate data must learn to recognize the lack of complete, robust data documentation, and learn to prepare robust data documentation based on any information they can gain about the disparate data resource.

VARIABILITY OVER TIME

The description of variability presented above applies to a point in time. The *first dimension of data variability* is the variability in data names, definitions, structure, integrity, and documentation that exists at any point in time with the operational data in a disparate data resource. The first dimension can be considerable and often overwhelming.

However, a data resource can change over time to reflect changes in both business and technology. For example, data names change, data definitions change, data structure changes, data integrity changes, the data documentation changes, and the data values captured and maintained can change. Variability over time due to business and technology changes is necessary and acceptable. What is not acceptable is change for change sake, and not properly managing the necessary and acceptable change.

The *second dimension of data variability* is the variability in data names, definitions, structure, integrity, and documentation that occurs over time with the operational data in a disparate data resource. The second dimension is in addition to the first dimension of data variability, meaning that the data variability at a point in time is magnified by the data variability over time. The result can easily be overwhelming and makes management of a disparate data resource nearly impossible. The overwhelming nature of the variability is the reason many organizations choose not to attempt understanding and resolution of a disparate data resource.

139

The first and second dimensions of data variability apply to operational data and their related data models, forms, screens, and reports. A similar situation is occurring with evaluational data, including both analytical data (the aggregation space) and predictive data (the influence and variation space). These evaluational data are following the same path of data variability as operational data.

The *third dimension of data variability* is the variability in data names, definitions, structure, integrity, and documentation that occurs with evaluational data in a disparate data resource. The third dimension of data variability magnifies the first and second dimensions, because the evaluational data are extracted from the operational data. In addition, the evaluational data are often analyzed in a variety of different ways and by different methods, both at a point in time and over time. No wonder the results are often questionable.

Take the variability of operational data at a point in time, add the variability to operational data over time, extract evaluational data from those operational data, analyze those evaluational data over time, and you have some serious data variability in a disparate data resource. What is the probability that those operational and evaluational data will adequately support the current and future business information demand?

SUMMARY

Data variability occurs with the semantics of a data resource (data names and definitions), the structure of the data resource (structure), the integrity of the data resource (quality), and documentation of the data resource. Data variability occurs with operational and evaluational data, structured and complex structured data, electronic and non-electronic data, logical and physical data models, and forms, reports, and screens. Data variability occurs at a point in time and over time.

One should be able to make five conclusions from the above descriptions of data variability. First, data variability exists throughout the entire disparate data resource. Second, data variability exists in all components of the data architecture. Third, the variability with data names and definitions, data integrity, and data documentation is largely due to a lack of complete and consistent management. Fourth, the variability with data structures is out of control with many things being done that should never be done. Fifth, the existing data disparity will continue, and will get worse, unless strong action is taken to stop further data disparity and to resolve existing data disparity.

These conclusions don't paint a very positive picture about an organization's data resource and its ability to support the current and future business information demand. Any of these conclusions would be difficult to accept, but accepting all five conclusions is almost beyond comprehension. No wonder people have trouble understanding their data and the business supported by those data. No wonder the current and future business information demand is not fully supported.

The table below summarizes the structural data variability for data files, data records, data instances, data items, and data codes.

Data File

Composition
Single Subject
Multiple Subjects

Completeness
Complete Subject
Partial Subject

Data Record

Completeness
Complete Occurrence
Partial Occurrence

Composition
Single Occurrence
Multiple Occurrences
    Subordinate Occurrence
    Parallel Occurrence

Data Instance

Time Frame
Current Data Instance
Historical Data Instance
    Complete Historical Data Instance
    Partial Historical Data Instance

History Location
Self-Contained Historical Data
Separate Historical Data

Data Item

Business Fact

Single Characteristic
Multiple Characteristic
Partial Characteristic

Composition
Consistent Characteristic
Variable Characteristic

Format
Fixed
Variable

Length
Fixed
Variable

Data Code

Data Properties
Single Property
Multiple Property

Data Subjects
Single Subject
Multiple Subject

Set of Data Codes

Data Properties
Complete Subject
Partial Subject

Data Subjects
Single Subject
Multiple Subject

Coded Data Code

Hidden Data Code Hierarchy

QUESTIONS

The following questions are provided as a review of disparate data variability, and to stimulate thought about understanding and documenting the variability of disparate data.

1. What is data variability?

2. What is the difference between acceptable and unacceptable data

variability?

3. Why does data variability exist in an organization's data resource?

4. What impacts does data variability have on the organization?

5 What component of the data architecture has the most data variability?

6. What are the dimensions of data variability?

7. How does data variability impact understanding?

8. Why is the Common Data Architecture used as the reference for understanding data variability?

9. Why should one expect data variability in the organization's data resource?

10. What can be done to stop further data variability?

Chapter 5

DATA INVENTORY CONCEPT

Inventorying data is the first step to resolving data disparity.

The first step toward integrating a disparate data resource is to inventory the existing data. The existing data may be in operational data files, in evaluational data files, in data models, on screens, reports, and forms, in a variety of documentation, or in people's minds. All of these sources need to be identified and documented to fully understand the existing disparate data resource.

Chapter 5 describes the concepts and principles for inventorying disparate data, the structure for documenting that inventory, and the various components of a disparate data resource that could be inventoried. Chapter 6 describes the actual process and techniques for inventorying and documenting disparate data using the material described in the current chapter.

CONCEPTS

The first major problem that public and private organizations face today, as mentioned in Chapter 1, is that they do not know all of the data that they have at their disposal. Various organization units and individuals know the data that they have available. However, the organization at large does not know all of the data it has at its disposal.

Most organizations do not have a complete inventory of their entire data resource, in one place that is readily available to anyone in the organization. I've found, after being involved with the disparate data in many public and private sector organizations, that only about 15% of the organization's data are inventoried or documented in any manner. When people can't find the data they need, they will likely create their own data, which increases the data disparity.

The first step to resolve data disparity and begin the data resource integration process is to inventory the existing disparate data. Inventorying disparate data solves the first basic problem of disparate data—a lack of awareness of data, within or without the organization, that

145

are at the organization's disposal. Inventorying disparate data sets the stage for understanding those data and transforming them to a comparate data resource.

The data inventory concept and data product concept describe what is captured during the data inventory process and how the data inventory is documented.

Data Inventory Concept

Inventory is an itemized list of assets; a catalog of the property of an individual or estate; a list of goods on hand; a survey of natural resources; a list of traits, preferences, attitudes, interest, or abilities; the quality of goods or materials on hand. It is also the act or process of taking an inventory.

A *data inventory* is the process of identifying and documenting all of the data at an organization's disposal so those data can be readily understood and used to develop and maintain a comparate data resource that supports the business information demand. It begins the process of understanding disparate data and developing a comparate data resource within a common data architecture.

The *data inventory concept* is that all data at the organization's disposal will be completely and comprehensively inventoried, and documented in one location that is readily available to anyone in the organization, so that the organization at large understands the content, meaning, and quality of those data.

The *data inventory objective* is to identify, inventory, and document all data that currently exist in the organization's data resource or are readily available to the organization so that those data can be readily understood and used to support the current and future business information demand. It raises the awareness of the data that exist and solves the first problem with disparate data.

The *data inventory process* identifies the existing data, collects the existing documentation, and enhances that documentation with additional insights. The data inventory process is sometimes referred to as *retro-documenting*. However, that term in not used because it implies documentation only and not a formal inventory.

The data inventory process identifies the existing data, collects the existing documentation, and enhances that documentation with additional insights.

Inventory Analogy

A traditional data inventory only lists the data available to the organization, but does not help the organization integrate those data because no common base exists for understanding that inventory.

For example, several different organizations keep inventories of plumbing items. Organization A installs plumbing systems and deals with only one-inch pipe, valves, and unions. It's implied within the organization that all plumbing items are one-inch steel and that all valves are gate valves. Organization B carries all types of valves and its interest is only in the types of valves, such as gate, ball, and so on, and the sizes of valves. It's implied within the organization that all items are steel valves. Organization C carries all types of pipe and its interest is in the size and composition of pipe, such as steel, copper, plastic.

A traditional inventory of plumbing items from these three organizations would produce three lists that could not be easily integrated. Organization A's inventory would list the number of pipes, valves, and unions, but would show nothing about size or material. Organization B's inventory would list quantities by size and type of valve, but indicate nothing about the material. Organization C's inventory would list quantities of pipe by size and material, but knows nothing about the item. Finding the proper plumbing item from these lists would be difficult and would require additional information.

A common nomenclature provides a base for identifying plumbing parts and for inventorying the items in each organization. Each organization's inventory shows the type of item, the size, the material, and the quantity. The individual inventory lists are easily combined to identify the existence of plumbing items available in each organization. Development of a common nomenclature requires the participation of all three organizations. It also requires that each organization cross-reference its item descriptions to the common nomenclature.

The same situation exists for data. Each organization, and often each organization unit, has its own data naming, data definition, and data structuring conventions. Any data inventory these organizations produce cannot be readily integrated into a common data inventory, any more than the plumbing inventories could be integrated. Therefore, a formal construct is needed for inventorying disparate data.

Data Product Concept

The formal construct for inventorying is the concept of data products. The ***data product concept*** is that the existing data resource, any documentation about the existing data resource, and any insights people have about the existing data resource are a product of some development effort. It's those products that need to be identified and documented to fully understand the existing disparate data.

The documentation of those products is done within a data product model. The *data product model* is a subset of data resource data architecture pertaining to documentation of an organization's disparate data resource. The input for the documentation comes from the data inventory process.

Semantics and Structure

Data resource integration is based on both semantic integration and structural integration, as described in Chapter 2. The data inventory starts that integration process by breaking down the existing data products to their basic components based on both meaning and structure. Any difference in meaning and any combination of business facts in data product items or data properties in data product codes are broken down into their basic components.

PRINCIPLES

The data inventory principles include recognizing that data disparity exists, increased understanding of the disparate data, a simple approach, a detailed approach, changes over time, and data provenance. Each of these principles is described below.

Data Disparity Exists

Data disparity exists in nearly every public and private sector organization. It's a fact that must be faced and resolved during data resource integration. Data disparity exists with all components of the data, including data names, data definitions, data structure, data integrity, and data documentation. The disparity is described in detail in Chapter 3 on Integrating the Data Resource.

Disparate data have very informal data names. Many disparate data names are short, inconsistent, and often meaningless. Disparate data names often create synonyms and homonyms. They provide little insight into the content or meaning of the data. A *disparate data name* is any informal data name in the disparate data resource. An *explicit disparate data name* is a disparate data name that exists in the data resource, such as a data file name. An *implicit disparate data name* is a disparate data name that is implied through a definition, contents, or use of the data.

The task of forming data names for disparate data is relatively easy. The Data Naming Taxonomy can be used to provide unique names for disparate data, as described below. I was able to uniquely identify any piece of data in public sector agencies in the State of Washington using the Data Naming Taxonomy.

Disparate data have very vague data definitions that are short, truncated sentences or phrases, if they exist at all. Disparate data definitions range from an elongated data name to data entry instructions and use of the data, but seldom provide any real understanding of the data with respect to the business.

A *disparate data definition* is any vague definition about the data in the existing data resource. An *existing disparate data definition* is a disparate data definition that currently exists in a data dictionary, database management software, or some other form of documentation. An *enhanced disparate data definition* is a disparate data definition that is enhanced in some way based on insight gained from another source, such as a person's memory.

The task of finding comprehensive definitions for disparate data can be frustrating and confusing for most people. However, developing good comprehensive data definitions for disparate data is necessary for a thorough understanding of the data and for accurate cross-referencing to a common data architecture.

Disparate data usually have improper data structures. A *disparate data structure* is any improper data structure that exists in the data resource. An *explicit disparate data structure* is a disparate data structure that is explicitly defined in the documentation or in a data model. An *implicit disparate data structure* is a disparate data structure that is not explicitly defined and is implied through the use of foreign keys.

The task of finding disparate data structures is also frustrating and confusing. Quite often, the foreign keys need to be identified and used to identify the disparate data structure. However, documenting the existing structure of disparate data is necessary for understanding those data and developing a comparate data resource.

Disparate data almost always have imprecise data integrity rules, if they even exist. The data integrity rules that do exist may be conflicting or incompletely defined. A *disparate data integrity rule* is any data integrity rule that exists in the data resource. An *explicit disparate data integrity rule* is a disparate data integrity rule that is explicitly stated in the data documentation or in a data model. An *implicit disparate data integrity rule* is a disparate data integrity rule that is not explicitly stated in the documentation or in a data model, but exists in database management systems or applications.

The task of finding the existing data integrity rules can be quite daunting. The data integrity rules may be buried in database edits or application edits, and may not be formally documented. The data integrity rules may even be buried as edits in the processes that people perform before the data are entered into the database. All of these existing data integrity rules need to be identified and documented.

Increased Understanding

Inventorying disparate data begins the process of understanding those data so they can be transformed into a comparate data resource. The *disparate data understanding principle* was described in the last chapter. That principle applies to understanding what data exist in the disparate data resource through the data inventory process.

Understanding what data exist raises awareness and begins lowering uncertainty. **Data awareness** is the knowledge about all of the data that are available to the organization and where those data are located. When people know what data are available, within or without the organization, they can readily use those data to support business activities. Data awareness often uncovers the hidden data resource that most organizations did not know existed.

The ***all-inclusive data inventory principle*** states that all existing data, or references to data, will be inventoried and cross-referenced to a common data architecture so they can be thoroughly understood in a common context. No existing data or references to data, such as data files, reports, screens, documents, dictionaries, data flows, and so on, will be exempt from the data inventory and data cross-reference processes, although priorities may be designated.

Simple Approach

Albert Einstein's simplexity principle was described in Chapter 2. That principle applies to the data inventory process. The data inventory process and documentation of that inventory in a data product model is the simplest approach possible to documenting the existing disparate data.

Albert Einstein also made the statement *We are seeking for the simplest possible scheme of thought that will bind together the observed facts.*[1] That statement readily applies to the inventorying and documentation of

---

[1] *The World As I See It*, 1934.

disparate data. The observed facts are details obtained during the data inventory process, and the data product model is the simplest possible scheme to bind those details together for understanding the disparate data.

Detailed Approach

The data inventory process, although very simple in principle, is very detailed. All of the detail possible must be identified and documented to fully understand the disparate data. The *opt for detail principle* states that when in doubt about the level of detail to document during the data inventory, always opt for greater detail. Experience has shown that more detail is needed to fully understand and integrate the data resource.

The best approach is to break down the detail during the data inventory process, not during the data cross-reference process. All of the data variability described in the last chapter is identified and broken down to an elemental level during the data inventory process, when the detail is readily available. Waiting until the data cross-reference process to break down the detail is difficult and time consuming because you have to return to the data inventory process to make the breakdown. Therefore, the most efficient approach is to break down all of the detail during the data inventory process.

Continuous Enhancement

Thoroughly understanding disparate data is a continuous process. The *continuous enhancement principle* states that documentation of disparate data should be continuously enhanced as additional insight is gained. Documenting and understanding disparate data is not a one-time process—it's an ongoing process through all phases of data resource integration. Any time additional insight about disparate data is gained, that insight must be documented.

The challenge with data resource integration is determining what the disparate data represent with respect to the business. Each piece of data and each insight into what those data represent must be captured and stored in the data product model. Identifying and documenting all of the detail is a continuous process that begins with the data inventory and continues through data transformation.

I hear some data modelers use the term *artifact* when referring to disparate data. They state that each artifact must be readily understood and documented. I prefer not to use the term *artifact* because the business professionals may not consider the disparate data as artifacts, because those data are key to the business, in spite of the disparity.

Philosophically, the disparate data may be artifacts, but professionally they should not be referred to as artifacts.

Changes Over Time

The data resource in most public and private sector organizations changes over time. The data values change to represent the current state of the business. New data are added and data that are no longer needed are removed. The disparity of the data may increase or decrease depending on data resource management activities.

Data names and definitions change, data structure changes, data integrity rules change, and data documentation changes. The changes may be slight or they may be major. The changes may be very obvious or they may be very transparent. The changes may improve the data resource or may make the data resource more disparate. The general trend is that these components tend to make the data resource more disparate.

Organizations must face data resource changes that occur over time, and make sure that those changes improve the data resource. One way to make sure that future changes are for the better is to document the past changes. The *change documentation principle* states that all changes to the data resource that occur over time must be identified and documented, no matter how slight or major those changes may be.

Data Provenance

Provenance comes from the French *provenir,* meaning *to come from.* It represents the origin or source of something, the history of ownership, or the current location of an object. The term is used mostly for precious artwork, but is now used in a wide range of fields, including science and computing.

Data provenance is provenance applied to the organization's data resource. The *data provenance principle* states that the source of data, how the data were captured, the meaning of the data when they were first captured, where the data were stored, the path of those data to the current location, how the data were moved along that path, and how those data were altered along that path must be documented to ensure the authenticity of those data and their appropriateness for supporting the business. Any gap along the pathway leads to questionable data integrity.

Heritage is property that descends from an heir, something transmitted by or acquired from a predecessor, or something possessed as a result of one's natural selection or birth. Heritage usually applies to biological or cultural descendants, but can be applied to data.

Data heritage is documentation of the source of the data and their original meaning at the time of data capture. It's the content and meaning of the data at the time of their origination and as they move from their origin to their current data location. It describes the original content and meaning of the data when initially captured.

Lineage is the direct descent from an ancestor or common progenitor to the descendants of a common ancestor that is regarded as the founder of the line. Lineage is commonly used for biological or cultural descendants, but can be applied to data.

Data lineage is a description of the pathway from the data source to their current location and the alterations made to the data along that pathway. It is a process to track the descent of data values from their origins to their current data sites. It includes determining where the data values originated, where they were stored, and how they were altered or modified. It's a history of how the content and meaning of the data were altered from their origin to their present location.

A *data origin* is the location where a data value originated, whether those data were collected, created, measured, generated, derived, or aggregated.

Data tracking is the process of tracking data from the data origin to their current location. It documents any alterations or modifications to the data, the addition of new data, and the creation of derived or aggregated data. It's a process to help understand and manage the movement of data within and between organizations.

Internal data tracking is data tracking in an environment where the organization has control of the data. It usually deals with data tracking within an organization, where changes to the data may be known. *External data tracking* is data tracking in an environment where the organization does not have control of the data. It usually deals with data tracking between organizations, where changes to the data may not be known.

Data provenance is very important for understanding data in a disparate data resource and must be documented. Data that have traveled a long pathway and have passed through many different data sites along that pathway tend to show semantic and syntactic drift. Different data origins and different pathways usually mean different data. How much difference is important to the organization depends on the particular data and the organization.

DATA INVENTORY DOCUMENTATION

Disparate data are quite variable, as described in Chapter 4. Documenting that variability is not an easy task; however, it is far from impossible. The structure for documenting an organization's disparate data is described below. How that structure is used during the data inventory process is described in the next chapter.

Note that some of the terms used for data inventory have been changed from previous books, articles, and presentations. The changes in terms represent a better understanding about how to inventory and document disparate data. That better understanding resulted from years working with the disparate data in a wide variety of public and private sector organizations.

Data Product Model

The structure of the data product model is shown in Figure 5.1. Only the structure portion of the data product model is shown because that's the most important for understanding how the data inventory is documented. The other details of the data product model are beyond the scope of the current book. Each of the data entities in the data product model is described below.

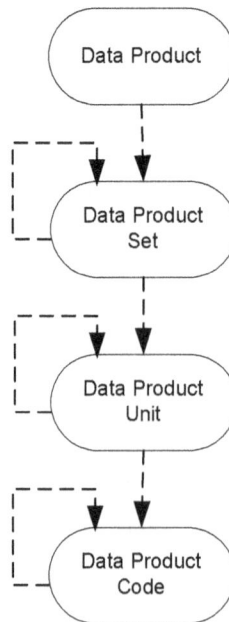

Figure 5.1. Data product model diagram.

Data Product

A *data product* is a major independent set of documentation of any type that contains the names, definitions, structure, integrity, and so on, of disparate data. It's anything about the data resource, electronic or manual, that is a product of some development effort. A data product can be an information system, a database, a data dictionary, a major project, a major data model, or anything else that provides insight into the existing disparate data. It is the highest level in the data product model.

Data Product Names

Data products must be uniquely named within the organization. Generally, a unique name does not exist for data products and needs to be created. A unique data product name is created when the data product is first identified to be inventoried. Organizations must plan ahead for developing consistent and unique data product names from the beginning of the data inventory process, with consideration for the ultimate scope of the data inventory.

If the data product names are not unique, the identification of disparate data will not be unique and the data inventory effort will not be successful. For example, using data product names like Health, County, Financial, and Traffic may initially seem unique, but will probably lose their uniqueness as additional data products are identified.

A unique data product name could include the organization, a location, a topic, and so on. For example, data product names like Health Department Data Dictionary, Johnson County Water Sampling Project, State Financial Information System, State Police Traffic Investigation System, and so on, are acceptable. Water Sample Logical Model, Vehicle Accident Logical Model, and Financial Account Physical Model might be typical data model names.

Data Product Definitions

Generally, data products do not have good definitions, if they have any definition at all. However, developing a good data definition is necessary for a thorough understanding of the disparate data and for accurate cross-referencing. Therefore, a comprehensive definition of the data product defining the data product and the scope of the data included in that data product must be developed.

If a data product definition does exist, it's a poor practice to assume that the definition is complete and accurate—it probably isn't. Most existing data product definitions were either developed early in a project and forgotten, or developed after the project was completed. Definitions developed early in the project probably changed during the project, but were never enhanced. Definitions developed after the project was completed were likely done quickly and were based on memory, which is poor, at best.

Data product definitions usually need to be developed, or at least enhanced, during data inventory. The data product definitions must comprehensively define a data product and the scope of data included in that data product. Other pertinent information, such as when the data product originated, who or was is responsible for the data product, and so on, is also quite useful.

Data Product Set

A data product contains one or more data product sets. A *data product set* is a major grouping of data within a data product. It may represent a data file, a data record, a data record type, a screen, a report, a form, a data entity, an application program, and so on.

Data Product Set Variations

A *data product set variation* is a recursion of a data product set to document multiple variations contained in a data product set. However, only one level of recursion is allowed. The data product set variation is not intended to document a hierarchy of data product sets. A data product set variation could be a data record type, a data entity type, changes over time, or any other breakdown of a data product set.

For example, a data file contains data items about computer hardware. Each hardware component does not contain the same data items. Different data items are placed in the same physical data fields, but their meaning depends on the record type. The three record types might be 1 for Computer Record, 2 for Controller Record, and 3 for Modem Record. The first data item in each record type might represent Hardware Computer Channel Count, Hardware Controller Port Count, and Hardware Modem Baud Rate, respectively. Each of these data record types would be documented as a data product set variation.

Data Product Set Names

Data product set names may exist, or are usually easy to identify. They may be physical data file names, report or screen names, or a data entity name. The data product set name must be unique within a data product. Similarly, the data product set variation name must be unique within a data product set. These names do not need to be unique within the scope of a disparate data resource. The task of creating unique data product set

156

and data product set variation names within a disparate data resource would be quite difficult.

For example, PERS_DATA_NEW, BUDGET_DATA, and WESTERN_REGION are typical data file names. Daily Financial Transaction Report, Monthly Vehicle Summary, and Water Sample Analysis Results are typical report, screen, or form names. Student, Stream Segment, and Timber Stand are typical data entity names.

When these data product set names are combined with the data product name according to the data naming taxonomy they become unique, as shown below.

> State Auditor: PERS_DATA_NEW
>
> Financial Information System: Daily Financial Transaction Report
>
> Woodland County: Water Sample

Data Product Set Definitions

Data product set and variation definitions usually do not exist for data records, data record types, screens, reports, forms, and so on. Similarly, data product set variation definitions seldom exist. Comprehensive definitions need to be prepared for data product sets and data product set variations to help people thoroughly understand what they represent.

A data product set definition must describe the data product set with respect to the data product. A data product set variation definition must describe the variation with respect to the data product set. These definitions can be enhanced any time additional insight is gained about their meaning.

If a data product set being inventoried is exactly the same as another data product set that has already been inventoried and documented, it does not have to be inventoried and documented any further. A statement is made in the data product set definition specifying the name of the other data product set to which it is equivalent. The inventory and documentation of that other data product set applies.

Data Product Set Scope

A data product set scope statement describes the scope or extent of the data product set or variation. The scope could be a subset of data, a selection of data, or the role of the data. The scope statement may contain a textual description of the scope of the data product set or variation, and it may contain data selection rules describing how the subset of data were obtained. The scope statement is separate from the data definition and the data integrity rules.

Data Product Set Integrity Rules

Any data integrity rules between data occurrences within a data product set or variation representing a data entity or data file need to be documented. Also, any data derivation of and data retention for a data occurrence need to be documented. Generally, these data integrity rules don't exist and need to be located and documented. They can usually be found in database management systems, applications, or ancillary documentation. If they do exist, they need to be verified to determine if they are actually enforced.

Data Product Unit

A data product set contains one or more data product units. A *data product unit* is any unit of data within a data product set, such as data attribute in a data model, a data item in a data record, a data field on a screen or report, a data item in a program, and so on.

Data Product Unit Variations

A *data product unit variation* is a recursion of a data product unit to document multiple variations contained in a data product unit. However, only one level of recursion is allowed. The data product unit variation is not intended to document a hierarchy of data product units.

A data product unit variation could be used to break down multiple, variable, and complex data items into their individual components. It could be used for changes over time. Each of these situations should be broken down to their lowest level and documented as a data product unit variation. The definition would describe the actual breakdown.

Data Product Unit Names

Data product units are uniquely named within a data product set. Usually, data product unit names are easy to identify and are shown as they appear in the source material. The name is not changed in any way, including, format, spelling, capitalization, underscoring, abbreviation, and so on. The reason the data product unit names are retained as they appear is for ready identification and to draw people into the data inventory process. If the name is changed in any way, it tends to alienate people and they won't become involved.

If the source is a database, the data product unit names are documented in the exact sequence shown in the database. They are not rearranged in any way. If the source is a screen, report, or form, try to follow a set sequence of right to left and then down. Keeping a regular sequence draws people into the data inventory process. Changing the sequence tends to alienate people.

Data product unit variation names usually need to be created because they don't appear in the source. The name needs to be unique within a data product unit, just like the data product unit name. A consistent routine should be followed for creating the data product unit variation names similar to the data product unit name.

For example, EMP_BD, SHIP_DT, TYPE, CODE, STATUS, and DATE are typical data product unit names. When these data product unit names are combined with the data product and data product set names according to the data naming taxonomy they become unique, as shown below:

> State Auditor: PERS_DATA_NEW. EMP_BD
>
> Financial Information System: Daily Financial Transaction Report. Total Expenditures
>
> Woodland County: Water Sample. Date Collected

Data Product Unit Definitions

Data product unit definitions are usually short phrases or single sentences, and are usually oriented to the capture, entry, storage, or use of the data. Seldom do data product unit definitions define the content and meaning of data with respect to the business because that wasn't the intent at the time the data were documented.

These definitions should be retained as they are stated in the original documentation. However, as insight is gained, the definitions should be enhanced to provide the meaning of the data with respect to the business. Enhancements could also include statements about the accuracy of data. The enhanced definitions should be comprehensive to aid in understanding and cross-referencing to the common data architecture, and should contain the date, the person making the enhanced definition, any source the person used, and so on,

Data Product Unit Integrity Rules

Any data integrity rules for a data product unit or between data product units need to be documented. Any data derivation and data retention rules should also be documented. Generally, some data integrity rules exist, usually as data edits, but are contained in database management systems or applications. In some situations, the data integrity rules are implemented by people reviewing the data before entry into the database. All data integrity rules must be identified and documented, and a determination made about the extent to which they are enforced.

Data Product Code

A data product unit or data product unit variation could contain many data product codes. A *data product code* is any coded data value that exists in a data product unit or data product unit variation. It represents a specific property of the subject of interest. For example, data product codes within a management level data product unit might be E for Executive, M for Manager, S for Supervisor, L for Lead worker, and W for Worker.

A data product code may have any combination of coded data values, names, and definitions. The data product code might not have a coded data value with only a name or a definition. It might have only a name or a code and a name. It might have a code, a name, and a definition. In some situations, it has a text field, which might be a name, a long name, or a short definition. All of these situations are considered data product codes.

Data Product Code Variations

A *data product code variation* is a recursion of a data product code to document multiple variations contained in a data product code. However, only one level of recursion is allowed. The data product code variation is not intended to document a hierarchy of data product codes.

A data product code variation could be used to break down multiple and complex property data product codes, multiple subject data codes, and mixed subject and complex subject data code sets to their individual components. It could be used for changes over time. Each of these situations should be broken down to their lowest level and documented as data product code variations. The definition would describe the actual breakdown.

Data Product Code Values

If the data product code has a coded data value, that data value is documented as a data product code. If the data product code has no coded data value, that field is left blank.

Data Product Code Names

If a data product code has a name, that name is documented with the data product code. The name is documented as it appears in the data resource, the same as with data product units. If the data product code has no name, that field is left blank.

Data Product Code Definitions

Many times it's difficult to determine whether a textual phrase for a data product code is a name or a short definition. In many situations, the name is considered to be the definition. If both a name and a definition exist, the definition is usually a short phrase that provides little meaning about what the data product code represents. Any definition that does exist must be retained and enhanced as additional insight is gained.

If a short textual phrase appears, a determination will need to be made whether that phrase is the name or a short definition. Usually by looking at the entire domain of data product codes, a determination can be made if the text represents a name or a definition.

Data Relation Diagrams

Diagrams may exist, or could be developed, to show data files and the data relations between those data files, or data entities and data relations between those data entities. Each of these situations is described below.

Data File-Relation Diagrams

A *data file-relation diagram* shows the arrangement and relationships between data files. It contains only the data files and the data relations between those data files. It does not contain any of the data items in those data files. Ideally, it is developed from the formal denormalization of a data entity-relation diagram that was developed during logical data modeling. Data entities are converted to data files according to formal data denormalization criteria. However, disparate data files are often developed without any formal data normalization or data denormalization.

Data file-relation diagrams seldom exist for disparate data. If they do exist, a variety of different symbols and notations may have been used, depending on what the developer decided to use at the time. The symbols and notations are seldom consistent across different diagrams, and may not be consistent on a single diagram. However, the diagrams do provide some insight into the data files and the data relations between those data files.

Existing data file-relation diagrams should be reviewed to determine if they accurately represent the disparate data. If they do adequately represent the disparate data, they can be documented. If they do not adequately represent the disparate data, they should be enhanced to adequately represent the disparate data.

If data file-relation diagrams do not exist, they should be developed. The best approach is to prepare an initial data file-relation diagram and continually enhance that diagram as additional insight is gained about the disparate data. Some organizations choose to redraw all the data file-relation diagrams so they use consistent symbols and notations.

A formal data file-relation diagram is developed using two symbols that are consistent with semiotic theory. An oval represents a data file, with the name of the data file inside the oval. A dashed line represents a data relation between data files. A dashed line with an arrow on one end designates a one-to-many data relation, which is the most prominent data relation for physical data. A dashed line with no arrows represents a one-to-one data relation, and seldom exists in disparate data. A many-to-many data relation does not exist between data files.

For example, a data file-relation diagram containing four data files for Employee, Department where the employee works, Position that the employee occupies, and Pay Checks that the employee receives is shown in Figure 5.2.

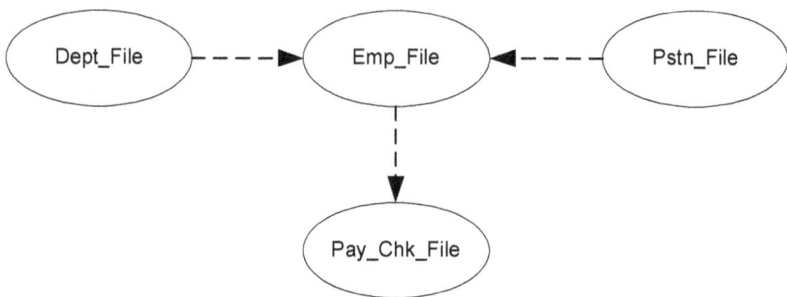

Figure 5.2. Data file-relation diagram example.

Data file-relation diagrams are documented in the data product. The documentation can either be storage of the actual data file-relation diagram, or reference to an external location where the diagram is stored.

Data Entity-Relation Diagrams

A ***data entity-relation diagram*** shows the arrangement and relationships between data entities. It contains only data entities and the data relations between those data entities. It does not contain any of the data attributes in those data entities, nor does it contain any roles played by the data attributes. Ideally, it is developed from the formal normalization of data that the business needs. However, disparate data are often developed without any formal data normalization.

Data entity-relation diagrams seldom exist for disparate data. If they do exist, a variety of different symbols and notations may be used, and are seldom consistent across diagrams. However, the diagrams do provide some insight into the data entities and the data relations between those data entities.

Existing data entity-relation diagrams should be reviewed to determine if they accurately represent the disparate data. If they do adequately represent the disparate data, they can be documented. If they do not adequately represent the disparate data, they should be enhanced.

If data entity-relation diagrams do not exist, they should be developed. The best approach is to prepare an initial data entity-relation diagram and continually enhance that diagram as additional insight is gained about the disparate data. Some organizations choose to redraw all the data entity-relation diagrams so that they have consistent symbols and notations.

A formal data entity-relation diagram is developed using two symbols that are consistent with semiotic theory. A box with bulging sides represents a data entity, with the name of the data entity inside the oval. A dashed line represents a data relation between data entities. A dashed line with an arrow on one end designates a one-to-many data relation, which is the most prominent data relation for logical data. A dashed line with no arrows represents a one-to-one data relation, and seldom exists in disparate data. A dashed line with an arrow on each end represents a many-to-many data relation. A typical data entity-relation diagram is shown in Figure 5.1 above.

Data entity-relation diagrams are documented in the data product. The documentation can either be storage of the actual diagram, or a reference to an external location where the diagram can be found.

Data Product Keys

Data relations are identified by data keys, specifically primary and foreign keys. A *primary key* is a set of one or more data attributes whose values uniquely identify each data occurrence in a data entity in a logical data model. In a database, a primary key is a set of one or more data items whose values uniquely identify each data record in a data file. In logical data models, a *foreign key* is the primary key of a data occurrence in a parent data entity that is placed in each data occurrence of a subordinate data entity to identify the parent data occurrence in that parent data entity. In data files, a foreign key is the primary key of a data record in a parent data file that is placed in each data record of a subordinate data file to identify the parent data record in that parent data file.

Ideally, the primary keys and foreign keys are defined in logical data models according to formal data normalization, and may be adjusted during formal data denormalization. In addition, more than one primary key may be defined during logical data modeling. During formal data denormalization, one of those primary keys is designated as the preferred primary key for the physical database, and the corresponding foreign key is defined.

However, that process seldom happened with disparate data. Formal data normalization and denormalization may or may not have occurred. Primary and foreign keys may or may not have been formally defined, or if defined, are not readily apparent. The result is often great difficulty identifying the primary and foreign keys and the corresponding data relations.

Data relations are not documented during in the data inventory. Only the primary and foreign keys are documented, and are used to identify the existence of a data relation. However, identifying primary keys and foreign keys in disparate data is not always an easy task because they are often not readily apparent. In some situations, they don't even exist because databases were built without the concept of a primary key.

Primary keys may exist, but be buried in another data item, such as a large control number. The corresponding foreign key may contain the entire data item, or only the portion of the data item that is necessary for unique identification. Primary keys may be designated, but may contain more data items than are necessary for unique identification. The corresponding foreign key may contain all of the data items, or only the data items necessary for unique identification. The primary key may be correctly defined, but the foreign key may have that primary key imbedded as part of a larger data item. The expect anything principle definitely applies to primary and foreign keys.

Both primary and foreign keys need to be identified and documented to understand the data relations and navigation in the database. The best approach is to identify data items forming a primary key that are required for uniqueness, and then look for those data items in subordinate data files. Remember, however, that the actual data names may be different.

Physical primary and foreign keys are documented in the data product set that represents a data file. The data product set name is Employee. The primary key is EMPL_SSN. The two foreign keys are to Department, using DEPT_ID, and to Job Class, using JBCLS_ID. The data primary and foreign keys are documented as shown below.

EMPL

Primary Key:	EMPL_SSN	
Foreign Key:	DEPT	DEPT_ID
Foreign Key:	JBCLS	JBCLS_ID

Logical primary and foreign keys are also documented in the data product set that represents a data entity, as shown below. The primary key has multiple data items. Foreign keys for Department and Academic Term are shown.

Education Course

Primary Key:	Department. Code Course. Identifier Academic Term. Code	
Foreign Key:	Department	Department. Code
Foreign Key:	Academic Term	Academic Term. Code

When multiple primary keys are identified, all are listed. Ideally, any data item or set of data items that uniquely identify a data record, or any data attribute or set of data attributes that uniquely identify a data occurrence, are listed as primary keys. Listing all possible physical primary keys helps identify foreign keys in other data files. Similarly, listing all possible physical foreign keys helps identify possible relations to other data files.

Any description of the data relation is listed with the foreign key, such as a name for the data relation, general data cardinality, or comment. Specific data cardinality is documented as a data integrity rule.

Primary keys and foreign keys may change over time, like other disparate data. These changes over time need to be documented so that people can thoroughly understand the disparate data.

Other Forms of Data

The material above deals largely with operational data in databases, data on traditional screens, reports, and forms, and with logical and physical operational data models. In other words, it deals largely with operational data in the data space.

However, operational summary data exist in the data space and need to be inventoried and documented. In addition, analytical data exist in the aggregation space, and predictive data exist in the influence and variation space. Complex structured data can be operational, analytical, or predictive. All of these types of data need to be inventoried and documented to provide a complete understanding of the entire data resource.

Dimensional Data – Fixed Data Hierarchy

Operational data often contain data in a hierarchy, such as company – department – division – section – unit, or United States – Region – State – County – City. These data hierarchies are fixed in the sense that the parent-child relationship cannot be changed and have any meaning. For example, units cannot be put between department and division, and cities cannot be put between state and county, and have any meaning.

The data totals in these fixed data hierarchies are commonly referred to as *summary data*. For example, if expenses were accumulated for a company, expense totals would exist for units, sections, divisions, departments, and the company as a whole. These summary data would be named according to their place in the hierarchy, such as unit expense, section expense, division expense, department expense, and company expense. Appendix B provides an example of a fixed data hierarchy with summary data.

The summary data in a fixed data hierarchy are documented in the Data Product Unit Model the same as operational data. The data sets are documented as data product sets, and the summary data are documented as data product units.

The data sets in a fixed data hierarchy are technically data dimensions, although that term was seldom used with fixed data hierarchies. The term *data dimensions* did not become prominent until data warehouses, OLAP (online analytical processing), and aggregated data became prominent.

Dimensional Data – Variable Data Hierarchy

A data hierarchy can also be variable in the sense that the data sets in the hierarchy can be rearranged so the parent – child relationships change. In other words, the hierarchy has no fixed sequence. These variable data hierarchies led to prominent use of the term *data dimensions*. The data in a variable data hierarchy could be aggregated in many different ways. The terms *data dimensions* and *aggregated data* became prominent.

Unlike a fixed data hierarchy, the aggregated data in a variable data hierarchy are not named by the data set in which they appear. The name of the aggregated data must represent the parent data sets, since those parent data sets can change. Appendix C provides an example of variable data hierarchies and how the aggregated data are named.

Aggregated data are often ignored because they are more difficult to identify, name, and define. However, they must be identified, named, and defined during the data inventory process. In many situations, a misunderstanding of aggregated data can be far more disastrous to the business than a misunderstanding of the elemental data.

The definition of aggregated data should include a description of what those data represent. The data integrity rules should show the data aggregation algorithm. A diagram showing the structure of the aggregated data is helpful for understanding the meaning of those data.

One of my consulting engagements was to identify the problems with widely different results for a variety of analytical analyses and the resulting aggregated data. Data were placed into different data warehouses and different analyses were performed on those data. Further, layer upon layer of slicing-and-dicing was done without any documentation of the aggregated data produced, and much of that was done on different selections of the data. The result was widely different aggregated data and confusion about their meaning. No business decisions could be made based on those data.

Therefore, the names, definitions, and integrity rules for aggregated data must be identified and documented to provide a complete understanding of the organization's data resource.

Predictive Data

The data used in predictive analysis are no different than operational data or analytical data. Additional data may be brought into the predictive analysis process that doesn't normally exist in the operational data resource. Data can be produced by the predictive analysis process, but those data are not magical or mythical in any way. They can be documented just like operational and analytical data.

The real power in predictive analysis comes in the processing used. The processing can be simple statistical analyses, like linear regression, chi square, multiple discriminate analysis, and so on; it can be very intensive, analysis using fractals and cellular automaton; or it could be anything in between. It's the predictive analysis process and the results of that process that are unique to the organization and are kept secret.

Predictive data are designed through rotational data modeling. The process is to move (rotate) through the dimensions of a dimensional data model. For each of those dimensions, the focus and non-focus measures, and the internal and external attributes are identified and documented. The focus and non-focus measures are with respect to the dimension being modeled. The internal and external attributes are with respect to attributes that are within the control of the organization or are outside the control of the organization. These measures and attributes are data attributes that belong to data entities, which have data relations, and can be modeled accordingly.

Therefore, documenting the data used in predictive analysis and the data produced by predictive analysis can be included in the data inventory relatively easily.

Complex Structured Data

A detailed inventory and documentation of complex structured data requires a different approach, using an expanded and enhanced Dublin Core model, and is beyond the scope of the current book. However, complex structured data can be documented in two different ways using the Data Product Model.

First, the complex structured data set, such as an image, a video, text, voice, and so on, are documented as a data product. The complex structured data set is named and the definition provides a comprehensive description of the contents of the data set. No additional documentation below the data product is captured.

Second, the complex structured data set can be broken down into its individual simple structured components. For example, a polygraph examination to determine if someone is telling the truth or showing deception. A polygraph examination consists of a series of questions asked by the examiner. The respondent can answer either *Yes* or *No* to each question. The blood pressure, pulse, perspiration, and respiration are measured during each question and answer to provide an indication of truth or deception. At the end of the session, the results are analyzed and a determination is made if the respondent was truthful or deceptive.

You can see how the data might be structured by polygraph examination, polygraph question, and the results of blood pressure, pulse, perspiration, and respiration during each question and answer. The polygraph examination would contain the examiner's data, the respondent's data, dates, times, location, machine, and so on. It would also contain the analog graph or a reference to it, and the conclusion for the examination. The polygraph question would contain the text of each question, the pulse, perspiration, and respiration details, and a conclusion about how the respondent answered the question.

Another example is a textual statement. Text can be analyzed by a variety of methods, either human or automated, to determine precedents and conclusion, who wrote the text, based on analysis and comparison with an author's known writing, and so on. Each of these parameters can be documented to provide additional insight into the text.

Video interviews can also be analyzed by a variety of methods. The video has voice, which can be converted to text and analyzed as mentioned above. In addition, the inflection and intonations in the voice can be analyzed, like the psychological stress evaluator often used in law enforcement. The body language can also be analyzed, such as eye movement, eyelid blinking, mouth, arms, posture, and so on, to determine the speaker's true feelings.

These brief examples show how complex structured data can be broken down into individual components that can be more easily interpreted and documented

The breakdown of complex structured data can be done by people or can be automated. The process applies to any complex structured data and can be performed to any level of detail desired by the organization. The resulting data entities and data attributes are documented as data product sets and data product units. The breakdown of complex structured data can be totaled to produce summary data, or analyzed to produce aggregated data. The breakdown can also be used in predictive analysis.

Time Relational Data

Time relational data involves relations between data entities based on time, usually referred to as time relations. A time relation is different from a data relation because it does not have fixed values in a primary key and foreign keys. The relation often depends on a point within a range of times.

For example, a person has many addresses over time. Each address has an effective date that is valid until another address that has a more recent effective data is entered. The set of current address and historical addresses provides an address history for a person.

A question might arise whether the person voted in the proper precinct based on their address. Since no direct match exists between the date of the election and the effective dates of the addresses, a data relation doesn't work. A search needs to be made of the effective data ranges for the addresses to determine which address was active at the time of the election.

Another situation is data reference sets, where each data reference item has a begin date and an end date. The appropriate data reference item must be used based on the effective dates of that data reference item and some corresponding date in the subordinate data entity. The data relation shows the data reference item, but not the effective date.

For example, student type codes frequently vary. Each student has a student type code that must be valid for the date that student registered with the school. The data relation is between Student and Student Type, based on the Student Type. Code. However, that data relation does not enforce the requirement for a valid student type code for the student's registration date. The date range of the Student Type. Code must be evaluated to determine if the data reference item is valid for the Student. Registration Date.

Time relations are documented as data integrity rules between data attributes in different data entities. The documentation is separate for the documentation of data relations.

Sources of Insight

Many people have asked me where to obtain insights into the disparate data resource. Any source of insight is useful for providing an understanding of disparate data. Sources of insight can be primary or supplemental.

The primary sources of insight about disparate data are databases, data models, application programs, and screens, reports, and forms. XML is treated as a screen or report. These primary sources of insight are documented as separate data products.

Databases provide insight into the meaning and structure of data in the database management system and data edits enforced by the database management systems. Logical and physical data models, whether electronic or manual, provide insight into either the logical design of the data or its physical implementation. Even hand-drawn diagrams can be useful. Generic data architectures and universal data models might provide some insight, but are often too generic and universal to be of much use.

Application programs, whether developed in-house or purchased, provide insight into the data they create or use, definitions about those data, and any data edits that are enforced.

Screens, reports, and forms provide insight about the data they contain and how those data are used by the business. Titles and headings provide clues to what the data represent. Screens, reports, and forms often contain summary data and aggregated data that are not in databases, but are still part of the organization's disparate data resource.

Supplemental sources of insight about disparate data are formal and informal documentation, and the tacit knowledge of individuals. Formal and informal documentation includes data dictionaries, project descriptions, data entry instructions, instruction manuals, standards, legislation, external reporting requirements, informal notes, e-mails, meeting minutes, memos, and so on. The tacit knowledge of individuals includes employees, business professionals, data management professionals, retirees, contractors and consultants, vendors, other people outside the organization, and anyone else with an insight into the disparate data.

People can be interviewed to determine what tacit knowledge they may have about the disparate data resource. Typically, people who have been with the organization a long time, both business professionals and data management professionals, have considerable knowledge about the data resource. Retired employees could be contacted for knowledge they may have about the data resource. Any providers of data from outside the organization can be contacted for their knowledge about the data. Vendors of purchased products can be contacted for additional knowledge about the data used in their applications or contained in their databases.

Seek out all possible sources of insight about the disparate data resource and document the insights obtained. When these sources have been exhausted, one can reasonably presume that the vast majority of insight about the organization's disparate data resource has been collected and documented. The point of diminishing returns has been reached and additional effort is not likely to produce substantial new insight.

SUMMARY

Inventorying disparate data is the first step toward achieving the formal data resource state. The existing data must be inventoried to determine the extent of the disparate data before any progress can be made toward resolving those disparate data. The data inventory concept emphasizes that a complete and comprehensive inventory of the disparate data resource must be done so those data are known and can be thoroughly understood. The data product concept provides the structure for documenting the inventory of disparate data.

The data inventory principles include:

Recognizing that disparate data exist and must be inventoried to know the extent of the disparate data.

The data inventory starts the understanding process that continues through the data transformation to a comparate data resource.

The data inventory process is relatively simple, yet very detailed.

The data inventory process requires continuous enhancement as new insight is gained about the data resource.

Changes to the data resource over time must be identified and documented.

The origin of data and changes made along the pathway to the current location must be documented.

The data product model provides the framework for documenting the results of the disparate data inventory. That structure consists of data products, data product sets, data product units, data product code sets, and data product codes. Existing data relation diagrams and new data relation diagrams can be stored or referenced in the data product model. The data key model provides the framework for documenting data relations through primary keys and foreign keys.

Documentation of summary data, analytical data, and predictive data is described. Documentation of complex structured data is briefly described, but is beyond the scope of the current book. Documentation of time relations is described. Sources of material for the disparate data inventory include:

Databases and database management systems.

Application programs, either developed in-house or purchased.

Formal and informal documentation about the data resource.

Logical and physical data models, generic data architectures, and universal data models.

Screens, reports, and forms.

Knowledge retained by people.

Data scanners and data profiling applications.

When all of the sources of material have been exhausted, the point of diminishing returns has been reached. The next step is to cross-reference the inventoried data to a common data architecture to enhance the understanding of those data within a common context.

QUESTIONS

The following questions are provided as a review of the disparate data inventory concept, and to stimulate thought about what is needed to inventory disparate data properly.

1. What is the data inventory concept?

2. How does the data product concept support the data inventory concept?

3. Why is continuous enhancement necessary when inventorying disparate data?

4. Why are changes over time important when inventorying disparate data?

5. Why is data provenance important to understanding disparate data?

6. How do primary and foreign keys define a data relation?

7. What's the difference between summary data and aggregated data?

8. Why can't complex structured data be inventoried and documented the same as tabular data?

9. What are the possible sources of insight for understanding disparate data?

10. Why is inventorying and documenting disparate data simple, yet very detailed?

Chapter 6

DATA INVENTORY PROCESS

How to go about inventorying disparate data.

Organizations seldom have a complete inventory of all data at their disposal. A data inventory process resolves that problem by providing a complete inventory of existing data maintained by the organization and at the organization's disposal. It also sets the stage for understanding the existing data so they can be cross-referenced to a common data architecture and a preferred data architecture can be designated.

Chapter 4, on Data Variability, described the different types of variability that could be encountered in a disparate data resource. Chapter 5, on Data Inventory Concept, described what needs to be done during the data inventory and the constructs for documenting the results of a data inventory. The current chapter describes how to conduct a data inventory and how to document the results of that inventory.

The data inventory process not only inventories the existing disparate data, but also breaks down any combined data into their basic components and begins documenting an initial understanding about disparate data. Both the breakdown and the initial understanding are needed to thoroughly understand the disparate data and resolve data disparity.

DATA INVENTORY PREPARATION

Data inventory preparation includes setting the scope of the data inventory, establishing the sequence of inventorying data, determining the involvement of people in the data inventory, and documenting the data inventory. Each of these topics is described below.

Data Inventory Scope

A data resource inventory must, ultimately, include all data at an organization's disposal. No data should be excluded from a complete data resource inventory. Many organizations consider only the data in databases, which is a start. However, inventorying databases is far from a complete inventory of disparate data. All data at an organization's disposal must ultimately be inventoried.

The data in an organization's data resource cannot be completely inventoried and documented at one time. A phased approach is established based on the problems that are critical to the business. Priorities for a phased approach are established based on benefits to the business and where the business is experiencing pain.

Major pain points are often the best place to start inventorying and understanding the existing data. If the business is experience many pain points, then a decision needs to be made about the most critical pain points, and the priorities need to be based on the severity of the pain to the business.

Priorities can also be based on business critical data. Business critical data are any data that are critical to operating the business. Business critical data are often referred to as vital data, high priority data, core business data, baseline data, crucial data, and so on. Essentially, business critical data are any data supporting the pulse of the business.

In most situations I've encountered, the major pain points occur with the business critical data. Pain with business critical data is often far more severe than pain with data that are not business critical. Therefore, the general approach to establishing priorities favors business critical data that are creating pain.

For example, if public works data is critical to the business and poor quality public works data is causing pain, that subject area becomes the initial scope. Similarly, if employee data, stream data, infrastructure data, and so on, are critical to the business and people are experiencing the pain of low quality data, those subject areas become the initial scope of the data inventory.

The initial scope of the data inventory may increase or decrease as the data inventory progresses. I've found that the initial scope actually increases in the majority of situations. What typically happens is that the initial scope is set based on pain with business critical data. However, as the data inventory progresses, additional data are discovered beyond the initial scope, and the scope is increased to include those additional data.

In *Data Resource Simplexity,* I mentioned a client that identified 16 databases with customer data that were critical to the business, and that the disparity was so bad, the organization had essentially lost track of their customer base. We established a scope and schedule based on those 16 databases. When I arrived, they had discovered an additional seven databases with customer data, for a total of 23 databases containing customer data. That situation is typical of what happens when organizations begin inventorying their disparate data.

I'm often asked how to continue data inventory and documentation when the first phase is over. In the vast majority of situations I've encountered, organizations have no problem continuing the data inventory process. People see the benefit and are literally *knocking at the door* to be the next data inventory phase.

Usually, organizations start waves of data inventory based on priorities. As one waves moves from data inventory into data cross-referencing, another wave of data inventory is initiated. Once the process is started, it is usually self-perpetuating, and is driven by the benefits.

Priorities may, and often do, change during the data inventory process. Balancing increased scope and changes in priorities can be difficult. However, it is not impossible if successive waves of data inventory are established. Formal project management can be implemented to track waves of data inventory, increased scope, and changing priorities.

Data Inventory Sequence

When the data inventory scope has been set, the sources of insight about disparate data within that scope are identified. Typically, the databases that contain any data that could conceivably be within the scope are identified. Not only are the major databases identified, but also any databases that contain data within the scope need to be identified. Even a database that has only a few data items within the scope must be identified and included. Better to err on the side of too many databases than too few to obtain as much understanding as possible.

Application programs, data models, screens, reports, and forms, formal and informal documentation, and knowledgeable people must also be identified and included in the data inventory. Even with the best guess about the sources of insight to be included in the data inventory, additional sources will be identified during the course of the data inventory.

A *horizontal phased approach* is to conduct a high-level data inventory and document all of the databases within the organization as data products. The high-level data inventory provides a good overview of the data the organization maintains in their data resource—the size of the breadbox. Next, the highest priority databases are inventoried and the data files are documented as data product sets. Finally, the highest priority data files are inventoried and the data items are documented as data product units.

A *vertical phased approach* is to conduct the data inventory starting with the highest priority database and documenting that database clear down to the data items. Then, the next highest priority database is inventoried and documented.

The horizontal phased approach may seem unnecessary in smaller organizations. However, it could be a valid approach in a very large organization. One state agency where I consulted had a monumental problem answering legislative information requests in less than six months, which was totally unacceptable. In addition, some of the information provided to the legislature was inconsistent and caused concern among the legislators.

One thing an organization does not want to do is to tell executives, superior courts, state or federal legislatures, and other regulatory organization that the request for information cannot be met in a timely manner. Even worse, is to provide conflicting information in a legal or political environment.

We followed a horizontal phased approach by inventorying all of the databases, then the data files in the high priority databases, then the data items in the high priority data files. The process took four people nearly a year just to inventory and document the high priority data. The result showed that the agency had far more data than they had ever expected, and that those data were more disparate than expected, which clarified the problems with disparate data. No wonder the agency had problems meeting requests for information.

The general sequence for a data inventory is to inventory and document the primary sources of insight first, followed by the supplemental sources of insight. The supplemental sources provide additional insight that can be used to enhance the documentation of the primary sources of insight. Usually, trying to document the supplemental sources of insight first produces confusing results and often leads to wasted resources.

Within the primary sources of insight, databases and data files are generally inventoried and documented first. Then the other primary sources of insight, such as data models, application programs, and screens, reports, and forms, are inventoried and documented. However, the sequence can be altered depending on the particular problems that an organization faces.

For example, understanding screens, reports, or forms may be a critical problem for the organization. In that situation, the screens, reports, or forms may be inventoried and documented first. Similarly, the data used and produced by application programs may be a critical problem for the organization. In that situation, the application programs are inventoried and documented. The same is true for data models.

Data Inventory Involvement

The people involved in a data inventory need to be identified and initial time commitments established. Typically, a core team is established and responsibilities are assigned. Ancillary team members are identified and their responsibilities are designated. Finally, anyone with insight about the disparate data is identified.

The core team often remains the same throughout the data inventory. However, additional ancillary team members and people with insight about the disparate data are frequently identified. Operating in an area of discovery often leads to the identification of many people who can contribute to understanding disparate data.

Initial time commitments can be established. However, these time commitments will likely increase as uncertainty about the disparate data increases. Not only are more people involved in the data inventory, but also the time commitment of those people frequently increases.

Each data inventory project takes on a life of its own. Even though an initial scope, involvement, and commitments are established, the project develops a life of its own as people become involved in understanding disparate data. The schedule should be general and not too rigid. The area of discovery requires that the schedule be flexible to allow the capture and documentation of all understanding about the data resource.

A large time commitment up front often turns people away from a data inventory because they don't see the benefit. However, when people see the benefit they will get involved and contribute as much time as necessary to resolve existing problems.

One situation I encountered was developing a new county property appraisal system. The existing appraisal system had massive problems with a plethora of data reference sets used to document and appraise residential and commercial property. The data reference sets had coded data values and names, but seldom had good definitions.

Appraisers were extremely busy appraising property and defending appraisals during appeals, but were contributing time to developing a new project. I set up an online system for the appraisers to enter the definitions they used, concerned that they had little time to contribute their definitions. To my surprise, massive definitions were being entered, and those definitions were in gross disagreement. My concern about involvement turned to concern about how to resolve the disparity in definitions. To my surprise, the chief commercial and chief residential appraisers went online to establish formal definitions for each data reference item in each data reference set.

The appraisers saw the benefit of resolving a problem that was contributing pain to the assessor's office. They contributed the time necessary, often their own time, to resolve the problem. Therefore, initial schedules and time commitments should be general and not too rigid. Rigid schedules and time commitments seldom work during data inventory.

A key point about involvement is to let people establish their own schedule. I've found that when people need to pause and think, they need to be allowed that time. When people are ready and willing to move ahead, they need to be given every opportunity to move ahead uninterrupted.

Another key point about involvement is to establish a no blame - no whitewash policy to encourage people to become involved. Whenever blame is placed, people are polarized and do not readily contribute to the data inventory. When bad situations are covered up, the understanding about the disparate data is compromised, and any subsequent tasks will likely be less than fully successful. Therefore, all contributions to the data inventory must follow a no blame - no whitewash policy.

I worked with one organization where the business people brought me in because they could not get the data they needed to support the business. The data had been physically manipulated to the extent that they didn't know what the data represented. The business had difficulty getting the data they needed, and the data they did get often conflicted.

My first task, which was not trivial, was to get the business and IT to sit down at the same table. The hostilities were obvious. The business attitude was how dare you mess up my critical business data. The IT attitude was how dare you question my ability to manipulate the data. The entire first session of several hours was spent shedding the hostilities and adopting a no blame - no whitewash approach. The situation existed—that was a fact. Let's get on with understanding the data and resolving the situation.

Data Inventory Documentation

The Data Product Model provides the construct for documenting the data inventory. Each organization needs to determine how and where that Data Product Model is implemented, based on their needs and physical operating environment. Software products for documenting the data inventory may be obtained, but those products must have the capability to document the data inventory as described in the current book. Organizations should not consider acquiring a software product that does not document the data inventory as described here.

The *opt for detail principle* emphasizes that all detail should be documented during the data inventory process. It's far better to have more detail than needed to thoroughly understand the disparate data than to have too little detail and not thoroughly understand the disparate data. More detail leads to better understanding and more informed decisions about creating a comparate data resource.

Data inventory is a dynamic discovery process and new insight is continually gained through the data inventory process, and even through the data cross-referencing and preferred data designation processes. The continuous enhancement principle recognizes that new insight is constantly gained and that the documentation needs to be constantly enhanced based on that new insight.

All enhancements to data inventory documentation should contain the name of the person entering the enhancement, the date of the enhancement, and the source of insight leading to the enhancement. These provide a way to track and verify the enhancement. The no blame - no whitewash policy ensures that people can enter enhancements without fear of any repercussion.

The data inventory documentation should be retained, even after data resource integration is complete. The documentation not only provides a history about the integrated data resource (data tracking), but old material may be found at any time. Retaining the documentation provides a way for people to understand that old material.

The data components that are captured during the data inventory are the four components of the Data Architecture Segment of the Data Resource Management Framework—data names, data definitions, data structure, and data integrity rules. All four of these components are needed to thoroughly understand the data.

Data names may or may not exist, as described in the last chapter. If a data name exists, that data name should be used as it appears. If a data name does not exist, an appropriate data name needs to be created.

Data definitions are often vague. Seldom are they complete or accurate.

Existing data definitions need to be documented, but do not assume that those data definitions are complete and accurate.

The scope of the data is often vague or unknown. The scope of the data must be documented in a scope statement, which describes any selection criteria, a subset of a larger set of data, or the role of the data.

Data integrity rules are often nonexistent. Most that do exist are data edits in database management systems or applications. Only the data integrity that actually exists should be documented during the data inventory, even though people have a tendency to list the desired data integrity rules. The desired data integrity rules are defined during the preferred data architecture designation process.

SUPPORTING TECHNIQUES

Two supporting techniques for the data inventory are data scanners and data profilers. Each of these techniques is described below.

Data Scanning

Data scanning is used primarily for capturing data to be stored in the data resource, such as document scanning, bar code scanning, and so on. However, data scanning also applies to scanning databases to identify the data items that exist in the database, or application programs to identify and document the data items that are used or produced. The scanning does not capture the actual data values—it only captures the data items so they can be properly documented.

Data scanning in the context of data resource integration is the process of electronically or manually scanning databases or application programs to identify the data stored by databases, or the data used or produced by applications. Data scanning can capture technical insight into the data, but cannot capture semantic insight into the data. Data scanning for data resource integration is often referred to as *data discovery scanning* because it supports increased understanding of the existing disparate data.

Data scanners are a source of insight about disparate data. Data scanners are good at inventorying existing data and documenting that inventory. Data scanners are good for capturing technical data contained in database management systems and for identifying changes in the databases that occurred since the last scan.

However, data scanners provide little semantic understanding of the data. Data scanners cannot integrate the inventory across multiple sources, such as scanning a database and then scanning an associated data dictionary, because they have no context for that integration. Data scanners do not work well with screens, reports, and forms, or for formal and informal documentation.

In other words, data scanners are good at inventorying the data that exist and changes to those data over time, but provide very little semantic understanding about those data. The semantic understanding comes from human intervention. Data scanners can do the inventory, but people need to interpret the meaning of that inventory.

I frequently receive questions about automated versus manual data scanning. Automated data scanning is faster, but does not provide the semantic understanding. Manual data scanning is slower, but comments that provide insight into the meaning of the data can be entered by the person doing the scanning. In addition, cross-referencing is generally easier and faster when done by the same person who did the manual scanning.

Data cross-referencing has not been described yet. However, data scanning and data cross-referencing can be done serially or in parallel. The process is serial when all of the data within the scope are inventoried and then all those data are cross-referenced to a common data architecture. The process is parallel when each piece of data or group of data is inventoried and then cross-referenced. When a person understands the processes of inventorying and cross-referencing data, those processes can be used in any manner to understand the data with minimum effort.

The risk with the serial approach is that the understanding gained during data inventory may be lost by the time the cross-referencing is performed. The risk with the parallel approach is that a cross-reference may be made without thoroughly understanding the data because not all of the sources of insight have been inventoried. The choice of a serial approach or a parallel approach needs to be made based on the relative risks. In many situations, a mixture of the serial approach and parallel approach are used based on the relative risks.

The choice of a serial or parallel approach also depends on whether data scanners were used for the data inventory. When data scanners are used for the data inventory, the serial approach is probably the best. When the data inventory is done manually, either the serial approach or the parallel approach may be used.

Each organization needs to make a choice about the degree of automated versus manual scanning that is done during the data inventory process. For example, automated scanning may be done for databases followed by manual scanning of data dictionaries, informal notes, and so on. The results of the manual scanning can be used to supplement the automated scanning.

Several organizations where I worked wrote their own automated scanners for database inventory, and ran those scanners periodically to identify changes in the databases. These custom scanners work well for an organization's unique operating environment, and can be built quickly and inexpensively. They can also be designed for easy entry of supplemental insight gained from other sources.

Data Profiling

Data profiling has many different definitions. It's an approach to data quality analysis using statistics to show patterns of usage, and patterns of contents, and automated as much as possible. Some profiling activities must be done manually, but most can be automated.[2]

Data profiling is also the process of examining the data available in existing databases and files, and collecting statistics about those data. The statistics can be used to identify uses of the data, improve data quality, understand the data for integration, document the data, and provide an inventory of the data. Data profiling can be used to identify candidate data sources for a data warehouse, clarify the structure of the data, and identify and understand data anomalies. The purpose of data profiling is to understand the data thoroughly so they support the business.

Data profiling is often referred to as data discovery. It is used to decipher and validate patterns in the data. It is used to identify problem areas so plans can be made to resolve those problem areas. It can be used to identify redundant data across data sources and preparing for the integration of those data. It can be used to identify the completeness and the accuracy of the data.

Data profiling, in the context of data resource integration, is the process of analyzing the data values in databases to determine possible data meaning, data structure, and data integrity rules in preparation for data resource integration. These determinations must be verified before they can be accepted as fact and used for data resource integration. Data profiling for data resource integration is often referred to as *data discovery profiling* because it supports increased understanding of the existing disparate data.

Data profiling can be useful for understanding disparate data if used properly. It's similar to psychological profiling of a criminal or the

---

[2] DAMA Dictionary of Data Management.

biochemical profiling of blood. Data profiling combines formal analysis with informal sleuthing to gain a better understanding of the data resource. It's preliminary and not absolute, but it does provide some insight into the data resource.

Data domain profiling analyzes the existing domain of data values for data items in a database. The existing data values, their frequency of distribution, variability, missing values, existence of multiple values, possibility of redundancy, and so on, are analyzed and documented. The analysis can identify the variability in data values, both within a data file and across data files. The variability in content and format, such as measurement units, forms of a person's name, and so on, can be identified. The existence of elemental and combined facts can be identified.

The analysis can identify the existence or lack of data integrity rules. However, the results of data domain profiling must be reviewed and verified before any data integrity rules are documented. In other words, the analysis is only a preliminary indication that must be verified.

Data domain profiling can identify data anomalies. A ***data anomaly*** is any data value that does not follow a pattern that matches a reasonable expectation of the business. It could be a correct data value, or it could be an error. If it's a correct data value, it could be acceptable or unacceptable to the business. Data anomalies can be used during the designation of preferred data to create precise data integrity rules.

Functional dependency profiling analyzes the data values for possible data relations between sets of data. If the same domain of data values is identified in different data files, a presumption can be made that those two data files might be related through a primary key – foreign key relationship. For example, the domain of values A through G appearing in data items in two different data files might indicate a subordinate data entity and a data reference set.

However, functional data profiling is an indication only and may not be correct. For example, two different data reference sets could exist with each having the domain of values A through G. Therefore, the results of functional dependency profiling must be reviewed and verified before a data relation is established.

Human data profiling identifies the pattern of actions different people exhibit when entering or editing data. Patterns about how people collect data, enter data, and edit data can be helpful for understanding disparate data. The patterns can also be useful for identifying data integrity rules that are not documented anywhere.

185

Automated tools can support data profiling. Existing data value can be analyzed by some very sophisticated techniques to identify candidate data integrity rules and functional dependencies. These tools, however, cannot capture understanding or meaning placed on data by people or organizations. They cannot determine intent or use of the data, and they cannot track the data from their source to their present location. Therefore, they only provide an indication that must be verified.

The verified results of data profiling are documented in the appropriate data product unit or data product code set. Preliminary results could be documented, but a statement should be made that the results are preliminary and need to be verified.

Data profiling is typically done during the data inventory so that all possible insights are available for data cross-referencing. However, some questions may arise during data cross-referencing, and even during the designation of preferred data, additional data profiling may be required. Therefore, data profiling could be done at any time that additional insight is needed.

INVENTORYING DISPARATE DATA

Data variability was described in Chapter 4. The last chapter described the data product model used for documenting the data inventory. The current section describes how to document the variability of disparate data according to the data product model, including how to split combinations of data down to their basic components.

Databases

Data products are any major independent set of documentation about disparate data, such as an information system, database, data dictionary, major project, data model, and so on. Data products are identified, named, and defined at the beginning of the data inventory process, or anytime during the data inventory process and a relevant data product is discovered.

For example, a Water Rights database is being inventoried. The data product name might be Water Rights Database. The initial data product definition might be something as simple as *A database containing a variety of data files documenting all of the water rights within the State of Washington*. The definition is enhanced as additional insight is gained.

No scope statement or data integrity rules are documented for data products. Data file-relation diagrams can be documented for data products. Diagrams can be formal or informal. They can be included in the definition or reference can be made to an external location.

Data Files

Data files can represent a single data subject or multiple data subjects, and they can represent a complete data subject or a partial data subject. These determinations cannot be made with certainty during the data inventory, because the complete scope of a data subject within a disparate data resource is not known. These determinations can only be made with certainty after data cross-referencing has been completed and the complete scope of a data subject has been determined.

However, indications as to the type of variability in a data file can be noted in the data product set definition during the data inventory process. For example, a person inventorying a data file may know or determine that the data file represents part of a data subject or multiple data subjects based on their experience. That insight can be documented in the data product set definition.

Data files are documented as data product sets. The physical data file name usually becomes the data product set name. A data file definition may exist, or an initial definition may need to be created. For example, a data file in the Water Rights Database might be the Water_Right_File, which becomes the name of the data product set. Usually, the data file name is entered as it appears for the physical data file. The initial definition might be as simple as *The Water Right File contains the basic features for each water right*. That definition is enhanced as additional insight is gained.

The Water Rights database and Water Right File are documented as shown below. The notation in parenthesis after each component indicates the data product model component used to document the data inventory. It's included here for understanding only, and does not appear when documenting disparate data.

> Water Right Database (DP)
> > Water Right File (DPS)

Data files can contain multiple data record types. Each of these data record types is documented as a data product set variation. For example, the Water Right File has two data record types, called Control_Number and AA_Transaction. Data product set variations are established for each of these data record types. The data product set variation names would be Control_Number and AA_Transaction. The initial definitions might be *A record of the control numbers for water rights* and *The location of the water right*, respectively. These definitions would be enhanced as additional insight is gained about each data record type.

The components of the data inventory are shown below.

```
Water Rights Database (DP)
   Water_Right_File (DPS)
      Control_Number (DPSV)
      AA_Transaction (DPSV)
```

A scope statement describes any selection criteria, how the data product set is a subset of a larger set of data, and/or the role of the data. For example, a data file may contain a subset of student data for middle school students, or for students from 2000 through 2010. The data file may contain data about plumbers, which are a subset of contractors. Any description of the scope of the data should be documented for a full understanding about what the data represents.

Data integrity rules that pertain to data records within the data file or between data files are documented for data product sets and data product set variations. The data integrity rules can be documented in the formal notation or in a textual description. The objective is to capture the data integrity rule, not necessarily have that data integrity rule in the formal notation.

Physical primary keys and foreign keys are documented for each data file, as described in the last chapter. The foreign keys are listed in alphabetical order by parent data subject name for ready identification. Data relations are documented with the foreign key, as described in the last chapter.

Primary and foreign keys are often difficult to identify. Some searching may need to be done because the primary and foreign keys are not readily apparent. Primary keys can be identified and used to find foreign keys in subordinate data files. Similarly, foreign keys can be identified and used to find primary keys in parent data files. However, finding data items with the same name in different data files does not always indicate a primary key – foreign key relationship.

Data Records

A data record can represent a complete data occurrence or a partial data occurrence. A data record can also represent a single data occurrence or multiple data occurrences. Multiple data occurrences can be either subordinate data occurrences or parallel data occurrences.

The determination of whether a data record represents a complete or partial data occurrence cannot be made with certainty during the data inventory, because the complete scope of the data instance within a disparate data resource is not known. The determination can only be made with certainty after data cross-referencing has been completed and the complete scope of a data occurrence has been determined. However, indications of the completeness of a data occurrence can be noted in the data product set or data product set variation definition during the data inventory process.

Partial data occurrences might be identified by multiple record types within a data file. For example, record type D might contain all of the detail data for a street segment, record type C might contain an initial comment, and record type E might contain an extension of that comment. Each of these three data record types would be documented as data product set variations, as described above.

The determination of whether a data record represents single or multiple data occurrences, and whether multiple data occurrences are subordinate or parallel, can usually be made during the data inventory. The determination is documented in the data product set or data product set variation definition.

The data items for subordinate data occurrences are only documented once, regardless of how many subordinate data occurrences are contained in the data record. For example, a data record contains multiple subordinate data occurrences for quarterly stream flow during the year. Each data occurrence contains data items for stream depth, stream width, total quarterly flow volume, and average daily flow volume. The data product set definition describes the quarterly data occurrences. Each of the four data items is only documented once.

Similarly, the data items for parallel data occurrences are only documented once, regardless of how many parallel data occurrences are contained in the data record. For example, a single data record for traffic collisions contains four data occurrences for four different traffic collisions. Each data occurrence contains the traffic collision number, the date, the number of injuries, the number of deaths, the number of vehicles, and the total damage. The data product set definition describes the four data occurrences. Each of five data items for a data occurrence is only documented once.

Note that the data file variability and the data record variability may not be the same. For example, a data file could represent a complete data subject, meaning data records for each data occurrence in that data subject, but the data occurrence may contain only part of the data items for that data subject.

Data Instances

Data records can represent current data instances or historical data instances. The historical data instances may either be complete and contain all of the data items, or may be partial and contain only the data items that changed and identifying data items. Historical data instances can be self-contained in the same data file or stored in separate data files.

Usually, these determinations can be made during the data inventory. They are documented in the data product set or data product set variation definition. The data items are documented as described below.

The importance of data product set and data product set variation definitions should be obvious. The comprehensive definitions covering data files, data records, and data instances will be most valuable for data cross-referencing, designating a preferred data architecture, and data transformation. Remember the *opt for detail principle* and document any insights about the data files.

Data Items

Data items are probably the most variable of any data in a disparate data resource. Each of the data item variability types must be identified and properly documented.

Data items are documented as data product units or data product unit variations. The data product unit name should be the name of the data item as it is contained in the data file. Ideally, the data item names should be listed in the exact format and sequence as they appear in the data file, which helps draw technical people into the data inventory process.

Data item definitions should be as comprehensive as possible. Any source of insight about a data item should be documented in the data product unit definition. Remember to opt for detail principle.

Data items can represent a single data characteristic, multiple data characteristics, or a partial data characteristic.

A single characteristic data item can be consistent, meaning it always contains the same data characteristic. For example, the single characteristic data items for the Water Rights File are each documented as data product units, as shown below. Initial data product unit definitions are entered, and are enhanced as additional insight is gained.

```
Water Right Database (DP)
    Water_Right_File (DPS)
        Control_Number (DPSV)
          Type_Water (DPU)
```

```
            Region (DPU)
            Old_New (DPU)
            Assigned_Number (DPU)
            Stage (DPU)
            Record Modifier (DPU)
            Reason_for_Modifier (DPU)
      AA_Transaction (DPSV)
            Trans_Code (DPU)
            County (DPU)
            Status (DPU)
            Name (DPU)
            Number_of_POD/W (DPU)
```

A single characteristic data item can also be variable, meaning it contains different data characteristics in different data records, but only one of those characteristics at any time. For example, a data item might contain a student's birth date, or the reason for no birth date. The variable data item needs to be broken down into two data product unit variations, as shown below. The data product unit definition states what the variable data item represents as it appears in the database. The data product unit variation names need to be created and should be as close to a reasonable name as possible. The data product unit variation definitions describe the real meaning of each variation.

```
   Std_Bth_Dt (DPU)
      Student Birth Date (DPUV)
      Birth Date Reason Code (DPUV)
```

A multiple characteristic data item contains two or more data characteristics that may or may not be closely related. When the data characteristics are closely related, such as a person's name or birth date, the data item is documented as a data product unit. However, when the data characteristics are not closely related, the individual components need to be broken down and documented as data product unit variations.

For example, a project data item contains the project member's responsibility on the project, the date the person was assigned to the project, and monthly time commitment. Each of these components needs to be defined as a data product unit variation, as shown below.

```
   Prjct_Dtl (DPU)
      Project Member Responsibility Description (DPUV)
      Project Member Assigned Date (DPUV)
      Project Member Monthly Hours (DPUV)
```

A partial characteristic data item contains only part of a data characteristic. For example, a vehicle accident description is broken down into three different data items due to a length limitation. Each of these data items is documented as a data product unit, as described above. However, an additional comment is made in the three data product unit's definitions that each of these data items are part of a complete data item.

Alternatively, a data product unit could be created for the combined data item with a definition that describes the individual data items as part of a combined data item, as shown below. The physical data items are documented as data product unit variations, with definitions describing that each is part of a combined data item.

    Vehicle Collision Description (DPU)
       Desc_1 (DPUV)
       Desc_2 (DPUV)
       Desc_3 (DPUV)

A data item can have a fixed or variable format. The format of the data item is documented in the data product unit definition, such as a fixed format date is MM/DD/YY, or a variable format mechanic's name could be in either normal or inverted sequence. If a companion data item identifies the format, then both definitions need to describe the relationship between the two data items. These definitions will assist in the data cross-referencing.

A data item can have a fixed or variable length. The data item length is documented in the data product unit definition. Any delimiters used for designating the data item length for variable length data items are also described. If a companion data item identifies the length, then both definitions need to describe the relationship between the two data items.

A data item can have a fixed or variable sequence within a data record. The data item sequence is documented in the data product unit or data product unit variation definition. Fixed sequence data items are relatively easy to describe. Variable sequence data items usually have a companion data item that provides a mnemonic identifying the variable sequence data item. Both data item definitions need to describe the relationship between the two data items.

Data integrity rules pertaining to the data item or the relation between data items are documented for each data item. The data integrity rules can be documented in the formal notation or in a textual description. The objective is to capture the data integrity rule, not necessarily have that data integrity rule in the formal notation.

A difference in data integrity rules does not represent a data product unit variation. Data integrity rules are often so weak and so variable that trying to document differences as data product unit variations only leads to additional work and confusion. Therefore, the data integrity rules are documented for their respective component.

Data Codes

Data codes are the second most variable data in a disparate data resource. Each of the data code variability types must be identified and documented. A comment can be made in the parent data product unit or data product unit variation regarding the variability of the data codes.

Data codes can be single property or multiple properties. A single property data code represents only one data property. For example, B for Brown Hair, M for Male, and E for Executive Manager are single property data codes.

Single property data codes are documented as data product codes with any combination of the coded data value, the data code name, and the data code definition, as shown below. Sometimes a decision needs to be made if a character string is a long data code name or a short data code definition. The best approach is for the person doing the data inventory to use their best discretion.

E	Executive	Above pay range 16 (DPC)
M	Manager	Pay range 12 to 1 (DPC)
S	Supervisor	Pay range 9 to 1 (DPC)
L	Lead Worker	Pay range 6 to (DPC)
W	Worker	Pay range 5 and below (DPC)

Multiple property data codes combine two or more data properties into a single data code, as shown below.

E	Executive	Above pay range 16
M	Manager, Supervisor	Pay range 9 to 15
W	Lead Worker, Worker	Pay range 8 and below

The multiple property data codes are broken down into single property data codes and documented as data product code variations, as shown below. Note that no data product code variations are defined for Executive. Note also that coded data values do not appear for Supervisor and Lead Worker data product code variations. It's sometimes difficult to identify the single properties. Usually, the best guess is made with adjustments during cross-referencing based on additional insight.

E	Executive	Above pay range 16 (DPC)
M	Manager, Supervisor	Pay range 9 to 1 (DPC)
M	Manager	Pay range 12 to 15 (DPCV)
	Supervisor	Pay range 9 to 11 (DPCV)
W	Lead Worker, Worker	Pay range 8 and below (DPC)
L	Lead Worker	Pay range 6 to 9 (DPCV)
	Worker	Pay range 5 & below (DPCV)

Data codes may represent a single data subject or multiple data subjects. Single subject data codes are documented as shown above.

A multiple subject data code includes more than one data property from different data subjects, as shown below. The data codes represent data subjects for gender, hair color, and eye color.

1	Male, Blond Hair, Blue Eyes
2	Female, Blond Hair, Blue Eyes
3	Male, Brown Hair, Blue Eyes
4	Female, Brown Hair, Blue Eyes

And so on.

These multiple data subjects need to be broken down into single property codes for single data subjects and documented as data product code variations, as shown below.

1	Male, Blond Hair, Blue Eyes (DPC)	
	1	Male (DPCV)
	1	Blond Hair (DPCV)
	1	Blue Eyes (DPCV)
2	Female, Blond Hair, Blue Eyes (DPC)	
	2	Female (DPCV)
	2	Blond Hair (DPCV)
	2	Blue Eyes (DPCV)
3	Male, Brown Hair, Blue Eyes (DPC)	
	3	Male (DPCV)
	3	Brown Hair (DPCV)
	3	Blue Eyes (DPCV)

And so on.

Note that when the documentation of data product code variations is complete, a single data property from a single data subject will be represented by many different coded data values. For example, Male is represented by data codes 1, 3, and so on. These multiple data codes will be resolved during data cross-referencing.

Set of Data Codes

A set of data codes may represent a complete data subject or a partial data subject. The determination of whether a set of data codes represents a complete or partial data subject cannot be made with certainty during data inventory, because the complete scope of the data codes within a disparate data resource is not known. Additional sets of data codes may be discovered that contain a larger domain of data codes. Therefore, the determination can only be made with certainty after data cross-referencing has been completed and the complete scope of data codes has been determined. An indication whether a set of data codes is complete or partial can be entered in the data product item or data product item variation.

A set of data codes may represent a single data subject or multiple data subjects. A single subject set of data codes was described above.

A multiple subject set of data codes is the situation where the data codes in a set of data codes represents more than one data subject. For example, a set of data codes for counties within a state contains 42 data codes. However, the state contains only 39 counties. Looking at the data codes in detail shows that codes 1 through 39 represent the counties, 40 represents outside the state, but within the United States, 41 represents outside the United States, but within North America, and 42 represents outside North America.

Clearly, the set of data codes represents something other than counties within a state. The data codes actually represent the source of revenue, which is within a county, outside the state but within the United States, outside the United States but within North America, and outside North America.

That set of data codes should be broken into two sets of data codes. The first set of data codes represents the revenue source as from a county, from the United States outside the state, from North America outside the United States, and from outside North America. The second set of data codes represents the only counties within the state.

Coded data codes are broken down as described above for multiple subject data codes and documented as data product code variations.

Data integrity rules are not documented for data product codes. The data integrity rules for data codes are documented as a data product unit or data product unit variation for the data item containing the data codes.

A set of data codes may contain a hidden hierarchy. Using the example in Chapter 4 with census codes, the data codes are broken down into components of the hierarchy: Census Race Category, Census Race Group, Census Race. The breakdown is done at the data product unit level. The parent data product unit represents the original set of individual data codes. The definition describes that the data codes represent a hidden hierarchy, and the data product unit contains detail codes representing the Census Race. The detail data codes are listed for the parent data product unit and two data product unit variations are created for Census Race Category Code and Census Race Group Code. The definitions describe the hierarchy and the position of the component within that hierarchy. Data product codes are listed for each data product unit variation.

The result of the breakdown of the hidden hierarchy is shown below. Note that the data codes for Census Race Category and Census Race Group contain a range of data code values.

> Census Race (DPU)
> > 653 Hawaiian (DPC)
> > And so on.
>
> Census Race Category (DPUV)
> > 653 – 699 Pacific Islander (DPC)
> > And so on.
>
> Census Race Group (DPUV)
> > 653 – 659 Polynesian (DPC)
> > And so on.

The full extent of data code variability may not be known until data cross-referencing, or even the designation of preferred data. Whenever data code variability is encountered, that variability must be documented, and appropriate adjustments must be made to the data cross-referencing and preferred data designations.

Changes Over Time

Many things evolve over time, like species evolution, changes in the Earth's geology, geographical and political boundaries, laws and regulations, and so on. The data resource is no different. It is dynamic and evolves over time in response to changes in the business.

Data resource evolution is the process where an organization's data resource changes over time in response to business needs. Data names, data definitions, data structure, and data integrity rules all evolve over time. It's not the same as the natural drift of the data resource toward disparity.

Data resource evolution must be identified and documented during the data inventory. Basically, any changes over time are documented as variations using the version notation from the data naming taxonomy.

For example, the scope of water rights might have changed over time. Those changes in scope, as reflected in the data definitions, would be documented as data product set variations, as shown below.

> Water Rights Database (DP)
> > Water_Right_File (DPS)
> > > Water_Right_File <Pre-1971> (DPSV)
> > > Water_Right_File <1971 – 1985> (DPSV)
> > > Water_Right_File <1986 – Current> (DPSV)

Minor changes in data definitions do not constitute a variation. The definition must be a substantial change in the scope of the data. A data definition threshold is reached when that substantial change occurs and a new variation is identified. For example, the definition of housing was changed to include temporary structures built by the homeless, or the change in employee to include volunteers. Similarly, the data may be split, resulting in the creation of variations.

The Water Rights file described above has two data records. The breakdown of the data records due to changes over time within the data record is shown below.

```
Water Rights Database (DP)
    Water_Right_File (DPS)
        Control_Number  <Pre-1978>(DPSV)
        Control_Number <1979 – 1982> (DPSV)
        Control_Number <1983 - Current> (DPSV)
        AA_Transaction <Pre1975> (DPSV)
        AA_Transaction <1976 – 1993> (DPSV)
        AA_Transaction <1994 – Current> (DPSV)
```

Since only one level of variation is allowed, any multiple variations must be broken down to their basic components. For example, if the Water Right file changes and the record type changes both occurred, the lowest level detail of the components would be documented.

Changes in primary and foreign keys are documented using the same version notation. For example, if the primary key for Education Course changed, both primary keys would be shown with their version notation. Changes in the foreign keys of a subordinate data file would be noted in a similar manner.

```
Education Course

    Primary Key:     <Pre-2005)
                     Department. Code
                     Course. Identifier
                     Academic Term. Code

    Primary Key:     <2005 – Current>
                     Education Course. System Identifier

    Foreign Key:     Department            Department. Code

    Foreign Key:     Academic Term         Academic Term. Code
```

Any changes in data items would be documented in a similar way. For example, if a general comment field for vehicle collision was changed to a description of the injuries, data product unit variations would be created as shown below. The data definitions would describe the different contents of the two data product unit variations.

```
Veh_Clsn (DPS)
    CMT (DPU)
        Comment <Pre-1998> (DPUV)
        Comment <1999 – Current> (DPUV)
```

Any changes in data codes would be documented in a similar way. For example, Management Level code E used to mean Executive, but now means Executive and Board Members.

```
E    Executive (DPC)

    E    Executive < Pre-1988> (DPCV)
    E    Executive & Board <1989 – Current> (DPCV)
```

Changes may also occur during the data resource integration process. The data resource does not remain static during data resource integration because the business does not remain static. Ideally, the changes should be kept to a minimum. Data files may be added or removed, data items may be added or removed, data codes may be added or removed, and so on. However, changes cannot be prevented during data resource integration. All of these changes need to be tracked and eventually used to enhance the documentation.

Data Models

Many different data models exist for an organization's data resource. These data models often have different names, definitions, primary and foreign keys, and data integrity rules; many overlap and conflict, resulting in disparate data models. Also, many generic and universal data models are used to start the initial common data architecture, as described in the next chapter. All of these data models need to be inventoried and documented.

Logical and physical data models, including generic data architectures and universal data models, are documented in the same way as described above for databases. The only difference is that the terms for logical data models are changed from data files, data items, and data codes to data entities, data attributes, and data reference items.

For example, multiple subject data files become multiple subject data entities. Multiple characteristic data items become multiple characteristic data attributes. Multiple property data codes become multiple property data reference items. The reader should begin to see the power of, and necessity for, a common data architecture.

Data models are documented as data products. Data entities and data files are documented as data product sets or data product set variations. Data attributes and data items are documented as data product units and data product unit variations. Data reference items and data codes are documented as data product codes or data product code variations.

Application Programs

The data used and produced by application programs are inventoried documented as described above for databases, except that the primary keys, foreign keys, and data relations are usually not known. More often, only the data that are input or output by the application program are documented. However, working data within the application program may be inventoried and documented if those data provide insight into the organization's disparate data resource.

The primary insight from application programs is the identification and documentation of data integrity rules. Data integrity rules pertaining to the domain of data values, data derivation, data retention, and so on, can only be identified by looking at application programs. The processing performed on the data may provide some meaning about the data. Definitions may be available in comments throughout the application program that may be useful in understanding disparate data.

An information system is documented as a data product. Application programs or program modules are documented as data product sets or data product set variations. Data items are documented as data product units or data product unit variations. Data codes are documented as data product codes or data product code variations.

Comments may be made in the data product set definition pertaining to the screens or reports produced by the application program. However, the documentation of screens and reports is separate from the documentation of the application program. Comments may also be made about the data files accessed or updated by the application program.

Purchased applications often contain far more data files than the organization uses. Only the data files used by the organization are documented, and only the data items in those data files used by the organization are documented. Inventorying the data files and data items not used by the organization, which often number in the thousands or tens of thousands, is a waste of resources, and serves no useful purpose.

Screens – Reports – Forms

Screens, reports, and forms are documented based on the data hierarchies shown in Appendices B and C. A data structure is prepared for each screen, report, or form, including summary or aggregated data, and that structure is used as the base for documentation. Documenting screens, reports, and forms without a corresponding data structure is difficult, if not impossible.

Typically, only data items are documented for screens, reports, and forms, including the elemental data items and any summary or aggregated data items. Any data definitions that exist should be documented. Data definitions are usually non-existent or vague, but column and row headings, and use of the data can provide insight into the meaning of the data. No primary or foreign keys exist on screens, reports, and forms, and no integrity rules exist.

The information system containing the screen, report, or form is documented as a data product. The screen, report, or form itself is documented as a data product set. The data items on the screen, report, or form are documented as data product units. Data items are documented as described above.

XML is inventoried and documented in the same way as a report. The information system containing the XML is documented as a data product. The set of XML is documented as a data product set, or data product set variation. The data items in the XML set are documented as data product units or data product unit variations. Any codes within XML are documented as data product codes or data product code variations.

Generally, the structure of XML is not documented. It's the XML data items that are of concern and need to be understood. However, the structure of the XML could be documented in the same way as a screen, report, or form so it can be better understood. Generally, no data integrity rules are documented for XML unless derivation rules appear in documentation about the XML.

Supplemental Documentation

Formal and informal documentation includes data dictionaries, project descriptions, data entry instructions, instruction manuals, standards, legislation, external reporting requirements, informal notes, e-mails, meeting minutes, memos, and so on. These supplemental sources of insight can either be documented as separate data products, or they can be used to enhance existing documentation from the primary sources of insight.

For example, if a standard is produced as a data model, it could be documented as a separate data product, as described above for data models. Data dictionaries could either be documented as a separate data product, or could be used to supplement existing documentation. Meeting minutes, memos, e-mails, and so on, would likely be used to supplement existing documentation.

The decision of whether formal and informal documentation should be entered as separate data products or used to supplement existing documentation can be difficult. Generally, if the documentation can stand alone, or relates to multiple primary sources of insight, it is documented as a data product. If the documentation does not stand alone or does not relate to multiple primary sources of insight, it is used to supplement existing documentation.

The tacit knowledge of individuals is used to enhance existing documentation from the primary sources of insight.

Other Forms of Data

Summary data in fixed hierarchies are documented based on data hierarchies described in Appendix B. The overall structure, such as a report, is documented as a data product. Each data set in the hierarchy is documented as a data product set within the data product. Each data item in the hierarchy is documented as a data product unit within its respective data product set. Any data codes are documented as data product codes within their respective data item.

The relationships of the data sets in the data hierarchy are documented with the primary keys for each data set. The primary key consists of the unique identifier for the data set being documented and the primary keys of all parent data sets, as shown in Appendix C. For example, the primary key for a Section within the Organization might be:

Section

Primary Key: Department. Identifier
                Division. Identifier
                Section. Identifier

Aggregated data in variable data hierarchies are documented as described in Appendix C. The overall structure, such as a report, is documented as a data product. Each data set in the hierarchy is documented as a data product set within the data product. Each data item in the hierarchy is documented as a data product unit within its respective data product set. Any data codes are documented as data product codes within their respective data item.

Unlike summary data in fixed hierarchies, the data items are named accordingly as manifestations of the data focus name, as described in

Appendix C. For example, the summary data items might be Timber Stand Analytics 6. Total Timber Volume.

Predictive data are documented in the same way as operational data, summary data, or aggregated data, depending on what the data represent. Generally, predictive data that are input to predictive analysis are documented in the same way as described for operational data. The data resulting from predictive analysis are documented in the same way as summary data and aggregated data.

Most spatial data are tabular data that are documented in the same way as operational data. The definition of the spatial data items representing the geography of the points, lines, and polygons can be documented, but the data values, data structure, and data integrity rules for these geographic data items are not documented.

Geographic information system databases are documented as a data product. The data layers, such as timber, soil, roads, and so on, are documented as a data product set. The data items in each data layer are documented as data product items.

Complex structured data are documented either in their complex structured form, or in a normally structured form resulting from breaking down the complex structure into simpler structures, as described in the last chapter. The complex structured form is documented as a data product where the definition contains the nature and contents of the complex structured data. Documentation of the simpler structures is done in the same way as described above for operational data or for screens, reports, and forms. Either approach is acceptable, but at the very least, complex structured data must be documented as a data product.

Non-electronic data should also be documented because they are part of the organization's data resource. Non-electronic data are documented in the same way as their electronic component, as described above. The definitions should specify the form and location of the non-electronic data, and any other insight that is useful for locating and understanding the non-electronic data.

SUMMARY

The scope of the data inventory is prioritized based on business critical data and where the organization is feeling pain over disparate data. Waves of data inventory can be established to keep the data inventory process moving ahead. Once data inventory is started in an organization, it becomes self-perpetuating as more and more people want to get their data integrated.

The general sequence for a data inventory is from the primary sources of insight to the secondary sources of insight. The secondary sources usually supplement the insights gained from the primary sources. Either a horizontal or a vertical phased approach may be used with the data inventory.

Involvement in the data inventory usually starts with identification of a core team and ancillary team members. Other people are brought into the process as needed. Since data inventory is a discovery process, a rigid project schedule and precise time commitments should be avoided. A no blame - no whitewash approach should be established so that people feel free to provide candid insights about the disparate data.

Documentation of the data inventory is done according to the Data Product Model. The opt for detail principle ensures that as much data as possible are captured and documented. The organization needs to determine where the data inventory documentation is stored, based on its particular operating environment. The data inventory documentation is retained after the data have been transformed to provide a history of the changes from disparate data to comparate data.

Supporting techniques include data scanning and data profiling, which can be automated or manual. Data scanning identifies the data in databases, application programs, screens, reports, and forms, and so on, but does not deal with data values. Data profiling documents the data values and makes predictions about the meaning of those data values. However, those predictions need to be reviewed and verified before they are accepted.

Databases are documented according to the Data Product Model, including data files, data records, data instances, data items, data codes, and sets of data codes. Changes over time are documented as variations. Data models are documented similar to databases, with a slight change in terms for logical data models. Application programs provide additional insight into the disparate data. Screens, reports, and forms show how the data are used or entered.

Supplemental insight can be either documented according to the Data Product Model, or as supplements to the existing documentation. Summary data, aggregated data, predictive data, complex structured data, and non-electronic data are all documented as part of the organization's data resource.

A data inventory starts the process of understanding the disparate data and sets the stage for cross-referencing those data to a common data architecture for further understanding and the designation of a preferred data architecture. A good job of inventorying and documenting all of the detail about disparate data results in good cross-referencing, a good preferred data architecture, and good transformation of data to a comparate data resource.

QUESTIONS

The following questions are provided as a review of the data inventory process, and to stimulate thought about how to adequately inventory and manage changes to disparate data.

1. Why are combined components broken down to their basic components during data inventory?

2. Why should the data definitions contain as much detail as possible about disparate data?

3. How are data relations documented?

4. How are changes over time documented?

5. What's the difference between summary data and aggregated data?

6. How are summary data named?

7. How are aggregated data named?

8. Why do non-electronic data need to be inventoried and documented?

9. How are complex structured data inventoried and documented?

10. What is the objective of inventorying existing disparate data?

Chapter 7

DATA CROSS-REFERENCING CONCEPT

Data cross-referencing greatly improves data understanding.

The next step after a data inventory is to cross-reference the inventoried data to a common data architecture. Cross-referencing data to a common data architecture solves the second problem with disparate data. Most organizations do not fully understand the content and meaning of their disparate data. Data cross-referencing builds on the understanding gained in the data inventory and provides organizations with a full understanding of the content, meaning, structure, and integrity of disparate data.

Chapter 7 describes the concepts and principles for cross-referencing the inventoried data to a common data architecture. The next chapter describes the techniques for cross-referencing the inventoried data to a common data architecture. Chapters 9 and 10 describe how to develop a preferred data architecture based on the cross-referenced data.

CONCEPT AND PRINCIPLES

The *data cross-reference concept* is the inventoried disparate data are cross-referenced to a common data architecture to further increase the understanding of those disparate data within a common context. An initial understanding of disparate data was gained during the data inventory process. That initial understanding is increased through a cross-referencing of the inventoried disparate data to a common data architecture.

Data cross-referencing is where the rubber meets the road. It's where a thorough understanding of the content, meaning, structure, and integrity of the data come together. Combined data were broken down to their individual components during the data inventory. Those components are put together in a normalized manner within a common data architecture.

Data cross-referencing solves the second problem with disparate data, which is the organization at large does not thoroughly understanding the disparate data. Cross-referencing disparate data to a common data architecture, and documenting that cross-referencing, provides a thorough understanding of the data and makes that understanding available to the organization at large.

The *data cross-reference objective* is to thoroughly understand the content, meaning, structure, and integrity of all data at the organization's disposal within the context of a common data architecture so that a comparate data resource can be developed that fully supports the current and future business information demand. The objective is to take the initial understanding of disparate data that was documented at an elemental level during the data inventory and increase that understanding within the context of a common data architecture at the organization level. That thorough understanding sets the stage for designating a preferred data architecture and developing a comparate data resource.

Cross-referencing disparate data to a common data architecture is a critical, non-trivial process. It requires a thorough understanding of both the disparate data and the common data architecture. It also requires tremendous patience and diligence to make sure that appropriate data cross-references are made.

Failure to make appropriate data cross-references affects the preferred data designations, the development of data transformation rules, and development of a comparate data resource. Decisions made during data cross-referencing have ripple effects through the entire data resource integration process.

A *data cross-reference* is a logical mapping between disparate data names and common data names. It's a link between components of the inventoried disparate data and components in a common data architecture. The three data cross-references are between data products and data subject variations, between data product units or variations and data characteristic variations, and between data product codes or variations and data reference set variations.

The terms *mapping* and *data mapping* are not used because they are often confused with cartographic mapping. The terms *cross-walking* and *data cross-walking* are not used because they represent a movement of data between two points that does not include formal data transformation or the application of data integrity rules. Data cross-referencing is a reference only, not a movement of data, and leads to formal data transformation with the application of data integrity rules.

Data resource integration is based on both semantic integration and structural integration, as described in Chapter 2. The data inventory started that integration process by breaking down the existing data products to their basic components based on both meaning and structure. The data cross-reference process continues by putting those components together in a normalized form within the context of a common data architecture.

Principles

Several principles apply to data cross-referencing, including understanding disparate data, the *umwelt principle*, organization agility, a discovery process, effective data cross-referencing, an interim common data architecture, enhancing the data inventory, enhancing a common data architecture, adjusting a common data architecture, a simple but detailed process, data cross-referencing is deterministic, data normalization, data cross-referencing sequence, and data cross-referencing involvement. Each of these principles is described below.

Data Understanding

The *disparate data understanding principle* was described in Chapter 4 as all disparate data variability, including data names, definitions, structure, integrity, and existing documentation will be understood and formally documented at a detailed level within the context of a common data architecture. Any attempt to resolve data disparity and integrate a disparate data resource without thoroughly understanding the disparate data will likely end in failure or a result that is less than fully successful. That principle applies to the entire data resource integration process.

Understanding is the key to high quality data resource integration. The question is *How* to understand the data—really understand the data. Not just an awareness gained during data inventory, but a deep understanding of the content, meaning, structure, and integrity of the data. Traditional data understanding is often done in an atmosphere of confusion, pressure, and conflicting descriptions. It's often done with limited documentation and limited input from knowledgeable individuals.

Real data understanding in a positive atmosphere begins with the data inventory process. That initial understanding is based on what is already known about the existing data based on primary and supplemental sources of insight. When the data inventory is complete, the extent of that existing data understanding has been reached, and another level of understanding needs to be achieved to further increase the data understanding.

That next level of understanding is the content, meaning, structure, and integrity of the data with respect to the business world where the organization operates. When people understand the data with respect to the business world as perceived by the organization, those data will support the business information demand. In fact, the use of data that are well understood is limited only by people's imagination.

The Umwelt Principle

The *organization perception principle* was stated in Chapter 3 as the comparate data resource developed to support an organization's business must be based on the organization's perception of the business world. If a comparate data resource is to support an organization's business activities, that comparate data resource must be based primarily on the organization's perception of the business world and how the organization chooses to operate in that business world.

Umwelt is a German word meaning the environment or the world around. It's the world as perceived by an organism based on its cognitive and sensory powers. It's the environmental factors collectively that are capable of affecting an organism's behavior. It's a self-centered world where organisms can have different umwelten, even though they share the same environment. It's an organism's perception of the current surroundings and previous experiences which are unique to that organism. It's the world as experienced by a particular organism.

Change *organism* to *organization*, which is really a collection of organisms, and change *environment* to *business environment* and you have an umwelt for an organization. The **organization umwelt principle** states that each organization has a particular perception of the business world in which they operate based on previous experiences that are unique to that organization. Those experiences affect the organization's behavior in the business world, and determine how the organization adapts to a changing business world and operates in that business world.

The *organization umwelt principle* supports the *organization perception principle* and emphasizes the importance of understanding both the business environment and the data supporting the business in that environment. The umwelt principle drives development of a common data architecture and the cross-referencing of the inventoried disparate data to that common data architecture.

The umwelt principle also emphasizes that each organization has a unique perception of the business world and chooses to operate according to that perception without being judged right or wrong. An organization can change their perception of the business world and how they operate in it based on experiences that are unique to that organization. One perception of the business world that is suitable for all organizations does not exist. Each organization has its own unique perception of the business world.

The umwelt principle explains why universal data models, generic data architectures, purchased applications, and so on, don't work. Simply, one perception of the business world does not work for all organizations. The common phrases are *How dare you force your umwelt on my organization? Who gave you the authority to tell me how to perceive the business world? Who had the authority to give that authority?*

The situation is like the difference between building codes and individual buildings. Building codes state the requirements for safe construction of buildings, but do not state the design of buildings. The design is based on the intended use of the building by the occupant. The same is true for bridges, airplanes, ships, cars, and so on. Codes specify requirements for safety, but the design is based on perceived use.

The umwelt principle also explains why *Party* does not appear in a common data architecture. Other than celebratory events or political parties, *Party* will not appear in an organization's perception of the business world where they operate. *Party*, if it exists at all, is a result of data denormalization, and will not be discussed further in data cross-referencing. All of the examples I've seen of *Party* are simply a data modeler forcing their umwelt on the organization.

Common perceptions of the business environment can be described for use by organizations as they see fit. However, these common perceptions are not standard or official, and cannot be forced upon an organization. Organizations are free to choose their perception of the business world—their own umwelten.

Organization Agility

Agility is the quality or state of being agile; marked by ready ability to move with quick easy grace; mentally quick and resourceful. The *organization agility principle* states that an organization must be agile to remain successful in their business endeavor. Agility depends on how the organization perceives the business world and how well it adjusts to changes in that business world. It depends on how well the organization understands the business world, how quickly the organization perceives changes in that business world, and how quickly they can respond to those changes.

Responding to changes in the business world depend, to some extent, on how quickly the data resource changes to reflect changes in the business world. The *data resource agility principle* states that an organization's data resource must be agile enough to change in a manner that supports the business change needed to remain successful in a dynamic business world. The data resource must change so that it provides one version of truth about the business world where the organization operates. How the data resource can be used to detect changes in the business world and how the data resource can be adjusted to reflect those changes are key issues for an agile organization. Thoroughly understanding the data resource supports real organization agility.

Discovery Process

The *data resource discovery principle* described in Chapter 2 states that data resource integration is a discovery process where any insights about the data resource are captured, understood, and documented. The process is performed by people, who may be supported by automated tools.

The data inventory process was a discovery process that uncovered the existing content, meaning, structure, and integrity of the disparate data. Data cross-referencing is also a discovery process that discovers and documents additional understanding of the data within the context of a common data architecture.

Effective Data Cross-Referencing

The *effective data cross-referencing principle* states that thoroughly understanding existing disparate data is only effective when those data are inventoried and documented at a detailed level and are cross-referenced to a common data architecture. Attempting to cross-reference disparate data to other disparate data is both inefficient and ineffective. The result is more confusion and a data resource integration process that either fails or is less than fully successful.

Interim Common Data Architecture

The *interim common data architecture principle* states that interim common data architectures may be developed in very large organizations where it is not possible to achieve a final common data architecture in one step because of the size of the task. Data products are cross-referenced to interim common data architectures, and those interim data architectures are cross-referenced to a final common data architecture. Only one level of interim data architectures is allowed.

Enhancing and Adjusting the Data Inventory

The *continuous enhancement principle* described in Chapter 5 states that documentation of disparate data should be continuously enhanced as additional insight is gained. Documenting and understanding disparate data is not a one-time process—it's an ongoing process through all phases of data resource integration. Any time additional insight is gained about disparate data, that insight must be documented.

Additional insight into disparate data may be gained during data cross-referencing. The data inventory was done one source of insight at a time, and an overall perspective was usually lacking. The data cross-reference looks at the total data inventory with respect to a common data architecture. That perspective often provides additional insight into the disparate data. That additional insight must be used to enhance the existing documentation.

The additional insight may be an enhancement to definitions or data integrity rules. The additional insight might lead to adjustments of the data inventory, such as a further breakdown of data product sets, data product units, data product codes, or possibly a combination of what was thought to be basic components. These additional insights are immediately documented while they are fresh in mind, rather than leaving the documentation until later or ignoring the insights altogether.

These enhancements and adjustments to the data inventory provide better understanding of the existing disparate data, provide better cross-referencing, and lead to better preferred data designations.

Enhancing the Common Data Architecture

The continuous enhancement principle also applies to a common data architecture. An initial common data architecture is established prior to data cross-referencing, as described later. That initial common data architecture is continually enhanced during the data cross-referencing process. As components from the Data Product Model are cross-referenced, the common data architecture needs to be enhanced. The details of that enhancement are described later in the current chapter and in the next chapter.

Adjusting the Common Data Architecture

A common data architecture needs to be reviewed periodically during data cross-referencing to ensure that it adequately represents the organization's perception of the business world. As a common data architecture is continually enhanced to cover the data cross-references, the organizations perception of the business world is sometimes forgotten. In addition, the data cross-referencing can result in the organization changing its perception of the business world. Therefore, a common data architecture needs to be reviewed periodically, and adjustments made to ensure that it adequately represents the organization's perception of the business world.

The ***common data architecture adjustment principle*** states that a common data architecture should be periodically reviewed and adjusted during data cross-referencing to ensure that it adequately represents the organization perception of the business world. Even though nothing appears to have changed, a good policy is to routinely review a common data architecture to determine if it needs to be adjusted.

Adjusting Data Cross-References

Adjustments to a common data architecture may lead to existing data cross-references becoming inappropriate. Therefore, whenever a common data architecture is adjusted, the existing data cross-references should be reviewed to ensure they are still correct. If the existing data cross-references are not correct, they need to be changed.

In addition, when additional insight is gained about the disparate data and a common data architecture, even though a common data architecture was not adjusted, a good policy is to review the data cross-references to ensure they are correct. If the existing data cross-references are not correct, they need to be changed.

Simple But Detailed Approach

Data cross-referencing is relatively simple, straight forward, and methodical, but it's very detailed. Although a simple task, data cross-referencing is time consuming and requires considerable thought and analysis to determine the real meaning and structure of the disparate data with respect to a common data architecture. However, it's not impossible. When the data cross-references have been made, the other tasks of data resource integration are relatively easy.

Some data cross-references are determined fairly easily, while others require considerable searching and analysis. Generally, about 70% to 80% of the data cross-referencing is relatively easy. About 10% to 15% of the data cross-referencing is more difficult and takes some thought and analysis. About 5% to 10% of data cross-referencing are extremely difficult and take real investigation. A small percentage of data cannot be understood or cross-referenced.

The best approach is to make data cross-references as soon as enough insight has been gained to make the cross-reference with reasonable certainty. The data cross-reference can always be changed when additional insight is gained.

Deterministic – Prospective – Descriptive

Data cross-referencing is deterministic because it formally breaks the disparate data down to their basic components and cross-references those components to a common data architecture. It ensures that data redundancy and variability are understood and resolved. It provides more benefit than probabilistic cross-referencing between data products.

Data cross-referencing is prospective because a common data architecture is established to support the data cross-referencing. That common data architecture will be used to designate a preferred data architecture. Therefore, the orientation is prospective toward a comparate data resource.

Data cross-referencing is descriptive because it continues describing the existing disparate data within the context of a common data architecture. Even though a common data architecture is prospective, understanding existing disparate data within a common data architecture is a descriptive process.

Data Normalization

Disparate data are often quite un-normalized at the data file level, the data item level, the data code level, and for time. Even some logical data models are un-normalized at the data entity level, the data attribute level, the data reference item level, and for time. These un-normalized data are normalized within the context of a common data architecture during data cross-referencing.

Data cross-referencing is based on both the data meaning and the data structure, which are based on the organization's perception of the business world according to the *organization perception principle* and the *organization umwelt principle*. The organization's perception of the business world is primary, and data normalization according to that perception is secondary.

Data cross-referencing normalizes data characteristics within data subjects, business facts within data characteristics, data properties within data reference items, and time into current and historical instances. The normalization is done as the basic components identified during data inventory are cross-referenced to a common data architecture. The result is a fully normalized data structure that can be used to designate a preferred data architecture.

Data Cross-Reference Sequence

The last chapter described the sequence of data inventorying and data cross-referencing. The entire scope of data could be inventoried and documented, and then the data cross-referencing could be done. Alternatively, the data cross-referencing could be done as soon as small sets of data are inventoried. When the techniques are understood, either approach is appropriate.

Several sequences could be followed by an individual within data cross-referencing. The first is to start at the beginning of the data inventory and cross-reference each data product unit or data reference set to a common data architecture. The second is to skip around and cross-reference the easiest components first, which builds success motivation for tackling more difficult components. The third is to tackle the most difficult components first and *crack the code*, then move on to the easier components.

Another approach is to use a group of knowledgeable people, where each contributes their understanding to the cross-reference. The group could meet and offer their knowledge in a group setting. The knowledge is shared, but the time commitment is higher. Alternatively, the data cross-referencing could cycle among individuals in the group and each would add the cross-references they understood. The knowledge is not readily shared, but the time commitment is lower.

All approaches work well, and are largely a personal preference. Rather than force a particular sequence, I let each group decide how they would prefer to sequence the data cross-referencing.

Data Cross-Referencing Involvement

Anyone knowledgeable about the disparate data should be involved in data cross-referencing. However, the more people that get involved in data cross-referencing, the greater the cost of data resource integration. More understanding requires more involvement, which increases the cost.

Some organizations tend to limit involvement in data cross-referencing to get the process completed quicker at a lower cost. However, acceptance of the data cross-referencing and enhancement of a common data architecture is lower. Less acceptance of a common data architecture usually means less acceptance of the preferred data architecture, and less acceptance of data resource integration.

Therefore, the best approach is to have a core team of knowledgeable people do the data cross-referencing, but make the results readily available to anyone in the organization interested in data resource integration. In addition, comments should be readily accepted from those interested people, because their insight may be quite valuable. The result is also more readily accepted.

Data Cross-Reference Approaches

Data cross-referencing can be done in three different ways: product-to-product, product-to-common, and common-to-common. The first is not a valid approach for several reasons, but the other two are valid approaches. Each approach is described below.

Product-To-Product

A typical approach to data integration is cross-referencing data products to other data products. A *product-to-product cross-reference* is a data cross-reference between data products without the benefit of a common data architecture. Product-to-product cross-references are between sets of disparate data, usually databases, bridges, or feeds between information systems. The result is layer upon layer of cross-referenced disparate data that provide little understanding of those disparate data.

Many of the product-to-product cross-references connect data items with different content, different format, different meaning, or different sets of coded data values. These cross-references result in comments like *nearly the same as*, *very close to*, *most of the codes used in*, and so on, that only add to the disparate data problem. The results are difficult to interpret and provide no base for real data transformation or integration.

Product-to-product cross-references will likely never be completed because of the number of databases, bridges, feeds, and ongoing changes in the data. The masses of data stored become unmanageable. I worked with one state attempting to conduct product to product cross-references with their databases. A quick calculation showed that storage was not available to handle the result, and ongoing changes would soon make the cross-references out of date.

Even if product-to-product cross-references were completed between databases, bridges, and feeds, the data on screens, reports, and forms, and all the derived, summary, and aggregated data are seldom included. Changes over time are seldom considered. Suggestions have been made that databases be considered primary sources and that screens, reports, and forms be considered secondary sources. The secondary sources are then cross-referenced to the primary sources. However, the derived, summary, and aggregated data, and changes over time, often can't be cross-referenced. These secondary-to-primary cross-references provide little understanding of disparate data and often lead to more confusion.

Therefore, directly cross-referencing disparate data to disparate data won't work, and often makes the situation worse. It does not lead to increased understanding and provides very little support for data transformation or data resource integration.

Product-To-Common

A far better approach is to make cross-references between data products and a common data architecture. A **product-to-common cross-reference** is a data cross-reference between data products and a common data architecture. The *effective data cross-referencing principle* emphasizes that disparate data must be inventoried at a detailed level and cross-referenced to a common data architecture for those data to be thoroughly understood and properly integrated. The product-to-common cross-references lead to increased understanding and directly support data resource integration.

When product-to-product references are needed, they are developed through the common data architecture. These indirect product-to-product cross-references are developed only when necessary and are easier to manage than direct product-to-product cross-references. They can be used as necessary to support data transformation.

The product-to-common cross-references are the cross-references described in the current chapter and the next chapter. Data product components are cross-referenced to corresponding components in the common data architecture to provide a complete understanding of the meaning, structure, and integrity of disparate data. That complete understanding fully supports data resource integration.

Common-To-Common

Normally, data products are cross-referenced to a final common data architecture through product-to-common cross-references. However, in very large organizations, such as governmental agencies or multi-national organizations, it's not always possible to achieve a final common data architecture in one step because of the size of the task. The interim common data architecture principle allows the development of one level of interim common data architectures, which are then cross-referenced to a final common data architecture.

Successive levels of interim common data architectures are not acceptable because they inevitably lead to additional effort with no corresponding increase in understanding. They unnecessarily delay achievement of a common view of disparate data.

An **interim common data architecture** is a common data architecture that is developed for cross-referencing one major segment of the data resource for a very large organization. When the interim common data architectures are completed, they are treated as data products and are cross-referenced to a final common data architecture. Interim common data architectures are usually coordinated by tactical data stewards.

A *common-to-common cross-reference* is a data cross-reference between an interim common data architecture that is treated as a data product, and the final common data architecture. A *final common data architecture* is a common data architecture that includes all data in the organization's data resource and is used to designate a preferred data architecture. It can be developed from product-to-common cross-references or common-to-common cross-references.

Developing interim common data architectures does not mean that those interim common data architectures are developed in isolation. Tactical data stewards should seek commonality as soon as possible between the interim common data architectures by discussing and exchanging thoughts on commonality during development of the interim common data architectures. That exchange makes the common-to-common cross-referencing easier and faster.

When all of the interim common data architectures are cross-referenced to a final common data architecture, the common-to-common cross-references are collapsed so that the data products are directly cross-referenced to the final common data architecture. The interim common data architectures may be maintained for reference, but data resource integration proceeds based on the final common data architecture. Performing data resource integration through a final common data architecture and interim common data architectures is extremely difficult.

The interim common data architectures must be cross-referenced to a final common data architecture before designating the preferred data architecture. Designating the preferred data architecture before all interim data architectures are cross-referenced to a final common data architecture could to be a wasted effort. Additional insight is often gained through cross-referencing additional interim data architectures to a final common data architecture.

COMMON DATA ARCHITECTURE COMPONENTS

The components of a common data architecture used for data cross-referencing are shown in Figure 7.1. The diagram is not intended to be a complete data model. It only shows the components of a common data architecture that are used for data cross-referencing and the data relations between those components. Each of the components is described below.

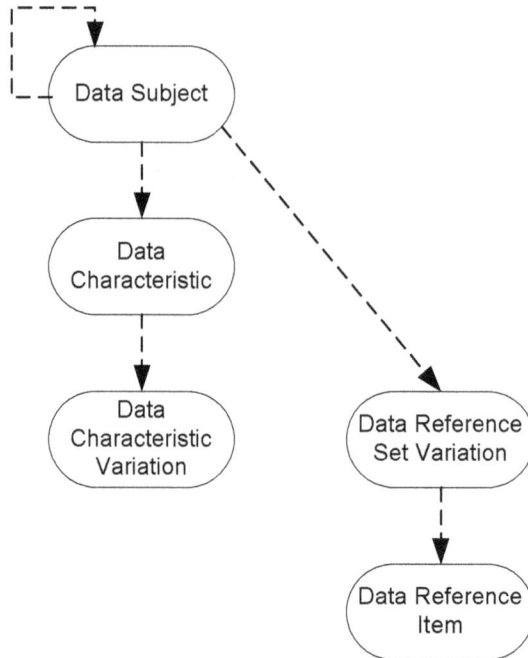

Figure 7.1. Common data architecture components.

Data Subject

A *data subject* was defined in Chapter 3 as a person, place, thing, concept, or event that is of interest to the organization and about which data are captured and maintained in the organization's data resource. Data subjects are defined from business objects and business events, making the data resource subject oriented based on the business. Data subject names are unique within a common data architecture. The definition describes the data subject.

Data Subject Variation

A data subject is recursive to provide data subject variations. A *data subject variation* is a variation of a data subject to support data selections, subsets of data, and data roles, and to support evaluational data subjects. Only one level of recursion is allowed, because the intent is to document variations of a data subject, not a hierarchy of data subjects.

A data subject variation can represent manifestations of a data focus in an aggregated data structure. For example, the Student Analytics Focus is the parent data subject. Student Analytics 1, Student Analytics 2, and so on, are the data subject variations. The data subject variation name is formed by an extension to the data subject name.

A data subject variation can also represent data selections, subsets of data, and data roles. The data occurrence group and data occurrence role notations of the Data Naming Taxonomy are used to name the data subject variation. For example, a subset of middle school students might be named [Middle School] Student. Plumbers that are a subset of Contractors might be named "Plumbing" Contractor. The subset of data aggregated for student analytics might be named [Selection 1] Student Analytics 4.

Data subjects contain all of the identifying data characteristics and their data characteristic variations. The data subject variation only inherits the identifying data characteristics as necessary. Attempting to document all of the data characteristics and data characteristic variations for each data subject variation would be a monumental task, and would provide little benefit for understanding the data. Therefore, data characteristics are documented only for data subjects.

Data subject variation names must be unique within the data subject, and are usually formed by a prefix to the parent data subject name, or by an extension to the parent data subject name, as shown above. The definition describes the data subject variation.

Data Characteristic

A *data characteristic* was defined in Chapter 3 as an individual fact that describes or characterizes a data subject. It represents a business feature and contains a single fact, or closely related facts, about a data subject, such as the make of a vehicle, or a person's height. Each data subject is described by a set of data characteristics.

Data characteristic names must be unique within a data subject. The same fact may have the same name across different data subjects, but the addition of the data subject name makes the data characteristic name unique. For example, data subjects for Student and Driver may each have a business fact for birth date. The addition of the data subject name makes those business facts unique, such as Student. Birth Date and Driver. Birth Date.

Data Characteristic Variation

A *data characteristic variation* was defined in Chapter 3 as a variation in the content or format of a data characteristic. It represents a variant of a data characteristic, such as different units of measurement, different monetary units, different lengths, different sequences in a person's name, and so on. Each data characteristic has at least one data characteristic variation, and may have many data characteristic variations.

Data characteristic names must be unique within a data characteristic. Data characteristic variation names show the variation in content or format as an extension to the data characteristic name. For example, variations in a student's birth date might be Student. Birth Date, CYMD or Student. Birth Date, M/D/Y.

Data characteristic variation names must be fully qualified to prevent any confusion about the exact format or content. For example, the data characteristic variation name for a student's name might be Student. Name Complete, Normal 56 Right All Caps, meaning the student's name is in the normal sequence, 56 characters long, right justified, in all capital letters. Even though the level of detail seems unnecessary and no closely related data characteristic variation is apparent, the *opt for detail principle* prevails. Additional data characteristic variation names may come along later and the detail avoids the need to go back and adjust previous data characteristic variation names.

A common mistake is to consider a difference in the business fact as a data characteristic variation. For example, a person's complete name is not a data characteristic variation. It's a data characteristic containing the person's first name, middle name, and family name. It's not the same as data characteristics for the individual components of a person's name. Similarly, the total depth of a well and the usable depth of a well are two different data characteristics, not variations of the same data characteristic. Therefore, a difference in a business fact is a different data characteristic, not a variation of a data characteristic.

Data Reference Set Variation

A *data reference set* is a specific set of data codes for a general topic, such as a set of management level codes in an organization. A data reference set is documented as a data subject containing data characteristics for at least the name, coded data value, definition, begin date, and end date. The data subject name for the data reference set is unique within a common data architecture and indicates the contents of the data reference set, such as Management Level or Vehicle Type.

A *data reference set variation* is a variation of a data reference set that has a difference in the domain of data reference items, their coded data values, their names, or substantial difference in the data definitions. Any difference, however slight, constitutes a different data reference set variation.

Data reference set variation names are unique within the parent data subject, and are usually formed by an extension to the data reference set name using the data naming taxonomy notation. For example, variations for a vehicle data reference set might be Vehicle Type. 1;, Vehicle Type. 2;, and so on.

Data Reference Item

A *data property* was defined in Chapter 4 as a single feature, trait, or quality within a grouping or classification of features, traits, or qualities belonging to a data characteristic. For example, gender has data properties for male, female, and unknown. Management level has data properties for executive, manager, supervisor, and lead worker.

A *data reference item* is single set of coded data values, data names, and data definitions representing a single data property in a data reference set variation. Each data reference set variation has many data reference items. Each data reference item represents a single data property. Each data property is characterized by a name, a definition, and possibly a coded data value.

Data Subject Thesaurus

A *data subject thesaurus* is a list of synonyms and related business terms that help people find data subjects that support their business information needs. It's a list of business terms and alias data entity names that point to the formal data subject name. For example, the following terms might appear in a data subject thesaurus.

Alias	Data Subject
Woodlot	Timber Stand
Forest	Timber Stand
Trees	Timber Stand
Timber	Timber Stand
Vegetation	Timber Stand
Pupil	Student
Attendee	Student
Personnel	Employee
Worker	Employee
Staff	Employee

A data subject thesaurus needs to be established before data cross-referencing begins, and needs to be continually enhanced through the data cross-referencing process. A good data subject thesaurus supports data cross-referencing, and supports full use of the data resource after data resource integration has been completed.

Common Data Name Words

A *common word* was defined earlier as a word that has consistent meaning whenever it is used in a data name. A *data name vocabulary* was defined earlier as the collection of all twelve sets of common words representing the twelve components of the data naming taxonomy. Each common word has a definition stating the meaning of that common word, which is very useful for understanding disparate data within a common context.

A data name vocabulary needs to be maintained while developing a common data architecture and cross-referencing inventoried data to that common data architecture. The common words used for data subjects, data characteristics, data characteristic variations, data reference set variations, and data reference items need to be defined, maintained, and consulted whenever a new data name is created in a common data architecture. The use of common words ensures consistency in data names within a common data architecture.

For example, a common word Variable is defined as meaning the format or content of the data value is variable. A data characteristic variation name for the names of streams might be Stream Segment. Name, Variable, and might contain S Nooksack River, Nooksack River South, South Fork Nooksack River, and so on.

PRODUCT-TO-COMMON CROSS-REFERENCE

The cross-references between data products and the common data architecture are shown in Figure 7.2. The three cross-references are between data product sets or variations and data subject variations, between data product units or variations and data characteristic variations, and between data product codes or variations and data reference set variations.

Data Product Cross-Reference

No cross-reference is made between the data products and a common data architecture. A data product represents a high level of data products and has no equivalent in a common data architecture.

Data Product Set Cross-Reference

A data cross-reference is not normally made between a data product set or variation and a data subject. The data product set or variation represents a data file, a data record type, a screen, report, or form, and so on. They are not equivalent to a data subject. Such a cross-reference would mean an exact match between the data product set or variation and a data subject, including all of the data characteristics in that data subject.

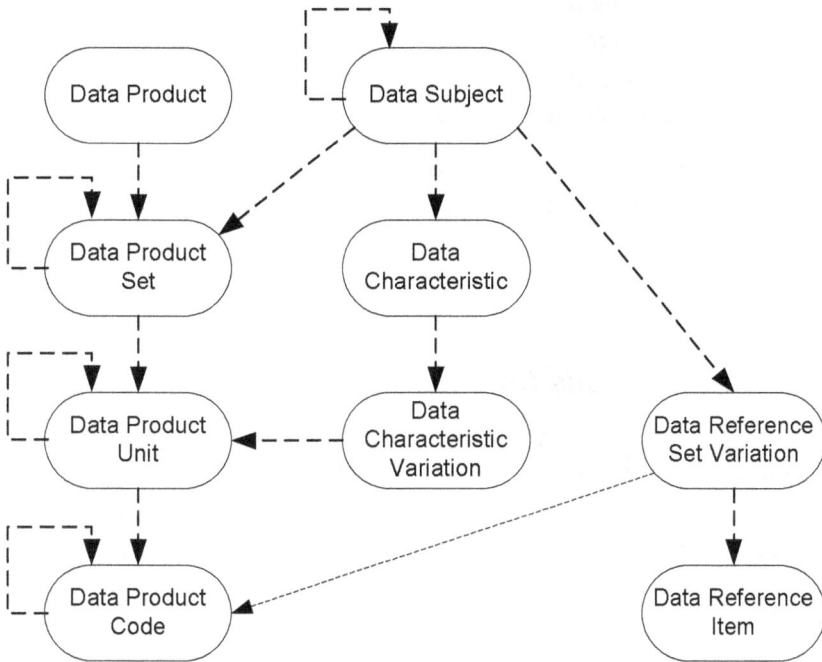

Figure 7.2. Product to common cross-references.

However, a data cross-reference can be made between a data product set or variation and a data subject for designating selections, subsets of data, and data roles. A *data product set cross-reference* is a cross-reference between a data product set or variation and a data subject variation solely for the purpose of designating data selections, subsets of data, and data roles, or for designating the manifestations of a data focus. Since data subject variations do not have any data characteristics, the cross-reference does not indicate an exact match between data product units and data characteristics.

Data Product Unit Cross-Reference

A *data product unit cross-reference* is a cross-reference between a data product unit or variation and a corresponding data characteristic variation. Each data product unit or variation is cross-referenced to a data characteristic variation. These are the primary cross-references between data products and a common data architecture.

If the data product unit variation is cross-referenced to a data characteristic variation, then the data product unit is not cross-referenced. If no data product unit variations exist, then the data product unit is cross-referenced to a data characteristic variation. In other words, only the lowest level of detail is cross-referenced. Cross-referencing combined data usually serves no purpose and may confuse the understanding, while delaying the breakdown of combined data. The best approach is to break down combined data during data inventorying and cross-reference only the detail data to a common data architecture.

The cross-reference is always made to a data characteristic variation, not to a data characteristic. Each data characteristic must have at least one variation, and may have many variations, depending on the variability of the disparate data. Therefore, the cross-references must be to a data characteristic variation.

Data Product Code Cross-Reference

A *data product code cross-reference* is a cross-reference between a data product code or variation and a data reference set variation. Each data product code or variation is cross-referenced to a data reference set variation to which it belongs. The data reference set variation must contain a set of data reference items that exactly matches the set of data product codes containing the data product code or variation being cross-referenced.

Only the lowest level of detail is cross-referenced to a data reference set variation. If data product code variations are cross-referenced to a data reference set variation, then the data product code is not cross-referenced. If no data product code variations exist, then the data product code is cross-referenced to a data reference set variation.

Data Keys and Data Relations

Primary keys and foreign keys are not cross-referenced to a common data architecture. Each primary key and foreign key found in the disparate data will have an equivalent primary key or foreign key in the common data architecture. The only cross-reference is with the data product units or variations forming the primary key or foreign key.

Data relations are implied through the primary keys and foreign keys and are not directly cross-referenced to a common data architecture.

Data Cross-Reference Comments

Each data product unit or variation cross-reference and each data product code or variation cross-reference may have an associated cross-reference comment that is separate from the data definition. The comment contains any insights about the cross-reference, problems or uncertainties with the cross-reference, insights needed to finalize the cross-reference, and so on. The cross-reference comment is useful for finalizing the data cross-references before the preferred data architecture is designated.

INITIAL COMMON DATA ARCHITECTURE

A common data architecture provides the common context for data cross-referencing. All disparate data that have been inventoried and documented are cross-referenced to a common data architecture. However, an initial common data architecture needs to be established before cross-referencing can begin.

The best way to establish an initial common data architecture is to look at the business world as perceived by the organization. The *organization perception principle* and the *umwelt principle* emphasize that the organization's perception of the business world is the initial starting point for establishing an initial common data architecture.

Business objects and business events that are critical to the business or support core business functions become data subjects in the initial common data architecture. Business features and traits of those business objects and business events become data characteristics in the initial common data architecture. Formal data names are used for the data subjects and data characteristics. Initial data definitions are entered for the data subjects and data characteristics.

Overgeneralizing an initial common data architecture should be avoided. The initial common data architecture is based on the business objects and events as perceived by the organization. Generalized concepts, like Party, and so on, are not business objects or events and are not part of an initial common data architecture. Any generalizations are done during formal denormalization of a preferred data architecture. Using generic data architectures or universal data models for creating an initial common data architecture should also be avoided. They seldom represent the way an organization perceives the business world.

Data characteristic variations, data reference sets, primary keys and foreign keys, and data integrity rules are not added to an initial common data architecture. These will be added during cross-referencing or during the preferred data architecture designation. Do not attempt to create a complete data model or a desired data model for the initial data architecture—it will be a waste of time and a detriment to cross-referencing. Just get the data subjects and data characteristics in place to get started.

An initial common data architecture will be enhanced as data cross-

225

referencing continues. As the product data are cross-referenced, the initial common data architecture is enhanced to support those cross-references. Additional data subjects, data subject variations, data characteristics, data characteristic variations, data reference set variations, and data reference items are added as needed.

The best approach is to establish an initial common data architecture with major business objects and business events as data subjects, and major features and traits as data characteristics. Then move ahead with data cross-referencing to enhance the initial common data architecture and gain additional understanding about the disparate data.

SUMMARY

Data cross-referencing continues the data understanding process by connecting the inventory of disparate data to a common data architecture. The data inventory provided an initial understanding of the disparate data. Cross-referencing the data inventory to a common data architecture increases that understanding within a common context.

The base for increasing the data understanding is first to understand the disparate data with respect to the organization's perception of the business world, and second to normalize the data according to the organization's perception of the business world. The normalization is done at four levels: data characteristics within data subjects, business facts within data characteristics, data properties within data reference items, and time.

Data cross-referencing is a discovery process that is very detailed and requires considerable thought. The process itself is relatively simple. The difficulty is with really understanding the existing disparate data.

An initial common data architecture is developed based on the major business objects and events that the organization perceives in the business world. That initial common data architecture is enhanced during the data cross-referencing process. Trying to develop a complete common data architecture before cross-referencing is usually a wasted effort.

The data inventory may need to be adjusted during data cross-referencing based on increased data understanding. The common data architecture may also need to be adjusted based on increased data understanding. An adjustment of the data inventory or common data architecture may require an adjustment of the data cross-references.

The primary approach to data cross-referencing is to cross-reference data products to the common data architecture. Cross-referencing data products to other data products is a complete waste of time and resources. Cross-referencing interim common data architectures to a final common data architecture is useful in very large organizations.

Cross-references between data products and a common data architecture include data product units or variations to data characteristic variations and data product codes or variations to data reference items. No other cross-references are made between data products and a common data architecture.

Data cross-referencing provides the base for designating a preferred data architecture and developing data transformation rules. The preferred data architecture and data transformation rules will be used to develop a comparate data resource that fully supports the current and future business information demand.

QUESTIONS

The following questions are provided as a review of the process to thoroughly understand disparate data, and to stimulate thought about how to understand disparate data.

1. What is the objective of data cross-referencing?

2. How are the *organization perception principle* and the *umwelt principle* related?

3. Why is data cross-referencing done to a common data architecture?

4. Why might it be necessary to enhance the data inventory?

5. Why might the common data architecture need to be adjusted?

6. What are the four levels of data normalization achieved during data cross-referencing?

7. What are the three basic approaches to data cross-referencing?

8. What are the three cross-references between data products and the common data architecture?

9. How is a data subject thesaurus helpful for data cross-referencing?

10. How is an initial common data architecture developed?

Chapter 8

DATA CROSS-REFERENCING PROCESS

How to go about cross-referencing disparate data.

Data inventorying began the process of thoroughly understanding disparate data. An initial understanding was gained from existing sources of insight about the disparate data. That initial understanding was documented during the data inventory process. Data cross-referencing expands on that initial understanding to understanding within a common context based on an organization's perception of the business world.

Chapter 7 described the concepts and principles for cross-referencing the data inventory to a common data architecture. Chapter 8 describes the process and techniques for performing the data cross-referencing between data products and a common data architecture. The extent of disparate data variability and redundancy can be determined after the cross-referencing has been completed.

Data cross-referencing is a non-destructive process that sets the stage for designating the preferred data architecture, which is used to build a comparate data resource. An initial common data architecture is developed based on the organization's perception of the business world, and is enhanced during the cross-referencing process. The cross-referencing normalizes the basic components of disparate data within that common data architecture.

DATA CROSS-REFERENCE PREPARATION

Preparation for data cross-referencing includes defining the scope of cross-referencing, defining the sequence of cross-referencing, determining who will be involved in cross-referencing, determining how the cross-references will be documented, establishment of an initial common data architecture, maintaining common data definitions, establishing a data subject thesaurus, and establishing a list of common data name words. Each of these topics is described below.

Data Cross-Reference Scope

Setting the scope of data cross-referencing is relatively easy. Data cross-referencing cannot be performed until the disparate data have been inventoried. Therefore, the scope of the data inventory sets the scope of data cross-referencing. Within that scope, the data can be cross-referenced to a common data architecture as soon as an initial common data architecture has been established and enough understanding is available to make the cross-reference.

Data Cross-Referencing Sequence

The sequence of data inventory and data cross-referencing was described in Chapter 6. The data inventory could be completed within the defined scope followed by data cross-referencing within that scope, or data cross-referencing could be performed during the data inventory process.

The primary criterion is that data cross-referencing can be performed as soon as enough understanding has been gained to make a reasonable determination about the cross-reference. Over the years, I've found that the sequence is largely a personal preference. Some people prefer to make a cross-reference during the data inventory as soon as sufficient understanding is available. Some people prefer to complete the entire data inventory and then proceed with data cross-referencing.

Either approach is acceptable because the option always exists to make changes to the data cross-references anytime additional insight is gained. Additional insight could lead to an enhancement of the data inventory, which could lead to changes in the data cross-references. The discovery nature of data inventory and data cross-referencing is the normal operating procedure.

Data Cross-Referencing Involvement

The data inventory process included anyone who had insight about the disparate data. Many different individuals were involved in the process because the objective was to gain as much insight about disparate data as possible. Literally dozens, or even hundreds, of people could be involved in the data inventory process. However, a core team drove the data inventory process.

A core team also drives the data cross-referencing process. Few additional people are involved in the data cross-referencing process because of the detailed nature of the cross-referencing. The core team members may reach out to individuals for clarifications before making the cross-references, but the actual cross-referencing is done by relatively few people.

The results of the data cross-referencing should be readily available for anyone to review and comment. Since data cross-referencing increases understanding of the disparate data in a common context, that increased understanding must be readily available to anyone in the organization. Making the data cross-referencing readily available not only encourages comments and additional insights, but it helps people understand the impacts of disparate data and encourages them to support creation of a comparate data resource.

Data Cross-Referencing Documentation

A common data architecture provides the construct for the data cross-referencing process and for documenting the cross-references. Each organization needs to determine how and where a common data architecture will be documented based on their physical operating environment. Software products could be obtained for documenting a common data architecture and the data cross-references, but those products must have the capability of documenting a common data architecture and the data cross-references as described in the current book. Organizations should not consider acquiring a software product that does not support a common data architecture and data cross-referencing as described here.

Many organizations develop their own software for documenting the data inventory, common data architecture, and data cross-references. Although the approach requires some initial resources, the result is a product that fits well with the organization's physical operating environment and a common data architecture, and is readily available to everyone in the organization.

Initial Common Data Architecture

An initial common data architecture is developed prior to beginning the data cross-referencing process. That initial common data architecture is based on an organization's perception of the business world and only includes major business objects and events within the scope of the data inventory and data cross-referencing. An initial common data architecture is not intended to be a complete data architecture for the organization. It is intended to provide a starting point for data cross-referencing.

An initial common data architecture is continually enhanced during data cross-referencing, based on the data that are being cross-referenced. The

231

result is a common data architecture that accurately represents the disparate data and can be used to designate a preferred data architecture.

For example, if the scope of data inventory and cross-referencing is about primary education, the major business objects and events might be Student, School District, School, Grade Level, and Academic Year. These business objects and events would be documented as data subjects and an initial definition would be prepared based on the business.

Major business features for each of the business objects and events would be documented as data characteristics with initial definitions. For example, Student. Name Complete, School District. Name, School District. State Identifier, School. Name, School. State Identifier, Grade Level. Name, Academic Year. Begin Date, and Academic Year. End Date might be the major business features.

Each wave of data inventory and data cross-referencing may require an enhancement to a common data architecture for the major business objects and events within the scope of that wave. However, that enhancement is only enough to start the data cross-referencing. It's not intended to produce a complete data architecture.

For example, the next wave of data inventory and cross-referencing might include all of the classes and teachers for primary education. Initial business objects and events might be Course, Course Section, Education Program, and Educator. These would be documented as data subjects in the initial common data architecture.

Initial business features might be Course. Identifier, Course. Name, Course Section. Identifier, Education Program. Identifier, Education Program. Name, and Educator. Name Complete. These would be documented as data characteristics.

Common Data Definitions

Data definitions are crucial for making the proper cross-references. Initial data definitions are prepared for components of the initial common data architecture. The data definitions should be as comprehensive as possible, including what is and what is not included. An initial data definition is prepared for any new common data architecture components, and those data definitions are continually enhanced during data cross-referencing.

Changes to a data definition, other than enhancements and clarifications, require careful consideration. All existing cross-references should be reviewed to determine if the changed definition would alter any of those cross-references. If the changed definition requires a change in the cross-references, then those changes are made.

Data Subject Thesaurus

A *data subject thesaurus* is a list of synonyms and related business terms that help people find data subjects that support their business information needs. It's a list of business terms and alias data subject names that point to the formal data subject, as described in the last chapter.

A data subject thesaurus needs to be established before data cross-referencing begins. Each data subject name is entered into the data subject thesaurus, and any business terms or alias data subject names are listed for that data subject name.

For example, Student would be entered into the data subject thesaurus. Related terms might be Pupil, Attendee, Participant, and so on. These terms would be entered as aliases pointing to Student. Similarly, Educator would be entered into the data subject thesaurus. Related terms might be Teacher, Instructor, Trainer, and so on. These terms would be entered as aliases to Educator.

The data subject thesaurus is continually enhanced during and after the data cross-referencing process. Anytime a new data subject is considered, the data subject thesaurus should be checked to determine if that data subject already exists. If the data subject does not exist, then the new data subject can be added to a common data architecture. Checking the data subject thesaurus before creating a new data subject ensures that no data subject synonyms or homonyms are developed.

Anytime a new data subject is added to a common data architecture, an entry is made into the data subject thesaurus, including all possible aliases for that new data subject. Anytime a new alias name for a data subject is encountered, an entry is made into the data subject thesaurus. The result is a comprehensive list of alias terms and formal data subject names.

Common Words

A *common word* is a word that has consistent meaning whenever it is used in a data name. A list of common words must be established for data subjects, data characteristics, and data characteristic variations before data cross-referencing begins. Any word used in a data name that has a common meaning is documented as a common word and is used consistently throughout a common data architecture.

For example, common data subject words might be Activity, History, and Suspense, meaning transaction data, historical data, and data pending some action, respectively. Common data characteristic words might be Number, Amount, Count, and Quantity, meaning an identifying number, a monetary amount, a count of items, and a capacity or size, respectively. Common data characteristic variation words might be Estimated, Measured, Normal, Inverted, and Irregular.

Establishing and maintaining a set of common words and using them consistently for all data names within a common data architecture, ensures that the data names are readily understood and have a consistent meaning.

DATA CROSS-REFERENCES

Three data cross-references are made between data products and a common data architecture, as shown in Figure 7.2. The first is between data product sets or variations and data subjects; the second is between data product units or variations and data characteristic variations; and the third is between data product codes or variations and data reference set variations. Each of these cross-references is described below.

Data Product Set Cross-References

A *data product set cross-reference* was defined in the last chapter. It is one of the three cross-references between data products and a common data architecture that identifies a data product set or variation as representing a specific subset of a data subject.

For example, a data product set named STDT_DATA references a data file containing a subset of student data representing middle school students. The data product set scope statement describes the subset of data for middle school students. The corresponding data subject would be Student, with a data subject variation for [Middle School] Student. The data subject variation definition describes the subset of middle school student data. A cross-reference is made between STDT_DATA and [Middle School] Student.

Note that the cross-reference in no way indicates that the data file represented by the data product set contains all of the data items for a student. The cross-reference only identifies the subset of data contained in the data file.

Another example is a data product set named Contractor, which represents a data file containing data about general contractors. General contractors are considered by the organization to be a role for contractors. A data subject variation is created within the Contractor data subject for "General" Contractor. A cross-reference is made between Contractor and "General"

Contractor.

A third example is data subject variations for manifestations of a data perspective involved in aggregated data analysis. The data subject might be Timber Analytics Focus for the analysis of the growth and harvesting of timber stands. The data subject variations might be Timber Analytics 1, Timber Analytics 2, and so on. The definition would explain the manifestations. The cross-reference might be between a data product set variation representing a data set in a data hierarchy and Timber Stand Analytics 4.

A fourth example is a selection of timber stand data for data analysis. Timber stands are selected for the Douglas fir species, above 2000 feet in elevation, that originated between 1920 and 1970. The data subject variation might be [Selection 3] Timber Stand Analytics. The definition would explain the selection. The cross-reference would be between a data product set representing the aggregated data hierarchy and [Selection 3] Timber Stand Analytics.

Data Product Set Cross-Reference Criteria

The following criteria are used for enhancing a common data architecture to provide cross-references between data product sets or variations and data subject variations. A common data architecture is searched for an appropriate data subject and data subject variation. The data subject thesaurus is helpful for finding data subjects.

> When an appropriate data subject variation is found, the cross-reference is made.

> When an appropriate data subject variation is not found, a new data subject variation is created and the cross-reference is made.

> When an appropriate data subject is not found, a new data subject is created, a data subject variation is created, and the cross-reference is made.

> When a new data subject is established, entries are made into the data subject thesaurus for that data subject and any aliases to that data subject.

Data Product Set Cross-Reference Comment

Cross-reference comments can be made at the time of the cross-reference or after the cross-reference. The comment may include any insight into the validity of the cross-reference, additional insight that needs to be gained, and so on. The comment should contain the name of the person making the comment, the date of the comment, and the source of any insight leading to the comment.

Data Product Unit Cross-Reference

A *data product unit cross-reference* was defined in the last chapter. It is one of the three cross-references between data products and a common data architecture that takes the basic disparate data product units and normalizes them within a common data architecture.

Data Product Unit Cross-Reference List

A **data product unit cross-reference list** shows the data product units or variations and their respective data characteristic variation. Data product units or variations are listed on the left in the order they appear in the data file. The corresponding data characteristic variations are listed on the right. The list shows the data product units exactly as they appear in the data product, including sequence, spelling, capitalization, and punctuation.

For example, data product unit cross-references for the Water Right File are shown below.

Water Right File

   Control Number
Type Water	Water Resource Category. Code, 1 Numeric
Region	Washington Ecology Region. Number, 3 Alpha
Old New	Water Right Number Status. Code, 1 Numeric
Assigned Number	Water Right. Number, 6 Numeric
Stage	Water Right Stage. Code, 1 Alpha
Record Modifier	Water Right Record. Modifier, 2 Numeric
Reason For Modifier	Water Right Record Reason. Code, 2 Alpha

   AA Transaction
Trans Code	Water Right Transaction. Code, 1 Numeric
County	Washington County. Number, 2 Numeric
Status	Water Right Status. Code, 1 Alpha
Name	Water Right Processor. Name, Variable
Number of POD/W	Water Right Removal Site. Count, 2 Numeric
Repeat POD/W	Water Right Removal. Repeat Count, 1 Numeric
Location of POD/W	Water Right Removal. Location Detail, 42 Text
WRIA	Water Resource Inventory Area. Number, 4 alpha
Section	Water Right Section. Number, 2 Alpha
Township	Water Right Tier. Number, 3 Alpha
Range	Water Right Range. Number, 3 Alpha
E or W	Water Right Range. Direction, 1 Alpha

The cross-referencing is based on reasoning, definitions, knowledge of the disparate data, and knowledge of a common data architecture. The data product units or variations are taken one at a time and a common data architecture is searched to find an appropriate data characteristic variation.

When an apparent match is found, the data product unit or variation is reviewed to make sure it fits within the data characteristic variation definition, and the data characteristic variation definition is reviewed to make sure it encompasses the data product unit or variation. If the review results in a match, the cross-reference is made. If a match is not found, the search continues, and may result in creation of a new data characteristic variation.

Any differences in format or content results in a different data characteristic variation. The data characteristic variation name must represent that difference in format or content. The name can include the format, content, length, or any other words representing the variation of a data characteristic, as shown below.

Person. Name Complete
  Person. Name Complete, Normal 48
  Person. Name Complete, Normal 55
  Person. Name Complete, Normal 60
  Person. Name Complete, Inverted 48
  Person. Name Complete, Inverted 55
  Person. Name Complete, Irregular

Vehicle. Model Name
  Vehicle. Model Name, 50 Right
  Vehicle. Model Name, 35 Right
  Vehicle. Model Name, 28 Left

Well. Depth
  Well. Depth, Measured Laser
  Well. Depth, Measured Physical
  Well, Depth, Estimated

Data Product Unit Cross-Referencing Criteria

The following criteria are used for enhancing a common data architecture to provide appropriate cross-references between data product units or variations and data characteristic variations:

> When an appropriate data characteristic variation is found, the cross-reference is made.

> When an appropriate data characteristic variation is not found, a new data characteristic variation is established and the cross-reference is made.

> When an appropriate data characteristic is not found, a new data

characteristic is established, a new data characteristic variation is established, and the cross-reference is made. The new data characteristic must not be a synonym or homonym of an existing data characteristic. The use of common words will help identify possible synonyms and homonyms.

When an appropriate data subject is not found after searching the data subject thesaurus for a possible match, a new data subject is established, a new data characteristic is established, a new data characteristic variation is established, and the cross-reference is made. The new data subject must not be a synonym or homonym of an existing data subject.

When a new data subject is established, entries are made into the data subject thesaurus for that data subject and any aliases to that data subject.

Any new data characteristic variations, data characteristics, or data subjects must be unique to ensure a common data architecture remains stable. Entering a new component to a common data architecture without checking for an appropriate component that already exists is often tempting. However, every effort should be made to ensure that each new component is unique.

Data product unit cross-referencing may take many iterations and many reviews by knowledgeable people to determine the appropriate cross-reference. Sometimes the cross-reference is a match, but the data characteristic variation definition does not fully encompass the data product unit or variation definition. In that situation, the data characteristic variation definition is enhanced.

Similarly, the data characteristic definition and data subject definitions need to be reviewed to determine if they encompass the data characteristic variation definitions. Those definitions may need to be enhanced accordingly. The process ensures that the common data definitions are always comprehensive.

If the data product unit or variation is found to represent multiple or variable business facts, then the data inventory needs to be adjusted to break the disparate data down into basic components. Then the data cross-referencing can proceed. For example, a data product unit for a stream size actually contains the width of the stream and the depth of the stream. Those two facts need to be defined as data product unit variations in the data inventory, and each of those basic components need to be cross-referenced to appropriate data characteristic variations.

Any difference in meaning results in a different data characteristic, not in a variation of data characteristic. For example, several data product units may exist for the depth of a water well, and cross-referencing those data product units to variations of a water well depth data characteristic might seem easy. However, a review of the definitions shows that some of those depths are the total depth of the well and others are the depth to water.

Data Product Unit Cross-Reference Comment

Cross-reference comments can be made at the time the cross-reference is made or after the cross-reference. The comment may include any insight into the validity of the cross-reference, additional insight that needs to be gained, and so on. That comment may be enhanced at any time during the cross-reference process.

Cross-reference comments are typically retained rather than being deleted. For example, if a cross-reference comment were made questioning the validity of the cross-reference, and it was later determined that the cross-reference was valid, an additional statement is added that the validity was confirmed. The process provides a good audit trail of concerns about cross-references and the resolution of those concerns.

Each cross-reference comment should contain the name of the person making the comment, the date of the comment, and the source of any insight leading to the comment.

Data Product Code Cross-Reference

A *data product code cross-reference* was defined in the last chapter. It is one of the three cross-references between data products and a common data architecture that takes the basic disparate data code properties and normalizes them to a data reference set variation within a common data architecture.

Data Reference Set Variation

A data reference set variation contains a specific set of data reference items. Even though individual data product codes or variations are cross-referenced to a data reference set variation, the complete set of data product codes for a particular data product unit or variation must match the complete set of data reference items in the data reference set variation. Any difference in the data product code values, data product code name, data product code meaning, or domain of data product codes results in a different data reference set variation.

Finding the proper data reference set variation requires looking at all the candidate data reference set variations to determine if they contain an exact match to the set of data product codes or variations being cross-referenced. If an exact match is not found, a new data reference set variation is created.

If a data reference set, which is a data subject, does not exist, then a new data subject is created and defined. The definition should describe the meaning of the set of codes contained in that data subject. As with any new data subject, an entry is made in the data subject thesaurus, including any alias data subject names. Then data reference set variations are created within that data subject.

The data subject name should reflect the contents of the data in the set of data reference items, such as Management Level, Gender, Ethnicity, and so on. The data reference set variation names include qualifiers to the data subject name using the data naming taxonomy notation, such as Management Level. Personnel; or Management Level. Finance;.

Data Reference Item List

A *data reference item list* is a listing of all of the data reference items in a data reference set variation, including the data reference item codes, data reference item names, and data reference item definitions.

For example, a data subject would be defined for Management Level with a definition of the meaning of management level. A data reference set variation would be created for Management Level. Personnel 1; that contained the data reference items shown below.

E	Executive	Above pay range 16
M	Manager	Pay range 12 to 1
S	Supervisor	Pay range 9 to 1
L	Lead Worker	Pay range 6 to
W	Worker	Pay range 5 and below

Data product codes or variations from a data product unit or variation that contained that exact set of codes (code value, name, domain, and meaning) would be cross-referenced to the data reference set variation.

For example, a data product unit contains the domain of codes E, M, S, L, and W, with names and definitions as shown above, which are defined as data product codes. Each of those data product codes is cross-referenced to the Management Level. Personnel 1; data reference set variation.

Another data product unit in another data file might contain the domain of names Executive, Manager, Supervisor, Lead Worker, and Worker, as shown above, which are documented as data product codes. Each of these data product codes would be cross-referenced to the Management Level. Personnel 1; data reference set variation.

When a data product unit contains a domain of codes E, M, S, and W, where W represents any worker, those four codes are documented as data product codes. Those data product codes are then cross-referenced to a different data reference set variation due to the difference in the domain and meaning of the codes. A new data reference set variation would be created for Management Level. Personnel 2; containing the four data reference items. The data product codes would then be cross-referenced to that data reference set variation.

The question always arises about a domain of data values. For example, a data product unit contained data product codes E, M, S, L, and W, with the names and definitions as shown above. A data product unit in another data file contained the data product codes E, M, S, and L, with the same names and definitions as shown above. Are these the same set of data codes?

Each of the data product units containing those data codes needs to be reviewed to determine if the two sets of data codes are identical, but the second set didn't have a value for Workers. A data dictionary, data edits, or application programs may be reviewed to make the determination. When the two sets of data codes are identical, the data product codes can be cross-referenced to the same data reference set variation. If the two sets of data codes are in fact different, then a new data reference set variation needs to be created.

The resolution of these situations is done during the preferred data architecture designation. The data cross-referencing only determines that the specific sets of data codes are identical or are different.

When the coded data values are different, such as EX, MN, SU, LW, and WR, even though the names and definitions are the same, then the data product codes are cross-referenced to a different data reference set variation. Similarly, when the data product code names are different, such as Big Boss, Little Boss, Trainee Boss, Leader, and Worker, even though the coded data values and definitions are the same, the data product codes are cross-referenced to a different data reference set variation.

When the meaning of the data product codes is different, the data product codes belong to different data reference set variations. For example, two sets of data product codes have the same coded data values and names, as shown below.

NA	North America
SA	South America
EU	Europe
AS	Asia

These two sets of data product codes appear to be identical and might be considered to be the same data reference set variation. However, the data code definition for North America in one set of data codes includes Central America because of the ease of distribution, but in the other set of data codes the definition for South America includes Central America because of the similarity in language. Therefore, these two sets of data codes belong to different data reference set variations.

The example from Chapter 6 for a combination of gender, hair color, and eye color is shown below. The complete breakdown of two genders, five hair colors, and five eye colors results in 50 individual codes. Twenty five of these codes represent each of the genders, 10 of these codes represent each of the hair colors, and 10 of these codes represent each of the eye colors.

```
1    Male, Blond Hair, Blue Eyes
  1    Male
  1    Blond Hair
  1    Blue Eyes
2    Female, Blond Hair, Blue Eyes
  2    Female
  2    Blond Hair
  2    Blue Eyes
3    Male, Brown Hair, Blue Eyes
  3    Male
  3    Brown Hair
  3    Blue Eyes
```
And so on.

Three data reference set variations are created within their respective data subjects for Gender. 1:, Hair Color. 1;, and Eye Color. 1;. The gender data reference set variation has 25 data reference items for each of the genders, the hair color data reference set has 10 data reference items for each of the hair colors, and the eye color data reference set variation has 10 data reference items for each of the eye colors.

Data cross-references are made between the gender data product code variations and the gender data reference set, between the hair color data product code variations and the hair color data reference set variation, and between the eye color data product code variations and the eye color data reference set variation.

The process may seem a bit too detailed, but the detail will be needed to prepare the data translation rules following the preferred data architecture designations.

The example from Chapter 6 for a hierarchy of census codes is shown below. Three data reference set variations are created within their respective data subjects for Census Race. 1;, Census Race Category. 1;, and Census Race Group. 1;. Data reference items are created in Census Race. 1; for each of the individual Census Race codes. Data reference items are created in Census Race Category. 1; for each distinct range of Census Race Category codes. Data reference items are created in Census Race Group. 1; for each distinct range of Census Race Group codes. Cross-references are then made between the data product codes and their respective data reference set variations.

```
Census Race
        653             Hawaiian
        And so on.

Census Race Category
        653 – 699       Pacific Islander
        And so on.

Census Race Group
        653 – 659       Polynesian
        And so on.
```

Again, the process may seem a bit too detailed, but the detail will be needed to prepare the data translation rules following the preferred data architecture designations.

Data reference set variations and data reference items are defined independent of the format of the data values. Only the data values are important for designating data reference set variations. The format of the data values is documented with the data product unit or variation and is reflected in the corresponding data characteristic variation.

When a data reference set is created as a data subject, the initial definition describes the contents of that data reference set. Each data reference set variation definition inherits its parent data reference set variation. The data reference set variation definition describes the particular variation of the data reference set, such as a larger domain, different definitions, and so on, but it does not list all of the data reference items.

The data reference item definitions must be within the scope of the data reference set definition. Whenever data product code or variations are cross-referenced to a data reference set variation, the definitions must be reviewed to ensure that the definitions of the data product codes fit within the scope of the definition for the data reference set and data reference set variation. When a discrepancy is encountered, the data reference set definition, data reference set variation definition, or data reference item definition must be enhanced. After any enhancement, the existing cross-references must be reviewed to ensure they are valid.

Whenever definitions of data product codes don't exist, the best determination of their meaning is made and entered as the definition. If a discrepancy is found later, the appropriate changes can be made to the definitions or the data cross-references.

Whenever any combination of data product codes is found, such as super sets or subsets, multiple property data codes, and so on, return to the data inventory and break the codes down into their individual components. Then cross-reference those data product codes to the appropriate data reference set variation.

Data reference item coded values and names may appear in several data reference set variations. That situation is normal and is part of the understanding process. The reason for the different data reference set variations may be a difference in the domain of data reference items, or in the meaning of the data reference items.

Data Product Code Cross-Reference Criteria

The data product code cross-reference criteria are summarized below.

> Review the set of data product codes or variations for a data product unit or variation.

> Search data reference set variations for a matching set of data reference items.

> When a match is found, cross-reference each data product code or variation to the data reference set variation.

> When no match is found, create a new data reference set variation with a matching set of data reference items. Then cross-reference each data product code or variation to the data reference set variation

> When no matching data reference set is found, create a new data subject for that data reference set. Consult the data subject thesaurus for the existence of a possible data reference set. Make appropriate entries in the data subject thesaurus. Create a data reference set variation with a matching set of data reference items. Then cross-reference each data product code or variation to the data reference set variation.

Data Product Code Cross-Reference Comments

Cross-reference comments can be made during or after data product code cross-referencing. Generally, no cross-reference comment is needed. However, in situations where a match between a set of data product codes and a set of data reference items is questionable, cross-reference comments should be made.

Cross-reference comments are typically retained rather than being deleted. For example, if a cross-reference comment questioning the validity of the match between the set of data product codes and data reference set items were made, and it was later determined that the cross-reference was valid, an additional statement is added that the validity was confirmed. The process provides a good audit trail of concerns about cross-referencing and the resolution of those concerns.

DATA PRODUCTS

Data cross-references are performed for data files, for summary data, for aggregated data, for screens, reports, and forms, for data models, for application programs, for complex data, and for changes over time. Each of these cross-references is described below.

Data Files

Data cross-references are not made between data product sets or variations and data subjects because data files seldom represent complete and single data subjects. Data files typically have a many-to-many relationship with data subjects. The cross-referencing must be done at a more detailed level to place data items within their appropriate data subject. Data cross-references are made between data product sets or variations and data subject variations, as described above.

Data cross-references are not made between data product units or variations and data characteristics because data product units or variations represent some variation of a data characteristic. Data cross-references are made between data product units or variations and data characteristic variations, and between data product codes or variations and data reference variations as described above.

Data cross-referencing at the detailed level splits multiple subject data files in to their respective data subjects, combines multiple file data subjects into one data subject, and resolves other data variability that exists between data files and data subjects.

Splitting Data Files

A data file may be split into many data subjects. For example, a data file has both vegetation data and river data. The organization desires to split the data file into the two different data subjects for vegetation and for rivers. Two data product set variations, for vegetation and for rivers, are created during the data inventory.

The appropriate data product units are documented for each data product set variation. In other words, data items appropriate for vegetation are documented as data product units for the vegetation data product set variation, and data items appropriate for rivers are documented as data product units for the river data product set variation. Data items that are appropriate for both vegetation and rivers are documented as data product units in both data product set variations. The data product units are then cross-referenced to the data characteristic variations within the appropriate data subject for vegetation or rivers.

Combining Data Files

Multiple data files may be combined into one data subject. For example, many different data files contain employee data. The organization desires to combine all employee data into one data subject. A data product set or variation is created for each data file and the employee data items are documented as data product units or variations. The data product units or variations are then cross-referenced to data characteristic variations within the employee data subject.

Combining Data Files with Types

Multiple data files may be combined into one data subject. For example, three data files contain data for prospective students, undergraduate students, and graduate students. The organization desires to combine these data files into one data subject for student, and retain whether the student is prospective, undergraduate, or graduate. Data product sets or variations and data product units or variations are documented for each data file during data inventory.

The data product set representing the data file would be cross-referenced to a data subject variation for "Prospective" Student, which is within the data subject for Student. That cross-reference indicates that all data in that data file pertain to prospective students. The data product units or variations are then cross-referenced to appropriate data characteristic variations within the student data subject, as described above.

A Student Type. Code would be defined to indicate the type of student.

However, that definition occurs during the preferred data architecture designation, not during data cross-referencing. The data cross-referencing process only connects existing disparate data to a common data architecture. Data subjects or data characteristics are only created to cover cross-referencing.

Data Records

Data records are not cross-referenced to a common data architecture. Only the data product units or variations contained in the data records are cross-referenced to a common data architecture for understanding. The data product sets and data product set variations document the data records with respect to the physical data files. The data subject containing the data characteristic variations to which the data product units or variations are cross-referenced represents the logical data record. The process complies with the normalization of data during cross-referencing.

Data Instances

Historical data instances are not cross-referenced to the common data architecture. Only the data product units or variations contained in the historical data instances are cross-referenced to a common data architecture for understanding. However, those data product units or variations are cross-referenced to a data characteristic variation that belongs to a history data subject.

For example, the data product units in a historical data instance for students would be cross-referenced to data characteristic variations that belong to the Student History data subject. Cross-referencing historical data instances to a history data subject complies with the normalization of time during data cross-referencing. A determination can be made during the preferred data architecture designation process whether the historical data instances should remain in a separate history file or combined with the current data instances.

Data Keys

Disparate primary keys and foreign keys are not cross-referenced to a common data architecture. The possible many-to-many relation between data product sets or data product set variations and data subjects makes it impractical to try cross-referencing primary and foreign keys. Only the data product units or variations are cross-referenced to a common data architecture for understanding.

However, primary keys and foreign keys can be listed for data subjects if they are relevant. For example, a data file represents employee data and has a primary key of EMPL_ID, defined as a department assigned unique identifier of an employee. The EMPL_ID is cross-referenced to Employee. Department Identifier, Numeric 6. That primary key is documented for the Employee data subject.

A data file for department data has the department name as a primary key. That department name is relevant and is documented as a primary key in a common data architecture.

Another data file for employee data has a primary key of EMP_SSN, which is cross-referenced to Employee. Social Security Number, Character 9. That data file also has a foreign key of DPT_NM, which is cross-referenced to Department. Name Complete, Alpha 24. That primary key can also be documented for Employee. The documentation of these primary keys and foreign keys is shown below.

> Department
>
>> Primary Key: Department. Name Complete
>
> Employee
>
>> Primary Key: Employee. Department Identifier
>>
>> Primary Key: Employee. Social Security Number
>>
>> Foreign Key: Department   Department. Name Complete

Note that the documentation of primary keys and foreign keys in a common data architecture does not include the data characteristic variation. Only the fact is important for primary keys and foreign keys, not the variation of that fact.

Primary keys are not documented for data subjects when they are not relevant. For example, a data file has a combination of student data, parent or guardian data, and class data. The primary key is a system-assigned identifier. The individual data items are cross-referenced to their respective data subjects for Student, Parent/Guardian, and Class. The system-assigned identifier is not documented for Student, Parent/Guardian, or Class because it only has meaning with respect to the disparate data file.

Data Integrity Rules

Data integrity rules are not cross-referenced to a common data architecture and are not involved in the data cross-reference process. Data characteristic variations are not dependent on variations in data integrity rules, because those rules are too variable and informally defined. The data inventory process documented the data integrity rules that exist in the disparate data. Those existing data integrity rules will be pulled together during the preferred data architecture designation process and used to develop formal data integrity rules.

Data Accuracy

Data accuracy can be documented during the data inventory process and can be used to determine the data characteristic variation name. For example, the lake size in one data file is estimated from aerial photographs at a scale of 1:24,000, but is surveyed on the ground in another data file. These two data items would be cross-referenced to Lake. Size, Acres Estimated 1:24,000 and Lake. Size, Acres Surveyed, respectively.

One alternative in a common data architecture is to create companion data characteristics for the size of the lake and the accuracy of the determination. For example, Lake. Size, Acres would be the data characteristic variation for the size of the lake, and Lake Size Determination. Code would be the data characteristic variation identifying how the lake size was determined. However, the determination is made during the preferred data architecture designation, rather than during data cross-referencing. Data characteristics are only created during data cross-referencing to support cross-references.

Summary Data Cross-Referencing

Summary data in fixed hierarchies usually appear on screens, reports, or forms, although those data could be stored in databases. A data hierarchy for summary data is shown in Appendix B. Since the summary data are named according to the data set in which they appear, they are cross-referenced to data characteristic variations in the data subject representing that data set.

For example, the department data on the data hierarchy shown in Appendix B would be cross-referenced as shown below.

Department

Department Identifier	Department. Identifier, Alpha 6
Department Name	Department. Name, Alpha 24
Department Employee Count	Department. Employee Count, Numeric 2
Department Annual Budget	Department. Annual Budget, Numeric 8
Department Expense To Date	Department. Expense To Date, Numeric 8

The other data on the report would be cross-referenced in a similar manner.

When summary data are stored in a data file, they are inventoried and documented as data product sets or variations and data product units or variations. These are cross-referenced as described above. In addition, the any primary and foreign keys are documented as described above.

Aggregated Data Cross-Referencing

Aggregated data in variable hierarchies may appear on screens, reports, or forms, or they may appear in databases. A data hierarchy for aggregated student analytics data is shown in Appendix C.

Within a common data architecture, a data subject is created for the data focus, such as Student Analytics Focus. The data definition describes the data focus, such as an accumulation of analytics about students. Data characteristics are created within that data subject, such as Enrollment Count, Average Student Age, and so on. The data definitions describe the meaning of the data characteristics.

Data subject variations are defined for each manifestation of the data focus, such as Student Analytics 1, Student Analytics 2, and so on. The data definitions describe the meaning of each manifestation. Primary keys and foreign keys are documented for each data subject variation.

The example below shows a portion of the Student Analytics data from Appendix C. Student Reporting System is the data product and is not cross-referenced to a common data architecture. Student Enrollment Summary is a data product set and could be cross-referenced to a data subject variation showing any selection or subset of the student data, such as [Selection A] Student Analytics. Funding School Disability Grade and Funding School data sets within the data hierarchy are documented as data product set variations. These would be cross-referenced to corresponding data subject variations showing the parent data sets, such as Student Analytics 1 and Student Analytics 3.

Student Reporting System	No cross-reference
Student Enrollment Summary	[Selection A] Student Analytics
Funding School Disability Grade	Student Analytics 1
Enrollment Count	
Average Student Age	
Funding School	Student Analytics 3
Enrollment Count	
Average Student Age	

And so on.

The data items in each data set of the data hierarchy are cross-referenced to corresponding data characteristic variations, as shown below.

Funding School Disability Grade
    Enrollment Count   Student Analytics. Enrollment Count, Numeric 5
    Average Student Age   Student Analytics. Average Age, Numeric 5

Funding School
    Enrollment Count   Student Analytics. Enrollment Count, Numeric 5
    Average Student Age   Student Analytics. Average Age, Numeric 5

And so on.

The process may seem detailed, but that detail provides the necessary understanding for making preferred data architecture designations and transforming the disparate data.

Predictive Data

Predictive data can be operational data, summary data, or aggregated data. The uniqueness with predictive data is not with the data themselves, but with the processing that is performed on those data. In other words, predictive analysis and data mining techniques are process issues, not data issues. Therefore, the data input to a predictive analysis and the data resulting from a predictive analysis are cross-referenced as described above.

Screens – Reports – Forms

The data on screens, reports, and forms can be operational data, summary data, or predictive data. Those data are cross-referenced as described above for data files, summary, aggregated data, or predictive data. Data hierarchies can be developed for screens, reports, and forms, and used to cross-reference the data.

Screens, reports, and forms don't have any primary keys or foreign keys. They also don't have any data integrity rules typically found with data files and data models. However, they do have data derivation rules for producing any summary data, aggregated data, or predictive data. Those data derivation rules need to be documented as data integrity rules.

XML structures typically contain operational data; however, XML structures can also contain summary data, aggregated data, and predictive data. XML structures do have a structure for the data that indicates the data subject. The data in XML structures are cross-referenced as described above.

XML structures have no primary or foreign keys. However, they do have data derivation rules for producing summary data, aggregated data, or predictive data. Those data derivation rules need to be documented as data integrity rules.

Data Models

Logical and physical data models can represent operational data, summary data, aggregated data, or predictive data. Logical and physical data models are cross-referenced as described above.

Application Programs

The data in application programs are cross-referenced as described above. The data read from and written to data files by application programs are not cross-referenced, because that cross-reference would be redundant with the cross-referencing of the data files themselves. Primary keys and foreign keys don't exist in application programs. However, any data integrity rules enforced by the application program need to be documented as data integrity rules.

The data in purchased applications that are used by the organization are cross-referenced to the data subjects as perceived by the organization, not by the definition of the data files in the purchased application. The data files and data items in many purchased applications are not used by the organization as defined in the application. For example, Party may contain people contributing aid, Product may contain people receiving aid, and Sales Region may contain sites where aid is rendered. The cross-references would be made to Aid Contributors, Aid Recipients, and Aid Sites accordingly.

Complex Structured Data Cross-Referencing

Complex structured data, such as spatial data, textual data, video data, image data, and so on, are not cross-referenced, because they were documented only as data products. The specific data subjects and data characteristics are not known, and cannot be inventoried or cross-referenced. However, the breakdown of complex structured data into the component data structures can be documented and cross-referenced, as described above.

Geographic information systems contain large quantities of operational data that are documented and cross-referenced as described for data files. The geographic component that contains the coordinates for points, lines, and polygons can be documented as a data item. However, the contents of that data item cannot be readily documented.

252

Changes Over Time

Changes over time for data product units and variations are cross-referenced to corresponding data characteristic versions in the common data architecture. For example, the changes in the Vehicle Collision Comment data item from a general comment to a comment about the injuries resulting from the collision is shown below.

```
Veh_Clsn (DPS)
    CMT (DPU)
        Comment <Pre-1999> (DPUV)
        Comment <1999 – Current> (DPUV)
```

The cross-references to corresponding data characteristic variations are shown below.

Comment <Pre-1998>	Vehicle Collision. Comment, Alpha 36 <Pre-1999>
Comment <1999 – Current>	Vehicle Collision. Injuries, Alpha 36 <1999 – Current>

Changes over time for data product codes or variations are not cross-referenced to corresponding data reference items. The data product codes or variations are cross-referenced to a data reference set variation that contains the same set of data product codes or variations, including the variations over time.

For example, the changes in data product codes for an Executive are shown below.

```
E    Executive
    E    Executive < Pre-1988>
    E    Executive & Board <1989 – Current>
```

These data product code variations are cross-referenced to a data reference set variation containing exactly the same set of data reference items with the same variations.

INTERIM COMMON DATA ARCHITECTURES

Data cross-referencing can be done by cross-referencing data products to an interim common data architectures, and then cross-referencing those interim common data architectures to the final common data architecture. The process is used only in very large organizations where it's difficult to go from data products to a final common data architecture in one process. It was never intended for small segments of a small data resource, because it is too time consuming. Only one level of interim common data architectures is used, because the process is quite detailed.

Two basic approaches can be used for interim common data architectures.

Each approach is described below.

The first approach is to inventory and document the data products for a major division or a major geographical area, and cross-reference those data products to an interim common data architecture. For example, a large multi-national organization could inventory and document the data products in major world regions, such as North America, South America, Europe, Asia, and so on. Those data products would then be cross-referenced to an interim common data architecture for that world region.

When the interim data architectures are completed, they are documented as data products. The interim common data architecture becomes a data product; the data subjects, including data reference sets, become data product sets; data subject variations become data product set variations; data characteristics become data product units; data characteristic variations become data product unit variations; and data reference items become data product codes.

The cross-references are then made to the final common data architecture, as described above. The final common data architecture is enhanced as necessary to cover the cross-references. The process is completed by changing the original data cross-references between the original data products and the interim common data architecture, to data cross-references between the original data products and the final common data architecture.

The first approach is very detailed, but is useful for very large organizations with relatively distinct sets of disparate data. The process is monitored by the tactical data stewards to ensure that a correct and complete final common data architecture is developed.

The second approach is to inventory and document data products as described above for the first approach. The interim common data architectures are then merged into a final common data architecture, combining any commonalities in the interim common data architectures. The data products are then merged together. Finally, the interim data cross-references are adjusted to the final common data architecture.

The second approach may be easier than the first approach, or it may be more difficult, depending on the similarity between the initial sets of data products. If the initial sets of data products are quite different, the approach is easier. If the initial sets of data products are very similar, the approach is more difficult. The approach requires close coordination among the tactical data stewards.

A third approach that is becoming more common with larger networks is to put the entire process online. The data products are inventoried and documented in one central location, the common data architecture is documented in one central location, and all data cross-references are done at that central location. The approach is much simpler than developing interim common data architectures and then cross-referencing those interim common data architectures into a final common data architecture. However, it requires constant coordination from the tactical data stewards. A lack of close coordination could lead to the entire approach failing.

ENHANCEMENT AND ADJUSTMENTS

Enhancements need to be made to the data inventory and to a common data architecture during data cross-referencing. Adjustments also need to be made to the data inventory, to the data cross-references, and to a common data architecture during data cross-referencing. Each of these situations is described below.

These enhancements and adjustments are a natural part of the data resource integration process. The uncertainty about disparate data makes a precise, one-time pass very difficult. Additional insight is continually gained during the data resource integration process that increases understanding about the organization's perception of the business world, how they operate in that business world, and the data needed to support that operation. That additional insight results in enhancements and adjustments.

Data Inventory Enhancement

Enhancements may need to be made to the data inventory during data cross-referencing. Enhancements to the data inventory include enhancing the data definitions and adding to the data integrity rules. Any time additional insight is gained about the existing disparate data, that insight must be documented.

People frequently think that additional insight can be remembered or is obvious, and therefore doesn't need to be documented. However, over time, that memory fades and the insight is lost. That loss could lead to difficulty making an accurate data cross-reference.

Common Data Architecture Enhancement

Enhancements are continually made to the common data architecture during data cross-referencing. Enhancements include adding new components to the common data architecture as needed to support cross-references, and enhancing data definitions. Adding new components is relatively easy, because those components must be in place to perform the cross-referencing. However, enhancing the definitions is more difficult.

As with data inventory definitions, people tend to become lax at enhancing definitions for thorough understanding. The data definitions need to be continually enhanced so that they adequately cover subordinate components and the data products being cross-referenced. The process is critical for the designation of a preferred data architecture. Any confusion or uncertainty about a common data architecture will impact the designation of a preferred data architecture.

Data Inventory Adjustments

Adjustments may need to be made to the data inventory during data cross-referencing. The adjustments are usually a further breakdown of the data products to their basic components. Data product sets may need to be further broken down into basic components. Data product units may need to be further broken down into basic components. Data product codes may need to be further broken down into basic components. All of these are normal occurrences during data cross-referencing.

Occasionally, the breakdown of a data product set, data product unit, or data product code is found to be invalid. That breakdown is eliminated from the data inventory and the data cross-referencing can continue.

Occasionally, the structure of the data inventory needs to be adjusted. That adjustment is made and the data cross-referencing can continue.

Common Data Architecture Adjustments

A common data architecture may need to be adjusted based on a better understanding of the business world and how the organization operates in that business world. As an initial common data architecture grows with the data cross-referencing, organizations often have a better understanding of how their data resource could support their business. That better understanding often leads to an adjustment of a common data architecture.

One of the reasons for not going too far with an initial common data architecture is that more adjustments may need to be made. An initial common data architecture may add components that are not needed for cross-referencing, and may create components that are not properly named or defined. A better approach is to let the data cross-referencing drive enhancement of a common data architecture. The result will be fewer adjustments.

Data Name Changes

Data names in a common data architecture can be changed. Changing a data name is relatively easy, because the change doesn't directly impact the cross-references. The name is simply changed. The data definition may need to be modified to reflect the data name change.

A data subject name may need to be changed from Contractor to Vendor, because more than contractors are included. The name is changed, the definition is adjusted accordingly, and the data subject thesaurus is updated.

A data characteristic name may need to be changed from Book. Cover Illustration to Book. Cover Layout because more than the illustration was included. The definition is changed accordingly.

A data characteristic variation name may need to be changed to further qualify the variation, such as Well. Depth, Measured to Well, Depth Measured Laser because the depth could also be measured with a less accurate measuring tape. The definition is changed accordingly.

A data reference set variation name may need to be changed to enhance understanding, such as Stream Gradient Type. 1; and Stream Gradient Type. 2: to Stream Gradient Type. Canadian; and Stream Gradient Type. American;.

Data Definition Changes

Data definitions are frequently enhanced, as described above. In some situations, however, a data definition needs to be changed, either because the definition is wrong or because the scope changed. Each data definition change must be evaluated to determine if the definition change will result in a name change, or a separation or a combination of components. A separation or combination of components might result in a change to the data cross-references.

Data Subject Changes

Data subjects may be combined. For example, two data subjects are created for Caregiver and Caretaker. These data subjects represent the same thing from the organization's perception of the business world and are combined into Caregiver. The data subject thesaurus is updated accordingly.

Data subjects may be separated. For example, volunteers were included in Employee due to State reporting requirements. However, the organization decided to separate volunteers because they are managed differently and have a substantially different set of data characteristics.

Therefore, Employee and Volunteer are created. The data subject thesaurus is updated accordingly.

Data Characteristic Changes

Data characteristics may be combined. For example, Patient. Weight Clothed and Patient. Weight Unclothed are combined into Patient. Weight, because all patients at the doctor's office were weighed with their clothes on. The data definition is adjusted accordingly.

Data characteristics may be separated. For example, Patient. Height was separated into Patient. Height Shoes and Patient. Height No Shoes, because patients to a hospital could be measured either way.

Common Data Architecture Reviews

A common data architecture should be reviewed periodically to ensure that it adequately represents the organization's perception of the business world and the data needed to operate successfully in that business world. Data subjects, data characteristics, data characteristic variations, and data reference set variations should be reviewed for similarities or differences that may result in combining or splitting of data subjects.

More frequent reviews may be necessary when multiple teams are working on the same data subject area. The teams may be diverging in their perception of the business world, and may be creating a diverging common data architecture. A good data subject thesaurus, and frequent checking of that data subject thesaurus help prevent a divergent common data architecture.

A final review should be done after the data cross-referencing has been completed, before the preferred data architecture designations. Discovery of changes during preferred data architecture designations result in a delay, and possible changes to those designations.

Data Subject Thesaurus

Keeping the data subject thesaurus up to date and referring to it regularly helps prevent data subject synonyms and homonyms. Fewer synonyms and homonyms result in fewer adjustments to a common data architecture. When a data subject thesaurus is not maintained and used, a common data architecture begins to deteriorate and frequent adjustments are needed.

Data Name Vocabulary

Keeping the vocabulary of common words up to date and referring to it regularly helps prevent synonyms and homonyms. A good vocabulary ensures consistency in data names. When no vocabulary exists, synonyms and homonyms are easily created, which is less than desirable and usually results in adjustments.

Data Cross-Reference Adjustments

Any changes to data definitions, changes to data names, splitting of components, combining of components, or adjustments to the data inventory may result in an adjustment to the data cross-references. Any data cross-references to components that have adjusted need to be reviewed for validity, and adjusted if necessary.

The data cross-references should also be reviewed periodically to ensure they are still valid. The data cross-reference comments should be reviewed to determine if all concerns about the cross-references have been resolved. If the concern has been resolved, a statement is entered stating how the concern was resolved.

A final review of the data cross-reference should be made prior to designating the preferred data architecture. Data cross-references that are not valid could lead to problems developing or implementing data translation rules or data transformation rules.

DATA REDUNDANCY AND VARIABILITY

An indication of the redundancy and variability of disparate data can be determined after data cross-referencing has been completed for a segment of the disparate data resource or for the entire disparate data resource.

Data Redundancy

When data cross-referencing has been completed for a segment of the disparate data resource or the entire disparate data resource, the data redundancy can be evaluated. *Data redundancy* was defined in Chapter 4 as the unknown and unmanaged duplication of business facts in a disparate data resource. It's the same facts, for the same data occurrence, for the same time period. It's the situation where a single business fact is stored in more than one location, and the locations may not be in synch. Data redundancy is typically determined for data files only.

Data redundancy can be difficult to determine because it's not known whether data occurrences are redundant or non-redundant. For example, a student's birth date may exist in two different data files. If those two data files contain redundant data occurrences for students, then the student's birth date is redundant. However, if those two data files represent different sets of students, such as middle school and high school, the student's birth date is not redundant.

Apparent data redundancy is the apparent existence of the same business fact in multiple data files, regardless of whether those data files contain redundant data occurrences. It's the redundancy of a business fact based on the data characteristic name. *Actual data redundancy* is the existence of the same business fact in multiple data files that contain non-redundant data occurrences. It's the redundancy of a business fact based on the data characteristic name and a determination of the redundancy in data occurrences. *Data occurrence redundancy* is the existence of multiple data occurrences for the same existence of a business object or happening of a business event.

Apparent data redundancy is relatively easy to calculate. The number of data product units or variations that exist in data product sets or variations representing data files is counted for each data characteristic. In other words, for each data characteristic, determine all of the data characteristic variations. For each of those data characteristic variations, determine all of the data product units or variations that belong to data files. Add up the number of data product units or variations for a data characteristic and that's the data redundancy.

For example, a data characteristic has six variations and those variations cross-reference to 14 data product units or variations that belong to data files, the data redundancy for that data characteristic is 14. The individual data characteristic redundancies can be averaged for all the data characteristics in a data subject to provide a data redundancy for that data subject. The individual data characteristic redundancies could be averaged for all the data subjects in a segment of the data resource to determine the redundancy for that segment of the data resource. The same could be done for the entire data resource.

Actual data redundancy is more difficult to calculate because non-redundant data occurrences may exist across the data files. Using the student example above, the data in two data files for middle school students and high school students do not contain redundant data. The only way to determine the actual data redundancy is to determine the data occurrence redundancy across data files and use that redundancy to calculate the actual data redundancy. That task is not easy and is seldom performed.

Actual data redundancy is also difficult to determine because data reference sets may qualify many different data subjects. For example, a gender code data reference set may qualify students, educators, bus drivers, and so on. The gender code would appear in each of these data files. However, that gender code does not represent actual data redundancy.

Actual data redundancy is difficult to determine because historical data instances contain the same data items. For example, a student's weight may be stored in a current data instance and in three historical data instances. However, those four existences of a student's weight do not represent actual data redundancy.

Apparent data redundancy could be determined for screens, reports, and forms, even though it is typically intended for data files. The same process described above is used, with the exception that the data products would be screens, reports, or forms, rather than data files. Actual data redundancy of screens, report, and forms is very difficult to determine because of data selections and time frames. However, the process is useful for identifying screens, reports, and forms that might contain redundant data and could be considered for elimination.

Apparent data redundancy is best used as an indicator, rather than an absolute. An apparent data redundancy of 10 or higher is a critical problem. An apparent data redundancy of 3 might be manageable. Each organization needs to determine the data redundancy level that is acceptable.

Data Variability

Data item variability, as defined earlier, is the variability in the format or content of data items representing the same business fact. It's a measure of how many different formats or contents exist for a particular data item across data files, and on screens, reports, and forms.

Data item variability is relatively easy to determine after data cross-referencing has been completed. The number of data characteristic variations for a data characteristic is the data item variability. For example, if Stream Segment. Name has six variations, the data item variability is six. Data item variability can be averaged for all the data characteristics in a data subject, or for all the data characteristics in a segment of the data resource, or for the entire data resource.

Data code variability, as defined earlier, is the variability in the coded data values, names, definitions, and domain of codes in a set of data codes. It's a measure of how many variations exist for a particular set of data codes across data files.

Data code variability is relatively easy to determine after data cross-referencing has been completed. The number of data reference set variations for a data reference set is the data code variability. For example, if a data reference set for Gender has eight different data reference set variations, the data code variability is eight. Data code variability can be averaged for all the data reference sets in a segment of the data resource, or for the entire data resource.

SUMMARY

Data cross-referencing continues the process of thoroughly understanding disparate data by cross-referencing the disparate data to a common data architecture. The data cross-reference scope is driven by the scope of the data inventory. The data must be inventoried before they can be cross-referenced. The data cross-referencing may be done in concert with the data inventory, or it may be done after the data inventory has been completed. The data cross-referencing is usually done by a core team, with input from others as needed.

Data cross-referencing is documented according to a common data architecture. The documentation is stored by whatever means is appropriate for the organization. An initial common data architecture is developed and is continually enhanced during data cross-referencing. The data subject thesaurus and a set of common words used in data names are maintained throughout the data cross-referencing.

Data cross-references are made between data product sets or variations and corresponding data subject variations, between data product units or variations and corresponding data characteristic variations, and between data product codes or variations and corresponding data reference set variations. No other cross-references are made between data products and a common data architecture.

Interim common data architectures may be developed for major segments of very larger organizations. These interim common data architectures are then treated as data products and are cross-referenced to a final common data architecture. Tactical data stewards must be actively involved in the process to ensure that it is performed appropriately.

The common data architecture is continually enhanced during data cross-referencing. The data inventory may also be enhanced as additional insight is gained about disparate data. The data inventory may also need to be adjusted based on insights gained during data cross-referencing. A common data architecture should be reviewed periodically and at the conclusion of data cross-referencing. Adjustments are made so that a common data architecture accurately represents an organization's perception of the business world. Data cross-references may need to be modified based on adjustments to the data inventory and common data architecture.

Data cross-referencing provides an understanding of disparate data within the context of a common data architecture. It sets the stage for designating a preferred data architecture, which is used for data transformation. The quality of data cross-referencing, like the quality of the data inventory, determines the quality of the preferred data architecture and data transformation.

QUESTIONS

The following questions are provided as a review of the process to thoroughly understand disparate data, and to stimulate thought about how to understand disparate data.

1. How is the scope of data cross-referencing established?

2. Who should be involved in data cross-referencing?

3. How is an initial common data architecture developed?

4. How detailed should an initial common data architecture be?

5. How is a data subject thesaurus useful?

6. How are common data words useful?

7. What's the purpose of interim common data architectures?

8. Why are data product codes or variations cross-referenced to a data reference set variation?

9. What is the purpose of a data cross-reference comment?

10. How are data redundancy and data variability determined?

Chapter 9

PREFERRED DATA ARCHITECTURE CONCEPT

Defining the to-be data architecture for the organization.

The next step after data cross-referencing is to designate the preferred data architecture for the organization. Designating the preferred data architecture sets the stage to solve the third problem, data redundancy, and fourth problem, data variability. The process builds on the understanding gained through the data inventory process and the data cross-reference process.

Chapter 9 describes the concepts and principles for designating the preferred data architecture. The next chapter describes the process and techniques for designating the preferred data architecture. Chapters 11 and 12 describe how to transform the disparate data resource to a comparate data resource based on the preferred data architecture.

CONCEPTS AND PRINCIPLES

Preferred means to put before; to promote or advance to a rank or position; to like better or best; to give priority; to put or set forward for consideration. *Preferred data* are data that have the preferred names, definitions, structure, integrity rules, format, and content acceptable for data sharing.

A *preferred data architecture* is a subset of the common data architecture that contains preferred data. It's the desired data architecture that provides a pattern for designing a comparate data resource and for transforming a disparate data resource to a comparate data resource.

The term *preferred* is used rather than *official* or *standard* because use of the preferred data architecture is a choice. The preferred data architecture does not have to be used, but anyone not using the preferred data architecture bears the responsibility for problems arising from not using it.

I settled on the term *preferred* after working with a university regarding their Help Desk problem. The Help Desk provided support for software products throughout the university. However, the variety of software products being purchased were more than the Help Desk staff could learn. The Help Desk produced a standard set of software products that could be purchased and that they would support.

Complaints about the standard were prolific and blunt—you can't tell me what software to buy with my grant money. A faculty senate committee asked if I'd help find a solution. After considerable discussion with all parties, we settled on a list of preferred software products that would be supported by the Help Desk. Preferred software products were defined as those prominently used throughout the university. Anyone could certainly use non-preferred software products, but could not expect routine support from the Help Desk. However, they could contract with the Help Desk for support of non-preferred software products.

The new approach worked great—nothing standard or official—just a list of preferred software products that would be routinely supported by the Help Desk, and the option to contract for additional non-preferred support.

The *preferred data architecture concept* is that the redundancy and variability of disparate data will be resolved through the designation of a preferred data architecture and the transformation of disparate data to comparate data according to that preferred data architecture. The data redundancy and variability may not be eliminated, but will be reduced to a known and manageable level. Formal documentation of the preferred data architecture allows people to readily understand and share common data to meet the business information demand.

The preferred data architecture is how the organization chooses to build and maintain their data resource. It's a preferred subset of their common data architecture that represents the most desirable to-be data architecture for the comparate data resource. It's the data architecture that works best for understanding and sharing common data.

The *preferred data architecture objective* is to designate the preferred representation of all data at the organization's disposal so those data can be readily understood and shared within and without the organization. The objective is to take a common data architecture that was enhanced to cover the data cross-references and designate preferred components that will become a pattern or template for designing and building a comparate data resource and transforming disparate data to comparate data.

The *preferred data designation process* is the process of designating and finalizing preferred data names, data definitions, data integrity rules, primary and foreign keys, data characteristic variations, data reference set variations, and data sources. Data translation rules between data characteristic variations and data reference items are based on the preferred data designations. It's a process that produces maximum benefit with minimal effort.

The preferred data designations are made within the context of a common data architecture after data inventorying and cross-referencing have been completed. The designations cannot be made during data inventorying or cross-referencing because the complete picture of disparate data is not known. The complete picture of disparate data is only available after data inventorying and cross-referencing have been completed.

Principles

Several principles apply to designating a preferred data architecture, including the preferred data designation principle, data understanding, enhancements and adjustments, a deterministic – prescriptive – prospective architecture, a resultant data architecture, and redundancy and variability resolution. Each of these principles is described below.

Preferred Data Designation Principle

The *preferred data designation principle* states that all preferred designations that comprise the preferred data architecture will be made within a common data architecture, after data cross-referencing has been completed, according to the organization's perception of the business world, by knowledgeable detail data stewards.

Data Understanding

The understanding of disparate data began with the data inventory, and increased through cross-referencing the inventoried data to a common data architecture. The understanding does not end with data cross-referencing. It continues through designation of a preferred data architecture, and even through data transformation to a comparate data resource.

The thorough understanding of both disparate data and comparate data is never completed. Additional understanding is continually gained through additional insights about existing disparate data, or about how the organization perceives the business world where they operate. Additional understanding is also gained as the business world changes and the organization changes in response to those changes.

During one class I as teaching, I was describing how to understand

267

disparate data and make the preferred data designations. One attendee summarized my explanation as preferred data designations were the most reasonable way the organization structures their data resource to meet their business information demand. Then that reasonable structure could be screwed up any way necessary to meet external reporting requirements. My response was, *In a nutshell, yes.*

Enhancements and Adjustments

Enhancements may be made to a common data architecture during designation of the preferred data architecture. New components may be added that were not identified through data inventory and cross-referencing, but are needed to support business operations. Enhancements may be made to the data definitions as additional insight is gained.

Adjustments may be made to a common data architecture during designation of the preferred data architecture. The increased understanding of the existing data may result in the organization having a different perception of the business world and the data they need to operate in that business world. A common data architecture would be adjusted accordingly. Adjustments can also be made to a common data architecture after the preferred data designations have been made to remove components that are not relevant.

Enhancements to the data inventory may be made based on insights gained during designation of the preferred data architecture. These enhancements usually included enhanced definitions so that people better understand the existing data. Enhancements could include inventorying additional data that were not known at the time of the data inventory.

Adjustments may also be made to the data inventory based on insights gained. These adjustments may be a further breakdown of combined data components, or a different breakdown of combined data components.

Adjustments may be made to the data cross-references based on adjustments to a common data architecture, adjustments to the data inventory, or a better understanding of the data cross-reference. Designation of the preferred data architecture often provides a better understanding of the existing disparate data, resulting in an adjustment to the data cross-references.

Adjustments may need to be made to the preferred data designations, as additional insight is gained through the preferred logical and preferred physical data designation processes. Adjustments may be made to any of the components of the logical or physical preferred data architectures, or to the data translation rules. Adjustments may also be made after the comparate data resource has been implemented, based on changing business needs.

Deterministic – Prescriptive – Prospective

Designating a preferred data architecture is deterministic because it formally designates the preferred data architecture by a set of principles and techniques. It provides a future data architecture for the organization's data that is different from the probabilistic data architecture of the disparate data resource.

Designating a preferred data architecture is prescriptive because it provides a direction for development of a comparate data resource. It prescribes the future to-be data architecture for the organization's comparate data resource that is different from describing the existing disparate data resource.

Designating a preferred data architecture is prospective because it looks ahead to what the organization needs to properly build and maintain a comparate data resource. It provides a to-be data architecture for the comparate data resource that is different from the as-is data architecture of the disparate data resource.

Resultant Data Architecture

The preferred data architecture is a result of the data inventory and cross-referencing processes. It is developed within the context of a common data architecture based on the understanding gained through data inventory and data cross-referencing, rather than independent of those processes. It may be considered a by-product of data inventorying and data cross-referencing, but that term sometimes implies waste material from a process. Also, additional effort is needed to make the preferred designations. The preferred data architecture does not happen automatically. Therefore, a resultant data architecture is the proper term.

Redundancy and Variability Resolution

Data redundancy is the third basic problem with disparate data and data variability is the fourth basic problem. Designating the preferred data architecture does not resolve these problems the way data inventory resolved the first basic problem and data cross-referencing resolved the second basic problem. However, designating the preferred data architecture sets the stage for resolving the third problem by designating preferred data sources, and the fourth problem by designating preferred data variations. Data resource transformation resolves those problems.

DATA ARCHITECTURES

Data architectures include the disparate data architecture, enterprise data architecture, preferred logical data architecture, preferred physical data architecture, and the comparate data resource. Each of these topics is described below.

Disparate Data Architecture

The existing disparate data does have an architecture, although that architecture is very disjointed and inconsistent, and is not readily visible. Most disparate data were developed in a probabilistic manner that was seldom planned or coordinated across the organization. The data inventory and cross-referencing processes documented that disparate data architecture, which becomes the as-is data architecture.

Enterprise Data Architecture

Enterprise data architecture is not clearly defined, has multiple definitions, and has been misused and abused to the point of being meaningless. It has become part of the lexical challenge and is not used during data resource integration. A similar situation exists with *enterprise data model. Enterprise architecture* and *enterprise data model* are an unqualified term and are not used in data resource integration.

An enterprise data architecture is usually developed independent of the existing disparate data. It's seldom done at the variation level, which prevents adequate cross-referencing. It provides little or no understanding if the existing disparate data, which makes any formal transformation from disparate data to comparate very difficult.

Even if an enterprise data architecture was complete and perfect, and accurately represented the organization's perception of the business world, which it usually doesn't, it's very difficult, if not impossible, to integrate disparate data according to an enterprise data architecture. Although it may be prospective, it is not based on a retrospective understanding of the existing disparate data. It provides little functionality for formal data transformation. The effort is often wasted, and frequently results in more disparate data through development of new databases.

If an enterprise data architecture has already been developed, it should be reviewed to determine if it was developed with formal data names, has comprehensive data definitions, used a formal data subject thesaurus, and used common data name words.

If an enterprise data architecture has the formality, then it is reviewed to determine how well it represents the organization's perception of the business world. If the representation is strong, then it could be used as an initial common data architecture for cross-referencing. However, the risk is that unnecessary components may be added to the initial common data architecture.

If an enterprise data architecture does not have the formality and does not represent the organization's perception of the business world, it should be discarded. If it appears to have some value, then it could be documented as a data product and cross-referenced to a common data architecture.

Generic data architectures and universal data models are often treated as enterprise data architectures. Most are not formal data architectures with formal data names, comprehensive data definitions, proper data structures, and precise data integrity rules. Most do not represent all of the organization's data or the organization's perception of the business world. None of them provides any understanding of the existing disparate data.

At best, generic data architectures and universal data models should be documented as data products and cross-referenced to a common data architecture. The data cross-referencing will prove or disprove their worth.

Preferred Logical Data Architecture

The *preferred logical data architecture* is the common, desired, to-be logical data architecture for the organization. It's a subset of a common data architecture developed from a thorough understanding gained through data inventorying and cross-referencing. It's developed through a formal process that normalizes the data based on the organization's perception of the business world.

The preferred logical data architecture covers all data, not just the data in databases. It's developed prospectively within a common data architecture according to the organization's perception of the business world, based on a retrospective understanding of the existing disparate data. It's a result of data inventorying and cross-referencing that avoids all the perceptions and misperceptions of an enterprise data architecture. It's not developed independently.

A preferred logical data architecture consists of preferred data characteristic variations, preferred data reference set variations, preferred data definitions, preferred primary keys and foreign keys, preferred data integrity rules, preferred data sources, and preferred data transformation rules. The preferred data names were established and maintained through the data cross-referencing process.

The preferred logical data architecture is a minimal effort approach to understanding and resolving disparate data. It leads to informed decisions about data resource integration, and sets the stage for developing the preferred physical data architecture, which will be used for data transformation.

The preferred logical data architecture is documented within a common data architecture by placing a preferred indicator on the appropriate data characteristic variations, data reference set variations, and primary and foreign keys.

Preferred Physical Data Architecture

The *preferred physical data architecture* is the common, desired, to-be, physical data architecture for the organization. It's developed from a formal denormalization of the logical preferred data architecture. It's the pattern or template for building the comparate data resource.

The preferred physical data architecture covers only the data stored in databases. It sets the stage for transforming disparate physical data to comparate physical data. Data names are abbreviated according to formal data name word abbreviations and a data name abbreviation algorithm. Data definitions and data integrity rules are adjusted to support the data denormalization. Primary keys and foreign keys are adjusted for physical implementation.

The preferred physical data architecture may include generalizations that the organization does not perceive in the business world, such as a legal entity. However, those generalizations must not be viewable by the business. The business should input data and acquire data based on specific data views of the generalized data entity. The data views show the data as the organization perceives the business world. Data integrity rules are placed on the data views, rather than on the generalized data entity.

The preferred physical data architecture is documented as a data product with a designation of preferred. No cross-references are made to a common data architecture, because the link can be made through the formal data names and their formal abbreviations.

Comparate Data Resource

The comparate data resource is developed according to the preferred physical data architecture. It is logically integrated within a common data architecture, but is physically deployed as necessary to be readily accessible. It supports the think globally – act locally principle.

PREFERRED DATA DESIGNATIONS

Preferred data designations are made for data names, data definitions, data characteristic variations, data reference set variations, data keys, and data sources, data occurrences and instances, data integrity rules, and multiple preferred designations. Each of these designations is described below.

A *preferred data designation* is a data variation that has been accepted by the consensus of knowledgeable people as being preferred for data sharing and development of a comparate data resource. A *non-preferred data designation* is a data variation that has not been accepted as preferred.

General guidelines can be established for making consistent preferred data designations. For example, dates will always be in a CYMD format, measurement units will all be metric, addresses will always be maintained at the individual component level, and so on. These guidelines help the data stewards make informed decisions about the preferred data designations.

The general approach is to look at the existing data resource within the context of a common data architecture and make preferred designations based on the guidelines and what is reasonable for the organization. The frequency of existence and frequency of use may be a consideration in making the preferred designations, but are not a primary criteria. Consistency and the desires of the organization are the primary concern.

Preferred data designations are identified with a preferred designation indicator. In situations where multiple preferred designations are made due to cultural, geographical, or political differences, a qualifier is added to the preferred designation indicator. Acceptable data designations are identified with an acceptable designation indicator. Obsolete data designations are identified with an obsolete designation indicator.

Preferred Data Names

A *preferred logical data name* is the data name developed according to the data naming taxonomy and approved by the business as the preferred name for the data. The preferred logical data names are the data names developed for an initial common data architecture and for enhancements to that common data architecture. They should have been developed using a data subject thesaurus and a set of data name common words.

A *preferred physical data name* is the data name developed from the

273

preferred logical data name during formal data denormalization according to a set of data name word abbreviations and a formal data name abbreviation algorithm.

Preferred Data Definitions

Data definitions were documented and enhanced through the data inventory and cross-referencing processes. These data definitions are an aggregate of existing definitions and insight gained during data inventory and cross-referencing. They need to be reviewed and finalized into preferred data definitions.

A *preferred data definition* is a comprehensive and denotative data definition developed from all of the insights documented during data inventory and cross-referencing that fully explains the data with respect to the business. That data definition may still be enhanced based on additional insights, but it is finalized with respect to pulling all current insights together into a comprehensive data definition.

Preferred data definitions are prepared for data subjects, data characteristics, data characteristic variations, data reference set variations, and data reference items. The general approach is to start with the data subject definitions, then proceed to data characteristic and data characteristic variation definitions. Then data reference set variation definitions are reviewed, followed by data reference items.

Data subject definitions are based on the organization's perception of the business world. Data characteristic definitions build on the definition of their parent data subject. The data subject definition is not repeated in each data characteristic, but the data characteristic definition must support the data subject definition. The same is true for data characteristic variations. It builds on the data characteristic definition by describing the specific variation in format or content.

Data reference set variation definitions also build on their parent data subject definition by describing the variation in the data reference items contained in the data reference set. The data reference item definitions describe the data property represented by the data item.

Preferred Data Characteristic Variation

Designation of preferred data characteristic variations apply to all data, not just the data in databases. The splitting and combining of data items was done during the data inventory process. No splitting or combining needs to be done within a common data architecture.

A *preferred data characteristic variation* is a data characteristic variation within a data characteristic that has been designated as the one preferred for data sharing and development of a comparate data resource.

A *non-preferred data characteristic variation* is a data characteristic variation within a data characteristic that has not been designated as preferred. A non-preferred data characteristic variation may be either acceptable or obsolete.

An *acceptable data characteristic variation* is any data characteristic variation that is not preferred, but is acceptable to use for an interim period until appropriate changes can be made to databases or application programs. However, its use should not be perpetuated.

An acceptable data characteristic variation may be designated until more insight is gained to make a preferred designation. However, a preferred data characteristic variation must be designated before data transformation can proceed.

An *obsolete data characteristic variation* is any data characteristic variation that is obsolete and can no longer be used. Ideally, all data characteristic variations, except the preferred, will become obsolete. However, that goal may not be achieved for many years, although substantial progress toward that goal can be made.

Preferred Data Reference Set Variation

Designation of data reference set variations apply to all data, not just the data in databases. The splitting and combining of data properties was done during the data inventory process. The splitting of a set of data codes was also done during the data inventory process. The combining of partial sets of data codes needs to be done during preferred data designations. If an appropriate data reference set variation does not exist for a combined set of data codes, one needs to be created.

A *preferred data reference set variation* is a data reference set variation within a data subject that has been designated as preferred for data sharing and development of a comparate data resource.

A *non-preferred data reference set variation* is a data reference set variation within a data subject that has not been designated as preferred. A non-preferred data characteristic variation may be either acceptable or obsolete.

An *acceptable data reference set variation* is any data reference set variation that is not preferred, but is acceptable to use for an interim period until appropriate changes can be made to databases or application programs. However, its use should not be perpetuated.

An acceptable data reference set variation may be designated until more insight is gained to make a preferred designation. However, a preferred data reference set variation must be designated before data transformation can proceed.

An *obsolete data reference set variation* is any data reference set variation that is obsolete and can no longer be used. Ideally, all data reference set variations, except the preferred, will become obsolete. However, that goal may not be achieved for many years, although substantial progress toward that goal can be made.

The preferred data reference set variation only shows the values for the data reference item code, name, and definition. The format for those values is defined by the preferred data characteristic variations. Each data reference set, defined as a data subject, has a preferred data characteristic variation for the coded data value, the name, and the data definition. Those preferred data characteristic variations designate the preferred format for the data reference item.

Preferred Data Keys

The disparate primary and foreign keys are reviewed during preferred data architecture designation and used to designate preferred primary and foreign keys. Designation of preferred primary keys and foreign keys applies only to the data in databases and data models. A check needs to be made to ensure that all appropriate primary and foreign keys from the data inventory have been documented in a common data architecture. Some disparate data primary keys that represent data from multiple data subjects are not appropriate and should not be documented in a common data architecture.

Preferred Primary Keys

Disparate data often contain more than one primary key for a data subject. These disparate primary keys are identified and documented during data inventory and cross-referencing. A disparate primary key may have meaning only for the data product set or variation in which it appears, and is not placed in a common data architecture. The disparate primary keys are reviewed and given a designation based on their validity and range of usefulness.

The *preferred primary key principle* states that each data subject in a common data architecture will have one and only one preferred primary key designated that uniquely identifies all data occurrences within that data subject in the organization's common data architecture.

A *candidate primary key* is a primary key that has been identified and considered as a primary key, but has not been verified. It has been documented during the data inventory and placed in a common data architecture, but has not been reviewed for its validity or range of uniqueness. All primary keys that originate from the data inventory are candidate primary keys.

A *preferred primary key* is a primary key that has been designated as preferred for use in a comparate data resource. It uniquely identifies all data occurrences in a data subject within a common data architecture for the organization and has been designated as preferred for data sharing and development of a comparate data resource. Only one preferred primary key is designated for each data subject.

An *alternate primary key* is a primary key that is valid and acceptable, but is not the preferred primary key. It uniquely identifies all data occurrences in a data subject within a common data architecture for the organization, but has not been designated as the preferred primary key. Multiple alternate primary keys may be designated for each data subject.

A *limited primary key* is a primary key that is available for all data occurrences, but has a limited range of uniqueness for data occurrences. For example, a primary key may uniquely identify vehicles within a state, but not across states. The limited range of uniqueness is specified as a comment for the primary key. A limited primary key is not perpetuated in the comparate data resource.

An *obsolete primary key* is a primary key that has no further use and should not be used. It no longer uniquely identifies each data occurrence in a data subject within a common data architecture for the organization, contains data characteristics that are not necessary for unique identification, or is not appropriate for some reason.

Preferred, alternate, limited, and obsolete primary keys may be either business keys or a non-business keys. A *business key* is a primary key consisting of a fact or facts whose values have meaning to the business. A business key is sometimes referred to as an *intelligent key*, however that term is not used because a primary key cannot possess intelligence. Generally, a business key is used for data normalization.

A *non-business key* is a primary key consisting of a fact or facts whose values have no meaning to the business. A non-business key is sometimes referred to as a *non-intelligent key*; however, that term is not used because a primary key cannot possess intelligence.

A *physical key* is a preferred or alternate primary key that may or may not be meaningful to the business, but is useful for physical navigation in the database. One of the primary or alternate, business or non-business keys is designated as the physical key during denormalization of the logical preferred data architecture to the preferred physical data architecture. That primary key becomes the physical key in the comparate data resource.

Preferred Foreign Keys

Disparate data often has more than one foreign key to the same parent data subject, whether explicitly stated or implied. These disparate foreign keys are identified and documented during data inventory and cross-referencing. When the primary keys have been designated, the disparate foreign keys are reviewed and given a designation based on the designation of primary keys.

The *preferred foreign key principle* states that each subordinate data subject in a common data architecture will have one and only one preferred foreign key designated that uniquely identifies the parent data occurrence in a parent data subject.

A *candidate foreign key* is a foreign key that has been documented during the data inventory and placed in a common data architecture, but has not been reviewed and given a specific designation. All foreign keys that originate from the data inventory are candidate foreign keys.

A *preferred foreign key* is a foreign key that matches the preferred primary key in a parent data subject. Only one preferred foreign key is designated for each parent data subject.

An *alternate foreign key* is a foreign key that matches an alternate primary key in a parent data subject. A *limited foreign key* is a foreign key that matches a limited primary key in a parent data subject. An *obsolete foreign key* is a foreign key that matches an obsolete primary key in a parent data subject.

Preferred Data Relations

Data relations are based on foreign keys, and only apply to databases and data models. General cardinalities can be documented for the data relation, but specific cardinalities are documented as data integrity rules. Data relation names are documented with the data relation. However, those data relation names should add meaning to the data relation, such as supplies, provides, purchases, and so on. Statements like is one of, has many, belongs to, and so on, add no meaning and are not appropriate data relation names.

Preferred Data Sources

Disparate data are very redundant with the same business fact being stored in a variety of different data files in different databases. The reasons for the data redundancy were described in Chapter 5 and in *Data Resource Simplexity*. An indication of the extent of data redundancy can be determined after data inventorying and cross-referencing, as described in Chapter 7. That data redundancy must be resolved before developing a comparate data resource.

The fact that data redundancy exists in a disparate data resource means that a specific location needs to be designated for obtaining each business fact. Therefore, the resolution of data redundancy begins with the designation of preferred data sources.

A *preferred data source* is the data product unit or variation within a data product set or variation representing a data file that will be the source for a business fact. It's the location where an individual business fact can be obtained that is the most current and most accurate. It's the location for the highest quality data that is sometimes referred to as the best-of-breed data.

The preferred data source is at a business fact level, not at a data occurrence or data file level. Combined business facts were broken down during data inventory and were cross-referenced to a common data architecture. The preferred data sourcing will be done at the business fact level.

Traditional data integration emphasizes a single system of reference, database of reference, or record of reference. Virtually no traditional data integration approaches emphasize the sourcing of data from a variety of different sources in a disparate data resource. The traditional approach is too simplistic because a single system, database, or record seldom has the highest quality data—the most current and most accurate data. The most current and most accurate data are often scattered across a variety of systems, databases, and records.

One traditional approach to data sourcing is the big behemoth approach where the biggest or the most prominent database becomes the preferred data source. However, size and frequency of use does not necessarily mean the most current or most accurate data. The best approach is to inventory a big behemoth as a data product, make cross-references to a common data architecture, and then determine if it is truly the preferred source for data.

The reality of disparate data is that the best sources of data are scattered throughout the disparate data resource. No one single location has the best data for a comparate data architecture. Identifying single sources of data will likely lead to lower quality data. The only reasonable approach to obtain the highest quality data possible is conditional data sourcing.

Conditional data sourcing is the process of selecting preferred data from a variety of different locations based on which location has the most current and most accurate data. It is done at a business fact level based on the data inventory and cross-referencing. Conditional data sourcing is sometimes referred to as *selective data sourcing*. Other appropriate terms would be *preferred source of value* or *preferred source of quality*.

Conditional data sourcing is based on the most current and most accurate data. It is not based on the format or content of the data. The format and content can be easily translated during data transformation and is not a concern in designating preferred data sources.

Conditional data sourcing is done at the data characteristic level, because data characteristics represent business facts. All of the data product units or variations for all the data characteristic variations within a data characteristic are identified. These data product units or variations are reviewed to determine which is most current and most accurate, regardless of their format or content.

The location that is the most current and most accurate is designated as the preferred source for that business fact. The situation frequently arises, even at the business fact level, that the most current and most accurate data come from different locations based on time or other conditions. The preferred sources are documented accordingly.

Conditional data sourcing may result in different sources for business facts within a data subject, and for different sources for a specific business fact. Both of the differences in data sourcing must be documented in a common data architecture. They will be used during data transformation to acquire the most current and most accurate data.

Preferred data sources are documented as data source rules. A ***data source rule*** specifies the preferred source from which a particular business fact is obtained and the conditions that determine the preferred source. The data source rule is stored with the data characteristic and applies to all data characteristic variations for that data characteristic.

An ***unconditional data source rule*** is a data source rule that specifies only one location as the preferred data source. A ***conditional data source rule*** is a data source rule that specifies multiple locations as the preferred data source and the conditions for selecting one of those locations.

Data source rules specify the preferred source for data, and the data characteristic variation specifies the format and content for each source. The data translation rules will change any non-preferred data characteristic variation to a preferred data characteristic variation.

The set of preferred data sources, as specified by the data source rules, becomes the *source of reference* for data transformation and development of a comparate data resource.

Preferred Data Occurrences

Redundant physical data occurrences frequently appear in a disparate data resource. ***Redundant physical data occurrences*** is the situation where the same logical data occurrence exists multiple times in different data files in a disparate data resource. Data product sets or variations may contain a complete set of redundant logical data occurrences, or may contain a combination of redundant and non-redundant logical data occurrences. The degree of physical data occurrence redundancy in a disparate data resource is a major problem that needs to be identified and resolved.

Data inventorying and cross-referencing to a common data architecture provided complete logical data occurrences for a data subject with respect to the business facts contained in the data occurrences. However, it did not identify redundant physical data occurrences in the disparate data resource.

A ***data integration key*** is a set of data characteristics that could identify possible redundant physical data occurrences in a disparate data resource. It's not a primary key because it does not uniquely identify each data occurrence. It's not a foreign key because no corresponding primary key exists. It's only used to identify possible redundant physical data occurrences in a disparate data resource.

A data occurrence may not include all of the data characteristics in a data integration key. However, it's a *fuzzy* indication of possible redundant data occurrence. It identifies the most likely redundant data occurrences. People ultimately need to make the final decision by verifying true redundancy and false positive matches.

The disparate primary keys, data product set or variation definitions, data cross-references, sets of data items, and integration key are used to integrate redundant physical data occurrences into one set of logical data occurrences within a common data architecture.

The same situation exists with historical data instances. ***Redundant*** *historical data instances* is the situation where redundant physical data occurrences may have corresponding physical historical data instances. Those physical historical data instances are probably not redundant within their parent physical data occurrence. However, they could be redundant across physical data occurrences in a disparate data resource.

Preferred Data Integrity Rules

Disparate data integrity rules were identified and documented during the data inventory process, including the data edits performed by database management systems and application programs. Those data integrity rules were listed with their respective data product set or data product unit, but were not cross-referenced to a common data architecture. During the preferred data designation process, those disparate data integrity rules are brought over to a common data architecture, reviewed, and finalized into preferred data integrity rules.

A *preferred data integrity rule* is a data integrity rule that has either been confirmed or created to ensure the integrity of a common data architecture. A *candidate data integrity rule* is a data integrity rule that was documented during the data inventory and brought over to a common data architecture. Note that each of the types of data integrity rules could be qualified with *candidate* or *preferred* for clarification.

Data integrity rules only apply to data subjects and data characteristics. All disparate data integrity rules for data product sets or variations are aggregated to their corresponding data subject. The corresponding data subject is identified by navigating through the data product units or variations within the data product sets or variations, to the corresponding data characteristic variation, to the parent data characteristic, to the parent data subject.

Similarly, all disparate data integrity rules for data product units or variations are aggregated to their corresponding data characteristic. The corresponding data characteristic is identified by navigating from the data product unit or variation, to the corresponding data characteristic variation, to the parent data characteristic.

These aggregated data integrity rules become the candidate data integrity rules that are reviewed and adjusted as necessary to ensure the integrity of preferred data. Generally, very few disparate data integrity rules are documented and aggregated to a common data architecture. Most preferred data integrity rules need to be created. The preferred data integrity rules may need to be adjusted throughout data transformation.

The preferred data integrity rules are documented with the appropriate data subject or data characteristic. The *data integrity rule normalization principle* states that data integrity rules are normalized to the data resource component that they represent or on which they take action. The data integrity rules are named accordingly. The data integrity rules are then documented with the data subject or data characteristic by which they are named. Sometimes, the specification of preferred data integrity rules results in movement from the component containing the candidate data integrity rule to another component that the preferred data integrity rule represents.

Multiple Preferred Data Designations

Multiple preferred data designations may need to be made based on differences in culture, geography, or politics. For example, a multi-national organization faces a difference in languages, social customs, monetary units, addresses, names, and so on. These differences need appropriate preferred data designations.

Multiple preferred data designations are not made for small segments of an organization that just want to have their own set of preferred data. For example, one department wants a preferred variation for a student's birth date in the normal sequence and another department wants a preferred variation for a student's birth date in the inverted sequence. The organization needs to come to a consensus for one preferred variation.

Multiple preferred data designations is the situation where multiple data characteristic variations or multiple data reference set variations are designated as preferred due to culture, geography, or politics. When multiple preferred data designations are made, a qualifier is added to the designation indicating the conditions for which each preferred designation is used.

Multiple preferred data designations pertain to the data values, not to the data architecture. For example, multiple preferred data characteristic variations could be designated for a course description in English, German, and French. Multiple preferred data reference set variations could be designated for management levels in different regions of the world.

The entire common data architecture could be in a different language, including the data inventory, data cross-referencing, and preferred data architecture. A *common data architecture variation* is a language variation in a common data architecture. The same common data architecture exists in a different language. A common data architecture variation is different from multiple preferred data designations. Multiple preferred data designations can exist across common data architecture variations.

Preferred Data Templates

Preferred data variations can be used to develop preferred data templates. A *preferred data template* is a subset of the preferred logical data architecture for a specific subject area that promotes data sharing within or between organizations, and helps organizations develop applications and databases using preferred data. The template is prepared from the logical data architecture so that organizations can implement that logical data architecture in their particular physical operating environment.

These preferred data templates are readily available to any organization that wants to either share data in the preferred form or maintain their data in the preferred form. Preferred data templates are very beneficial in the public sector for sharing data across many different organizations. They result in savings on original development, savings on edge matching data between jurisdictions, and savings on sharing data. They are a good way to prevent data disparity, improve data quality, and effectively use limited resources.

Preferred data templates are an excellent example of how data standards should be presented, and how data registries should be managed. When standards are prepared from preferred data, and registries document preferred data, the data disparity can be substantially reduced. Organizations using the preferred data templates from data standards and data registries can readily share data.

DATA TRANSLATIONS

When the preferred data designations have been made, data translation rules can be prepared between the preferred data and the non-preferred. The *data translation principle* states that data translation rules are prepared between preferred data designations and non-preferred data designations to assist in the transformation between disparate data to comparate data. Data translation rules are prepared both ways between the preferred data and the non-preferred data. Data translation rules may be prepared between non-preferred data, but only when necessary.

Data Translation Rules

A *data translation rule* is a data rule that defines the translation of a data value from one unit to another unit. It represents the translation of the values of a single fact to different units, and is not considered to be a data derivation rule. It's an algorithm for translating data values between preferred and non-preferred data designations, or between different non-preferred data designations, when necessary. It only specifies translations in format or content between data variations. It cannot specify a translation in meaning.

A *preferred data translation rule* is a data translation rule between a preferred data designation and a non-preferred data designation. Preferred data translation rules are routinely prepared to assist data transformation.

A *non-preferred data translation rule* is a data translation rule between different non-preferred data designations. Non-preferred data translation rules are very time consuming and are not often used. Therefore, they are only prepared when needed and are used on an interim basis.

A *forward data translation rule* is a data value translation rule from a non-preferred data designation to a preferred data designation. A *reverse data translation rule* is a data translation rule from a preferred data designation to a non-preferred data designation. Both forward and reverse data translation rules are prepared between preferred and non-preferred data designations. Forward and reverse data translation rules between different non-preferred data designations are created only when necessary.

A *fundamental data translation rule* is a basic data translation rule that can be applied to many specific data translations. The data translation rule is specified once and can be inherited for many specific data translations. For example, fundamental data translation rules can be prepared for changes in measurement units or dates.

A *specific data translation rule* is a data translation rule that applies directly to the data translations. It may inherit a fundamental data translation rule, or it may specify a unique data translation rule. For example, the translation between Street Segment. Length, Feet to Street Segment. Length, Meters can inherit a fundamental data translation rule for feet to meters.

The data sharing vision emphasizes that data are shared in their preferred form, and that the contributing organization or receiving organization that does not maintain data in the preferred designation is responsible for translation. The sharing of common data translation rules assists the data sharing process.

Data Translation Approaches

Data translation can be performed three different ways: common to

285

physical data translations, physical to physical data translations, and common to common data translations. Each of these approaches is described below.

Common-to-physical data translations are data translations between a common data architecture and the disparate data documented as data products. Specifically, data translations are prepared between the preferred data characteristic variations and data product units or variations, or between the data reference items in a data reference set variation and the data product codes or variations. The problem with preparing common-to-physical data translations is that a translation needs to be prepared for each physical manifestation of the data in the disparate data resource, resulting in a tremendous effort.

Physical-to-physical data translations are data translations between the disparate data documented as data products and the compare data resource. Specifically data translations are prepared between data product units or variations and the preferred physical variation in the comparate data resource, or between data codes or variations documented as data products and corresponding preferred codes in the comparate data resource. The problem with physical-to-physical data translations is that data translation rules need to be prepared for each physical manifestation of the data in the disparate data resource, resulting in a tremendous effort.

Common- to-common data translations are data translations between the preferred and non-preferred data designations within a common data architecture, and applied as needed to physical data translation. The common-to-common approach specifies the minimum set of data translations that can be applied to physical data translations, as needed. The approach is much more efficient and is the recommended approach.

Data Characteristic Translations

A *data characteristic translation rule* is a data translation rule that translates data values between non-preferred and preferred variations of a data characteristic. Each data characteristic translation rule has a source data characteristic variation, a translation algorithm, and a target data characteristic variation. Since data translation rules are prepared both ways between preferred and non-preferred data characteristic variations, two data characteristic translation rules are routinely prepared. Others may be prepared between non-preferred data characteristic variations as needed.

Data characteristic translation rules for irregular data characteristic variations can often be difficult. For example, a person's name in any format could require an extensive algorithm, or may need human intervention to interpret the irregularity and translate it to a specific format. Translating data from a specific format to an irregular form is not possible. Since the format is irregular, the best approach is to use the specific format as the irregular format.

Data translation rules may be coded into one or more programming languages and made available to organizations involved in data sharing. Sharing common translation routines saves resources and promotes data sharing.

Data Reference Item Translations

A *data reference item translation rule* is a data translation rule that translates coded data values and names between data reference items in preferred and non-preferred data reference set variations within a data subject. The rule translates only the data values, not the format of those data values. The preferred data characteristic variation identifies the format for the data values.

Since data translation rules are prepared both ways between data items in preferred and non-preferred data reference set variations, two data reference item translation rules are routinely prepared. Others may be prepared between data items in different non-preferred data reference set variations as needed. Like data characteristic variations, the translation rules may be coded in several programming languages and made available to organizations involved in data sharing.

Data reference item translations can be more difficult than data characteristic variation translations, because of the relationship between data properties and data reference items.

A *one-to-one data reference item translation rule* translates the coded data value and/or the name from one data reference item in the source to one data reference item in the target. These translations are very routine.

A *many-to-one data reference item translation rule* translates the coded data value and/or the name from many different data reference items in the source to one data reference item in the target. These translations are very routine.

A *one-to-many data reference item translation rule* translates one coded data value and/or name from the source to many data reference items in the target. These translations are difficult and require additional input to make the split from one source value to many target values.

SUMMARY

Preferred data can be designated after data inventorying and cross-referencing have been completed for a major segment of the data resource or for the entire data resource. The preferred data designations set the stage for transforming the disparate data to a comparate data resource. They bring all of the understanding accumulated through data inventorying and cross-referencing together to make the preferred designations.

The data designation process is deterministic, prescriptive, and prospective. The preferred data designations identify the preferred logical data architecture. That preferred logical data architecture is formally denormalized to a preferred physical data architecture, which becomes the template for the comparate data resource.

Preferred data characteristic variations, data reference set variations, primary keys, and foreign keys are designated based on precise criteria. Preferred data sources are designated, including conditional data sources. Comprehensive data definitions are finalized, and precise data integrity rules are developed. Multiple preferred designations can be made based on cultural, geographical, or political differences.

Redundant data occurrences and data instances are identified for consolidation. Data translation rules for common to common data translations are prepared for data characteristic variations and the data items in data reference set variations. Those data translation rules are used as necessary to translate between the disparate data and comparate data.

Designating preferred data ends the process of identifying, documenting, and understanding disparate data. The next step is to begin transforming the disparate data to a comparate data resource, and eliminating the disparate data.

QUESTIONS

The following questions are provided as a review of preferred data designations and translation schemes, and to stimulate thought about defining the preferred data architecture for an organization

1. What is the preferred data designation principle?

2. What is the difference between a preferred logical data architecture and a preferred physical data architecture?

3. Why is the preferred data architecture considered a resultant data architecture?

4. Why is the traditional enterprise data architecture not developed?

5. Why might multiple preferred data designations be made?

6. What types of preferred data designations are made?

7. What's the purpose of the preferred physical data architecture?

8. What's the purpose of preferred data templates?

9. What are data translation rules?

10. Why are data translation rules done from common variations to common variations?

Chapter 10

PREFERRED DATA ARCHITECTURE PROCESS

How to define the to-be data architecture.

Chapter 9 described the concepts and principles for designating the preferred data architecture. Designating the preferred data architecture sets the stage for solving the third problem, data redundancy, and fourth problem, data variability. The process builds on the understanding gained through the data inventory process and the data cross-reference process.

Chapter 10 describes the techniques for designating the preferred logical data architecture by making all of the preferred data designations within a common data architecture. The preferred physical data architecture is developed based on the preferred logical data architecture and the organization's operating environment. The techniques for developing data translation rules between data characteristic variations, and between data reference items in data reference set variations are described. These techniques are based on the concepts and principles presented in the last chapter.

PREFERRED DATA DESIGNATION PREPARATION

Preparation for making preferred data designations includes the scope of preferred data designations, the sequence of preferred data designations, the involvement in making preferred data designations, and adjustments to a common data architecture. Each of these topics is described below.

Scope

The scope for preferred data designations is the same as for data inventorying and data cross-referencing. However, all disparate data within the scope must have been included in data inventorying and data cross-referencing. If preferred data designations are made and another segment of disparate data is found within that scope, the preferred data designations could change based on insights gained from the additional disparate data.

Therefore, the scope must be with respect to subject areas within a common data architecture, not with respect to the disparate data resource. For example, all stream data, or all public works data, or all student data must be included in the data inventorying and data cross-referencing processes. Selecting a segment of the disparate data for data inventorying and data cross-referencing may not include all of the disparate data for a subject area. A check should be made to ensure that all disparate data within a specific subject area are included in the process so that the preferred data designations will be correct and will not need to be changed.

Sequence

The preferred data architecture is designated after data cross-referencing has been completed for the entire disparate data resource, or for a major subject area of the disparate data resource. Preferred data designations cannot be made before data cross-referencing is completed, because all of the insights for preferred data designations may not be available. Preferred data designations could be made that would need to be changed based on additional insights.

Developing and enhancing an initial common data architecture should not be confused with predetermining data designations. A common data architecture is based on the organization's perception of the business world. However, establishing an initial common data architecture according to an organization's perception of the business world is not predetermining any preferred data designations.

For example, an organization could decide to put all contractors in one data subject, with a contractor type designation showing plumbers, electricians, fabricators, general contractors, and so on. The data cross-references would be made accordingly. The process establishes a desired common data architecture, but does not establish preferred data designations.

Preferred data designations are not made in any particular sequence. However, the preferred data designations must be made before the data translations rules can be prepared, because the preferred data designations must be known to develop the data translation rules between the preferred and non-preferred data designations.

The general approach for preferred data designations is to work from preferred data names, through preferred data definitions, preferred data characteristic variations, preferred data reference set variations, preferred primary and foreign keys, preferred data sources, preferred data occurrences and instances, and preferred data integrity rules. The data characteristic variation translation schemes and the data reference item translation schemes are designated after the preferred data designations.

Involvement

Designating the preferred data architecture is done by the core team with input from the detail data stewards. The data steward's knowledge of the organization's perception of the business world where the organization operates, and their knowledge of the data needed to support business operations, help them designate the preferred data architecture. The core team and detail data stewards may reach out to others in the organization for insights or clarification about the preferred data architecture.

The people involved in designating the preferred data architecture must be knowledgeable about the organization's perception of the business world, the data the organization needs to operate in that business world, and data normalization and denormalization. Business professionals should be included to verify the data needed to support their business activities. Two good approaches are to use business cases and reporting requirements to verify the data needed and the preferred designations for those data.

Common Data Architecture Adjustment

A common data architecture may need to be adjusted during the preferred data designation process and after the preferred data process has been completed. Adjustments during the preferred data designation process could include adding data characteristic variations or data reference set variations when existing ones are not acceptable for a preferred data designation. Adjustments could include grouping or splitting data subjects based on changes in the organization's perception of the business world resulting from additional insights gained.

Adjustments could include deletions of data subjects or data characteristics that are no longer relevant. Deletions usually result when an enterprise data architecture is prepared ahead of time and used as an initial common data architecture, but components of that enterprise data architecture have no data cross-references. Deletions may be removal from a common data architecture, with proper entries into a data subject thesaurus, or may be leaving the components in a common data architecture with a notation that they are obsolete.

When a common data architecture is adjusted, data cross-references may need to adjusted accordingly, and data inventorying may even need to be adjusted. The discovery nature of understanding and resolving disparate data requires moving forward and backward through all the processes until the desired result is achieved.

PREFERRED DATA DESIGNATIONS

Making preferred data designations includes designating preferred data names, data definitions, data characteristic variations, data reference set variations, data subjects, data keys, data sources, data occurrences and instances, data integrity rules, and multiple preferred data designations. Each of these preferred designations is described below.

Preferred Data Names

The data names within a common data architecture are likely to be correct when the data naming taxonomy, a data subject thesaurus, and a list of data name common words are used. However, when these techniques are not used, the common data architecture names may not be correct.

The data subject and data characteristic names should be reviewed to determine if they were formed properly and if they represent the data according to how the organization perceives the business world. Any changes to the data names should be made before proceeding with making preferred data designations. The data subject thesaurus and the list of common data name words should also be enhanced if necessary.

Preferred Data Definitions

Developing preferred data definitions can be a challenging task. The traditional approach is to create a short data definition that provides little meaning with respect to the business, which is often a tautology. The data definitions must be comprehensive, denotative, and business oriented, as described in Chapter 3 and *Data Resource Simplexity*.

The general approach is to pull all of the data definitions accumulated during the data inventory process through the data cross-references to a common data architecture. Data product set definitions are pulled over to the corresponding data subjects, and data product unit definitions are pulled over to the corresponding data characteristic variations.

The set of definitions for each data subject is reviewed and a comprehensive data definition is prepared for that data subject. Data characteristic definitions and data reference set variations can be reviewed to provide insight into a data subject definition. Business professionals can be involved to ensure the data subject definition is complete and correct with respect to the business.

The set of definitions for all of the data characteristic variations within a data characteristic is reviewed and a comprehensive data definition is prepared for the data characteristic. The data subject definitions can help focus the data characteristic definitions, since the data characteristics qualify a data subject. Business professionals should also be involved to ensure that the data characteristic definition is complete and correct with respect to the business.

When the preferred data definitions have been developed and accepted by the business professionals, the data product definitions that were pulled over through the cross-references do not need to remain in a common data architecture. They can be removed from the common data definitions, but are still maintained with the data products to help people understand the existing disparate data.

In some situations, a comprehensive data definition cannot be developed because business professionals disagree. When disagreement occurs, the definition should be expanded until agreement is achieved. If agreement cannot be achieved with an expanded definition, the data subject or data characteristic likely represents two or more components that need to be separated, or separate components that need to be combined.

Try combining or subdividing data subjects or data characteristics to see if consensus can be gained. When consensus is gained by combining or subdividing, the data cross-references may need to be adjusted accordingly, and the data inventory may even need to be adjusted. Those adjustments are part of the discovery process.

Developing preferred data designations is an excellent opportunity to develop fundamental data definitions and inherit those fundamental data definitions. The development and use of fundamental data definitions is described in Chapter 3 and in *Data Resource Simplexity*.

Preferred Data Characteristic Variations

The set of data characteristic variations for each data characteristic is reviewed to determine which variation is most appropriate for the business as the preferred data characteristic variation. General guidelines can be prepared for designating preferred data characteristic variations, such as all dates will be in the CYMD format, all measurement units will be metric, people's names in the normal sequence, monetary units in US Dollars, and so on.

The criteria for designating a preferred data characteristic variation are listed below.

When only one data characteristic variation exists within a data characteristic and it is appropriate for the business, it is designated as the preferred data characteristic variation.

When multiple data characteristic variations exist within a data characteristic and one is appropriate for the business, it is designated as the preferred data characteristic variation.

When multiple data characteristic variations exist within a data characteristic and several are appropriate for the business, the most reasonable one is designated as the preferred data characteristic variation.

When none of the existing data characteristic variations within a data characteristic is appropriate for the business, a new data characteristic variation is created that is appropriate for the business and is designated as the preferred data characteristic variation.

All other data characteristic variations become non-preferred data characteristic variations. The non-preferred data characteristic variations are designated as acceptable or obsolete.

Data Characteristic Variation List

A *data characteristic variation list* is a list of all the data characteristic variations within a data characteristic. The list is useful for reviewing all of the data characteristic variations and designating the preferred data characteristic variation.

For example, the employee birth date variations listed below were identified during data cross-referencing. The general guidelines state the CYMD format is the preferred variation for date, and that variation is designated as preferred. The designation is made with an asterisk after the name.

```
Employee. Birth Date
    Employee. Birth Date, YMD
    Employee. Birth Date, MDY
    Employee. Birth Date, M/D/Y
    Employee. Birth Date, CYMD *
```

Well depth data characteristic variations are listed below. The general guidelines state that metric units are the preferred variation for measurements, but that variation does not exist. A new data characteristic variation is defined for meters and is designated as the preferred data characteristic variation, as shown below.

Well. Depth
    Well. Depth, Inches
    Well. Depth, Yards
    Well. Depth, Feet
    Well. Depth, Meters *

The well location data characteristic variations are listed below. A review of these variations shows that a preferred data characteristic variation cannot be designated due to the wide range in accuracy and the difficulty of developing data translation schemes. Therefore, no data characteristic variation is designated as preferred, and a companion data characteristic is established to show the format of the well location. Note that the companion data characteristic could be a data reference set with data reference items for the different formats and accuracies of the well location.

Well. Location
    Well. Location, PLS 40 Acres
    Well. Location, Lat/Lon 5 Degrees
    Well. Location, SPC 50 Feet
    Well. Location, Lat/Lon 1 Degree

Well. Location
    Well Location. Format

Data Product Unit Cross-Reference List

A *data product unit cross-reference list* is a list of the data product units or variations and their corresponding data characteristic variations. The list could be useful for understanding the source of the variation and determining the preferred variation.

For example, the data product cross-reference list for equipment identification is s below. On closer inspection, the first data product unit is actually the serial number of the equipment, while the latter two data product units are identifiers assigned by the organization.

EQP: EQUIP_ID	Equipment. Identification Number, Char 16
EQUIP: EQUIP_ID_NUM	Equipment. Identification Number, Num 8
EQ: EQUIPMENT_NUM	Equipment. Identification Number, Char 5

The data cross-references were adjusted as shown below, and two preferred data characteristic variations were designated.

EQP: EQUIP_ID	Equipment. Serial Number, Char 16 *
EQUIP: EQUIP_ID_NUM	Equipment. Identification Number, Num 8
EQ: EQUIPMENT_NUM	Equipment. Identification Number, Char 5 *

The data product unit cross-reference list below shows the building values that were thought to be the same values. However, on closer inspection the values were actually different.

FAC: BLDG_VAL	Building. Current Value, Dollars 6
BLDG BLD_VAL	Building. Current Value, Thousands 4
BLD: STRCT_VAL	Building. Current Value, Dollars 8

The data cross-references were adjusted as shown below, data characteristic variations were added, and preferred designations were made.

FAC: BLDG_VAL	Building. Current Value, Dollars 6
	Building. Current Value, Dollars 8 *
BLDG BLD_VAL	Building. Original Value, Thousands 4
	Building. Original Value, Dollars 8 *
BLD: STRCT_VAL	Building. Replacement Cost, Dollars 8 *

The reverse situation could also exist. The data product unit cross-references below show cross-references from a truck data file and an auto data file. On closer inspection, these are all vehicles and should be cross-referenced accordingly.

TRK_FLE	
ACQ_DT	Truck. Acquisition Date, YMD
MFG	Truck. Manufacturer Name Complete, 16
MDL_NM	Truck. Style Name Complete, 12
AUTO_FLE	
DT_PCH	Auto. Purchase Date, MDY
M_NM	Auto. Manufacturer Name Complete, 14
STYL	Auto. Style Name Complete, 14

The data cross-references are adjusted to vehicle data characteristic variations as shown below. Data characteristic variations were added to support the general guidelines, and the preferred data characteristic variations were designated.

TRK_FLE	
ACQ_DT	Vehicle. Acquisition Date, YMD
	Vehicle. Acquisition Date, CYMD *
MFG	Vehicle. Manufacturer Name Complete, 16 *
MDL_NM	Vehicle. Style Name Complete, 12 *
AUTO_FLE	
DT_PCH	Vehicle. Purchase Date, YMD
M_NM	Vehicle. Manufacturer Name Complete, 12
STYL	Vehicle. Style Name Complete, 8

Designating preferred data characteristic variations for irregular data is often difficult. The best approach is to designate a preferred data characteristic variation and then try to make the appropriate data characteristic variation translation. For example, existing employee names may be irregular, but the organization desires to have the complete name in the normal sequence. The addition of a preferred data characteristic variation is shown below.

EMP: EMPL_NM   Employee. Name, Irregular 18
                                Employee. Name Complete, Normal 20 *

These examples show how data product unit cross-reference lists can be used to evaluate the data characteristic variations, make adjustments, and designate the preferred data characteristic variations.

Preferred Data Characteristic Name

The formal data name of a preferred data characteristic in the preferred logical data architecture does not carry the variation name. The appearance of a data characteristic in the preferred logical data architecture means that the preferred data characteristic variation is used. That specific variation does not need to be designated in the data characteristic name.

Using the variation name in the preferred logical data architecture makes the name longer than necessary. Using a variation name of Preferred also makes the name longer than necessary, and does not indicate the actual preferred format or content. Therefore, the data characteristic name in the preferred logical data architecture means the preferred data characteristic variation.

The preferred format and content of the data characteristics are stated in the data characteristic definition, as shown below.

The employee's name is in the normal sequence.

The well depth is in meters.

The format of the data characteristics is also described in the data integrity rules where appropriate, as shown below.

Employee. Name, Domain! 5 <= Character <= 20

Well. Depth, Domain! 1 <= Integer <= 5

Preferred Data Reference Set Variations

Making preferred data reference set variations is more difficult than making preferred data characteristic variation definitions, because of the variability in the data reference item code, name, and domain of values. The set of data reference set variations for each data subject is reviewed to determine which variation is the most appropriate for the business as the preferred data reference set variation. The codes, names, definitions, and domain of values are all reviewed to make that determination.

The criteria for designating a preferred data reference set variation are listed below.

When only one data reference set variation exists within a data subject and it is appropriate for the business, it is designated as the preferred data reference set variation.

When multiple data reference set variations exist within a data subject and one is appropriate for the business, it is designated as the preferred data reference set variation.

When multiple data reference set variations exist within a data characteristic and several are appropriate for the business, the most reasonable one is designated as the preferred data reference set variation.

When none of the existing data reference set variations within a data subject are appropriate for the business, a new data reference set variation is created that has the desired data reference items, and is designated as the preferred data reference set variations.

All other data reference set variations become non-preferred data reference set variations. The non-preferred data reference set variations are designated as acceptable or obsolete.

Data Reference Item List

A *data reference item list* is a listing of all the data reference items in a data reference set variation, including the data reference item codes, data reference item names, and data reference item definitions. For example, a data reference set variation for disability is shown below.

Disability. Set 1;

S	Sight	A person with sight impairment.
H	Hearing	A person with hearing impairment.
P	Physical	A person with physical impairment.
D	Development	A person with developmental impairment.

Note that the format for data reference item coded values, names, and definitions is not a concern for designating a preferred data reference set variation. Only the values of the code and name, and the meaning of the data reference item are important for making a preferred designation. The format is determined by the data characteristic representing the code, name, and definition.

A preferred data reference set variation is designated with an asterisk after the name, in the same way as a preferred data characteristic variation. For example, the data reference set variation shown below is the one that exists in the disparate data and is appropriate for the business. Therefore, it is designated as the preferred data reference set variation.

Stream Gradient. Set 1; *

1	Flat	Less than 4.99 percent gradient.
2	Slight	5 to 9.99 percent gradient.
3	Moderate	10 to 19.00 percent gradient.
4	Steep	20 to 39.99 percent gradient.
5	Extreme	40 percent or steeper gradient.

A *data reference item matrix* is a matrix of all of the data reference items, for all of the data reference set variations, for a single data subject, including the coded data values, data reference item names, and data reference item definitions. It identifies the variability between disparate data reference set variations for the same data subject.

For example, four data reference set variations for disability are shown below. The names and the codes are different. The definitions were left off of the example due to space, but would normally be included.

Disability. School:	Disability. Employment;	Disability. Health;
10 Sight	A Seeing	V Vision
20 Hearing	H Hear	S Sound
30 Physical	P Physical	A Accidental
40 Develop	D Developed	G Genetic

None of these data reference set variations meet the criteria for a preferred data reference set variation. Therefore, a new data reference set variation is developed with the preferred codes, names, and definitions, and is designated as the preferred data reference set variation.

Disability.

School;	Employment;	Health;	New; *
10 Sight	A Seeing	V Vision	S Sight
20 Hearing	H Hear	S Sound	H Hearing
30 Physical	P Physical	A Accidental	P Physical
40 Develop	D Developed	G Genetic	D Developmental

The data reference items in the above examples represent the same domain of data properties. However, that is not always the case. Different data reference set variations may represent a different domain of data properties within the same data subject.

For example, two disparate data reference sets were found for small vehicle horsepower and large vehicle horsepower, as shown below.

301

Vehicle Horsepower. Small;

Below 100	A	Below 100 Horsepower
100-199	B	100-199 Horsepower
200-349	C	200-349 Horsepower
350-499	D	350-499 Horsepower

Vehicle Horsepower. Large;

500-749	1	500-749 HP
750-999	2	750-999 HP
1000-1499	3	1000-1499 HP
1500+	4	1500+ HP

The two data reference sets represent different domains of data properties for vehicle horsepower and need to be combined into one data reference set. The new preferred data reference set is shown below with the two disparate data reference sets. The combined disparate data reference set variations are shown on the left, and the preferred coded data values and definitions are shown on the right.

Vehicle Horsepower. New; *

Below 100	A	1	Below 100 Horsepower
100-199	B	2	100-199 Horsepower
200-349	C	3	200-349 Horsepower
350-499	D	4	350-499 Horsepower
500-749	1	5	500-749 Horsepower
750-999	2	6	750-999 Horsepower
1000-1499	3	7	1000-1499 Horsepower
1500+	4	8	Above 1500 Horsepower

A similar situation exists with management level data reference items. Two disparate data reference sets of management level data reference items are shown below. Neither the codes nor the names match, and no definitions were provided.

Management Level. Personnel;

OP	Owner / Partner
EX	Executive
MN	Manager
SP	Supervisor
LW	Lead Worker

Management Level. Finance;

041	Senior Manager
163	Line Manager
239	Unit Manager
157	Team Manager
445	Team Member

A new data reference set was defined to include all of the management-level data reference items, as shown below. The new data reference item names and coded data values are shown, along the corresponding disparate coded data values.

Management Level. New; *

Owner	01	OP	
Senior Executive	02	EX	041
Line Manager	03	MN	163
Unit Supervisor	04	SP	239
Lead Member	05	LW	157
Team Member	06		445

Existing data reference set variations may be too detailed for the business. The data reference items may need to be combined to better represent the business. For example, current ecological regions are show below.

Ecological Region. Wildlife;

1	Northeast
2	East Central
3	Southeast
4	Southern Midwest
5	Central Midwest
6	Northern Midwest
7	Southwest
8	Northwest

These eight detailed ecological regions need to be combined into three general ecological regions, as shown below. A new data reference set variation is created and designated as preferred.

Ecological Region. Wildlife;		Ecological Region. New *	
1	Northeast	E	East
2	East Central	E	East
3	Southeast	E	East
4	Southern Midwest	M	Midwest
5	Central Midwest	M	Midwest
6	Northern Midwest	M	Midwest
7	Southwest	W	West
8	Northwest	W	West

Preferred Data Reference Set Name

The formal data name of a preferred data reference set variation is the data subject name without any variation name, the same as a preferred data characteristic variation. The appearance of a data reference set in the preferred logical data architecture means that the preferred data reference set variation is used. That specific variation does not need to be designated in the name.

The preferred format of the coded data value, data reference item name, and data reference item definition are defined in their corresponding preferred data characteristic variations. For example, a data subject that represents a data reference set for Animal Species has a preferred data characteristic variation for Animal Species. Code, for Animal Species. Name, and for Animal Species. Definition. Those preferred data characteristic variations define the format and integrity rules for the data reference items in the preferred data reference set variation.

Preferred Data Subjects

Data subjects are designated as preferred when they contain a preferred data reference set variation, or one or more preferred data characteristic variations. Other data subjects become non-preferred. The situation occurs when an enterprise data architecture is developed independent of the existing disparate data and used as an initial common data architecture. After data cross-referencing, some of the data subjects do not have a preferred data reference set or preferred data characteristic variations, and remain non-preferred.

The non-preferred data subjects may remain in a common data architecture, but a note should be added to the data definition that it is non-preferred. An entry should also be made in the data subject thesaurus with the data subject name referring to a preferred data subject. Alternatively, the non-preferred data subject may be removed from a common data architecture.

Preferred Data Keys

Primary keys are important for uniquely identifying each data occurrence in a data subject, and for navigating the data resource. Disparate data have many different primary keys for the same data subject, different ranges of uniqueness, and unnecessary data characteristics not required for uniqueness. Understanding these disparate primary keys and designating preferred primary keys is often a challenging task.

A *primary key list* is list of the primary keys for a data subject that exists in the disparate data. Only the data characteristic is listed for each primary key, not the data characteristic variation. Designating preferred primary keys is not dependent on the format or content of the data. It's only dependent on the value of the primary key. The content and format will be translated to the preferred data characteristic variation during data transformation.

The example below shows the primary keys that have been identified for vehicle data in a disparate data resource. The data characteristics are listed for each primary key.

```
Vehicle
    Primary Key:
        Vehicle. Identification Number

    Primary Key:
        State. Code, ANSI
        Vehicle. License Number

    Primary Key:
        Vehicle. License Number

    Primary Key:
        Vehicle. License Number
        Vehicle. Model Name
```

The **primary key range of uniqueness** is the range of data occurrences for which the primary key provides a unique identification. The primary keys in disparate data may have different ranges of uniqueness that must be identified before a preferred primary key can be designated.

For example, the primary keys identified for a vehicle are shown below with a statement of their range of uniqueness. The range of uniqueness is placed after the Primary Key label. Unnecessary data characteristics are also indicated to provide insight into designating a preferred primary key.

```
Vehicle
    Primary Key: Unique for all vehicles manufactured.
        Vehicle. Identification Number

    Primary Key: Unique for vehicles in the United States.
        State. Code, ANSI
        Vehicle. License Number

    Primary Key: Unique for vehicles in a state in the United States.
        Vehicle. License Number

    Primary Key: Unique for vehicles in a state in the United States.
        Vehicle. License Number
        Vehicle. Model Name – Unnecessary data
```

A **primary key matrix** is a matrix of the primary keys that shows all of the disparate primary keys for a data subject and across related data subjects. The matrix is helpful for evaluating disparate primary keys, designating a preferred primary key, and combining data occurrences and data instances.

The primary key matrix is useful for identifying commonality across related data subjects in the public sector where data sharing is common. Public sector organizations need to share data to operate effectively and

305

efficiently, and primary keys can be used for that data sharing.

For example, a primary key matrix is shown below for drivers, employees, inmates, welfare recipients, and businesses in a state. The corresponding primary key lists can be used to identify range of uniqueness, unnecessary data characteristics, and other primary keys that could be useful for data sharing.

	Driver	Employee	Inmate	Welfare	Business
Social Security Number		X			X
Business Identifier					X
Driver's License Number	X				
State Identifier			X		
Fingerprint Identifier			X		
Person Name Complete	X	X		X	
Person Birth Date	X	X		X	

A primary key matrix could be prepared for all data subjects in the organization's data resource, or within the scope of data integration. The matrix is not particularly useful for operational data, because the matrix would be relatively sparse. However, the matrix is very useful for aggregated data in variable hierarchies to identify the primary keys for each data set in those variable hierarchies.

Preferred Primary Key

All of the primary keys in a data subject are reviewed to determine the preferred primary key. The criteria for designating primary keys are listed below.

Each primary key identified in the disparate data becomes a candidate primary key for a data subject.

Each candidate primary key in a data subject is reviewed to determine its range of uniqueness for identifying each data occurrence in a data subject and any unnecessary data characteristics.

When a candidate primary key is unique within the scope of the organization's business, it remains a candidate primary key.

When a candidate primary key does not uniquely identify each data occurrence within the scope of the organization's business, it is designated as an obsolete primary key.

When a candidate primary key has limited uniqueness within the scope of the organization's business, it is designated as a limited primary key and the range of uniqueness is noted.

When a candidate primary key is meaningful within the scope of the organization's business, it is designated as the preferred business primary key. Any remaining candidate primary keys meaningful for the business are designated as alternate business primary keys.

When a candidate primary key is not meaningful within the scope of the organization's business, but is useful for database management, it is designated as the preferred physical primary key. Any remaining candidate primary keys that are not meaningful for the business, but are useful for database management, are designated alternate physical primary keys.

When no candidate primary keys exist for a data subject, a new primary key that is meaningful within the scope of the organization's business is created and designated as the preferred business primary key.

When no candidate primary keys exist for a data subject, a new primary key that is meaningful within the scope of the organization's business for database management is created and designated as the preferred physical primary key.

No candidate primary keys are deleted from a common data architecture, even though they are obsolete. They are retained to show that they had been identified and determined to be obsolete.

Using the vehicle example above, all four primary keys become candidate primary keys. The first primary key becomes preferred because it uniquely identifies all vehicles manufactured. The second primary key is an alternate in the United States because it is readily identifiable and is used in nationwide law enforcement systems. The third primary key is an alternate because it could be useful within a specific state. The fourth primary key is obsolete because it contains unnecessary data characteristics.

```
Vehicle
    Primary Key: Unique for all vehicles manufactured.
                Preferred
        Vehicle. Identification Number

    Primary Key:  Unique for vehicles in the United States.
                Alternate
        State. Code, ANSI
        Vehicle. License Number

    Primary Key:  Unique for vehicles in a state in the United States.
                Alternate
        Vehicle. License Number
```

Primary Key: Unique for vehicles in a state in the United States.
     Obsolete
  Vehicle. License Number
  Vehicle. Model Name – Unnecessary data

Both business and physical primary keys can be designated. Business primary keys are used for data normalization and physical primary keys are used in database management systems. Each has a specific purpose and needs to be identified.

For example, the primary keys identified for employees are shown below. The first is preferred and is a business primary key. The second is an alternate and is a business primary key. The third is preferred and is a physical primary key.

Employee

Primary Key: Unique for all employees in organization.
     Preferred. Business.
     Employee. Social Security Number

Primary Key: Unique for all employees in organization.
     Alternate. Business
     Employee. Organization Identifier

Primary Key: Unique for all employees in organization.
     Preferred. Physical.
     Employee. System Identifier

Data Integration Key

Primary keys are used to uniquely identify data occurrences within a data subject. However, the primary keys in disparate data may not be useful for integrating data occurrences from different data files representing the same data subject. Those disparate primary keys may be unique within their data file, but are not unique across multiple data files, making the integration of data occurrences difficult.

For example, student data in different data files at the school level, the district level, and the state level may have different primary keys. Integrating student data, particularly when students move between schools, districts, and states can be a difficult task. Some means of uniquely identifying students across all schools, districts, and states is needed to provide accurate student data.

A *data integration key* was defined in the last chapter as a set of data characteristics that could identify possible redundant physical data occurrences in a disparate data resource. A data integration key is not a primary key because it does not uniquely identify a specific data occurrence. It is only used to identify possible identical data occurrences.

The reason that most traditional data integration approaches use a system of record or system of reference is that the lack of a primary key across multiple data sources is not an issue. One primary data source is used and the other secondary data sources are largely ignored. However, that approach is often not acceptable to the business, because data occurrences could be lost in the integration process.

A data integration key for student data might include the student's birth name, birth date, birth location (hospital, city, state, and country), race, ethnicity, mother's maiden name, and so on. The data integration key could be many different data characteristics contained in a data occurrence that might be useful for identifying identical data occurrences. Although it doesn't uniquely identify identical data occurrences, it provides insight for making a judgment call about whether data occurrences represent the same student.

A data integration key is documented in the same way as a primary key, but is labeled as a data integration key. The data integration key for student data is shown below. The data values of a data integration key are used to identify possible matches between students in different data files. Some data values may not exist in all data files, but the existing data values help identify possible matches.

Student

    Integration Key: Ethnicity. Code
                          Race. Code
                          Student. Birth Date
                          Student. Birth City Name
                          Student. Birth Country Name
                          Student. Birth Name Complete
                          Student. Birth State Name
                          Student. Mother Maiden Name

A *data integration key index* is a table showing the values of a data integration key for each data occurrence, in all data files, within a data subject. A data integration key index is created for each data subject and is labeled with the data subject name. The index may be quite large, since it contains the data integration key values for each data record, in each data file, within a data subject.

Possible matching data occurrences across the data files within a data subject can be identified electronically, but the final determination of identical data occurrences may need to be made manually. Using a data integration key with too few data characteristics may result in unreasonable matches. Using a data integration key with too many data characteristics may result in unnecessary processing time and no matches. The best approach is to identify a data integration key that will most likely identify realistic matches.

Preferred Foreign Key

All foreign keys in a data subject are reviewed to determine the preferred foreign keys that match the preferred primary keys. The criteria for designating foreign keys are listed below.

When a candidate foreign key matches the preferred business primary key in a parent data subject, it is designated as a preferred business foreign key.

When a candidate foreign key matches the preferred physical primary key in a parent data subject, it is designated as a preferred physical foreign key.

When a candidate foreign key matches an alternate business primary key in a parent data subject, it is designated as an alternate business foreign key.

When a candidate foreign key matches an alternate physical primary key in a parent data subject, it is designated as an alternate physical foreign key.

When a candidate foreign key matches a limited primary key in a parent data subject, it is designated as a limited foreign key.

When a candidate foreign key matches an obsolete primary key in a parent data subject, it is designated as an obsolete foreign key.

Remaining candidate foreign keys are reviewed to determine if a parent data subject has a possible corresponding primary key that has not been designated.

When a parent data subject has a corresponding primary key that has not been designated, that designation is made, and the candidate foreign key is designated accordingly.

When a parent data subject has no corresponding primary key, the candidate foreign key is designated as obsolete.

When no candidate foreign keys exist, and one or more parent data subjects exist, foreign keys are created for the parent data subjects based on the primary keys in those parent data subjects.

A *foreign key list* is a list of the foreign keys for a data subject that exists in the disparate data. Only the data characteristic is listed for each foreign key, not the data characteristic variation. Designating foreign keys, like primary keys, is not dependent on the format or content of the data. It's only dependent on the value of the foreign key. The content and format will be translated to the preferred data characteristic during data transformation.

Using the employee example above, each employee receives many pay checks. The foreign key list for pay checks is shown below. The first foreign key is to Employee using Employee. Social Security Number, and it is a preferred business foreign key. The other foreign keys are listed accordingly.

Pay Check

Foreign Key: Employee   Employee. Social Security Number
              Preferred. Business.

Foreign Key: Employee   Employee. Organization Identifier
              Alternate. Business

Foreign Key: Employee   Employee. System Identifier
              Preferred. Physical.

Generally, identifying the primary key referenced by a foreign key is not difficult when the formal data names are used. The data subject name in the foreign key identifies the parent data subject, and the data characteristic names match the data characteristics in the parent data subject. The additional data subject name after the Foreign Key label is a routine practice for designating foreign keys, and is very useful for documenting foreign keys in disparate data.

A common practice is to list all implicit foreign keys. For example, if a class is identified by the course identifier and the academic year identifier, then foreign keys are defined for both the class and the academic year. The practice is routine for documenting all possible navigations between data subjects.

Preferred Data Relations

Data relations between data subjects are designated by the foreign keys. However, only one data relation exists between a parent and subordinate data subject even though many foreign keys may exist between those two data subjects. That data relation becomes the preferred data relation, and represents both a business data relation and a physical data relation.

Preferred Data Sources

A *preferred data source* was defined in the last chapter as the data product unit or variation that will be the source for a business fact. It's the location where an individual business fact can be obtained that is the most current and most accurate, and has the highest quality. Data sources that are not designated as preferred data sources become non-preferred data sources.

Conditional data sourcing was defined in the last chapter as the process of selecting preferred data from a variety of different locations based on which location has the most current and most accurate data. The source is based on the most current and most accurate data, not on the format or content of the data, as specified in a preferred data characteristic variation. The format and content can be easily translated during data transformation and is not a consideration in designating data sources.

In other words, the preferred data characteristic variation and the preferred data source are not necessarily the same. The preferred data source is determined independent of the preferred data characteristic variation.

Data source rules were defined in the last chapter as rules specifying the preferred data source where a particular business fact is obtained, and the conditions that determine the preferred source for each business fact. As described in the last chapter and above, a single system or record of reference seldom exists. The typical situation is conditional data sourcing, which is specified by data source rules.

An *unconditional data source rule* specifies one location where a business fact is obtained. A conditional data source rule specifies multiple locations where a business fact is obtained, and the conditions for specifying the location.

Possible insights for identifying redundant data occurrences in a disparate data resource are listed below. These insights provide some indication of possible redundant data occurrences.

> Disparate primary keys could be used to indicate possible redundant data occurrences. However, the primary keys for the same data occurrence are often different in different data files for the same data subject. In addition, the same primary key, such as a system assigned identifier, may appear in data files representing different data subjects.

> The data product set or variation definitions could provide some indication of the data occurrences contained in that data product set or variation and whether they might be redundant with data occurrences in another data product set or variation.

The cross-references to a common data architecture could be reviewed to find all of the data product sets or variations for each data subject, either through cross-references to a data subject variation, or through cross-references to data characteristic variations within the data subject.

The same set of data items in a data file could indicate redundant physical data occurrences. However, the same of set of data items does not necessarily mean those data occurrences are redundant.

A *data characteristic source list* is a list of all the data sources for each data characteristic. The data characteristics are listed for each data subject, and the data sources are listed for each data characteristic. The data sources for each data characteristic are compiled from the cross-references between data product units or variations and data characteristic variations. The data subject and data characteristic names are the logical common data architecture names, and the source names are the physical data product set or variation and data unit or variation names.

For example, the data characteristic source list for a few of the employee data characteristics is shown below. The data product units or variations are listed for the data characteristics within the employee data subject.

```
Employee
    Employee. Name
        PYRL.EMPL_NM
        AA.EMP_NAME
        TRAIN.EMPLYE_NM

    Employee. Birth Date
        PYRL.EMPL_BD
        AA.EMP_BIRTH
        TRAIN.EMPLYE_BDATE

    Employee: Race. Code
        PYRL.EMPL_RACE
        AA.EMP_RC
        TRAIN.EMPLYE_ETH
```

The criteria for specifying the data source rules are listed below.

Prepare a data characteristic source list for the scope of data being integrated to determine data source rules.

For each data characteristic, look at each source of the data and determine which is the best source based on whether data values are present and on the quality of the data, such as the currentness and accuracy of the data.

Develop the unconditional or conditional data source rule according

313

to the availability and quality of the data.

Data source rules use the data rule notation. The data rule identifier is Source! and any conditions follow the When notation. The double left carets (<<) indicate the source of the data, meaning *comes from*.

The data source rules for the employee data are shown below. The unconditional source for Race. Code is PYRL.EMPL_RACE. The conditional sources for Employee. Name between January 1, 1990 and December 31, 1999 is PYRL.EMPL_NM, and after January 1, 2000 is AA.EMP_NM. The conditional source for Employee. Birth Date is based on the parent Department. Identifier.

```
Employee: Race. Code
    Source! << PYRL.EMPL_RACE

Employee. Name
    Source ! When Employee. Hire Date >= 'January 1, 1990'
            & <= 'December 31, 1999' << PYRL.EMPL_NM

            When Employee. Hire Date >= January 1, 2000
            << AA.EMP_NAME

Employee. Birth Date
    Source!  When Department. Identifier ^ Employee = '62' | '63' | '64'
            << PYRL_EMPL_BD
            When Department. Identifier ^ Employee <> '62' | '63' | '64'
            << TRAIN.EMPLYE_BDATE
```

In some situations, a data value may not exist in the preferred source designated by the data source rule. If missing data values are likely to occur, alternate data sources may be defined in the data source rules. For example, the data source rule for Employee. Birth Date may designate alternate sources, as shown below. The last two conditions were added so that when the data value for birth date was missing, another data source would be used.

```
Employee. Birth Date
    Source!  When Department. Identifier ^ Employee = '62' | '63' | '64'
            << PYRL_EMPL_BD
            When Department. Identifier ^ Employee <> '62' | '63' | '64'
            << TRAIN.EMPLYE_BDATE
            When TRAIN.EMPLYE_BDATE = ' ' << PYRL.EMPL_BD
            When PYRL.EMPL_BD = ' ' << AA.EMP_BIRTH
```

An alternate notation for data source rules can be used where the data source rules are listed for a data subject rather than for a data characteristic, and the data characteristics are listed within the data source rule criteria. The alternate notation avoids repeating the conditional criteria. For example, the student data sources are shown below.

314

Student

Source!

Student. Race. Code << PYRL.EMPL_RACE

When Student. Registration Date <= 'December 31, 1999'
Student. Birth Date << STDT.BRTH_DT
Student. Name Complete << STDT.NAM
And so on...

When Student. Registration Date >= 'January 1, 2000'
Student. Birth Date << REG.STD_BD
Student. Name Complete << REG.STD_NM
And so on...

The examples above are simple, but show how data source rules can be written. The conditional criteria could be a date, a type of entity, a country or region, age, residence, date or date range, or any other combination of criteria. The conditional criteria could be from the data entity receiving the source data, or from a parent data entity. Virtually any criteria can be specified to designate the source of the data. The rules can be structured in any manner that is easy to interpret and uses the fewest notations.

Data Occurrences and Data Instances

The examples above show data source rules for a single non-redundant data occurrence in disparate data, and for multiple redundant data occurrences in disparate data. In other words, if stream data for all streams exist in only one data file, that data file becomes the unconditional source for stream data. However, if stream data for all streams exist in more than one data file, then conditional data sourcing needs to be specified for which data items are sourced from each of those data files to form the preferred data occurrence.

A problem arises when not all data occurrences for a data subject exist in any single data file. For example, different data files may contain grade school students, middle school students, and high school students. Also, multiple data files exist for grade school, middle school, and high school students. Student data occurrences are redundant across the data files within a grade level, but not across data files for different grade levels. All of these student data occurrences need to be brought together into a single data file for all students.

The preferred business primary key uniquely identifies each student, but does not appear in the existing data files. A primary key index can be prepared to show the existing primary keys for students in the existing data files and the preferred business primary key for each student. Data source rules are then prepared to define the preferred data sources for each student within each grade level.

A more intricate problem arises when the student data occurrences are redundant across data files within a grade level, and are redundant across data files for different grade levels. For example, several data files contain data for grade school and middle school students, and several data files contain data for middle school and high school students. The middle school students are redundant both within and across grade levels.

Again, the preferred business primary key uniquely identifies each student, but does not appear in the existing data file. A primary key index can be prepared to show the existing primary keys for students in the existing data files and the preferred business primary key for each student. In addition, a data integration key index can be prepared to show possible matching students in the existing data files. Data source rules are then prepared to define the preferred data sources for each student.

The examples above describe current non-redundant and redundant data occurrences between existing data files—current data instances. The situation can become quite detailed, but can be resolved with the use of a primary key index, a data integration key index, and data source rules. However, the situation becomes even more detailed with historical data instances.

Historical data instances are subordinate to current data instances in a one-to-many relationship. In other words, each data occurrence has a current data instance and could have many historical data instances. These historical data instances can be as redundant as the current data instances described above, and they can represent different times.

Historical data instances will have the same business and physical preferred primary key as their parent current data instance, plus a time component. The time component depends on the particular data subject. Geologic events, such as continental drift, may be a decade or century, timber stand growth may be a year, a person's name change may be a day, a vehicle accident may be an hour, a chemical reaction may be a second, a nuclear reaction may be a micro-second, and so on.

Data source rules are first defined to bring the current data instances together, as described above. Then data source rules are defined to bring the historical data instances together within their parent data occurrence. The additional parameter for defining the historical data source rules is the time component. A different time results in a different historical data instance, regardless of the source of that data instance or the historical data captured.

The historical data source rules specify which historical data items are to be sourced. The data source rules can specify a subset of the historical data items, such as only those data items whose value changed, or they can specify all data items in the historical data instance.

Preferred Data Integrity Rules

A *preferred data integrity rule* was defined in the last chapter as a data integrity rule that has either been confirmed or created to ensure integrity of a common data architecture. A *candidate data integrity rule* was defined as a data integrity rule that was documented during the data inventory and brought over to a common data architecture.

Generally, very few data integrity rules exist in the disparate data resource, which is the reason that most disparate data have very low quality. A complete set of precise data integrity rules usually need to be specified within a common data architecture. However, the data integrity rules that do exist in disparate data can be a start to developing precise data integrity rules within a common data architecture.

The best approach is to bring all data integrity rules documented during the data inventory process over to a common data architecture. These candidate data integrity rules are then reviewed to determine if they can become preferred data integrity rules, or if preferred data integrity rules need to be developed.

Preferred data value rules, conditional data value rules, data structure rules, conditional data structure rules, data derivation and rederivation rules, and data retention rules all need to be defined within a common data architecture as described in Chapter 3 and in *Data Resource Simplexity*. These preferred data integrity rules define the quality needed in a comparate data resource, based on business needs.

The preferred data integrity rules must have a violation action and violation notification defined. Many people resist defining violation actions and notifications because it's too time consuming. However, the default for data that fail the data integrity rules is to delete and ignore. That default is not practical for data resource integration. Therefore, the violation actions and notifications must be defined.

Many people resist defining a complete set of precise data integrity rules because it's a time consuming process. However, it's usually these same people who complain about the low quality of the existing disparate data. The time must be spent developing a complete set of precise data integrity rules if the comparate data resource is to contain high quality data to support business needs.

The preferred data integrity rules are identified with the word *Preferred*. For example, a preferred data integrity rule for a student's birth date would be specified as shown below.

```
Student. Birth Date, Domain! Preferred
     January 1, 1986 <= Date <= December 31, 1998
```

Data integrity rules that are not preferred do not have the preferred designation. They usually remain in a common data architecture as an indication of the data integrity that exists in the disparate data.

Multiple Preferred Data Designations

Multiple preferred data designations was defined in the last chapter as the situation where multiple data characteristic variations or multiple data reference set variations are designated as preferred due to culture, geography, or politics.

For example, multiple data characteristic variations could be designated for a course description in English, German, and French, as shown below. The preferred data characteristic variations can be used as necessary for international students.

```
Course. Description, English *

Course. Description, German *

Course. Description, French *
```

Similarly, multiple data reference set variations could be designated for management levels in different regions of the world, as shown below. The data reference set variations can be used as appropriate for the world region.

```
Management Level; Europe *

Management Level; Asia *

Management Level; North America *
```

Changes Over Time

A common data architecture often changes over time as the business world changes, or as an organization chooses to operate differently in the business world. Those changes need to be represented in the preferred data designations. The criteria for designating changes over time are listed below.

When a data subject name changes, a version stating the relevant dates is added to the former data subject name, and the data subject new name is established with a version stating the relevant dates. All of the data characteristics and data reference set variations are moved to the new data subjects, with appropriate name changes.

When a data characteristic name changes, a version stating the relevant dates is added to the former data characteristic name, and a new data characteristic name is established with a version stating the relevant dates. All of the data characteristic variations are moved to the new data characteristic.

When a data definition changes, the new definition is placed ahead of the old definitions with the effective date. The former definition is retained for historical purposes.

When a preferred data characteristic variation changes, a version notation is added to the former preferred data characteristic variation stating the relevant dates. A new preferred data characteristic variation is designated as preferred, with a version notation stating the relevant dates.

When a preferred data reference set variation changes, a version notation is added to the former preferred data reference set variation stating the relevant dates. A new preferred data reference set variation is designated as preferred, with a version notation stating the relevant dates.

When a data reference item in a preferred data reference set changes, the end date for that data reference item is added. The former data reference item is not removed from the data reference set. The begin date is added for a new data reference item.

When primary or foreign key designations are changed, a version notation is added to the former key stating the relevant dates. New designations are made, with a version notation stating the relevant dates.

When a preferred data source changes, which seldom happens, a version notation is added to the former preferred data source stating the relevant dates. A new preferred data source is designated, with a version notation stating the relevant dates.

When a preferred data integrity rule changes, a version notation is added to the former preferred data integrity rule stating the relevant dates. A new preferred data integrity rule is established, with a version notation stating the relevant dates.

319

Preferred Data Architecture Adjustment

Components may have been added to a common data architecture during the preferred data designation process to develop a comparate data resource that supports how the organization desires to do business. However, some components placed in an initial common data architecture, or components added during the preferred data designation and never used, may no longer be relevant for the way the organization desires to do business.

A common data architecture can be reviewed after the preferred data designations have been made to identify all non-relevant components and either remove them or note that they are no longer relevant. The two approaches are described below and either approach is acceptable.

The first approach is to remove all non-relevant components so that the common data architecture represents only components that support data cross-references and preferred data designations. The approach results in a smaller common data architecture, but does not indicate thoughts and insights gained during the preferred data designation process.

The second approach is to retain the non-relevant components and label them as non-relevant with an explanation as to why they are not relevant. The approach results in a larger common data architecture, but documents the thoughts and insights gained during the preferred data designation process.

DATA TRANSLATION RULES

Data translation rules set the stage to actually convert the data values between disparate data and comparate data. A *data translation rule* was defined in the last chapter as specifying the algorithm for translating data values between preferred and non-preferred data designations, or between different non-preferred data designations when necessary. *Preferred data translation rules* are between preferred and non-preferred data designations. *Non-preferred data translation rules* are between non-preferred data designations.

Forward data translation rules are between non-preferred data designations and preferred data designations. *Reverse data translation rules* are between preferred data designations and non-preferred data designations.

Data translation rules apply to data characteristic variations and data reference set variations. Each of these types of data translation rules is described below.

320

Data Characteristic Variation Translation

A *data characteristic translation rule* was defined in the last chapter as a data translation rule that translates data values between non-preferred and preferred variations of a data characteristic. It consists of a source data characteristic variation, a translation algorithm, and a target data characteristic variation.

A data characteristic translation rule is designated with the keyword Translation!. The notation >> is used to indicate *goes to* or *converted to*. The notation << is used to indicate *comes from* or *converted from*. The data translation rule is normalized to the data characteristic variation on which it takes action, meaning the receiving data characteristic variation.

Data characteristic translation rules are prepared both ways between preferred and non-preferred data characteristic variations. Measurements, such as feet to inches or miles to kilometers, are relatively easy. For example, the translation between well depth in inches and well depth in meters is shown below.

    Well
        Well. Depth, Meters << Inches Translation!
        Well. Depth, Meters = Well. Depth, Inches / 39.39

Names are more difficult to translate, such as a person's name from normal to inverted sequence. For example, the name of drivers who receive licenses is translated from an inverted sequence to a normal sequence.

    Driver
        Driver. Name Complete, Normal << Inverted Translation!
        Algorithm for parsing and rearranging the driver's name

A person's name in an irregular format would require an extensive algorithm to translate that name to a regular format, and many need human intervention to interpret the irregularity and translate it to a specific format. Translating a person's name from a regular format to an irregular format would not be possible.

Some translations, such as state plane coordinates to latitude and longitude, are the most difficult and require a detailed mathematical algorithm.

Some specific locations can be translated to more general locations. For example, a construction accident location specified by latitude and longitude to 1 minute accuracy could be translated to a more general location, such as a 40-acre parcel. However, it would not be possible to translate a well location from a general 40-acre parcel to a specific latitude and longitude location with 1 minute accuracy.

Some location translations require more than one source data characteristic and more than one target data characteristic. For example, translating a well location specified as latitude and longitude (Lat / Lon) to a well location specified as a section, tier, and range (PLS for Public Land Survey) requires two source data characteristics and three target data characteristics.

```
Well

    Well Location PLS << Lat / Lon Translation!
        Well. Latitude Degrees, 2 Digits
        Well. Longitude Degrees, 2 Digits
        Well. Section Number
        Well. Tier Number
        Well. Range Number
        Algorithm for converting Lat / Lon to PLS
```

The translation of data value length variations is relatively easy, if the data value does not need to be truncated. Translating from a shorter data value to a longer data value is easy. Translating from a longer data value to a shorter data value can be difficult if the source data value is longer than the target. If the data value needs to be truncated, the translation algorithm becomes very detailed, or human intervention is needed.

Translating data values from right to left justified, or from left to right justified is relatively easy. The translation algorithm specifies the shifting of the data value either right or left.

Translating data values that have different meaning is not valid. For example, translating Well. Depth, Estimated Feet to Well. Depths, Measured Meters is not valid because the data values have different meanings.

Data characteristic translation rules are maintained until all disparate data have been permanently translated to a comparate data resource. The rules then become inactive, but are retained for historical purposes.

Fundamental Data Translation Rules

The fundamental data concept can be used for defining data translation rules. *Fundamental data translation rules* are basic translation rules that can be inherited in many specific data translations. *Specific data translation rules* apply directly to the data and can inherit fundamental data translation rules.

Fundamental data translation rules are stored in a Translation Rule data subject. The data characteristics are the specific translation rules. Since data translation rules are specified both ways between non-preferred and preferred data characteristic variations, two translation rules are defined.

For example, the two data translation rules for translating between a date CYMD and a date YMD are shown below. The algorithm for making the translation is shown in the contents of each data characteristic.

    Translation Rule. Date CYMD >> Date YMD
    Translation Rule. Date YMD >> Date CYMD

Similarly, the translation between meters and inches is shown below.

    Translation Rule. Meters >> Inches
    Translation Rule. Inches >> Meters

However, in the case of measurement, the translation could have different accuracies. The data characteristic variation indicates the accuracy, as shown below.

    Translation Rule. Meters >> Inches, 0.001
    Translation Rule. Meters >> Inches, 0.1

An alternative notation is to show the number of significant digits as the data characteristic variation. For example, the translation from meters to inches could be 39.3900787401575, or 39.4, or 39.0. The data translation rule notations are shown below.

    Translation Rule. Meters >> Inches, 13 Digits
    Translation Rule. Meters >> Inches, 1 Digit
    Translation Rule. Meters >> Inches, 0 Digits

Fundamental data translation rules can be used for specific data translations. For example, translating an employee's birth date from MDY format to CYMD format using a fundamental data translation rule is shown below.

    Employee
        Employee. Birth Date, CYMD << MDY Translation!
            Translation Rule. CYMD << MDY

Similarly, Pi could be defined in a data translation rule as 3.14159265 or 3.14, as shown below.

    Translation Rule. Pi, 8 Digits
    Translation Rule. Pi, 2 Digits

Pi can then be used in specific data translation rules. For example, a survey plot area is calculated from its radius using the Pi translation rule.

    Survey Plot
        Survey Plot. Area << Radius Translation!
            Survey Plot. Area, 2 Digits = Survey Plot. Radius, 3 Digits ** 2
                * Translation Rule. Pi, 2 Digits

Fundamental data translation rules can be developed for a majority of the data characteristic variation translations. Very few specific data characteristic translation rules need to be defined. Fundamental data translation rules minimize the documentation and maximize the consistency of data characteristic variation translation.

Data Reference Item Translation

A *data reference item translation rule* was defined in the last chapter as translating coded data values and names between data reference items in preferred and non-preferred data reference set variations in a data subject. The data reference set translation rule only translates the data value, not the format of the data value. The data characteristic translation rule for the coded data value and name translates the format.

A *one-to-one data reference item translation rule* translates the coded data value and/or the name from one data reference item in the source to one data reference item in the target, which is relatively easy. A *many-to-one data reference item translation rule* translates the coded data value and/or the name from many different data reference items in the source to one data reference item in the target, which is relatively easy. A *one-to-many data reference item translation rule* translates one coded data value and/or name from the source to many data reference items in the target, which can be difficult and may require additional input.

Data reference item translation rules are usually a matrix of the coded data values and names that shows both the non-preferred and the preferred sets of data reference items. The matrix is the translation rule that can be used to translate from the non-preferred to the preferred data reference items, and from the preferred to the non-preferred data reference items.

The data reference item translation rule is named by the data subject containing the data reference set variations. For example, the matrix for disability data reference item translations is named Disability. Translation!, the matrix for vehicle horsepower data reference items translations is named Vehicle Horsepower. Translation!, and the matrix for management level data reference item translations is named Management Level. Translation!. The matrix is documented with the data subject containing the data reference set variations.

The data reference item translation rule for disability is shown below. The coded data values and names are shown for the three disparate data reference set variations, and for the new preferred data reference set variation. The coded data values and names can be translated either way based on the matrix of values.

Disability. Translation!

School;		Employment;		Health;		New; *	
10	Sight	A	Seeing	V	Vision	S	Sight
20	Hearing	H	Hear	S	Sound	H	Hearing
30	Physical	P	Physical	A	Accidental	P	Physical
40	Develop	D	Developed	G	Genetic	D	Developmental

The data reference item translation rule for vehicle horsepower is shown below. The matrix shows the combination of two distinctly separate disparate data reference set variations combined into one all-inclusive preferred data reference set variation. The coded data values and names can be translated either direction.

Vehicle Horsepower. Translation!

Small;		Large;		New; *	
A	Below 100			1	Below 100 Horsepower
B	100-199			2	100-199 Horsepower
C	200-349			3	200-349 Horsepower
D	350-499			4	350-499 Horsepower
		1	500-749	5	500-749 Horsepower
		2	750-999	6	750-999 Horsepower
		3	1000-1499	7	1000-1499 Horsepower
		4	1500+	8	Above 1500 Horsepower

The data reference item translation rule for management level is shown below. The matrix shows the combination of two overlapping disparate data reference set variations combined into one all-inclusive preferred data reference set variation. The coded data values and names can be translated either way.

Management Level. Translation!

New; *		Personnel;		Finance;	
Owner	01	Owner/Partner	OP		
Senior Executive	02	Executive	EX	Senior Manager	041
Line Manager	03	Manager	MN	Line Manager	163
Unit Supervisor	04	Supervisor	SP	Unit Manager	239
Lead Member	05	Lead Worker	LW	Team Manager	157
Team Member	06			Team Member	445

The data reference item translation rule for ecological regions is shown below. The matrix shows a reduction of a detailed disparate data reference set variation into a new, more general preferred data reference set variation. The coded data values and names can be translated from the non-preferred to the preferred, but cannot be translated from the preferred to the non-preferred without additional input.

Ecological Region. Translation!
  Wildlife;   New; *

1	Northeast	E	East
2	East Central	E	East
3	Southeast	E	East
4	Southern Midwest	M	Midwest
5	Central Midwest	M	Midwest
6	Northern Midwest	M	Midwest
7	Southwest	W	West
8	Northwest	W	West

These data reference item translation rules are simple, but they cover the range of possibilities, and can be used to develop more detailed data reference item translation rules.

PREFERRED PHYSICAL DATA ARCHITECTURE

The preferred physical data architecture can be developed when the preferred logical data architecture designation has been completed. The preferred physical data architecture is developed according to a formal set of data denormalization criteria. These data denormalization criteria were discussed in Chapter 3 and described in detail in *Data Resource Simplexity*.

The primary objective of formal data denormalization is to develop a physical data architecture that is optimum for a particular operating environment, without compromising the logical data architecture. Note that the entire data architecture is adjusted, not just the structure. The major problems with traditional data denormalization are that only structure is adjusted, and the logical data model is often compromised. The result is a data resource that does not have high quality and does not meet business needs.

All four components of a data architecture are denormalized. First, the data structure is denormalized according to the formal data denormalization criteria. Second, the logical data names are changed to physical data names on the denormalized data structure using a set of data name word abbreviations and an abbreviation algorithm. Third, the logical data definitions are adjusted to the physical data structure. Fourth, the data integrity rules are adjusted to the physical data structure and become the data edits that need to be implemented to ensure data quality.

The resulting physical data architecture is documented as a data product with a designation of preferred. No data cross-references are made between the preferred physical data architecture and a common data architecture. That preferred physical data model is then used to design the comparate data resource, and for data transformation between disparate data and comparate data.

PREFERRED DATA TEMPLATES

A *preferred data template* was defined in the last chapter as a subset of the preferred logical data architecture for a specific subject area to promote data sharing between organizations and help organization develop applications and databases. Generally, a preferred data template is prepared for the preferred logical data architecture so an organization can formally denormalize that architecture for their particular operating environment.

Preferred data templates are most useful in the public sector where data are common across many different public sector organizations. For example, geologic data, topographic data, streams, roads, power lines, and so on, benefit from preferred data templates. Similarly, crime and criminal data, vehicle registration data, business license data, and so on, benefit from preferred data templates.

SUMMARY

Preferred data designations are the next step after data cross-referencing has been completed. Preferred data designations include preferred data names, preferred data definitions, preferred data characteristic variations, preferred data reference set variations, preferred data subjects, preferred primary and foreign keys, preferred data sources, and preferred data integrity rules. Specific criteria guide the preferred data designation process.

A data integration key is used to identify possible matching data occurrences in data files that contain redundant data. Historical data instances are designated as data subjects subordinate to the data subject containing the current data instance. Multiple preferred data designations may be made for cultural, geographical, or political differences. Changes over time for data names, data definitions, data structure, and data integrity rules are designated with the version notation.

Data translation rules are developed for translating data values between preferred and non-preferred data characteristic variations, and between preferred and non-preferred data reference set variation. Fundamental data translation rules are developed to support specific data translation rules. Fundamental data translation rules provide maximum consistency with minimum effort.

A preferred physical data architecture is developed after the preferred logical data architecture has been designated based on formal data denormalization criteria. Preferred data templates to support data sharing between organizations can be prepared based on the preferred logical data architecture. Preferred data templates are most useful for sharing data between public sector organizations.

The preferred data designation process provides a preferred logical data architecture and a preferred physical data architecture for developing a comparate data resource and transforming disparate data to comparate data. The process ends the documentation and understanding aspects of existing disparate data and sets the stage for physically transforming the disparate data and building a comparate data resource that has high quality and meets business needs.

QUESTIONS

The following questions are provided as a review of preferred data designations and translation schemes, and to stimulate thought about defining the preferred data architecture for an organization.

1. What preferred data designations are made during the preferred data designation process?

2. How is a data integration key useful for making preferred data designations?

3. How are preferred data definitions prepared?

4. How are preferred primary keys and foreign keys determined?

5. What is done with primary keys and foreign keys that are not designated as preferred?

6. How are preferred data sources determined?

7. How are preferred data integrity rules prepared?

8. How are redundant data occurrences and data instances identified?

9. How is a preferred physical data architecture prepared?

10. How are data translation rules prepared?

Chapter 11

DATA TRANSFORMATION CONCEPT

Where the rubber meets the road!

When the preferred physical data architecture has been designated for one segment of the data disparate data resource, or for the entire disparate data resource, the existing disparate data can be transformed to comparate data according to that preferred physical data architecture. The last six chapters described the concepts and processes in the formal state that were used to understand the existing disparate data and designate a preferred data architecture. Now it's time to transform those disparate data to comparate data, either in the virtual state or comparate state, based on the preferred data architecture designations.

Chapter 11 describes the concepts and principles for transforming disparate data to comparate data based on the preferred data architecture and the current operating environment of an organization. The concepts and principles for transforming comparate data to disparate data to maintain those disparate data until all applications using those disparate data can be transformed are also described. The techniques and processes for transforming disparate data to comparate data, and comparate data to disparate data, are described in the next chapter.

CONCEPTS AND PRINCIPLES

The concept for formal data transformation and the principles supporting the concept are described below.

Data Transformation Concept

The *data resource integration concept* was defined in Chapter 2 as resolving the disparate data to produce a comparate data resource that meets the current and future business information demand. *Data resource integration* was defined as the thorough understanding of existing disparate data within a common data architecture, the designation of preferred data, and the development of a comparate data resource based on those preferred data. *Data integration* was defined as the merging of data from multiple, often disparate, sources, usually based on some record of reference, to provide a single output. It does not resolve any data disparity, and may further increase data disparity.

Data resource transition was defined in Chapter 2 as the transition of an organization's data resource from a disparate state, through the formal data resource state and virtual data resource state, to a comparate data resource state. It's the pathway that is followed from a disparate data resource to a comparate data resource that is unique to each organization. *Formal data resource integration* was defined as any data resource integration done within the context of a common data architecture. *Informal data resource integration* was defined as any data resource integration done outside the context of a common data architecture.

The only difference between the virtual state and the comparate state is whether the data transformation is done temporarily, on an as-needed basis, or is done permanently. The virtual state is the temporary transformation of data and the comparate state is the permanent transformation of data.

Data resource transformation is the formal process of formally transforming a disparate data resource to a comparate data resource within the context of a common data architecture according to the preferred data architecture designations. It's a subset of overall data resource transition that is based on the preferred physical data architecture. It's a metamorphosis of the physical disparate data to form physical comparate data.

Data resource transformation includes transforming disparate data to comparate data to achieve a comparate data resource, and transforming comparate data to disparate data to maintain existing applications until they can be transformed to use comparate data. It's a very detailed process that requires careful planning, but it's far from impossible. Data resource transformation is absolutely necessary to achieve a high quality data resource that meets the current and future business information demand, but is often ignored by most traditional data transformation approaches.

The **data resource transformation concept** states that all data transformation, whether disparate data to comparate data or comparate data to disparate data, will be done within the context of a common data architecture, using the preferred data architecture designations, according to formal data transformation rules. The best existing disparate data are extracted and transformed to comparate data to create a single, high quality version of truth about the business.

The **data resource transformation objective** is to transform the best of the existing disparate data to a high quality comparate data resource so it can support the current and future business information demand. The objective is more than just connecting a few databases and merging the data, building bridges between databases, or sending electronic messages over a network. It's a precise, detailed, and very rigorous process that creates a high quality comparate data resource.

Data transformation is the process of transforming disparate data to comparate data, or comparate data to disparate data, within the context of a common data architecture. It's one step in the overall extract-transform-load process that is done during data resource transformation. *Formal data transformation* is done within the context of a common data architecture and follows all of the concepts, principles, and techniques for formal data resource integration. *Informal data transformation* is done outside the context of a common data architecture, seldom follows formal concepts, principles, and techniques, and seldom resolves data disparity. The traditional data transformation done today is informal data transformation.

Forward data transformation is the formal transformation of disparate data to comparate data. Data are extracted from the preferred data source, transformed, and loaded into the data target. Forward data transformation can eventually be eliminated when the disparate data resource has been completely transformed to a comparate data resource. *Reverse data transformation* is the formal transformation of comparate data to disparate data. It's necessary to maintain disparate data that supports disparate applications until they can be converted to comparate data. Reverse data transformation can eventually be eliminated when applications are no longer based on disparate data.

The data transformation concept is shown in Figure 11.1. The existing disparate data are shown on the left. The existing disparate operational data are used to create disparate historical data and disparate evaluational data, as shown by the dashed lines. The disparate historical data can also be used to create disparate evaluational data. The initial data disparity is perpetuated throughout the data resource and impacts the business information demand.

The desired comparate data are shown on the right. Comparate operational data are used to create comparate historical data and comparate evaluational data, as shown by the solid lines. Comparate historical data can also be used to create comparate evaluational data. Comparate data are perpetuated throughout the data resource to support the business information demand.

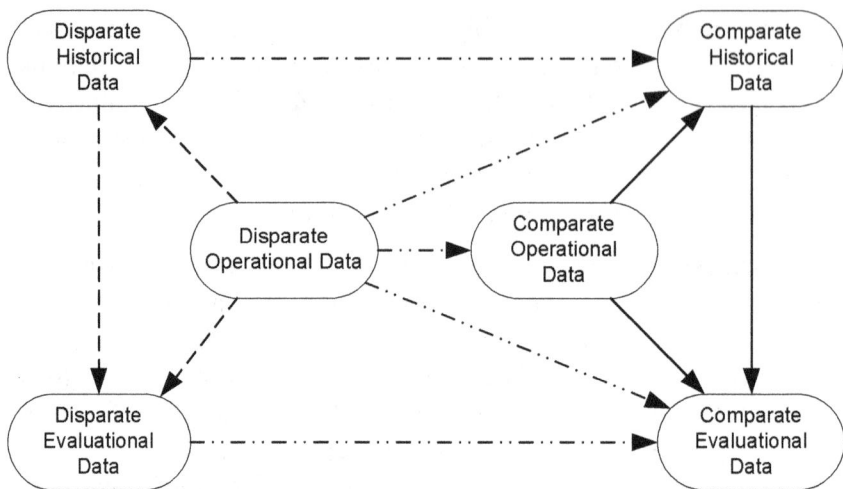

Figure 11.1 Data transformation concept.

Data transformation is shown in the center with dashed-dotted lines. Disparate historical data are transformed to comparate historical data. Disparate evaluational data are transformed to comparate evaluational data. Disparate operational data are transformed to comparate operational data, and may be transformed to comparate historical and comparate evaluational data. Each of these data transformations follows the same principles and techniques.

Data transformation is not the same as deploying data or replicating data. Deploying and replicating data simply moves or copies the existing data to another location. Data transformation is not the same as merging or combining existing data. Data transformation actually changes the data structure and data values from a disparate state to a comparate state.

Data Transformation Principles

Data transformation principles include a formal process, a destructive process, a technical process, application data transformation, data transformation rules, data bridges, data broker, data depot, and data integration key. Each of these principles is described below.

Formal Process

The *formal data transformation principle* states that formal data transformation will be used to create a comparate data resource. Informal data transformation will not be considered or used. The emphasis will be on forward data transformation, with reverse data transformation only to the extent needed to maintain disparate data until applications can be transformed to use comparate data. Formal data transformation is deterministic, prospective, and prescriptive.

Formal data transformation is performed between the existing physical disparate data and the desired physical comparate databases that were developed according to the preferred physical data architecture. The data inventory, cross-referencing, and preferred logical data architecture provide the link between the existing physical disparate data and the desired physical comparate data. Accordingly, the physical data names are used for data transformation.

Both data integration and data resource integration can use the same data transformation techniques. The difference is that data integration is generally less formal and has not gone through the formal processes of data inventory, cross-referencing, and preferred data architecture designations, and does not result in a permanent comparate data resource. Data resource integration has gone through the formal processes and results in a permanent comparate data resource.

Formal data resource integration relies on insights gained through the formal processes to make informed decisions about selecting the best disparate data and transforming those data to build a comparate data resource. It's not perfect, but it's the best that can be done based on the existing disparate data.

Destructive Process

Data transformation is a destructive process because it actually changes the data structure and data values from their disparate state to a comparate state. All of the previous processes for data inventorying, data cross-referencing, and preferred data designations were non-destructive because they did not alter the data in any way. They only provided an understanding and made preferred data designations within the context of a common data architecture. Data transformation takes the disparate data apart and builds a comparate data resource.

Detailed Process

Many people believe that data transformation is a difficult, or impossible, process and resort to a traditional Extract-Transform-Load process that seldom transforms the data. The traditional Extract-Transform-Load process may provide some superficial cleansing of the data, but seldom provides any robust transformation of the data structure or data values. It seldom produces a comparate data resource.

Formal data transformation is a very detailed process, but is far from impossible. It's based on very sound concepts and principles that produce a comparate data resource. It takes thought, effort, and time, but the result is a comparate data resource that meets the business information demand.

When the data transformation process is understood, each organization develops their own techniques for performing the data transformation based on their particular operating environment. My experience has been that when the formal data transformation rules have been developed, the database technical staff and application programmers are infinitely clever at performing the data transformation. When they see the specifications of what needs to be done, they know how to implement those specifications in their operating environment.

Application Data Transformation

A *disparate data application* is any application that reads and stores disparate data. A *comparate data application* is any application that reads and stores comparate data. *Application data transformation* is the process of transforming disparate data applications from reading and storing disparate data to reading and storing comparate data. The entire application may not be changed, but the data read and data store routines of the application can be changed from disparate data to comparate data.

Weak application data transformation is the use of routines to read and store comparate data while the application still operates with the disparate data. *Strong application data transformation* is the complete transformation of an application to read and store comparate data as well as operate with comparate data. Typically, weak application data transformation is done during data resource transformation.

Data Transformation Rules

A *data transformation rule* is a data rule that specifies how the data will be transformed within the context of a common data architecture based on the existing disparate data and the preferred physical data architecture. Data transformation rules can be specified both ways between disparate data and comparate data.

Data transformation rules can be explicit or implicit. *Explicit data transformation rules* are stated as a formal data rule using specific notations. *Implicit data transformation rules* are stated in the form of a table or matrix for data value translations.

Data transformation rules can be specified as data reconstruction rules, data translation rules, data recast rules, and data derivation rules. Each of these data transformation rules will be described below with their respective data transformation process.

Data Bridges

A *data cross-walk* is the physical movement of data from one data file to another data file without any formal data transformation or the application of data integrity rules. The analogy is like using a cross-walk at an intersection where people cross, but are not altered in the process. The term is not used with data resource transformation because it implies an easy task of moving the disparate data to a comparate data resource without any transformation.

A *data bridge* is an application that moves data from one disparate data file to another disparate data file to keep the two data files in synch. The primary purpose is to maintain redundant data in a disparate data resource. When one data file is updated, those data are moved across the data bridge to update other data files. Data bridges are basically a data cross-walk between two data files to keep those data files in synch.

Data bridges can work in only one direction, from a primary data file to a secondary data file to keep the secondary data file in synch with the primary data file. Data bridges can also work in both directions when both data files receive updates, to keep those data files in synch with each other.

Many data bridges exist in a disparate data resource and considerable effort is spent building and maintaining data bridges. Most of these data bridges can be replaced with data brokers during data resource transformation, or can be eliminated when the disparate data resource has been transformed to a comparate data resource, often resulting in significant savings.

Data Broker

A *broker* is one who acts as an intermediary; an agent who makes arrangements. A *data broker* is an application that acts as an intermediary between disparate data and comparate data in databases or applications. It performs formal data transformations in both directions between disparate data and comparate data. *Data brokering* is the process of using data brokers to perform formal data transformation.

A data broker can operate between disparate databases to replace existing data bridges. It can manage multiple data bridges more efficiently, and can handle formal data transformation rules, when necessary.

A data broker can operate between disparate data applications and comparate databases by formally transforming the data. A data broker can also operate between comparate data applications and disparate databases by formally transforming the data.

A data broker can operate between disparate data applications and comparate data applications by formally transforming the data in messages between those applications.

Data brokers operate until all disparate data have been transformed to comparate data, and all disparate data applications have been transformed to comparate data applications. Data brokers are slowly eliminated as databases and applications are transformed to comparate data. They are eventually gone when all databases have comparate data and all applications use comparate data.

Data Depot

A *depot* is a place for storing goods; a store or cache; a place for storing and forwarding supplies; a building for railroad or bus passengers or freight. A *data depot* is a place for storing data for formal data transformation. It's a staging area or work area for transforming data independent of the data source or data target. It's not intended to store data or to be a working database for production operation.

A data depot can be used for either forward data transformation to build comparate databases, or for reverse data transformation to maintain disparate databases until applications can be transformed to use comparate data.

A data depot is a staging area for the formal transformation of data between disparate and comparate databases. Application code is developed to perform the data transformation within a data depot according to formal data transformation rules. A data broker differs from a data depot because it's an application that performs formal data transformation on small sets of data moving between applications and databases. It does not perform formal data transformation between comparate and disparate databases.

A *data converter* is an application that changes the data between heterogeneous databases. It does not transform the data in any way. It only changes the physical form of the data from one database environment to another database environment. A data converter may need to be used when extracting disparate data to a data depot, or when loading transformed data into a comparate data resource.

Data Integration Key

A *data integration key* was defined in the last chapter as a set of data characteristics that could identify possible redundant physical data occurrences in a disparate data resource. It's not a primary key because it does not uniquely identify a specific data occurrence. It's not a foreign key because no corresponding primary key exists. It's only used to identify possible redundant physical data occurrences in a disparate data resource.

A data integration key supports various algorithms and techniques for identifying redundant data in disparate databases. The data integration key, and the algorithms and techniques used for identifying possible redundant data occurrences, must be documented during the data transformation process.

DATA TRANSFORMATION PHASES

Many organizations are not formally transforming their data resource. What transformation they may do is usually incomplete or inconsistent transformation to meet current needs. Most follow a traditional Extract-Transform-Load approach, a suck-and-squirt approach, or a brute-force-physical approach. Some believe that a simple extract, superficial cleansing, and loading will solve all the disparate data problems. These approaches make a very big problem look very easy to resolve, but usually result in more disparate data.

Formal data transformation consists of three formal phases with formal steps in each phase. The phases are based on the traditional Extract-Transform-Load approach, but have been substantially enhanced to support formal data transformation. The enhancements avoid traditional approaches mentioned above that lead to additional disparate data.

The diagram in Figure 11.2 shows the three formal data transformation phases and the eleven formal data transformation steps. At a high level, data are extracted from the data source according to data source rules and are placed in a data depot for transformation. The data source and data target remain unaltered during the data transformation process, because all data transformation is done within a data depot.

The data are transformed within the data depot according to a formal set of data transformation rules. If any problem occurs during data transformation, the data depot is emptied, the problem is corrected, the source data are re-extracted, and the data transformation continues. When the data transformation is successful, the transformed data are loaded into the data target.

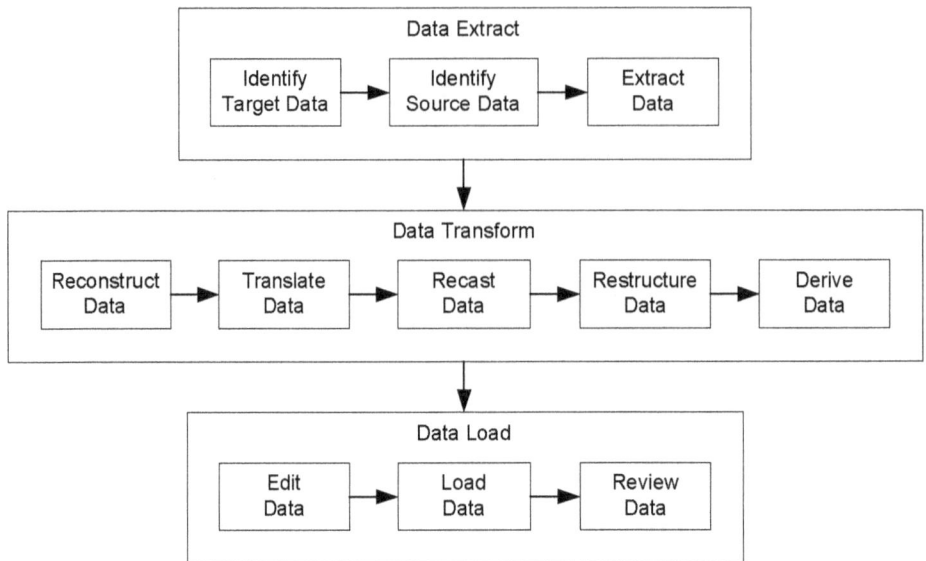

Figure 11.2. Data Transformation Phases.

Data Extract Phase

Data extract is the formal process of identifying and extracting the preferred disparate data and loading those data into a data depot for data transformation. It consists of target data identification, source data identification for those target data, and source data extraction to a data depot. Any data needed from the data target to support the data transformation are also extracted and placed in the data depot.

Data extract can be used for current operational data to build comparate operational databases. It can also be used for current and historical data instances to develop comparate evaluational databases for analytical processing. When data extract is used to develop comparate evaluational databases, the lowest level of source data detail must be extracted to provide for summarizing data to the lowest level evaluational data desired.

Data extract consists of specifications for developing the code to extract the source data. It is not the actual coding that performs the data extract. When the specifications have been developed, the technical staff can develop the specific coding based on the particular operating environment.

Identify Target Data

Identify target data is the formal process of determining the desired target data. The desired target data are specified as the preferred physical data structure and will be used throughout the data transformation process. The preferred logical data structure can be included in the specification if it is useful. The process sets the scope of data transformation.

Identify Source Data

Identify source data is the formal process of determining the source data that will be needed to prepare the target data. The source data are specified as a physical data structure of the disparate data as documented during data inventorying. The logical data structure, based on the data cross-references, can be included in the specification if it is useful. The preferred data source rules are used to identify the source data.

One of the most frequently ignored steps in traditional data transformation is formal data source rules, including conditional data sourcing. Emphasis is often placed on a system of reference or system of record to avoid the details of conditional data sourcing. However, that approach seldom results in the most current or most accurate data, and can impact the target data quality.

Extract Source Data

Extract source data is the formal process of extracting the source data from the preferred data source based on the specifications, performing any database conversions necessary between the data source and the data depot, and placing the source data into a data depot for data transformation.

Data Transform Phase

Data transform is the formal process of transforming disparate data into comparate data, in the data depot, using formal data transformation rules. It consists of data reconstruction, data translation, data recasting, data restructuring, and data derivation. Data transform is where the disparate data are actually transformed to comparate data.

Data transform can be used for both operational data and for evaluational data transformation. Some of the steps within data transform apply to both operational and evaluational data, and some of the steps apply only to evaluational data.

Transforming data is the really difficult part of data resource transformation, because of the detail involved in both the specifications and the coding. Data transform consists of specifications for developing the code to transform the data. It is not the actual coding that performs the data transformation. When the specifications have been developed, the technical staff can develop the specific coding based on the particular operating environment.

Reconstruct Data

Reconstruct data is the formal process of rebuilding complete historical data that are not stored as full data records. It is typically used for developing comparate evaluational data, and is seldom used for developing comparate operational data. It is an optional step for creating comparate evaluational data.

When operational data change, the old data value may be saved as a historical data instance, containing either the changed data values or a full data instance. Historical data instances that are full data instances do not need to be reconstructed. However, historical data instances containing only the changed values do need to be reconstructed to full historical data instances.

A *data reconstruction rule* is a data rule that specifies the reconstruction of historical data into full historical data instances in preparation for data transformation. The data reconstruction rule shows the conditions for data reconstruction and the data reconstruction that is performed. The data reconstruction rules are designated with the keyword Reconstruction!.

Translate Data

Translate data is the formal process of translating the extracted data values to the preferred data values, if they are not already in the preferred format or content, using appropriate data translation rules. It's an important step to put all data in the preferred form to reduce the variability inherent in disparate data and ensure consistency in the comparate data resource. It needs to be done after data reconstruction and before recasting, restructuring, or deriving data.

Translating data is done for both operational data and evaluational data, including current and historical data instances. All data must be translated into the proper format or content in a comparate data resource.

Data translation rules were defined in Chapter 9 as specifying the algorithm for translating data values between preferred and non-preferred data designations. They only specify translations in format or content between data variations. Their development was described in Chapter 10. Those data translation rules are used in the translate data process.

Recast Data

Recast data is the formal process of adjusting data values for historical continuity. It aligns data values for a common historical perspective using data recast rules. Data recasting follows data translation so that the proper data values are recast. Data recasting is not a translation of data values. It's an adjustment of the data values, after they have been translated, to provide historical continuity.

Recasting data only applies to certain data, such as financial data to analyze trends independent of monetary inflation. Recasting data is typically done only for evaluational data. Recasting current operational data could destroy their integrity for operational decision making. Recasting data can be done to any current or past time period, and could be done for multiple time periods. Each organization must determine the appropriate time period for recasting data depending on their specific needs.

A *data recasting rule* is a data rule that specifies the adjustment of data values to a specific time period, such as adjusting financial data values to a specific time period for a comparison of trends independent of monetary inflation. The recasting time period may be in the present or the past. The rule is designated with the keyword Recast!. It contains the time period for the recasting, the point for recasting, and the algorithm used for recasting.

Restructure Data

Restructure data is the formal process of changing the structure of the disparate source data to the structure of the comparate target data. It takes physical disparate data structures that have existed in the past and changes them to a preferred physical data structure. Data restructuring can be performed any time during data transformation, but is best performed after data recasting and before data derivation.

Many structural problems need to be overcome during data restructuring. The physical data structure may be different, primary keys often change over time, the meaning of data often change over time, data may be missing for certain time periods, and so on. These problems result from different perceptions of the business world, changes in perceptions of the business world, lack of formal logical and physical data modeling, different product implementations, and so on, and need to be resolved during data restructuring.

Data restructuring applies primarily to current data instances in operational data, but can be used for current and historical data instances in evaluational data if the restructuring is not too difficult. When restructuring disparate operational data to preferred evaluational data becomes too difficult, the best approach is to restructure only the operational data first. In a subsequent process, preferred physical operational data are renormalized to preferred physical evaluational data.

When evaluational data originate from multiple disparate data sources that are restructured in separate data restructuring processes, the best approach is to perform the operational data restructuring first, followed by renormalizing the preferred physical data to the preferred evaluational data. Trying to perform data restructuring from disparate operational data directly to comparate evaluational data in multiple data restructuring processes often leads to different results. Therefore, the best approach is to restructure all of the operational data first, followed by a renormalization to preferred physical data.

Derive Data

Derive data is the formal process of deriving target data from source data according to formal data derivation rules. It applies to deriving individual data values, to summarizing operational data, and to aggregating evaluational data to the lowest level of detail desired. Data derivation is the last step in the data transformation phase, because all of the data need to be available for derivation.

Data derivation is not the same as data translation. Data derivation creates data values from existing data values. Data translation changes existing data values.

A *data derivation rule* was defined in Chapter 3 as a data integrity rule that specifies the contributors to a derived data value, the algorithm for deriving the data value, and the conditions for deriving the data value. Data derivation can be a *generation data derivation,* where the data derivation algorithm generates the derived data values without the input of any other data values. It can be a *single contributor data derivation* when one data value is the contributor to an algorithm that generates the derived data. It can be a *multiple contributor data derivation* where many data attributes from the same data entity or different data entities contribute to the derived data. It can be an *aggregation data derivation* where two or more values of the same data attribute in different data occurrences contribute to the derived data.

Data Load Phase

Data load is the formal process of loading the target database after the data transformation has been completed. The transformed data are edited according to the preferred data integrity rules, loaded into the target database, and reviewed to ensure the load was successful before the data are released for use.

When the data load is successful, the data depot can be cleared for additional data transformation. Alternatively, the contents of the data depot could be archived as a record of the data transformations that were made. That record may be important for data provenance in large organizations or between organizations. However, it cannot be used for operational processing.

Edit Data

Edit data is the formal process of applying the preferred data edits to the transformed data to ensure the quality of the data before they are loaded into the target database. The process applies to both operational and evaluational data. The data edits are applied within the data depot so that any data that fail the preferred data integrity rules remain in the data depot and do not enter the target database. The target database may be accessed for data that are involved in the data editing, but the data edit process remains in the data depot.

The preferred data edits should specify the violation action and the notification action to be taken when data fail the edit. The preferred data integrity rules may specify the violation and notification actions for normal processing, but may not apply to data transformation. If these actions have not been specified for data transformation, they need to be specified before data editing begins.

Data quality improvement applications, such as address cleansing applications, may be run while data are in the data depot. These applications must be run before the preferred data edits are performed so that the results of the improvement pass through the data edits. The data quality improvement applications generally improve the chances that data pass the preferred data edits, but may result in the data not passing the preferred data edits. Therefore, they must be run before the preferred data edits are applied.

Applying the preferred data edits only verifies the data integrity. It does not verify the data accuracy—how well the data represent the business world. No data integrity rules or data edits can be specified to evaluate the accuracy of the data.

Load Data

Load data is the formal process of loading the data from the data depot into the target database. Any database conversion that is necessary is done during the data load process. Only data records that pass the preferred data edits are loaded into the target database. The violation action may be to hold the record that contains a violation in the data depot until the violation is corrected, or it may be to hold the entire set of data within the data depot until all violations are corrected. The choice is up to the organization and their particular operating environment.

Review Data

Review data is the formal process of reviewing the data that have been transformed and loaded into the target database to ensure they are appropriate for production use. The review is generally focused on whether or not the load was successful. However, it can focus on other aspects of data transformation and integrity to ensure that the data are appropriate for use. In some situations, the preferred data edits are applied after the data have been loaded as a final verification that the data are appropriate for production use.

When the data fail the review process, the load is reversed and the transformed data are removed from the target database. Adjustments are made to the data transformation, data edits, and data load processes to correct the failure. The data are then reloaded and reviewed to ensure they are appropriate for production use.

Reverse Data Transformation

The above discussion applied largely to forward data transformation. However, reverse data transformation can be used during the virtual data resource state to maintain disparate databases until the applications can be transformed to use comparate data. The process is essentially the same, except that the comparate-to-disparate data transformation rules are reversed to become disparate-to-comparate data transformation rules.

The process may seem like excessive documentation, but it eases the process of transforming data in the virtual state. Eventually, all of the disparate data will be converted to comparate data and all of the disparate data applications will be converted to comparate data applications. Then the reverse data transformation rules need only be retained for historical purposes.

In some situations, the reverse data transformation rules may be needed for the transformation of comparate data to meet disparate external reporting requirements. Creating a comparate data resource for an organization does not eliminate the need to provide data to external organizations as disparate data. The reverse data transformation rules need to be retained to meet these external requirements.

SUMMARY

Formal data transformation begins the process of changing the structure and values of disparate data to comparate data based on the preferred physical data architecture. Data transformation can be done formally within the context a common data architecture or informally, outside of the context of a common data architecture. It can be forward from disparate data to comparate data, or reverse from comparate data to disparate data.

Formal data transformation is a destructive process because it actually changes the data. It's a detailed process that takes thought, effort, and time, but is achievable. It's based on formal data transformation rules that are implemented through a data broker between databases and applications until the applications can be transformed to operate on comparate data. Data transformation between databases is done in a data depot that is independent of the source data and target data.

Formal data transformation consists of three formal phases containing eleven formal data steps, shown in the outline below.

Data Extract Phase
    Identify Target Data
    Identify Source Data
    Extract Source Data
Data Transform Phase
    Reconstruct Data
    Translate Data
    Recast Data
    Restructure Data
    Derive Data
Data Load Phase
    Edit Data
    Load Data
    Review Data

Formal data transformation is the only way for an organization to move from a disparate data environment to a comparate data environment in an effective and efficient manner. Traditional approaches seldom provide any real benefit and often result in an increase in disparate data. The best approach is formal data transformation within the context of a common data architecture.

QUESTIONS

The following questions are provided as a review of transforming disparate data, and to stimulate thought about the process of transforming disparate data.

1. What is the data transformation concept?

2. Why is data transformation considered a destructive process?

3. What's the difference between data bridges, data converters, and data brokers?

4. What is the purpose of a data depot?

5. What is the purpose of the three formal phases of data transformation?

6. What are the five formal steps of the data transformation phase?

7. When are data integrity rules applied to the transformed data?

8. What are the different types of data transformation rules?

9. What is the purpose of reverse data transformation?

10. What does formal data transformation accomplish?

Chapter 12

DATA TRANSFORMATION PROCESS

Managing the transformation of data and applications!

The last chapter described the concepts and principles for transforming data during the virtual data resource state and the comparate data resource state based on the preferred physical data architecture, the existing disparate data, and the organization's operating environment. The concept of a data broker was described for managing data transformation until applications using disparate data could be transformed to using comparate data. The three formal phases and their eleven formal steps for extracting, transforming, and loading data were described.

Chapter 12 describes the techniques for transforming disparate data to comparate data to build a comparate data resource and support applications using comparate data. It also describes the techniques for transforming comparate data to disparate data to support applications using disparate data until they can be transformed. These techniques are based on the concepts and principles described in the last chapter and solve the third basic problem of data redundancy and the fourth basic problem of data variability found in a disparate data resource. The ultimate result of data transformation is a comparate data resource that supports the current and future business information demand of an organization.

DATA TRANSFORMATION PREPARATION

Preparation for data transformation includes the scope of data transformation, the sequence of data transformation, and the involvement in data transformation. These topics are different than described for data inventorying, data cross-referencing, and preferred data designations, because they involve actually changing the data, rather than understanding the data.

Data Transformation Scope

The scope of data transformation can be different from the scope for data inventorying, data cross-referencing, and preferred data designations.

However, the data transformation scope must be within the scope of data that have already been inventoried and cross-referenced, and for which preferred data designations have been made, because data transformation is based on the preferred physical data architecture. Data transformation cannot proceed without a preferred physical data architecture.

The scope of data transformation must also include the scope of application transformation. The development of a comparate data resource and the transformation of applications to using comparate data must be carefully integrated. In other words, the scope has expanded from understanding the disparate data and designing a comparate data resource, to building the comparate data resource, transforming the disparate data, and transforming existing applications using those comparate data.

Data Transformation Sequence

The sequence of data transformation depends on the organization's plans to develop a comparate data resource and transform applications from using disparate data to using comparate data. An organization can perform the data inventory and data cross-reference steps to understand their existing disparate data. An organization can also make the preferred data designations to understand how a comparate data architecture would be developed. Then plans can be made to actually transform the data.

For example, data inventorying, data cross-referencing, and preferred data designations may have been done for all public works data. Those processes provide a complete understanding of the disparate public words data within the context of a common data architecture. However, only public water system data will be transformed, to be followed later by sewer data, power data, street data, and so on. The plans for transforming disparate data must be integrated with the plans for transforming applications to using comparate data. Those tasks cannot be done independently.

Data Transformation Involvement

Involvement in data transformation includes data stewards, database professionals, application analysts and programmers, business professionals, and project managers. Data stewards have knowledge of the data and how those data are used by the business. Database professionals know the existing disparate data resource and develop the comparate data resource. They develop and maintain the data depot for data transformation, and the data brokers. Application analysts and programmers know how the applications can be transformed to use comparate data, and can assist with the development and maintenance of data brokers.

Business professionals provide input about the processes performed in the applications and the data needed by the business. They develop the business cases and reporting requirements to verify the comparate data and applications. Project managers ensure that the entire process is orchestrated so that the business operations are not impacted. The entire data transformation process becomes much more involved than understanding the disparate data.

One caution about transforming data and applications is that the process should not be hampered by extensive application changes. Business professionals and application managers often see an opportunity to make extensive application changes during data transformation. Although those changes seem feasible, extensive application changes during data transformation could be difficult unless very carefully planned. A better approach is to transform the data with only the application transformations necessary to use comparate data, and then make additional application enhancements at a later date.

DATA TRANSFORMATION

Data transformation includes the three formal phases and eleven formal steps described in the previous chapter. It uses the general extract-transform-load approach, but includes specific steps for transforming disparate data based on a physical preferred data architecture and applying data integrity rules to ensure high quality data to support the business.

Data transformation is unique to each organization, their disparate data, and their operating environment. Considering all of the different organizations, all of the different forms of disparate data, and all of the different operating environments, literally tens of thousands of unique situations exist. Describing each of these unique situations, or even a few of them, is way beyond the scope of the current book, and could fill many books on specific data transformation.

Therefore, the techniques described below are general techniques that can be applied to specific situations by people knowledgeable about those situations. The specific logic for performing the processes depends on database professionals, application programmers, and the particular operating environment. Many complaints I've received about unique situations not being described are valid, but knowledge of specific situations must be combined with general techniques to form specific techniques for each unique situation.

Data Extract Phase

Data extract was defined in the last chapter as the formal process of identifying and extracting the preferred disparate data and loading those data into a data depot for data transformation. Data extract consists of identifying the target data, identifying the source data needed to prepare those target data, and loading the source data into a data depot for data transformation.

Identify Target Data

Identify target data is the formal process of determining the desired target data. The target data are documented as a data set, as shown below. Since data transformation is based on the physical preferred data architecture, the physical data names are used. Note that the preferred physical data names do not show the variation name. The preferred variation is always used during data transformation.

```
DEPTMT
   DEPTMT_NM
   DEPTMT_ACRNM
   DEPTMT_TYP_CD

EMPLYE
   EMPLY_SSN
   EMPLY_NM
   EMPLY_BRTH_DT
   DEPTMT_NM
```

The logical target data names could also be shown for business professionals accustomed to looking at the preferred logical data architecture. Note that the data characteristic variations are not shown. Since data transformation is based on the preferred data, the preferred data characteristic variation is always used.

```
Department
   Department. Name
   Department. Acronym
   Department Type. Code

Employee
   Employee. Social Security Number
   Employee. Name Complete
   Employee. Birth Date
   Department. Name
```

Identify Source Data

Identify source data is the formal process of determining the source data that will be needed to prepare the target data. The preferred data source for each target data item is determined based on the data source rules. The process is to take each target data item and determine the preferred source for that data item using the data source rules and the data cross-references. The example below shows the sources for each target data item identified in the target data.

```
DEPTMT
    DEPTMT_NM              DEPT:DEPT_NM
    DEPTMT_ACRNM          DEPT:ACRONYM
    DEPTMT_TYP_CD         CODES:DTYPE

EMPLYE
    EMPLY_SSN             EMPL:SSN
    EMPLY_NM              PYRL:PYRL_NM
    EMPLY_BRTH_DT        AA:BDATE
    DEPTMT_NM             EFILE:DNM
```

Multiple data sources may need to be identified when conditional data source rules exist. For example, an employee's birth date may be obtained from two sources based on their hire date. The example below shows how the sources would be designated.

```
EMPLY_BRTH_DT
    When EMPLY_HRE_DT <= December 31, 1999   << PYRL:PYRL_BD
    When EMPLY_HRE_DT >= January 1, 2000,    << TNG:BRDT
```

Disparate data often contain combined data, which were broken down to data product unit variations during data inventorying. The breakdown of those combined data are used to identify the data item that needs to be sourced from the disparate data.

For example, a disparate data comment field contains the project name and the project start date, which need to be separated in the comparate data resource. The source data is the same for both the project name and project start date, as shown below.

Target Data

```
PRJCT_NM
PRJCT_STRT_DT
```

Source Data

```
PRJCT_NM                   PRJ:CMT
PRJCT_STRT_DT              PRJ:CMT
```

Contributing data items may need to be obtained to support derived data,

351

even though those contributing data items may not appear in the target data. The situation may apply to operational data or to evaluational data. All of the source data needed to support the derived data are identified as source data.

For example, all of the vehicle trip miles may need to be obtained for deriving the total miles a vehicle was used for business. The example below shows the target data is Vehicle. Business Miles and the source data are the individual Vehicle Trip. Miles, which are obtained from the miles in the vehicle trip disparate data file.

Target Data

    VEHCL:BUSNS_MILS

Source Data

    VEHCLTRP:MILS   VCLTRP:MLS

Non-redundant data records may exist in different disparate data files. All of these data records need to be identified and brought into the data depot for transformation. For example, student records need to be sourced from data files for grade school students, middle school students, and high school students, and combined into one comparate data file for all students. In addition, the data names are different in the disparate data files.

The designation of target data and source data are shown below. If conditional data sourcing were needed for data from multiple disparate data files, the conditions would be designated as described above.

Target Data

    STDNT_NM_CMPLT
    STDNT_BRTH_DT
    STDNT_HGHT
    And so on.

Source Data – Elementary School

    STDNT_NM_CMPLT   ESTD:NM
    STDNT_BRTH_DT   ESTD:BD
    STDNT_HGHT   ESTD:HT
    And so on.

Source Data – Middle School

    STDNT_NM_CMPLT   MDL:NAME
    STDNT_BRTH_DT   MDL:BIRTH
    STDNT_HGHT   MDL:H
    And so on.

Source Data – High School

STDNT_NM_CMPLT	STD:NME
STDNT_BRTH_DT	STD:BDT
STDNT_HGHT	STD:TALL

And so on.

Note that the data integration key could be used to identify possible redundant data occurrences between the disparate data files. For example, a particular student may appear in both the middle school and the high school disparate data files. Since the primary keys are different in those disparate data files, the data integration key would be used to identify those redundant data occurrences. Data would then be sourced from those redundant data occurrences based on the conditional data source rules.

The examples above are simple examples. However, the disparate data situation in most organizations is often quite confusing. A combination of unconditional data sourcing, conditional data sourcing, combined facts in disparate data, derived data contributors, and non-redundant and redundant data occurrences is usually the norm for most data transformation processes. The above notations are combined to form a complete statement of the data that need to be sourced.

Extract Source Data

Extract source data is the formal process of extracting the source data from the preferred data source based on the specifications, performing any database conversions necessary between the data source and the data depot, and placing the source data into a data depot for data transformation. The data extract is based on the source data specified in the Identify Source Data step described above.

Data are extracted from the source by some type of routine, either within a database management system or from an application outside a database management system. Individual routines for extracting source data from a specific data source or database are shown in Figure 12.1. Each routine extracts data from one database and places those data in the data depot.

One routine for extracting data from multiple data sources or databases is shown in Figure 12.2. One routine extracts data from multiple data sources and places those data in the data depot. Both approaches are valid, and a combination of approaches can be used, depending on the specific operating environment.

The data extract routine uses a primary key matrix and existing physical primary keys to extract the appropriate data occurrences or data instances.

It can use the data integration key to identify possible redundant data occurrences and either use the appropriate data occurrence, or flag the redundant data occurrences for evaluation and decision. It can extract current data instances and corresponding historical data instances.

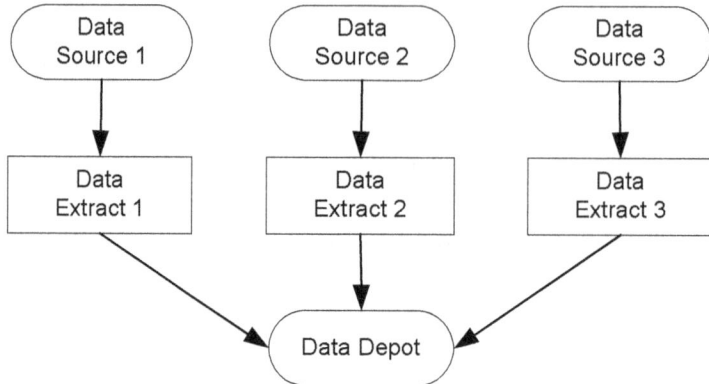

Figure 12.1. Individual data extract routines.

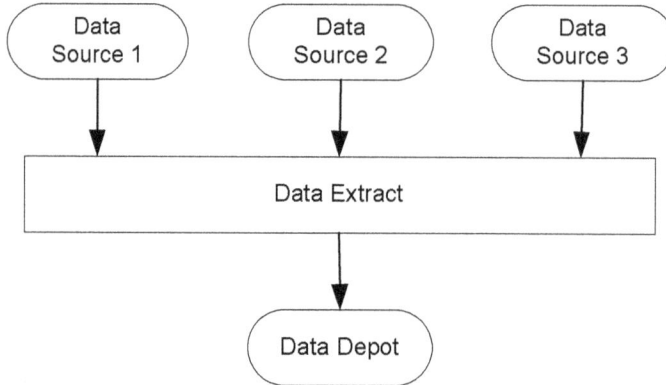

Figure 12.2. A single data extract routine.

The data extract routine can break down combined disparate data and place the specified source data in the data depot. The breakdown is based on the specifications placed in the data product unit variation during the data inventory process.

A *data converter* is an application that changes the data between heterogeneous databases. It does not transform the data in any way. It only changes the physical format of the data from one database environment to another database environment. The data extract routine uses a data converter, when necessary, to change the physical format of the data from the disparate database to the data depot database.

Specific data extract routines need to be written based on the disparate data and the operating environment. Database technicians and application programmers are usually very skilled at developing data extract routines, once they know the exact specifications. The key is to develop the exact specifications before building the data extract routines. Proceeding with any data extract without complete specifications often leads to low quality data and creates more disparate data.

After the source data have been extracted and processed according to the specifications, the data are placed in the data depot for data transformation, using their disparate data names so the connection can be made to any documentation done during data inventorying. Combined disparate data that are broken down during data inventorying use the data product unit variation name.

Historical data instances are extracted similar to current data instances. The only difference is that the primary key contains some type of time or date indication. Otherwise, the same specifications for data sourcing, breaking down combined disparate data, contributors to derived data, and redundant data instances apply.

Data Transform Phase

Data transform was defined in the last chapter as the formal process of transforming disparate data into comparate data, in the data depot, using formal data transformation rules. It consists of data reconstruction, data translation, data recasting, data restructuring, and data derivation.

Reconstruct Data

Reconstruct data is the formal process of rebuilding complete historical data that are not stored as full data records. It is typically used for developing comparate evaluational data, and is seldom used for developing comparate operational data.

When operational data values change, the former data value may be saved as history. Either the changed data values, and the appropriate key, or all data values may be saved as history. When all data values have been saved, data reconstruction does not need to be done.

A *data reconstruction rule* is a data rule that specifies the reconstruction of historical data into full historical data instances in preparation for data transformation. The data reconstruction rule shows the conditions for data reconstruction and the data reconstruction that is performed.

For example, student data need to be reconstructed from the present back through 1984. The reconstruct rule is shown below, showing the dates for data reconstruction and the data that need to be reconstructed. Note that the preferred physical data names are used in the data reconstruct rule, since the data reconstruction can involve many different physical data names across multiple current and historical data files.

```
Student
    Reconstruct! Current back through January 1984
        STDNT_NME
        STDNT_BRTH_DT
        STDNT_WGHT
        STDNT_CHNG_DT
    And so on.
```

The reconstructed data may be all of the extracted source data or only a subset of the extracted source data. The data reconstruct rule shows only the data that are to be reconstructed.

The typical approach is to start with the current historical data instance and work backward in time through the historical data to create the historical data instances. Whenever a data value changes for any of the data shown in the data reconstruct rule, an historical data instance is created for each of the data attributes shown in the data reconstruct rule. The appropriate primary key is formed and the historical data instance is saved. The process continues until the limit of historical data is reached, or until the time limit stated in the data reconstruct rule is reached.

Multiple non-redundant data files may each have their own history. The data reconstruct rule needs to be applied to each of these data files. The resulting historical data occurrences represent the changes from all of the non-redundant data files.

For example, the student data from an elementary school data file, middle school data file, and high school data file each have their own history data files. Historical data instances are created from each of those data files and merged as one set of historical data instances that apply to the current data instances.

Multiple redundant data files that have their own history need to be treated differently. Only the data sourced from each data file are involved in the creation of historical data instances. Data that are not sourced from a data file are not used to create historical data instances.

For example, several data files contain redundant student data occurrences. The data source rules show which data are extracted from those data files. The data reconstruct rule shows which of those extracted data are used to create historical data instances. Data that are not extracted are not used to create historical data instances.

Translate Data

Translate data is the formal process of translating the extracted data values to the preferred data values, if they are not already in the preferred format or content, using appropriate data translation rules. *Data translation rules* were defined earlier as specifying the algorithm for translating data values between preferred and non-preferred data designations.

For example, a student's birth date could be translated from the MDY format to the CYMD format, as shown below.

```
STDT
   BRTH_DT  Translation!  MDY >> CYMD
```

Similarly, a student's name could be translated from the inverted sequence to the normal sequence, as shown below.

```
STDT
   NM  Translation!  Name Inverted >> Name Normal
```

A student's height could be converted from inches to millimeters, as shown below.

```
STDT
   HT  Translation!  Inches >> Millimeters, 1 Digit
```

The data names are the physical disparate data names that were loaded from the data source. The data translation rules are shown in their formal notation. Fundamental data translation rules can be used where appropriate. When the format is variable, algorithms could be used to identify the format so the appropriate data translation rules could be used.

Data reference items are translated to the preferred data reference set variation using a matrix. For example, a student's disability data reference item coded data values and names would be translated to the preferred data reference set variation as shown below.

Disability. Translation!

School;	Employment;	Health;	New; *
10 Sight	A Seeing	V Vision	S Sight
20 Hearing	H Hear	S Sound	H Hearing
30 Physical	P Physical	A Accidental	P Physical
40 Develop	D Developed	G Genetic	D Developmental

The translated data values can be placed back into the existing data item, or a new data item can be created. In the examples above, the student's birth date, name, height, and disability would be translated back into the same data item that was extracted from the data source.

The process is to work through each data item extracted from the data source to determine if the data value is in the preferred format or content. When the data value is not in the preferred format or content, a data translation rule is specified. When all of the data translation rules have been specified, the process of data translation can begin.

Recast Data

Recast data is the formal process of adjusting data values for historical continuity. It aligns data values for a common historical perspective using data recast rules. A *data recasting rule* is a data rule that specifies the adjustment of data values to a specific time period, such as adjusting financial data values to a specific time period for a comparison of trends independent of monetary inflation.

For example, 30 years of budget data could be recast to the beginning of the 30 year period for an analysis of trends independent of inflation, as shown below. The 30 year period is from 1970 through 1999, the values are recast to 1970, using Recast Algorithm 6. Recast Algorithm 6 specifies the adjustments applied to each year during the 30 year period

```
Recast! 1970 through 1999 to 1970 using Recast Algorithm 6
  BDG:OBJ
  BDG:SOB
  BDG:PRG
  BDG:SPRG
And so on.
```

The data names are the physical disparate data names that were loaded from the data source. The recast data values can be placed back into the existing data item, or new data items can be created for the recast data values.

The process is to identify any data that needs to be recast, determine the time period for recasting, determine the point for recasting, and specify the algorithm for recasting the data values during the time period. When the data recasting rules have been specified, the process of recasting can begin.

Restructure Data

Restructure data is the formal process of changing the structure of the disparate source data to the structure of the comparate target data. It takes physical disparate data structures that have existed in the past and changes those structures to the preferred physical data structure. Data restructuring may involve combining data into fewer data entities, or splitting data into more data entities.

The data restructuring is shown as a list with the physical source data names on the left and the preferred physical data names on the right. The physical source data names may be either the names of the data extracted from the source, or the names of the data resulting from data translation or data recasting.

The example below shows a data restructure list. The employee's name obtained from the payroll data file becomes the employee's name in the new employee data file. The birthdate from the affirmative action data file becomes the employee's birth date. The ethnicity code obtained from the training file becomes the employee's ethnicity code.

```
EMPLYE
    PYRL: NAM                    NM
    AA:BIRTH_DATE                BRTH_DT
    TNG:ETHNICITY                ETHNTY_CD
    And so on.
```

The process is to go through all of the extracted, translated, and recast data and place those data according to the preferred physical data architecture. The data restructure list may be more detailed than the example above, but the process is the same. When the data restructure list has been completed, the data can be moved according to that list.

Derive Data

Derive data is the formal process of deriving target data from source data according to formal data derivation rules. It applies to deriving individual data values, to summarizing operational data, and to aggregating evaluational data to the lowest level of detail desired. A *data derivation rule* was defined in Chapter 3 as a data integrity rule that specifies the contributors to a derived data value, the algorithm for deriving the data value, and the conditions for deriving the data value.

For example, an employee's years of service is calculated annually on the employee's increment date, based on their yearly increment date and their hire data, as shown below. The data in the data depot have their preferred physical data name, but the derivation algorithm uses the logical data names according to a common data architecture.

```
    EMPLYE
        SVC_YRS
            Derivation! Annually on Employee. Yearly Increment Date
            Employee. Yearly Increment Date – Employee. Hire Date
```

Similarly, the Vehicle. Business Miles are derived from all of the Vehicle Trip. Miles that were extracted as described above.

VEHCL
 BUSNS_MLS
  Derivation! January 1{Sum VEHCLTRP:MLS}December 3

Many different types of data derivation rules can be prepared, as described in Chapter 3 and shown in Appendix A. Data derivations rules are described in more detail in *Data Resource Simplexity*.

The process is to specify all of the data derivation rules that apply to the restructured data in the data depot. When those rules have been specified, they can be applied to the data.

Data Load

Data load was defined in the last chapter as the formal process of loading the target database after the data transformation has been completed. The transformed data are edited according to the preferred data integrity rules, loaded into the target database, and reviewed to ensure the load was successful before the data are released for use.

Edit Data

Edit data is the formal process of applying the preferred data edits to the transformed data to ensure the quality of the data before they are loaded into the target database. The process is to apply the preferred data integrity rules as defined in a common data architecture to the transformed data in the data depot. Any data that fail the data integrity rules trigger a violation action and a notification action.

Data that fail the data edits remain in the data depot until the failure can be resolved. Algorithms could be implemented to resolve the failure so that the data pass the data integrity rules, or the data could be held in suspense for a person to review and resolve. Data that fail the data edits should never be loaded into the target database.

Some people allow data that fail the data edits to enter the comparate database with a flag showing that the data failed the edit. Those flags are later reviewed and corrections are made to the data. However, in the vast majority of situations, those flags are seldom reviewed and the failed data are seldom corrected. The result is a lower quality comparate data resource. Therefore, only data that successfully pass the data edits should be placed in the comparate data resource.

Load Data

Load data is the formal process of loading the data from the data depot into the target database. Any database conversion that is necessary is done during the data load process. Only data that pass the preferred data edits are loaded into the target database. Data that fail the preferred data edits remain in the data depot until the problem is resolved.

Review Data

Review data is the formal process of reviewing the data that have been transformed and loaded into the target database to ensure they are appropriate for production use. The review makes the final determination of whether the transformed and loaded data are appropriate for use. If all of the data transformation processes were successful, the data passed the data integrity rules, and the load was successful, the data can be released for use.

The failure is identified and the data are re-transformed or re-edited before another data load is attempted. The worst scenario is that the data need to be removed from the data depot, the source data need to be re-extracted, and the data transformation process needs to be performed on the new set of data.

DATA TRANSFORMATION SUPPORT

Support for data transformation includes reverse data transformation, data brokering, managing evaluational data, managing missing data and default data, and maintaining data transformation documentation. Each of these topics is described below.

Reverse Data Transformation

Forward data transformation is the formal transformation of disparate data to comparate data. Data are extracted from the preferred data source, transformed, and loaded into the data target. The processes described above are forward data transformation. *Reverse data transformation* is the formal transformation of comparate data to disparate data. It's necessary to maintain disparate data that supports disparate applications until they can be converted to comparate data.

Reverse data transformation follows the same phases and steps described above. The only difference is that the source data are extracted from the comparate data resource and the target data are loaded into the existing disparate data resource. The process is performed only for new data that are initially entered into the new comparate data resource and need to be placed into the existing data resource to support disparate data applications.

The data extract phase identifies new data that have been added into the comparate data resource, identifies where those new data will be placed in the existing disparate data resource, and extracts the new data to the data depot for transformation. Data converters are used as necessary to change the data from one database management system to another. The physical data names are used during the load data phase.

The data transform phase follows the same general sequence described above, although the processes may be different. Historical data may need to be reconstructed when the disparate data contain full historical data instances and the comparate data contain partial historical data records. Historical data may need to be de-constructed when the disparate data contain partial historical data instances and the comparate data contain complete historical data instances.

The data values may need to be translated from the preferred variation in the comparate data resource to a non-preferred variation in the disparate data resource. Data translation rules are prepared using the same notation described above.

Data seldom need to be recast during reverse data transformation, and also seldom need to be un-recast during reverse data transformation. If those situations do occur, the same process described above is used.

The comparate data are restructured to the disparate data as described above for restructuring the disparate data to the comparate data. The same process described above is used for the data restructuring.

Data derivation may need to be done, but is usually minimal. The same process described above is used for data derivation.

The data load phase usually does not perform any data edits. The comparate data generally have much higher integrity than the disparate data, eliminating the need for applying any data edits. The data are loaded into the disparate data resource from the data depot using a data converter when necessary. A review of the loaded data is made prior to releasing the data for use.

Some reverse data transformations cannot be performed, such as splitting coded data values. Data transformation that goes from specific to general is easy to perform, but data transformation that goes from general to specific is difficult to perform without additional insight.

Reverse data transformation may need to break down or combine data values in the disparate data resource. The original data inventory documentation can be consulted to determine how data values need to be combined or broken down. Those specifications are added to the processes described above for reverse data transformation.

Data Brokering

A *data broker* is an application that acts as an intermediary between disparate data and comparate data in databases or applications. It performs formal data transformations in both directions between disparate data and comparate data. *Data brokering* is the process of using data brokers to perform formal data transformation.

The data brokering process is shown in Figure 12.3. The forward and reverse data transformations described above are shown vertically in the center of the diagram. Forward data transformation is down from disparate data to comparate data, and reverse data transformation is up from comparate data to disparate data.

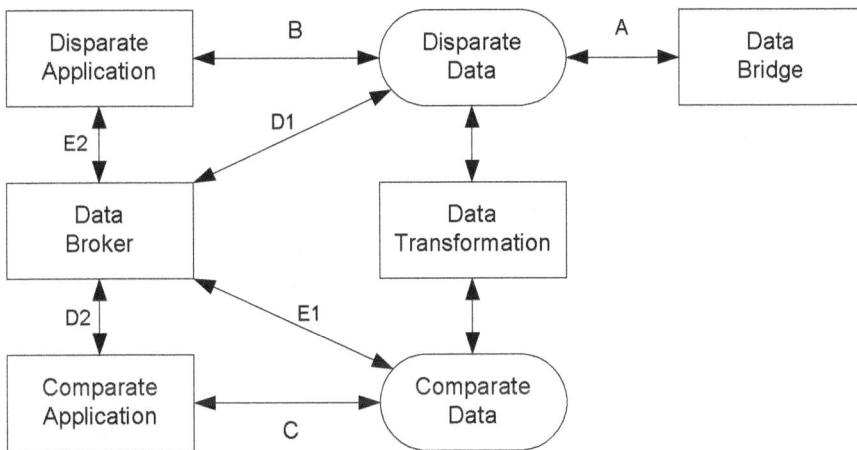

Figure 12.3. Data brokering process.

A *data bridge* is an application that moves data from one disparate data file to another disparate data file to keep the two data files in synch. The primary purpose is to maintain redundant data in a disparate data resource. Route A shows the data bridges, which will likely be replaced by more formal data bridges.

The data brokering process is shown on the left side of the diagram. Route B represents a disparate data application using disparate data, and requires no data brokering. Route C represents a comparate data application using comparate data, and requires no data brokering.

Routes D1 and D2 are the transformation of data from a disparate data resource, through a data broker, to a comparate data application, and the transformation of data from a comparate data application, through a data broker, to a disparate data resource. Routes E1 and E2 are the transformation of data from a comparate data resource, through a data broker, to a disparate data application, and the transformation of data from a disparate data application, through a data broker, to a comparate data resource. Route D1 replaces the data bridges.

The data broker uses the same transform data processes described above for forward and reverse data transformation. The basic difference is that the data transformation in the center of the diagram maintains the disparate and comparate databases independent of any applications, while the data broker transforms data between applications and databases.

Databases and applications are often tightly coupled, which could be difficult to manage. The tight coupling is one source of disparate data and low quality data. The data broker concept can break that tight coupling to maintain the application-specific databases until the applications can be transformed to use comparate data.

The terms *wrapping*, *encapsulation*, and *middleware* have been used for data transformation. These processes, when done with formal data transformation as described above, are essentially the same as a data broker. However, doing these processes outside of formal data transformation and a common data architecture leads to a perpetuation of disparate data, or an increase in disparate data. Therefore, the best approach is to use formal data transformation within a common data architecture as described above.

Evaluational Data

The question about evaluational data always comes up during data transformation. The basic question is whether disparate evaluational data should be transformed to comparate evaluational data, or whether the disparate operational data should be transformed to comparate operational data and then renormalized to comparate evaluational data. The typical approach is to transform the evaluational data, or to simply ignore any transformation of evaluational data.

However, the primary problem with most existing disparate operational and evaluational data is the quality of those data. The data seldom went through any formal data integrity rules or data edits. The low quality of the disparate operational data was perpetuated into the evaluational data obtained from those operational data.

In addition, the disparate evaluational data have been sliced, diced, and stored, which has perpetuated the low quality into the analysis of evaluational data. The resulting analytical data is seldom documented as to the source data, the selection criteria, and the analysis performed. The result is questionable analytical data, making the transformation of those analytical data questionable.

Attempting to transform the existing disparate operational data and the existing disparate evaluational data inevitably leads to a mismatch between the resulting comparate operational data and comparate evaluational data. Data integrity can be applied to the disparate operational data during data transformation, but it's extremely difficult to apply data integrity to the disparate evaluational data during data transformation.

The best approach, for those organizations interested in high quality operational and evaluational data, is to formally transform the disparate operational data as described above. Then, those high quality comparate operational data are formally renormalized to comparate evaluational data, which retain the high quality. Finally, the analysis of the evaluational data is performed with formal documentation of the source data, the selection criteria, and the analysis performed. The result is high quality analytical data.

Missing and Default Data Values

Missing data values are a frequent problem during data transformation, because disparate data often have missing data values. The data integrity rules need to include the possibility of missing data values. Where appropriate, algorithms can be implemented to replace missing data values. When missing data values are determined by an algorithm, a companion data characteristic needs to be created showing how the missing data value was created. When missing data values cannot be replaced with any degree of certainty, then the missing data values need to be accepted.

Default data values are another problem encountered during data transformation. Some default data values, such as {'Y' | 'N'} Default 'N' are appropriate in many situations. However, default data values such as when no ethnicity code, enter C for Caucasian, or when no birth date, enter January 1, 1900 are not acceptable. When possible, unacceptable default data values should be eliminated during data transformation.

Retiring Disparate Data

Disparate data can be retired when those data are no longer needed. When all disparate data applications have been transformed to comparate data applications, and all disparate databases have been transformed to comparate databases, the disparate data can be retired. In most situations, the disparate data are retired one database or one subject area at a time as applications and databases are converted.

When disparate data are retired, the associated data bridges and data brokers can be retired. Forward and reverse data transformation routines can also be retired. However, the specification for forward and reverse data transformation may be retained as a historical record of the data transformations that were made. If questions arise about the data transformations, the specifications can be reviewed to determine how the data were transformed.

When disparate data are retired, the documentation of those disparate data made during data inventorying, data cross-referencing, and preferred data designation should be retained as a historical record. Questions always arise about disparate data in databases, on screens, reports, and forms, in applications, and so on. These questions can usually be answered by referring to the documentation of those disparate data. Eventually, that documentation may be retired, but organizations should not be too hasty in retiring the documentation of their disparate data.

SUMMARY

The scope of data transformation can be different from the scope of data inventorying, data cross-referencing, and preferred data designations, but the data transformation process must follow those other processes and must include application transformation. The sequence of data transformation depends on the organization's plans to transform both the disparate data and the applications using those disparate data. Involvement in data transformation includes data management professionals, application professionals, and business professionals.

The data extract phase identifies target data, identifies the source data to prepare those target data, and extracts those source data to a data depot for transformation. The data transform phase reconstructs historical data, translates data values to the preferred variation, recasts data for historical continuity, restructures the data into the comparate data structure, and derives data. The processes are based on precise specifications, including data transformation rules. The data load phase edits the transformed data based on the preferred data edits, loads data that pass the data edits into the comparate data resource, and reviews the loaded data to ensure they are appropriate for operational use.

Reverse data transformation transforms comparate data to disparate data to support disparate data applications, following the same general sequence as forward data transformation. Data brokers support the forward and reverse data transformation of data between applications and databases, and replace many of the existing data bridges. Comparate evaluational data are usually developed from comparate operational data, rather than from transformed disparate operational data to ensure high quality data for analysis.

Disparate data can be retired when all applications using those disparate data have been transformed to using comparate data and all disparate databases have been transformed to comparate databases. Data brokers and data bridges can also be retired when they are no longer needed. Data transformation specifications are retained as a historical record of how the data were transformed. Disparate data documentation is retained as a historical record of the understanding of disparate data.

Data transformation ends the process of identifying, understanding, and resolving disparate data. The two major benefits of resolving disparate data are providing a high quality comparate data resource that meets the business information demand, and showing that disparate data are a waste of resources and can severely impact the business. Hopefully, an organization that goes through the process of understanding and resolving disparate data will never again allow the creation of disparate data.

QUESTIONS

The following questions are provided as a review of data transformation, and to stimulate thought about how to implement data transformation.

1. How does the sequence of data transformation compare to the sequence of data inventorying, data cross-referencing, and preferred data designations?

2. Who is involved in data transformation?

3. What processes are performed in the data extract phase?

4. Why are data extracted to a data depot?

5. What data transformations could be performed in the data depot?

6. What processes are performed in the data load phase?

7. Why should data that fail the data edits never be placed in the comparate data resource?

8. What processes are done differently in reverse data transformation.

9. What benefits does data brokering provide?

10. When can disparate data be retired?

Chapter 13

INTEGRATING THE DATA CULTURE

Culture must be integrated the same as architecture.

Chapter 1 described the rampant data disparity that exists in most public and private sector organizations today and how to create a comparate data resource that meets the business information demand. Chapter 2 described the integration of data resource management, including data architecture and data culture. Chapters 3 through 12 described the concepts, principles, and techniques for developing a comparate data resource with a Common Data Architecture.

The current chapter describes the concepts, principles, and techniques for developing a cohesive data culture with a Common Data Culture. Complete data resource integration must include development of both a comparate data resource and a cohesive data culture. Developing either without the other will not achieve data resource integration and will not provide substantial, persistent benefit to the organization.

The human side of data resource management must be included with the architectural side to ensure success. Many organizations have attempted architectural change without cultural change, with less than fully successful or persistent benefits and increasing disparate data. Culture change must be included with architectural change to achieve persistent benefits.

CONCEPTS AND PRINCIPLES

The data culture concepts and principles were presented in Chapters 1 and 2. Those concepts and principles are summarized below in preparation for integrating the data culture of an organization.

Data Culture Concepts

Culture is the act of developing the intellectual and moral faculties; expert care and training; enlightenment and excellence of taste acquired by intellectual and aesthetic training; acquaintance with and taste in fine arts, humanities, and broad aspects of science; the integrated pattern of human knowledge, belief, and behavior that depends upon man's capacity for learning and transmitting knowledge to succeeding generations; the customary beliefs, social forms, and material traits of a racial, religious, or social group.

Data culture (1) is the function of managing the data resource as a critical resource of the organization equivalent to managing the financial resource, the human resource, and real property. It consists of directing and controlling the development, administering policies and procedures, influencing the actions and conduct of anyone maintaining or using the data resource, and exerting a guiding influence over the data resource to support the current and future business information demand.

Data culture (2) is the component of the Data Resource Management Framework that contains all the activities, and the products of those activities, related to orientation, availability, responsibility, vision, and recognition of the data resource.

The *data culture integration concept* is to resolve the fragmented data culture and create a cohesive data culture for the management of a critical data resource. A thorough understanding of the current fragmented data culture leads to its resolution and the creation of a cohesive data culture. That cohesive data culture, along with a comparate data resource, support formal data resource management.

A *fragmented data culture* is a data culture that is broken apart into separate pieces that are unrelated, incomplete, and inconsistent. It is similar to a disparate data resource, and leads to the creation of a disparate data resource. A fragmented data culture cannot effectively or efficiently manage an organization's data resource.

A *cohesive data culture* is a data culture composed of business processes that are integrated to effectively and efficiently manage an organization's data resource. The business processes are seamless, consistent, and work together in a coordinated manner to develop and maintain a comparate data resource.

The *Common Data Culture* is a single, formal, comprehensive, organization-wide data culture that provides a common context within which the organization's data culture is understood, documented, and integrated. It includes all components in the Data Culture Segment of the Data Resource Management Framework for a reasonable data orientation, acceptable data availability, adequate data responsibility, expanded data vision, and appropriate data recognition.

A *common data culture* (lower case) is the actual data culture built by an organization for the proper management of their data resource. It's based on the concepts, principles, and techniques of the Common Data Culture. It provides the overarching construct for a common view of the organization's data culture. All variations in the data culture are understood within the context of a common data culture. The preferred data culture is defined within the context of a common data culture. Data culture integration is done within the context of a common data culture.

Data culture integration is the thorough understanding of the existing fragmented data culture within a common data culture, the designation of a preferred data culture, and the transition toward that preferred data culture. It's the act or process to integrate and coordinate the organization's data management function and processes into a cohesive data culture. It resolves a fragmented data culture by getting people to work together to build and maintain a comparate data resource.

Formal data culture integration is any data culture integration done within the context of a common data culture. *Informal data culture integration* is any data culture integration done outside the context of a common data culture. It usually does not resolve variability in the data culture and seldom leads to a cohesive data culture.

An *integrated data culture* is a data culture where all of the data management functions and processes in an organization are integrated within a common context, and are oriented toward developing and maintaining a comparate data resource. Data culture variability has been resolved and data resource management is performed consistently across the organization.

Data culture transition is the transition of an organization's data culture from a fragmented data culture state, through a formal data culture state, to a cohesive data culture state. It's a pathway that is followed from a fragmented data culture to a cohesive data culture. It's unique to each organization, depending on their existing data culture and desired data culture.

Data Culture Principles

The following data culture principles are summarized from Chapter 2. Specific principles are described below for each of the data culture components.

Data culture integration must be done in concert with data resource integration. Ideally, data culture integration should be done before data resource integration. However, that approach is seldom feasible because it's difficult to implement a new data culture, then wait before applying that new data culture to management of the data resource.

All components of the cohesive data culture, including data orientation, data availability, data responsibility, data vision, and data recognition, must be implemented at the same time. Implementing only a subset of those components does not fully resolve the fragmented data culture.

Data culture integration must be performed organization-wide. Little good comes from implementing the cohesive data culture to only part of the organization. Other parts of the organization simply continue creating disparate data. Since the data are usually orthogonal to the organization structure, the disparate data cannot be resolved as long as some of the business units have not been included in data culture integration.

Data culture integration is simpler than data resource integration, yet is more difficult to implement. It's simpler in the sense that it is not as detailed as data resource integration, fewer steps are involved, the steps are relatively straight forward, the variability is lower than the data resource, the understanding process is easier, and the documentation is easier.

It's more difficult in the sense that changing the culture is more difficult than changing the architecture. Having the culture change the architecture is difficult enough, but having the culture change the culture can be quite difficult. People show some resistance to change when integrating the data resource. However, people show great resistance to change when integrating the data culture.

Implementing a cohesive data culture must be persistent. If the data culture transition is not persistent, people will drift back to their old ways of managing data and data disparity will increase. A considerable effort must be made to understand the resistance that people have and address that resistance. A considerable effort must be made to show people how a cohesive data culture develops a comparate data resource and how reversion to the fragmented data culture creates disparate data.

Implementing a cohesive data culture is not data governance. Data governance seldom has specific concepts, principles, and techniques, and seldom addresses the issue of a common data culture. It does not address a preferred data culture or the development of a cohesive data culture. It's not as robust as formal data culture integration.

Data culture integration must be done both within and without the organization. The internal aspect is with the employees that must buy into data culture integration and commit to making data resource management work if a comparate data resource is to be developed and maintained. The external aspect is with consultants, vendors, trainers, and so on, that the organization utilizes to support their data resource management effort. The external people have their own thoughts, ideas, and agendas, which are often not in synch with the organization and should not be allowed to alter the cohesive data culture of the organization.

Data Culture States

The *fragmented data culture state* is the situation where every organizational unit, and possibly every person, is managing data in their own way, with their own orientation, vision, processes, and software tools. The data culture is highly variable and exhibits all of the characteristics of a fragmented data culture. The management is informal and seldom documented, and the fragmentation is not known. It is the least desirable state and is the initial state for data culture integration.

The *formal data culture state* is a necessary state where the data culture is readily understood within the context of a common data culture. The variability of the fragmented data culture is understood and documented, the preferred data culture is designated, and the data culture integration is prescribed. No changes to the data culture have yet been made pending review and approval by the organization.

The *cohesive data culture state* is the desired state, where the fragmented data culture has been transformed substantially and permanently to a cohesive data culture. It's a persistent transformation according to the preferred data culture prescription. A single set of processes has been established across the organization. It's the ideal, mature state for management of the organization's data resource.

The fragmented data culture state is retrospective, descriptive, and probabilistic due to its fragmented and uncoordinated development. The formal data culture state understands that fragmented data culture and prepares a prospective, prescriptive, and deterministic preferred data culture. The cohesive data culture state implements the preferred data culture to provide an integrated data culture that works in concert with an integrated data resource to formally manage an organization's data resource.

DATA CULTURE COMPONENTS

The problems, criteria, and principles for the five components of the Data Culture Segment of the Data Resource Management Framework are summarized below. *Data Resource Simplexity* should be consulted for a more detailed description.

Data Orientation

Data orientation is the first component of the Data Culture Segment. *Orientation* means the act or process of orienting or being oriented; the state of being oriented; the general or lasting direction of thought, inclination, or interest; the change of position in response to external stimulus. *Data orientation* is the orientation of data resource management in response to business information needs which allows the business to operate effectively and efficiently in the business world.

Unreasonable Data Orientation

Unreasonable means not acting according to reason, not conforming to reason, or exceeding the bounds of reason or moderation. An *unreasonable data orientation* is an unreasonable attitude about developing the data resource that is physically oriented, short term, and narrowly focused. Most public and private sector organizations have an unreasonable data orientation that results in high quantities of disparate data.

The problems with an unreasonable data orientation are summarized below.

A physical orientation is a profound orientation toward physical design, data storage, and hardware performance. Little or no consideration is given to developing data that completely support the current and future business information demand.

A short term orientation is focused on short term objectives to the detriment of long term needs. The major concern is current performance of hardware and software applications. A short term orientation usually results from a physical orientation.

A multiple fact orientation places multiple business facts or multiple values of the same business facts in a single data attribute. The orientation is toward short term data needs of current applications, not the long term needs of future applications.

A process orientation is a focus on the process performed on the data rather than on the data as a resource. The orientation is toward physically processing the data rather than on supporting the business information demand.

An operational data orientation is a focus on discarding operational data when their operational usefulness is over. No consideration is given for retaining historical data for analytical processing.

An independent database orientation focuses on developing individual databases without concern or interest for developing a data resource within a consistent organization-wide data architecture.

An inappropriate business orientation is any orientation that is not appropriate for business professional involvement. It can range from the exclusion of business professionals to business professionals developing their own databases.

Reasonable Data Orientation

Reasonable means agreeable to reason, not extreme or excessive, having the faculty of reason, and possessing sound judgment. A *reasonable data orientation* is an orientation toward the business and support of the current and future business information demand. It depends on the architectural concepts, principles, and techniques, but more importantly, it depends on the culture of the organization.

The reasonable data orientation criteria are summarized below.

Development of a comparate data resource must include both architectural principles and cultural principles.

Development of a comparate data resource must be business oriented.

Development of a comparate data resource must include business professionals and their knowledge of the business.

Development of a comparate data resource must include data management professionals, and their knowledge and skills with design and development.

Development of a comparate data resource must be done within a common data architecture.

Development of a comparate data resource must follow the Five-Tier Five-Schema concept.

Development of a comparate data resource must follow a proper sequence where appropriate people are involved at the appropriate time.

Development of a comparate data resource must include teamwork and synergy.

The reasonable data orientation principles are summarized below.

The *business orientation principle* states that the data resource must

375

be oriented toward business objects and events that are of interest to the organization and are either tracked or managed by the organization. Those business objects and events become data subjects in a subject-oriented comparate data resource.

The *business inclusion principle* states that business professionals must be directly involved in the development of a comparate data resource. The understanding and knowledge that business professionals have about the business must be included to ensure development of a comparate data resource that supports the current and future business information demand.

The *teamwork synergy principle* states that the appropriate business and data management professionals must be involved at the appropriate time, in any project, to ensure that development or enhancement of a comparate data resource supports the business information demand.

The *proper sequence principle* states that proper design proceeds from development of logical data structures that represent the business and how the data support the business, to the development of physical data structures for implementing databases.

The *single data architecture principle* states that the entire data resource of an organization must be developed and managed within a single, organization-wide, common data architecture.

The *Five-Tier Five-Schema orientation principle* states that development of a comparate data resource within a common data architecture must be done according to the Five-Tier Five-Schema Concept.

Data Availability

Data availability is the process of ensuring that the data are available to meet the business information demand, while properly protecting and securing those data. The data must be readily available to support business activities, but they must be protected to ensure proper access and recoverability in the event of a natural or human caused disaster.

Unacceptable Data Availability

Unacceptable means not acceptable, not pleasing, or unwelcome. *Unacceptable data availability* is the situation where the data are not readily available to meet the business information demand or are not properly protected or secured.

The problems with unacceptable data availability are summarized below.

Data are not readily accessible when anyone needing data to support their business cannot readily access those data. The data can be totally unavailable or very difficult to access, or a person could not be authorized to access those data.

Data are inadequately protected when anyone who does not have business authority can gain unauthorized access to the data to alter or destroy it, or to make unauthorized use of the data.

Data are inadequately recoverable when the frequency of backups is not sufficient to match the fast pace of changes in a dynamic business environment, or when data are not backed up.

A person's or organization's right to privacy and confidentiality is unprotected when data are released that should not be released. In some situations, data that should be released are withheld when those data are not privileged by law.

Data are used inappropriately for purposes other than legitimate business activities.

Acceptable Data Availability

Acceptable means capable or worthy of being accepted. ***Acceptable data availability*** is the situation where data are readily available to meet the business information demand while those data are properly protected and secured. The data must be readily available so they can be shared across business activities. The data must also be adequately protected from unauthorized access, alteration, and deletion.

The acceptable data availability criteria are summarized below.

The data resource must be readily available to business and data management professionals needing data to perform their business activities.

The data resource must be adequately protected from unauthorized access, alteration, or destruction.

The data resource must have an appropriate balance between ready accessibility to meet business needs and adequate protection.

The data must be protected against reasonable failures in accordance with the critical nature of the data

The data resource must be recoverable from failure in accordance with the critical nature of the data.

377

The privacy and confidentiality of people and organizations must be protected.

The data must be used for ethical purposes.

The acceptable data availability principles are summarized below.

The *adequate data accessibility principle* states that access to the data resource must be sufficient to allow people to perform their business activities, and for citizens and customers to obtain the data they need regarding services and products.

The *adequate data protection principle* states that the data resource must be protected from unauthorized access, alteration, or destruction.

The *proper balance principle states* that a proper balance needs to be maintained between allowing enough access for people to perform their business activities, and limiting access to protect the data from unauthorized alteration or deletion.

The *adequate data recovery principle* states that the data resource must have reasonable protection against reasonable failures, and must be recoverable as quickly as possible with the data are altered or destroyed by human or natural disasters.

The *privacy and confidentiality principle* states that the data resource must be protected from any disclosure that violates a person's or organization's right to privacy and confidentiality.

The *appropriate data use principle* states that an organization must constantly review the use of data to ensure the use is appropriate and ethical.

Data Responsibility

Responsibility is the quality or state of being responsible; moral, legal, or mental accountability; reliability and trustworthiness; something for which one is responsible. *Data responsibility* is the assignment of appropriate responsibility for development and maintenance of the data resource to specific individuals.

Inadequate Data Responsibility

Inadequate means insufficient, or not adequate to fulfill a need or meet a requirement. *Inadequate data responsibility* is the situation where the responsibility, as defined, does not fulfill the need for properly managing a comparate data resource. The responsibility is casual, lax, inconsistent, uncoordinated, and not suitable for the current environment of a shared data resource.

The problems with inadequate data responsibility are summarized below.

No centralized control is the situation where any formal, centralized control over the data resource does not exist. People are thinking locally and acting locally.

No management procedures is the situation where few procedures exist for managing the data resource. Some degree of control may exist, or appear to exist, but minimal procedures are in place for people to follow.

No data stewardship is the situation where no formal responsibility for developing and managing the data resource for the good of the organization has been assigned.

Adequate Data Responsibility

Adequate means sufficient for a specific requirement; sufficient or satisfactory; lawfully and legally sufficient. *Adequate data responsibility* is the situation where the responsibility, as defined, meets the need for properly managing a comparate data resource. The responsibility is formal, consistent, coordinated, and suitable for a shared data environment.

The adequate data responsibility criteria are summarized below.

Formal responsibilities must be defined for data stewardship at all levels of the organization.

Reasonable management procedures that can be easily and readily followed must be established.

Centralized control of a common data resource must be imbedded in the organization.

The Data Resource Guide must provide support for data stewardship responsibility.

The adequate data responsibility principles are summarized below.

The *data stewardship principle* states that data stewards will be assigned at all levels of an organization, with appropriate responsibilities for developing and maintaining a comparate data resource.

Steward came from the old English term sty ward; a person who was the ward of the sty. They watched over the stock and were responsible for the welfare of the stock, particularly at night when the risks to the welfare of the stock was high.

A *data steward* is a person who watches over the data and is responsible for the welfare of the data resource and its support of the business information demand, particularly when the risks are high.

A *strategic data steward* is any person who has legal and financial responsibility for a major segment of the data resource. That person has decision-making authority for setting directions, establishing policy, and committing resources for that segment of the data resource.

A *detail data steward* is a person who is knowledgeable about the data by reason of having been intimately involved with the data. That person is usually a knowledge worker who has been directly involved with the data for a considerable length of time.

A *tactical data steward* is a person who acts as liaison between the strategic data steward and the detail data stewards to ensure that all business and data concerns are addressed.

The *reasonable management procedures principle* states that reasonable procedures for development and maintenance of a comparate data resource must be established.

The *centralized control principle* states that centralized control of a comparate data resource within a common data architecture evolves from the assignment of data stewards and the development of reasonable data management procedures.

Data Vision

A *vision* is the act or power of imagination, a mode of seeing or conceiving, discernment or foresight. A *data vision* is the power of imagining, seeing, or conceiving the development and maintenance of a comparate data resource that meets the current and future business information demand.

Restricted Data Vision

Restricted means to confine within bounds; subjected to some restriction; not general; available to particular groups and excluding others; not intended for general circulation or use. A *restricted data vision* is the situation where the scope of the data resource is limited, the development direction is unreasonable, or the planning horizon is unrealistic.

The problems with a restricted data vision are summarized below.

Scope pertains to the range of a person's perceptions, the breadth or opportunity to function, or the area covered by a given activity. The *data resource scope* is the total data resource available to an organization. The *actual data resource scope* is the portion of the data resource that is actually formally managed. The *perceived data resource scope* is the portion of the data resource that is perceived to be formally managed. In most organizations, the perceived data resource scope is far larger than the actual data resource scope.

The *data resource direction* is the course of data resource development toward a particular goal or objective. In many organizations, the data resource direction is incompatible with the business direction, or is incompatible with the database technology direction.

A *horizon* is the distance into the future which a person is interested in for planning. The *data resource horizon* is the distance into the future that an organization is interested in planning for its data resource development. An *unrealistic planning horizon* is the situation where the data resource horizon is too nearsighted, too farsighted, or overly optimistic.

A *nearsighted planning horizon* is the situation where an organization's data resource horizon is very short term. Data resource development is focused on short term objectives to the detriment of long term goals.

A *farsighted planning horizon* is the situation where an organization's data resource horizon is very long term. The vision is too far over the horizon to be of interest to most people.

An *overly optimistic horizon* is the situation where the data resource horizon is the best, and can be easily and quickly achieved. The vision may be valid and realistic, but the horizon is too optimistic. In spite of the good intentions, the vision cannot be achieved within the designated horizon.

Expanded Data Vision

Expanded means to increase the extent, number, volume, or scope of something; to enlarge; to express fully or in detail; to write out in full; to increase the extent, number volume, or scope. An *expanded data vision* is an intelligent foresight about the data resource that includes the scope of the data resource, the development direction, and the planning horizon. It's the situation where the scope of the data resource includes the entire data resource, the development direction is aligned with the business and technology, and the planning horizon is realistic.

The expanded data vision criteria are summarized below.

Increase the scope of data resource management to include the entire data resource at the organization's disposal.

Set a reasonable direction for development of a comparate data resource that is aligned with the business direction and the technology direction.

Establish reasonable planning horizons that encourage people to become involved.

Develop a cooperative environment where all stakeholders work together as a team to achieve a comparate data resource.

The expanded data vision principles are summarized below.

The *wider scope principle* states that data resource management must ultimately include all data at the organization's disposal.

The *reasonable development direction principle* states that the direction of data resource development must focus primarily on the business direction and secondarily on the database technology direction.

The *realistic planning horizons principle* states that realistic planning horizons must be challenging, yet achievable, and must be developed to cover all audiences in the organization. The horizons must stretch the imagination slightly, but not unrealistically. It must be understandable and achievable, but not too close or too distant.

The *cooperative development principle* states that the stakeholders of the data resource must be involved in developing the vision for a comparate data resource. An expanded data vision must be developed collectively by all the stakeholders of the data resource, through the strategic, tactical, and detail data stewards. It must be acceptable by the stakeholders after it is established.

Data Recognition

Recognition means the action of recognizing; the state of being recognized; acknowledgement; special notice and attention. *Data recognition* is the situation where management of the data resource is recognized as professional and directly supporting the business activities of the organization.

Inappropriate Data Recognition

Appropriate means especially suitable or compatible; fitting. *Inappropriate* means not appropriate. *Inappropriate data recognition* is the situation where the organization at large does not recognize data as a critical resource of the organization, the fact that the data resource is disparate, or the need to develop a comparate data resource.

The problems with inappropriate data recognition are summarized below.

The wrong target audience is where an initiative is targeting the wrong audience or trying to convince the wrong people that a serious situation exists with disparate data. The targeted audience may be too high in the organization or too low in the organization to be effective.

Requiring unnecessary justification is the mistaken perception that an initiative to understand the disparate data and develop a comparate data resource requires extensive justification.

Searching for a silver bullet is an attempt to achieve some gain without any pain. The result is minimal gain with considerable pain. The resulting situation may be worse than the initial situation.

An attempt to automate understanding is a mistaken perception that the understanding of disparate data and development of a comparate data resource can be automated.

A reliance on data standards is a mistaken perception that standards can resolve existing disparate data or prevent future disparate data. Data standards cannot resolve existing disparate data, and many data standards themselves are disparate.

A reliance on generic data models or universal data architectures is a mistaken perception that they can resolve the existing disparate data or prevent future disparate data. Those data models and architecture cannot resolve disparate data. They often create additional disparate data by forcing an organization to warp their perception of the business world into a generic data model or universal data architecture.

Appropriate Data Recognition

Appropriate data recognition is the situation where the organization recognizes that data are a critical resource of the organization, the data resource is disparate, and an initiative to develop a comparate data resource is needed. The recognition is organization wide and the data resource is managed with the same intensity as the financial resource, human resource, and real property.

The appropriate data recognition criteria are summarized below.

Start an initiative that targets vested interests.

Seek the direct involvement of business professionals.

Tap the hidden knowledge base in the organization that understands the data resource.

Start an initiative within the current budget.

Incrementally improve that initiative based on benefits gained. Provide a proof positive perspective for improving data resource quality.

Be opportunistic and take every opportunity to sell a comparate data resource.

Build on any lessons learned with each successive phase of the initiative.

Adopt a no blame – no whitewash attitude for resolving the disparate data situation.

Avoid requiring any unnecessary justification for beginning an initiative to manage data as a critical resource of the organization.

The appropriate data recognition principles are summarized below.

The *vested interest principle* states that the audience with a vested interest in managing data as a critical resource of the organization should be targeted for supporting any quality improvement initiative.

The *knowledge base principle* states that the existing, often hidden, base of knowledge about the data resource must be tapped to ensure a complete and thorough understanding of the data. Any initiative to improve data resource quality must include people who have an intimate knowledge of the data resource by reason of having worked with the data for a long period of time.

The *current budget principle* states that any first initiative to improve data resource quality should begin within current budget. Most initiatives that start lower in the organization and within the current budget get very early recognition.

The *incrementally cost effective principle* states that any data management initiative to resolve disparate data and create a comparate data resource should begin small, produce meaningful results, and continue to grow to a fully recognized initiative.

The *proof positive principle* states that when you go to executives for approval with proof of positive results, you are more likely to gain their support than if you ask for support based on a promise to deliver.

The *opportunistic principle* states that every opportunity should be taken to promote the initiative in the organization, regardless of the size of the opportunity.

The *lessons learned principle* states that every initiative has some failures and some successes, and the lessons learned can be included in the next initiative.

The *no blame – no whitewash principle* states that the disparate data situation exists, that laying blame for that situation only polarizes and alienates people, and whitewashing the situation only allows it to continue.

The *unnecessary justification principle* states that an extensive justification is not needed to begin an initiative for developing a comparate data resource. An extensive justification is *not* needed to improve data resource quality.

DATA CULTURE INTEGRATION

Data culture integration includes description of data culture variability, data culture integration approach, data culture survey, the preferred data culture designation, and data culture transformation. Each of these topics is described below.

Data Culture Variability

The fragmented data culture has a high degree of variability, just like a disparate data resource. The data culture variability applies to all five components of data culture, just like data resource variability applies to all five components of data architecture. The data culture variability must be understood if a fragmented data culture is to be integrated into a cohesive data culture.

Data culture variability is a state where all aspects of data management are inconsistent, characterized by variations, and are not true to the concepts and principles for managing data as a critical resource. The management procedures are highly variable, and that variability is pervasive throughout the organization.

The larger the organization and the more geographically or functionally diverse an organization is, the greater the data culture variability. The longer an organization has been in business, and the more mergers and acquisitions the organization has endured, the greater the data culture variability. Greater data culture variability makes the task of developing a cohesive data culture more difficult. Greater variability causes greater uncertainty and greater resistance to creation of a cohesive data culture.

Explicit data culture variability is the variability that can be readily visible, or identified in documented procedures and data management actions pertaining to data orientation, data availability, data responsibility, data vision, and data recognition. *Implicit data culture variability* is the variability that is not readily visible, or identified in documented procedures and data management actions.

The *presumed data culture variability principle* states that an existing fragmented data culture is highly variable and should be considered as the norm in most public and private sector organizations. Seldom is any organization free from some degree of data culture variability.

Acceptable data culture variability is the acceptable level of variability in management of the data resource. *Unacceptable data culture variability* is any unacceptable level of variability in management of the data resource. Any data culture variability that is unacceptable and impacts management of the data as a critical resource must be resolved.

The *data culture variability principle* states that every organization has a level of variability that must be accepted and clarified, and that any variability above that acceptable level must be resolved. Data culture integration seeks to resolve the unacceptable variability and clarify the acceptable variability. The *expect anything principle* applies to data culture the same as it does to the data resource. One should expect any data management procedure, even if it seems irrational.

Data Culture Integration Approach

The data culture integration approach includes the common data culture, the scope of data culture integration, the sequence of data culture integration, the involvement in data culture integration, sources of insight about the current data culture, and adjustments to a common data culture. Each of these topics is described below.

Common Data Culture

The Common Data Culture consists of the five Data Culture Components of the Data Resource Framework: data orientation, data availability, data responsibility, data vision, and data recognition. It's the common context for understanding and resolving fragmented data management practices in an organization. The existing fragmented data management practices are documented within these five components, the preferred designations are made within these five components, and the transformation is planned within these five components.

The data management practices may be grouped within these five components based on each individual organization. Public and private sector organizations vary considerably in their organization and business practices, making designation of a specific grouping of data management practices within each of the five components difficult. Therefore, each core team leading the data culture integration can develop any structure for grouping the data management practices that is appropriate for the organization.

Scope

The scope of data culture integration is the entire organization. Since the organizational structure is usually orthogonal to the data architecture, the entire fragmented data culture of the organization must be understood and integrated into a cohesive data culture. When only part of the organization is involved in data culture integration, the other part of the organization retains a fragmented data culture and continues creating disparate data. Therefore, the entire organization must be involved in integrating the data culture.

Sequence

The overall sequence of data culture integration is generally prioritized based on the organizational units that are most involved in managing or using the data resource. Organization units that are responsible for developing and maintaining the data resource should be involved first, followed by those organizational units that use the data resource to support their business activities. Finally, organizational units that are minimally involved in using the data resource can be included in data culture integration

The specific sequence for data culture integration is to start by surveying and documenting the existing fragmented data culture, much like inventorying and documenting the disparate data resource. When the existing data culture has been surveyed and documented, a preferred data culture can be designated, based on the business goals and objectives of the organization. When the preferred data culture has been designated, the data culture transformation can be planned and then implemented.

Data culture integration must be performed across the entire organization, and must be integrated with data resource integration. In the ideal situation, data culture integration should precede data resource integration so that the people are prepared to manage data resource integration properly. However, that ideal is not easily achieved and data culture integration often proceeds in concert with data resource integration.

Involvement

Anyone in the organization who develops, manages, or uses the data resource, or manages people who develop, manage, or use the data resource, must be involved in data culture integration. In most public and private sector organizations, that involvement includes virtually everyone in the organization, from executives to knowledge workers, and from business professionals to data management professionals.

A core team is usually designated to manage data culture integration. That core team typically has different members from the core team that manages data resource integration, although the two teams need to work together. The core team needs to establish the priorities for conducting the data culture survey and the people that need to be contacted. Then the core team moves through the process of surveying, documenting, making preferred designations, determining the transformation, and finally implementing the data culture transformation.

Data culture integration must be based on a no blame – no whitewash principle. People cannot be blamed for past practices and the existent of a fragmented data culture. Blame only polarizes people, alienates them from the data culture integration process, and hampers effective development of a cohesive data culture. Similarly, whitewashing the existing fragmented data culture prevents any effort to develop a cohesive data culture. Therefore, a no blame – no whitewash attitude must be adopted to encourage people to become involved in developing a cohesive data culture.

Sources of Insight

Insight into the current data culture in an organization comes from two primary sources. The first is any formal or informal documentation about the data management practices that should be followed. Formal documentation is generally approved by some person or group within the organization and is readily available to everyone in the organization. Informal documentation may not be approved by some person or group in the organization and may not be readily available to everyone in the organization. Informal documentation usually exists within a specific group or for a specific person.

The second source of insight is what each person in the organization is actually doing when developing, managing, and using the data resource.

People may be following formal or informal documentation, or they may be doing their own thing, independent of any formal or informal documentation. The worst-case scenario in many public and private sector organizations is that people are doing their own thing when developing, managing, or using the data resource.

Adjustments and Enhancements

Adjustments and enhancements often need to be made during data culture integration. As the data culture integration process moves through the fragmented, formal, and cohesive data culture states, additional insights may be gained. Those insights need to be documented, and adjustments or enhancements made to the survey results, the preferred data culture, or the data culture transformation process. Like data resource integration, data culture is a discovery process and insights are continually gained.

Data Culture Survey

A *survey* is the act or instance of surveying; something that is surveyed; the examination of a condition, situation, or value; appraise, inspect, scrutinize. A *data culture survey* is the act of surveying the current data management practices in an organization and documenting the results of that survey. It identifies and documents the current data management practices within each of the five data culture components, including the explicit and implicit data management practices. It documents the fragmented data culture state and begins the process of formally understanding the existing data culture in an organization.

The term *survey* is used rather than *inventory* because specific items to be inventoried do not exist as they do in the data resource. The existing data culture is a set of explicit and implicit practices that must be identified and documented.

The *data culture survey concept* is that the existing fragmented data culture in an organization is leading to the creation of increasing quantities of a disparate data resource that are impacting business activities. That fragmented data culture must be identified and documented as the first step to understanding that fragmented data culture and transforming it to a cohesive data culture that leads to creation and maintenance of a comparate data resource that supports business activities.

The *data culture survey objective* is to survey and document all of the fragmented data management practices that are explicitly and implicitly being performed by people within and without the organization. Those fragmented data management practices will be used to designate preferred data management practices that will then be implemented to properly develop and maintain a comparate data resource.

Data Culture Survey Process

The data culture survey process is to identify the existing fragmented data culture and the problems created by that fragmented data culture within the five data culture components in the Data Culture Segment of the Data Resource Management Framework. The basic problems with a fragmented data culture were described above for each of the five data culture components. Those basic problems are a guide to gaining input from business professionals and data management professionals about the explicit and implicit data management practices currently being performed.

The data culture survey is a fact-finding mission to identify the specific problems with an organization's fragmented data culture and what needs to be done to create a cohesive data culture. Existing formal documentation is collected during the data culture survey. Informal documentation is identified and formally documented.

People are interviewed about the organization's management practices and the problems those practices are creating. Anyone in the organization involved in data resource management is interviewed to gain insight about the existing data culture. The basic problems start the interview process. When people start with the basic problems, they begin to see specific problems in the organization and begin to identify those problems.

The data culture survey does not include the architectural problems and principles. However, it can address problems with not having formal data architecture principles and techniques, or not following established data architecture principles and techniques. In other words, not having formal data architecture principles and techniques is a data architecture problem, but not establishing or following the formal data architecture principles and techniques is a data culture problem

Data Culture Survey Documentation

The existing documentation is brought together in one place as data culture insights. *Data culture insights* are any insights necessary for thoroughly understanding the organization's existing fragmented data culture and developing a cohesive data culture for properly managing data as a critical resource of the organization.

Data culture insights gained during the data culture survey are documented according to the five components of data culture. Documentation of the data culture survey is relatively simple compared to documentation of the data resource. The documentation consists of textual statements about the data culture practices actually being performed and the conditions under which they are performed. The data culture practices are documented within each data culture component, and specific problems are documented within those data culture practices. The data culture insights are stored in one readily accessible place so that anyone in the organization can review and comment on those insights.

Data Culture Survey Components

Brief examples of data culture insights are shown below for the five data culture components. The specific insights obtained during the data culture survey vary with each organization and are far more extensive than those shown below. The reader can likely add more insights to the list.

Data Orientation:

> Orientation of the data resource is purely physical without any logical design based on how the organization perceives the business world.

> The business is unclear about the orientation of the business, making orientation of the data resource very difficult. Frequent changes are needed because the business lacks a long term orientation.

> New employees need to receive a thorough orientation about the data resource before they are allowed to use or update the data.

> Data warehouse and data analytical processes are severely hampered because operational data are not saved. Historical data cannot be found for longitudinal analysis.

> Data files are developed based on business processes, which leads to redundant data and many bridges to maintain those redundant data.

> Data management practices are in place, but very few people follow those practices, either because they choose not to or because they are not aware that formal practices exist.

> Business professionals have absolutely no say in how the databases are designed or managed. The data often do not meet business needs.

Data Availability:

> I know the data are there, but I can't access those data. I end up

creating my own data.

I assure my clients that their private data will be protected, only to find out that other employees have released those data. My clients are quite unhappy.

We have no idea what data are privileged and what data can be released. We need guidelines for privileged data.

Our system goes down frequently. I try to do business manually, but find it difficult to get those manual data back into the system.

I know other employees are using our data inappropriately for their own gain, but don't want to create problems by naming those people.

It seems that anyone can change the data any time, which causes problems with the integrity of the data. Specific procedures need to be implemented for who can change data and when the data can be changed.

Data Responsibility:

I have no idea who is responsible for the data. It seems that anybody can do anything with the data.

Management allows a free-for-all with the data. I create my own data to protect its integrity.

I don't know who to go to for information about the data. Everyone is referring me to someone else.

We need people who have a formally designated responsibility for the data.

Data Vision:

The people in my unit have no idea what the direction for data resource development might be. I'd like to follow that direction, but find it difficult.

All of the plans I see are so far in the future that it's impossible for me to adapt to those plans. I need some near- term plans that I can follow.

Apparently management has plans, but I can't find them. If I can't find them, I certainly can't follow them.

The plans I see are great, but it's impossible to meet their deadlines. It takes time to implement the plans and I still need to perform my regular business tasks.

When people make plans, they need to consult the work force to see if those plans are reasonable and can be implemented. Dictated plans just don't work.

Data Recognition:

We seem to be continually acquiring new software packages that will make our work better, but it always makes things worse.

Management keeps asking for justification to improve data quality. I could spend that time actually improving data quality rather than justifying the need.

We keep telling executives the problem, but they never listen. We explain a situation and then ask them later about that situation, but they don't seem to remember.

I'm continually presented with purchased models that don't fit the data I need to support my tasks. Why can't we get a model that matches the data I need?

I keep being asked to be involved in writing data standards. That takes my time, but seldom seems to product any results.

Just when I get my data organized and understood, a new package comes along that treats my data differently. I have to adjust to the package, but it doesn't fit my business.

Preferred Data Culture Designation

A *preferred data culture* is a subset of a common data culture that contains the preferred practices for managing data as a critical resource. It's the desired data culture that provides the pattern for building a cohesive data culture and transforming the fragmented data culture to that cohesive data culture. It's how the organization chooses to manage their data as a critical resource.

The *preferred data culture concept* is that the variability of the existing fragmented data culture will be resolved through the designation of a preferred data culture and the transformation of the fragmented data culture to a cohesive data culture. The variability may not be eliminated, but it will be reduced to a known and manageable level. Formal documentation of the preferred data culture allows people to readily understand what's needed to formally manage data as a critical resource.

The *preferred data culture objective* is to designate the preferred practices for managing data as a critical resource, so that those practices are readily understood and consistently performed throughout the organization. Those preferred practices are then used for data culture transformation.

Preferred Data Culture Process

The preferred data culture process is to consolidate the data survey insights and to designate the preferred data culture based on the consolidated insights. The specific criteria and principles for making the preferred data culture designations were described above for each of the five data culture components. Those criteria and principles must be met when designating a preferred data culture for the organization.

The preferred data culture process defines the formal data culture state based on the data culture survey, the specific data culture criteria, and the data culture principles. It reduces the unacceptable level of data culture variability to a known and manageable level of variability. It sets the stage for transformation of the data culture from the fragmented state to the cohesive state.

The variability in the data culture identified during the data culture survey is relatively easy to identify. The insights obtained during the data culture survey often provide a wide range of differences in the existing data culture. That variability needs to be resolved to develop a cohesive data culture.

Note that data culture integration has no cross-referencing equivalent to the data cross-referencing in data resource integration. A common data culture does not exist like the common data architecture. Therefore, a preferred data culture variation is not designated from a set of data culture variations. The process is to state the preferred data culture based on the insights from the data culture survey, and the criteria and principles stated above.

The first step in the preferred data culture designation process is to consolidate similar insights into basic insights about the data culture. The data survey usually produces many insights that are similar, but are worded slightly different. These similar insights are combined into a set of basic insights that are used to prepare the preferred data culture designations.

The second step in the preferred data culture designation process is to review the basic data culture insights and prepare the preferred data culture practices within each of the five data culture components. If the basic insights don't cover all of the criteria and principles, then preferred data culture practices are created to cover those criteria and principles. The result is the designation of a complete set of data culture practices for properly managing the data resource.

Preferred Data Culture Documentation

Documenting the preferred data culture is done in the same way as documenting the results of the data culture survey. The preferred data culture practices are stated within each of the five data culture components. Those preferred data culture designations are stored in one readily accessible place so that anyone in the organization can review the data culture practices.

Preferred Data Culture Components

The preferred data culture practices must meet the criteria and the principles provided above, and must meet or resolve the data culture survey items. Additional data culture criteria, data culture principles, and data culture practices may be added as necessary, to provide a complete set of data culture practices for the organization.

A complete list of all possible preferred data culture practices for all types of organizations would fill a book. Therefore, a few key considerations for developing the preferred data culture practices for a specific organization are listed below for each of the data culture components.

Orientation:

> The data culture orientation practices must provide one formal orientation for managing the data resource, or several formal orientations for very large organizations with a wide range of business activities.

> The data culture practices must focus on the business and how the business perceives the business world in which the organization operates.

> The data culture orientation practices must focus on business goals and business objectives as laid out in the business intelligence value chain.

> The data culture practices must provide support for the business plan and strategies.

> The data culture orientation practices must support the entire data resource of the organization, including data within and without the organization.

> The data culture orientation practices must support a critical area approach, where data are maintained for core business data and

critical business areas.

The data culture orientation practices must be business professional focused, where the data resource is oriented to the business professional's way of thinking, draws the business professional into the process, and taps the business professional's knowledge and skills.

The data culture orientation practices must encourage business professional involvement, particularly in the logical design of the data resource, which leads to commitment, acceptance, and success.

The data culture orientation practices must focus on the people performing the business tasks, not on the processes, including business experts, domain experts, data experts, and any other stakeholders in the data resource.

The data culture orientation practices must focus on getting people to interact and share their problems, techniques, vision, options, and solution, as well as their data.

The data culture orientation practices must use acceptable terms that are appropriate for the business, are readily understood by the business, and draw business professionals into the process of managing the data resource.

The data culture orientation practices must not be tool driven or allow the data perceived by the business to be warped into a software product.

Availability:

The data culture availability practices must provide one formal view of availability for the data resource related to access, security, privacy and confidentiality, backup and recovery, and ethical use of the data.

The data culture availability practices must meet all rules and regulations for releasing data and withholding data

Responsibility:

The data culture responsibility practices must define formal responsibilities for managing the data resource, such as strategic data stewards for legal / financial responsibility, tactical data stewards for liaison in large organizations, and detail data stewards for developing the data architecture.

Vision:

> The data culture vision practices must define a formal long term strategic vision for the organization's data resource, and one or more short term tactical visions for major segments of the data resource.

> The data culture vision must ensure that the vision is a very vivid picture of the future data resource, and includes steps to achieve that vision.

> The data culture vision must describe an architecture approach to managing the data resource, and integrate that data architecture with the information technology infrastructure.

> The data culture vision must describe the tangible and intangible benefits of managing data as a critical resource of the organization.

Recognition:

> The data culture recognition practices must describe how the data can be recognized as a critical resource of the organization, including how management should be made aware of the critical nature of the data resource and how data management professionals should become more professional.

> The data culture recognition practices must emphasize a sharable data resource that is developed within a single common data architecture.

> The data culture recognition practices must emphasize that data and processes are orthogonal to each other, and that the data resource is not developed based on processes.

> The data culture recognition practices must emphasize that problems exist with a disparate data resource, that blame cannot be laid for those problems, and that the problems cannot be covered up.

> Data culture recognition practices must emphasize the advantages of a comparate data resource and the advantages of formal data resource management.

Data Culture Transformation

Data culture transformation is the formal process of transforming a fragmented data culture to a cohesive data culture, within the context of a common data culture, according to the preferred data culture. It's a subset of overall data culture transition that includes transforming the data orientation, data availability, data responsibility, data vision, and data recognition. It's a very detailed process that requires careful planning, but it is absolutely necessary to achieving a cohesive data culture.

The ***data culture transformation concept*** is that all data culture transformation will be done within the context of a common data culture using the preferred data culture. The best existing data culture practices are combined with new data culture practices to provide a cohesive data culture.

The ***data culture transformation objective*** is to transform the existing fragmented data culture to a cohesive data culture to support management of data as a critical resource of the organization. The objective is more than just documenting the existing fragmented data culture. It's a precise, detailed process that creates a cohesive data culture.

Data Culture Transformation Process

The data culture transformation process is to move the organization from a fragmented data culture state to a cohesive data culture state based on the preferred data culture practices. It resolves the existing data culture fragmentation by implementing a cohesive data culture. It's a forward transformation process that does not have a reverse data culture transformation equivalent to reverse data transformation.

The data culture transformation process is based on a formal plan, like the formal plan for any project. It includes data orientation transformation, data availability transformation, data responsibility transformation, data vision transformation, and data recognition transformation. It must be done either before data transformation or in concert with data transformation. The key considerations for developing a data culture transformation plan are listed below.

> The data architecture concepts, principles, and techniques are important for creating a comparate data resource. However, the data culture concepts, principles, and techniques are needed to ensure that a cohesive data culture is in place so the organization can properly manage data as a critical resource.

> Most people want the data resource to support the business, but past practices have prevented that from happening. Transformation to a cohesive data culture will ensure that the data resource meets the current and future business information demand.

> Data culture transformation is based on success motivation, which requires a people orientation. People created the past data disparity and only people can resolve that disparity through implementation of a cohesive data culture.

People are uncertain about change and tend to resist it. Data culture transformation must recognize the resistance to change, reduce the resistance with a vivid vision, and manage the expectations of business professionals and data management professionals.

Most people are willing to change, but don't know how to go about it and are concerned about impacts on the business during change. Data culture transformation must minimize these concerns by reducing impacts on the business.

People don't mind changing, but they do mind being changed. They mind it very much. Therefore, business professionals and data management professionals must be actively involved in preparing a data culture transformation plan and implementing that plan.

Success is contagious. The data culture transformation plan must ensure that successes occur regularly and are visible. Those successes encourage people to continue with the transformation.

The data culture transformation plan should encourage involvement and change, not mandate that change. Mandates imply compliance, enforcement, and punishment, and should be avoided in any data culture transformation.

Data culture transformation should be the easiest route to follow toward a cohesive data culture and a comparate data resource. The easiest route to follow creates a win-win situation for the business and the employees.

The data culture transformation plan is a people issue, not a technical issue. Just writing the plan doesn't achieve the end result. People must be involved in developing and achieving the plan.

Implementing the data culture transformation plan takes a very personal and emotional commitment. It takes trust in a clear, compelling, and credible vision of a cohesive data culture.

Many people concentrate on data architecture integration and ignore data culture integration. An organization cannot achieve complete data resource integration without having both data architecture integration and data culture integration.

Not creating both a comparate data resource and a cohesive data culture at the same time allows the data resource to drift back to disparity and the resulting impacts on the business. Many of the best-intentioned data architecture integrations fail because the data culture was not integrated. Both are needed for complete data resource integration.

SUMMARY

Data culture is the second segment of the Data Resource Management Framework, consisting of data orientation, data availability, data responsibility, data vision, and data recognition. The current data culture in most public and private sector organizations is fragmented, just as the data resource is disparate. That fragmented data culture needs to be integrated to form a cohesive data culture, just like the disparate data resource needs to be integrated to form a comparate data resource.

Data culture integration must be done either before or at the same time as data resource integration. All components of the data culture must be integrated at the same time to create a cohesive data culture. Data culture integration must be done organization wide since data and processes are orthogonal to each other.

Data culture integration is simpler than data architecture integration because there are fewer components to integrate. However, it is more difficult because the existing organization data culture must change that culture. A culture changing the architecture is relatively easy compared to a culture changing the culture.

Data culture integration is done within the context of a common data culture. The scope is the entire organization and the sequence is to survey the existing data culture, designate the preferred data culture, and transform the data culture. Anyone involved in developing, maintain, or using the data resource is involved in data culture integration. Insights into the existing fragmented data culture is obtained from formal and informal documentation, and from anyone involved with the data resource.

Data culture integration goes through three states: the existing fragmented state, the formal state, and the cohesive state. The fragmented state is the existing stat. The formal state is an understanding of the fragmented state through a data culture survey and the designation of a preferred data culture. The cohesive state results from a transformation of the fragmented state based on the preferred data culture designations. The formal criteria and principles for each of the five data culture components guide data culture integration.

Creating a cohesive data culture is a choice, just like creating a comparate data resource. Organizations can choose whether to create a cohesive data culture and a comparate data resource that supports the business information demand, or they can choose to all the disparate data resource and fragmented data culture to impact the organization's business. The responsible choice that's in the best interest of the public sector citizens and private sector customers is a cohesive data culture and a comparate data resource.

QUESTIONS

The following questions are provided as a review of data culture integration, and to stimulate thought about the need for data cultural integration.

1. Why is data culture integration needed in addition to data architecture integration?

2. What is the purpose of the three data culture states?

3. What are the five components of data culture?

4. How is a data culture survey performed?

5. How is the data culture survey documented?

6. How are the results of the data culture survey used to designate the preferred data culture?

7. How does the Common Data Culture differ from a common data culture?

8. How is the fragmented data culture transformed to a cohesive data culture?

9. Why is there no reverse data culture transformation like there is with data transformation?

10. Why must data culture transformation be persistent?

Chapter 14

MANAGING THE DATA RESOURCE

Getting started and keeping it going.

The previous chapters summarized the contents of *Data Resource Simplexity* and described the theory, concepts, principles, and techniques for data resource integration. Data resource integration develops a comparate data resource within a common data architecture. Data culture integration creates a cohesive data culture within a common data culture.

Chapter 14 briefly describes the management problems that must be addressed and overcome to achieve complete data resource integration and data culture integration. It provides a direction for establishing a formal data management profession responsible for managing data as a critical resource of the organization. All of the theory, concepts, principles, and techniques described in earlier chapters will be relatively useless unless formal data resource management can be established.

HALTING AND RESOLVING DISPARITY

The theme of *Data Resource Simplexity* was to stop the headlong charge over the event horizon of disparity. That charge, which continues today, has severely impacted both public and private sector organizations. If that charge continues, which it appears to be doing, the service to citizens and customers will reach a critical point where business survival becomes an issue.

The theme of *Data Resource Integration* is to repair the damage that has been caused by that headlong charge toward disparity. The best way to repair the damage is to recognize data as a critical resource of the organization and to begin formally managing data accordingly. The best way to gain respect for data resource management is to step up to the task of resolving the disparity that has been created and to ensure that it never happens again.

Managing Data

Understanding and resolving an organization's disparate data resource has been adequately described in the previous chapters. However, situations with data from outside the organization must be handled, such as multiple data models, multiple data documentation sources, universal models and generic architectures, data standards, application acquisition, data registries, and acquired data. Each of these situations is described below.

Multiple Data Models

Data models, regardless of their source from within or without the organization, often conflict and do not adequately represent the organization's perception of the business world. Many organizations have modeled their critical data numerous times using different techniques and perceptions based on the modeler, not on the organization. None of these data models should be used as a common data architecture for the organization, or even as an initial common data architecture. The best approach is to document each data model as a data product, make cross-references to a common data architecture, and use the insight to designate a preferred data architecture.

Multiple Data Documentation Sources

The existing data documentation in most organizations, whether developed by the organization or obtained from outside the organization, resides in an assortment of formal and informal dictionaries. The dictionaries may come from a variety of different sources and exist in a variety of different forms. Virtually none of these dictionaries are useful for formally managing the data resource. The best approach is to document each of these dictionaries as a data product, make cross-references to a common data architecture, and use the insight to designate a preferred data architecture. The result is a formal documentation of the organization's data resource.

Universal Models and Generic Architectures

Universal data models and generic data architectures seldom provide any real insight into how an organization perceives the business world where they operate. Using models and architectures as a common data architecture does not help development of a data resource that supports the organization's business information demand. The best approach is to document these data models and data architectures as data products, make cross-references to a common data architecture, and use the insight to designate a preferred data architecture.

Data Standards

Data standards cannot resolve the existing data disparity, and it's even questionable if they can prevent further data disparity. Seldom do they provide any real insight into how the organization should build a data resource to support its business activities based on its perception of the business world. In many situations, data standards are simply a reporting requirement between different organizations. The best approach is to document these data standards as a data product, cross-reference them to a common data architecture, and use the insight to designate a preferred data architecture. Data transformations can then be specified to meet the reporting requirements.

Application Acquisition

Application acquisition is a prominent trend today, but a purchased application can substantially increase data disparity and could warp the organization's perception of the business world. The proactive approach is to document the data architecture of an application before the application is purchased, cross-reference it to a common data architecture, and determine how different it is from the preferred data architecture. Then an informed decision can be made as to whether or not to purchase that application. If the application does not have a complete data model, the application is in question and should not be considered.

If the application has already been purchased, the reactive approach is to document the data architecture of the application, cross-reference it to a common data architecture, and then determine how that application should be used to support the organization's business. Data should not be indiscriminately dumped into an application (a brute-force-physical approach) without formally determining how those data should be managed.

Data Registries

Data registries are often viewed as a standard data model that should be used. However, the data model in those data registries are, at best, the perception of one organization and how that organization perceives the business world. The data may not represent how another organization perceives their business world. Again, the best approach is to document a data registry as a data product, cross-reference it to a common data architecture, and use the insight to designate a preferred data architecture.

Acquired Data

Data are often acquired from outside the organization, or through mergers and acquisitions. These data are typically quite disparate and seldom support an organization's perception of the business world. These data should be documented as data products, cross-referenced to a common data architecture, and used to designate a preferred data architecture. Then the data can be transformed accordingly to become part of the organization's comparate data resource to adequately support the business.

Approach

Several approaches to halting and resolving data disparity, include stopping hype-cycles, resolving the lexical challenge, changing attitudes, and stop warping the business. Each of these approaches is described below.

Stop the Hype-Cycles

The current trend of one hype-cycle after another must be stopped to achieve formal data resource management. Hype-cycles are a form of silver bullets, and usually become tarnished bullets that often make the disparate data situation worse. Hype-cycles have not helped data resource management become professional, and lead to much of the lack of respect for formal data management.

Some organizations attempt to make hype-cycles persistent, through declaration, standards, certifications, and so on. However, hype-cycles seldom lack any real foundation in theories, concepts, principles, and techniques. They are typically current centric, trendy, and often have profit motives. In due time, they all fail and are replaced by another hype-cycle.

The best approach is to establish formal data resource management based on sound theories, concepts, principles, and techniques. Formal data resource management becomes persistent and pervasive, and leads to a formal data management profession. Standards, certifications, and initiatives are built around formal data resource management, and can change as technology changes. Organizations can then create initiatives to implement formal data resource management, and can use any theme or logo they desire to carry that initiative within their organization.

Resolve the Lexical Challenge

The current burgeoning lexical challenge in data resource management must be resolved. Formal terms must be established based on roots, prefixes, and suffixes in a language (English, German, and so on), must have a comprehensive and denotative definition, and must be used consistently throughout the data management profession. The data management professionals themselves must be actively involved in creating a formal lexicon of terms and must be willing to use those terms.

Many formal terms have been presented in *Data Resource Simplexity* and the current book to help achieve the goal of a formal lexicon for data resource management. A combined Glossary has been provided in the current book and is readily available to anyone wanting to use formal terms. Hopefully, professional organizations will endorse these terms, begin using them, and will promote their use.

I ran across an interesting term a while ago—*integrating data integration*. Actually, it was about data integration, not data resource integration. However, the approach was to combine all of the individual data integration efforts in an organization into a single data integration effort. The idea was good—with respect to disparate data integration. The point that was being made was exactly the same as the data resource integration described in the current book. A formal approach is needed to integrate all of the disparate data in an organization and create a comparate data resource.

Change the Attitudes

Many people have attitudes about data resource management that must be changed. After *Data Resource Simplexity* was published, I had several people approach me and really get on my case about my comments on attitudes. They tore me up one side and down the other. Who did I think I was? Attitudes—really? People standing around me were waiting to see how I would respond. After listening to these outbursts, I calmly replied, *I rest my case*.

An enlightening situation occurred a number of years ago with a fellow manager in another organization. He commented that his programmers were very good at programming, but were not so good with the business. He made the statement that they were super compiler writers and amateur human beings. I wouldn't be quite that severe, but many of the data management professionals today are certainly super technicians that are weak on business understanding.

I see similar situations with business professionals' attitudes toward data management professionals. What went wrong with data resource management? Why do data management professionals create a disparate data resource that doesn't meet business needs? How did the business allow a critical resource to be mismanaged?

These attitudes must be changed and teamwork must prevail. Business professionals and data management professionals must bring their collective knowledge and skills together in a team approach to building and maintaining a comparate data resource. A good analogy is building an airplane. Professionals on passenger comfort, wiring, hydraulics, aerodynamics, structure, instrumentation, and so on, must come together to build an airplane. No independent actions.

Stop Warping the Business

Business professionals and data management professionals, alike, must stop warping-the-business to fit an application or data model. I've seen *golf-course decisions* by business professionals where an application was acquired, sometimes against the recommendations of data management professionals, and data management professionals were left with implementation. I've seen data management professionals *play with the technology* to the detriment of the business.

Similar situations are brute-force-physical development, paralysis-by-analysis, and suck-and-squirt techniques. I recently ran across a brute-force-physical data warehouse that had low quality and didn't meet business needs. In one meeting, the database technician asked what the business needed and one business manager explained the data needed. The database technician said, *Oh, I can just stuff another column in the table to do that.* No edits, no integrity, no definition, no understanding of the data hierarchy, and so on.

An analogy is an airplane that doesn't have enough power. Let's just bolt another engine on each wing, or cut the tail smaller to reduce drag, and so on. All brute-force-physical approaches create disparate data and ultimately impact the business.

None of these approaches is appropriate for the business or for formal data resource management. The data resource must be formally designed, built, and implemented to meet business needs. The effort must include both business professionals and data management professionals working together toward a common goal.

No Quick Fixes

Business professionals and data management professionals must stop looking for quick fixes. Quick fixes do not exist, and every attempt at a quick fix only delays a real fix, often making the situation worse. Quick fixes can't understand the data, resolve data disparity, and create a comparate data resource. Only people can understand disparate data and build a comparate data resource.

Many ETL products offer a quick solution to disparate data. When I describe the data integration process to ETL vendors, they claim their product covers that process. Then I go into the real detail and usually get the answer something like *Oh, we can do that, but you have to write the specs*. The ETL products don't, and can't, develop the specs because they can't understand the disparate data or perceive the comparate data resource needed to support the business.

The best approach is to recognize that only people can understand the disparate data and develop a comparate data resource. Only hard work— real hard-thinking kind of work—can understand the disparate data, perceive the comparate data, and develop the specs for data resource integration. Only people can perform that kind of hard work, and products can provide the support.

ON GAINING RESPECT

Respect is a common theme in most organizations, both for business professionals and data management professionals. Respect comes from looking at the situations that result in a lack of respect and taking an initiative to resolve those situations and earn respect.

Most Frequent Complaint

The most frequent comment I hear from data management professionals is that they don't get any respect from the business. I agree, but the question is why don't they have any respect? What have they done, or not done, to have a lack of respect? *Data Resource Simplexity* and the current book provide many examples.

The next most frequent comment I hear from data management professionals is that someone needs to get to the executives and convince them that data management and the data resource deserve more respect. Many of my consulting engagements start with a request that I meet with executives and convince them that the data resource needs to be properly managed. However, the problem isn't necessarily with the executives.

Stop Telling and Start Listening

Data management professionals must stop telling the business and start listening to the business. All too often I hear data management professionals tell the business what's wrong and the resolution. Seldom do data management professionals really listen to the business.

I've heard many people mention creating an elevator pitch, so that when they have a couple of minutes with an executive or business professional they can throw that pitch and gain some respect. The bottom line is that most of those elevator pitches are not within the other person's problem set, are poorly received, and don't work. Here we go, data management professionals telling me what to do again.

A far better approach is to take the opportunity and ask an executive or business professional what problems they are facing. Engage them in their problem set, rather than adding something new to their problem set. In many situations their problem has roots in a data problem, which can be pursued to a successful conclusion. If not, at least that executive or business professional had an opportunity to discuss their problems, and the data management professional may just have learned something about the business.

Stop Demanding and Start Earning

Data management professionals must stop demanding respect and start earning it. Demanding respect seldom achieves any true benefits, and often alienates people. Earning respect provides lasting benefits for both data management professionals and the business. The proper approach is to *command respect, not demand respect*.

All of the concepts, principles, and techniques in *Data Resource Simplexity* and the current book, if followed, will go a long way toward earning respect. Real hard-thinking kind of work to stop further data disparity and resolve the existing data disparity will allow both business professionals and data management professionals to command respect.

Other IT Component Disparity

All four components of the information technology infrastructure have disparity. The worst disparity is with business activities, and the next worst disparity is with the data resource. The least disparate is usually the platform resource. The business activities are the most dynamic component because they must reflect changes in the business world. The data resource is the next most dynamic because it must maintain historical data as well as current data. The platform resource is the least dynamic.

Stabilizing the data resource through data resource integration assists in stabilizing the business activities through business activity integration. Many well-intentioned business activity integration initiatives, sometimes known as business process reengineering, have failed because of a disparate data resource. Formal data resource integration, the use of data brokers, and forward and reverse data transformation provide a stable environment for business activity integration.

Therefore, the best approach is to resolve the data resource disparity to provide some stability in the organization. Then tackle the business activity disparity based on a stable data resource. Any platform disparity can then be resolved to handle a stable data resource and stable business activities.

Take The Initiative

I'm often asked how long it will take to resolve a disparate data resource and create a comparate data resource. The reasonable answer is that it will take ten years to substantially resolve a disparate data resource if the organization is diligent. However, in all likelihood the entire disparate data resource will never be completely resolved. A point of diminishing returns is reached where it's not feasible to expend the effort to resolve the remaining disparate data.

I've seen organizations take their data redundancy from a factor of ten to a factor of four and be ecstatic about the results. I've seen other organizations take their data redundancy from a factor of eight to a factor of three and not be satisfied until the disparity is reduced further. The choice is up to the organization and their perception of the point of diminishing returns.

Generally, when data redundancy reaches a factor of two or three, the point of diminishing returns has been reached. The organization can concentrate on maintaining the comparate data resource and prevent further data disparity. The remaining data redundancy will disappear over time without much additional effort.

I often ask people what it's like after they have resolved data disparity and created a comparate data resource. The response is always something like they can't believe how easy it is to maintain the data resource and support the business information demand. They fully understand the power of a comparate data resource and its support for the business. They wish they had managed the data resource properly from the beginning, and can't understand how they ever let a disparate data resource evolve.

Getting Started

I'm frequently asked what's a good starting point for starting data resource integration. The starting point varies for each individual organization and is based on specific problems with the data resource. The best starting point is where the organization is feeling the most pain with data quality or data availability.

411

Finding the pain points is relatively easy if one listens to the business problems—remember to stop talking and start listening. Engage business people in a discussion about the problems they have and how those problems might be related to the data resource. Meet business professionals in their offices or a neutral place and start discussing their problems. You may be surprised at what you learn.

A real incentive to getting started is readily sharable data. When the pain of not meeting business needs exceeds the pain of crossing organizational boundaries and sharing data, people will begin integrating the data resource. When the pain of existing low quality data exceeds the pain of creating a comparate data resource, people will begin interacting and creating a comparate data resource.

One approach to getting started is to sell the benefits of disaster reduction or disaster avoidance. Disparate data create a risk for an organization by being large and costly to maintain and by not supporting a rapidly changing business. That risk could lead to a disaster if an organization misses opportunities or fails to fully utilize an opportunity. Developing an integrated data resource can prevent a disaster or reduce the impact of a disaster by reducing the risk.

Talk to business professionals about impact avoidance and cost avoidance. I used to say that long term benefits has lost its meaning and short term benefits was more appropriate. I'm now realizing that even short term benefits has begun to lose its meaning. I now talk about impact avoidance and cost avoidance, which seems to have a much better reception.

Getting started may be a perception problem. Creating a comparate data resource is intangible to most people. They can't visualize the benefits of developing a comparate data resource. The perception is that if a process does not produce code, it does not provide any benefit to the organization.

Building a comparate data resource is often perceived as an esoteric process where *the rubber meets the sky*. Past data management practices have enforced that perception. The perception needs to be overcome by selling the disadvantages and benefits of a comparate data resource.

Paint a Vision

The initiative must provide a very vivid vision about what's wrong with a disparate data resource and how a comparate data resource can support the current and future business information demand. A vision must describe the future and focus people on the benefits of a comparate data resource. It must include creative ideas from a wide variety of people, including visionaries and knowledge workers.

The vision must bring order out of chaos, comparity out of disparity, and orderliness out of disorder. It must be so powerful, so compelling, so overwhelmingly beneficial in its simplicity that the organization can only respond with *Yeah, that's what I need*.

Avoid Excuses

Many organizations use the excuse that data resource integration is too difficult and too expensive. They can't afford the resources or the perceived impact on the business. They seem to be in a comfort zone, in spite of the pain they are feeling due to low quality data and the business information demand that is not being met.

One thing I've noticed over the years is that when business is good and revenue is up, organizations don't see a need for data resource integration. When business is bad and revenue is down, organizations don't have the resources available for data resource integration. There never seems to be a point where the business is just right and the revenue is just right for data resource integration.

Organizations must avoid the excuses, recognize the pain that is caused by disparate data, and establish an initiative for data resource integration. The result will be much like the person who's eyesight slowly diminishes and finally gets their first pair of glasses. They never realized things could look so clear.

No organization can afford to shut down business for several months, let alone several years, to develop a comparate data resource. Any organization that shuts down that long will likely go out of business. Data resource integration must be done on-the-fly, while conducting normal business activities.

Going Out of Business

I'm often asked if an organization will go out of business due to a disparate data resource. The answer is possibly yes for private sector organizations. I've been involved with several private sector organizations that have either lost their customer base or lost control of their customer base due to improper management of the data resource. These organizations were in grave danger of going out of business, had they not regained control of their customer data.

The answer is probably not for public sector organizations. Most business functions in public sector organizations are legislatively mandated. Those business functions can only be eliminated by legislative mandate. However, a disparate data resource can result in poor management of a business function and a waste of resources, which brings public scrutiny in these tough economic times.

Therefore, the best approach for both public and private sector organizations is to properly manage the data as a critical resource so that it adequately supports the current and future business information demand.

Techniques Exist

One comment I frequently hear is that no techniques are available to stop the creation of disparate data and create a comparate data resource. People say the profession has not matured enough to handle these complex problems. Well, the profession will never mature with that attitude.

The techniques are available and have been proven. They are easy to use and produce results. They are relatively easy to implement, although real hard-thinking work is needed to produce results. They provide the easiest route to follow that assures success.

The techniques provide a success motivation that becomes contagious. They lead to involvement, which leads to commitment, which leads to acceptance, which leads to success. One only needs to start using the techniques—maybe as early as tomorrow.

Keeping it Going

I used to wonder how I would keep a data resource integration effort going after the current project was completed. How would I keep the momentum going? How would I get the next project started?

In the majority of situations, I've been pleasantly surprised. The issue was not going out and finding another data resource integration project, it was choosing which one of those waiting in line would be the next. People continually approached me to ask if they could be the next project for data resource integration.

Once the initiative was started and people saw the benefit of integrating disparate data and creating a comparate data resource, they wanted their data integrated. I frequently started one team in one subject area, got it moving, and then started another team in another subject area. Often I took a key person from a successful project and put them on a new project to keep it moving.

Business Involvement

Business professionals should, and will eventually, become more involved in managing the data resource that supports their business activities. They are the people knowledgeable about the business and the rapid changes that occur in the business. They will become more data management enabled to design, build, maintain, and use a comparate data resource.

Data management is likely to go to the business, rather than remain in IT. The same skills and techniques will be required, regardless of where the data management function is placed. However, placing that function in the business will ensure that it more readily supports the business.

I've had a relatively easy time teaching business professionals the skills and techniques for managing data, and a relatively difficult time getting traditional data modelers and architect to understand the business. I've had a relatively easy time getting business professionals to understand data quality with respect to the business, and a relatively difficult time getting traditional data modelers and architects to really understand data quality.

I've had a relatively easy time getting business professionals to take both a people orientation and a business orientation. I've found it easier to get business professionals involved in a teamwork approach. I've found it easier to get business professionals involved in a business survival orientation.

I've found it easier to convince business professionals that quality is not free, but it's far less expensive if built in from the beginning, than adding it later. I've found it easier to convince business professionals that data quality improvement and data resource integration has a point of diminishing returns.

SUMMARY

The task of managing data as a critical resource of the organization requires patience and understanding. It's difficult and challenging, but it's far from impossible. The situation will get worse before it gets better, but it will get better. The benefits of a comparate data resource more than pay for the data resource integration effort.

The approach and the benefits vary from organization to organization, from project to project, and from year to year. The process for starting and maintaining an initiative to create a comparate data resource varies from organization to organization. The secret is to start on a pathway toward success and learn along the way. Follow the concepts, principles, and techniques described in *Data Resource Simplexity* and the current book.

Seize the opportunity to stop further data disparity and create a comparate data resource that supports business survival. Seize the opportunity to begin formal data resource management and manage data as a critical resource of the organization that supports the current and future business information demand.

Don't delay! Start today!

QUESTIONS

The following questions are provided as a review of managing the data resource, and to stimulate thought about what's involved in formally managing a data resource.

1. How are data from outside the organization managed?

2. What needs to change to establish formal data resource management?

3. How can data management professionals start earning respect?

4. How can resolving data resource disparity help resolve disparity in the other IT components?

5. How does an organization get started with data resource integration?

6. Why is a vivid vision necessary for starting data resource integration?

7. How is an initiative to integrate the data resource maintained once it has been started?

8. Why is business involvement in data resource management necessary?

9. Why is data resource management likely to become a business function rather than an IT function?

10. How can data management professionals help establish a formal data management profession?

Appendix A

DATA INTEGRITY RULE EXAMPLES

Appendix A contains examples of data integrity rules to show the types and formats of the various data integrity rules. For a detailed description of data integrity rules, refer to *Data Resource Simplexity*.

Data Integrity Rule Symbols

Mathematical symbols:

+	addition
-	subtraction
*	multiplication
/	division
**	exponentiation
=	equals

Logical symbols:

<	less than
>	greater than
<=	less than or equal to
>=	greater than or equal to
=	equal to
<>	not equal to
><	must be equal to, or must be
^	hierarchy (parent – child)
&	logical and
|	logical or
||	concatenated with
::	valid for
~	relationship
<<	comes from, translates from
>>	goes to, translates to
Blank	means a blank data value
' '	means a blank data value

Set symbols:

{ }	a set

n{ }m   a set with minimum and maximum values
( )   grouping of elements
n\ \m   substring from n to m

Data Integrity Rule Common Words

Cardinality!   Proactive Update!

Constraint!   Rederivation!

Change!   Retroactive Update!

Comment: Selection!

Condition!   Source!

Constraint!   Translation!

Delete!   Unique!

Derivation!   Violation!

Notification!

Employee
    Cardinality!
    Change!

Street Segment
    Cardinality 1!
    Cardinality 2!

Customer
    Inactive Delete!
    Active Delete!

Product
    Product. Market Value
        Domain!   1 <= integer <= 1000
        Need!   Required

Class – Student
    Cardinality!
    Constraint!

Data Value Rules

20 <= Trailer. Length <= 60

Trailer. Length
    Domain! 20 <= Integer <= 60

Company. Name
        Domain! 5 characters <= Text <= 30 characters & first
        character <> Blank

Domain! 5 <= alphanumeric characters <= 128 & right justified

Domain! -180.0 <= real <= +180.0

Driver. Birth Date, Domain! >< Valid Date

Candidate. Birth Date
　　　Domain! January 1, 1996 <= Date <= December 31, 1998

Sample Tree. Height, Domain! 36.75 <= Real <= 72.25

Product. Audit Indicator
　　　　　　Domain! {'Y' | 'N'}   Default 'N'
　　　When default value entered
　　　Product. Audit Indicator Default Value Entry = "Y"

Region. Code
　　　Domain! {'AK' | 'BK' | 'CD' | 'RQ' | 'XT'}

Customer
　　　Region. Code, Domain >< Region. Code

Conditional Data Value Rules

　　　　　Need! Region. Code is Required

　　　　　Need! 1{Region. Code}1

　　　　　Need! Prevented

　　　　　Need! Region. Code is Optional

　　　　　Need! 0{Region. Code}1

　　　　　Need! Optional

　　　　　Need! Region. Code is Prevented

　　　　　Need! 0{Region. Code}0

　　　　　Need! Prevented

Product Order. Value Condition!
　　　When Product Status. Code = 'Confirmed'
　　　　　Product Order. Sale Date is Required
　　　　　Product Order. Ship Date is Prevented
　　　　　Product Order. Delivery Date is Prevented
　　　When Product Status. Code = 'Shipped
　　　　　Product Order. Sale Date is Required
　　　　　Product Order. Ship Date is Required
　　　　　Product Order. Delivery Date is Prevented
　　　When Product Status. Code = 'Delivered
　　　　　Product Order. Sale Date is Required
　　　　　Product Order. Ship Date is Required
　　　　　Product Order. Delivery Date is Required

Product Order. Value Condition!
　　　Product Order. Ship Date >= Product Order. Sale Date

Product Order. Delivery Date >= Product Order. Ship Date

Employee Seniority - Employee Type Integrity!
When Employee Type. Code = '1' Employee Seniority. Code >< 'B'
When Employee Type. Code = '2' Employee Seniority. Code >< {'B' |
'C'}
And so on...

Domain! Employee Type. Code & Employee Seniority. Code ><
Employee Seniority – Employee Type Integrity.

Employee Seniority – Employee Type Integrity
Employee Seniority – Employee Type Integrity. Begin Date
Need! Required
Employee Seniority – Employee Type Integrity. End Date
When Employee Seniority – Employee Type is valid
Employee Seniority – Employee Type. End Date is Prevented
When Employee Seniority – Employee Type is not valid
Employee Seniority – Employee Type. End Date is Required

Data Structure Rules

Stream - Stream Segment Cardinality!
1{Stream}1 ~ 2{Stream Segment}M

Employee
Employee. Social Security Number
Need! Required
Department. Number
Need! Required
Domain! Department: Department. Number
Ethnicity. Code
Need! Optional
Domain! {Blank | Ethnicity: Ethnicity. Code}

Employee – Ethnicity Cardinality!
1{Employee}1 ~ 0{Ethnicity}1

Class ~ Professor Cardinality!
1{Professor}1 ~ 0{Class}3

Conditional Data Structure Rules

Degree ~ Student Cardinality!
When a Student is an Undergraduate Student a Degree is
Prevented.
When a Student is a Graduate Student a Degree is Required.

Student >< {[Undergraduate] Student | [Graduate] Student}

Degree ~ [Undergraduate] Student. Cardinality!
1{[Undergraduate] Student}1 ~ 0{Degree}0

Degree ~ [Graduate] Student. Cardinality!
1{[Graduate] Student}1 ~ 1{Degree}M

Prospective Student ~ Student Constraint!
Prospective Student <> Student

Data Derivation and Data Rederivation Rules

Employee
Employee. Age, Years- Derivation!
Employee. Age, Years = Current Date - Employee. Birth Date

Well Type. Code, Derivation!
Derive: On initial data entry
Rederive: When contributor's data value changes
When Well Casing Type Code = 'Black Steel' & Well. Depth <= 10 Feet
Well Type. Code = '1'
When Well Casing Type Code = 'Black Steel' & Well. Depth > 11 Feet & <= 100 Feet
Well Type. Code = '2'
When Well Casing Type Code = 'Black Steel' & Well. Depth > 300 Feet
Well Type. Code = '3'
And so on…

Product Shipment
Product Shipment. Product Count, Derivation!
Product Shipment. Product Count = Count of unique Products in Product Shipment
Derive: When Product Shipment Status. Code ='C'
Rederive: None
Product Shipment. Total Weight, Derivation!
Product Shipment. Total Weight = Sum of all Product Load. Weight in Product Shipment
Derive: When Product shipment Status Code = 'C'
Rederive: None
Product Shipment. Average Product Weight, Derivation!
Produce Shipment. Average Product Weight = Product Shipment. Total Weight / Product Shipment. Product Count
Derive: When contributors have been derived.
Rederive: None

Vehicle
Vehicle. Yearly Miles, Derivation!
January 1 {Sum Vehicle Trip. Miles} December 31
Derive: January 15 of following calendar year
Rederive: None

Data Retention Rules

Employee
Employee. Name, Change!
Move Employee. Name to Employee History. Name
Enter effective date of name change in Employee History. Date

421

Enter new employee name in Employee. Name

Employee
Employee. Name, Change!
Move Employee to Employee History
Enter effective date of name change in Employee History. Date
Enter new employee name in Employee. Name

Employee
Employee. Birth Date, Change!
Change allowed with no History

Customer. Retention!
Customer. Inactive!
When Customer has not Purchased a Product for 12 months
Delete Customer
Customer. Left Country!!
When Customer has left the country
Delete Customer
Customer. Deceased!!
When Customer has deceased
Delete Customer
Customer. Delete!
Move Customer to Customer History
Enter current data in Customer History. Date
Delete Customer

Customer History
When Current Date >= Customer History. Date + 36 Months
Delete Customer History

Data Selection Rules

[Retirement Eligible] Employee. Selection!
Employee. Age, Years >= '50' & Employee. Service Years >= '25'

[Management Level] Employee. Selection!
Management Level. Code = {'2' | '4' | '5'}

[Preferred] Employee. Selection!
[Retirement Eligible] Employee & [Management Level] Employee

Product. Style, Selection!
3 \ Product. Comment \ 8

Data Translation Rules

Pole
Pole. Length, Inches- Translation!
Pole. Length, Meters * 39.39

Product
Product. Price, US Dollars- Translation!
Exchange Rate. Euro = current exchange rate
Exchange Rate. Date = current Date

Product. Price, Euro = Product. Price, US Dollars * Exchange Rate. Euro

Traffic Accident
Traffic Accident. Location, State Plane Coordinate- Translation!
Traffic Accident. Location, Latitude Longitude- = Traffic Accident. Traffic Accident Location, State Plane Coordinates- & Geographic Coordinate. Algorithm Six.

Translation
Translation. Algorithm Twelve

Driver
Driver. Complete Name, Inverted- Translation!
Driver. Complete Name, Normal- & Translation. Algorithm Twelve

Translation
Translation. Miles – Kilometers
Translation. Meters – Feet
And so on.

Road Segment
Road Segment. Length, Kilometers- Translation!
Road Segment. Length, Miles- & Translation. Miles - Kilometers

Translation. Pi, Seven Decimals = 3.14159623

Road Segment
Road Segment. Length, Kilometers
Road Segment. Length Significant Digits

Inheritance

Coordinate
Coordinate. Longitude Degree, Domain!
-180.0 <= value <= 180.0

Well Head
Well Head. Longitude Degrees, Domain! >< Longitude. Degree, Domain!

Coordinate
Coordinate. Longitude Degrees, Washington Federal- Domain!
122.234 <= value <= 123.615

Coordinate. Longitude Degrees, Washington State- Domain!
122.197 <= value <= 123.675

Well Head
Wellhead. Longitude Degrees, Domain! >< Coordinate. Longitude Degrees, Washington Federal- Domain!

Versions

Customer
Customer. Left Country Duration! <Pre-1995>

Customer. Left Country Duration! <January 1995>

Student
Student. Name
Student. Name, Change! < Through 1997>
Student. Name, Change! <1998>

Customer
Customer. Deceased Retention! <Pre-2001>
Customer. Left Country Retention! <Pre-2001>

Customer. Inactive Retention! <2001>

Class ~ Professor. Cardinality! <Pre 2007>
1{Professor}1 ~ 0{Class}3

Class ~ [Full] Professor. Cardinality! <2007>
1{Professor}1 ~ 0{Class}2

Class ~ [Associate] Professor. Cardinality! <2007>
1{Professor}1 ~ 0{Class}4

Failure and Notification

Trailer. Length
Domain! 20 <= Integer <= 60
Violation! Move Trailer to Trailer Suspense

Trailer
Violation! Move Trailer to Trailer Suspense

Trailer. Length
Domain! 20 <= Integer <= 60
And so on.

Trailer
Violation! Move Trailer to Trailer Suspense
Notification! Entry into Vehicle Error Log.

Trailer. Length
Domain! 20 <= Integer <= 60

Data Source Rules

Employee: Race. Code
Source! << PYRL.EMPL_RACE

Employee. Name
Source ! When Employee. Hire Date >= 'January 1, 1990'
& <= 'December 31, 1999' << PYRL.EMPL_NM

When Employee. Hire Date >= January 1, 2000
<< AA.EMP_NAME

Employee. Birth Date
Source! When Department. Identifier ^ Employee = '62' | '63' | '64'
<< PYRL_EMPL_BD

424

When Department. Identifier ^ Employee <> '62' | '63' | '64'
<< TRAIN.EMPLYE_BDATE

Employee. Birth Date
Source! When Department. Identifier ^ Employee = '62' | '63' | '64'
<< PYRL_EMPL_BD
When Department. Identifier ^ Employee <> '62' | '63' | '64'
<< TRAIN.EMPLYE_BDATE
When TRAIN.EMPLYE_BDATE = ' ' << PYRL.EMPL_BD
When PYRL.EMPL_BD = ' ' << AA.EMP_BIRTH

Hierarchy

The up-caret is used to denote a hierarchy. The example below is read as "Report is parent to Site Class, which is parent to Age Category, which is parent to Species, which is parent to Timber Stand." The hierarchy could also be read in the other direction as "Timber Stand is subordinate to Species, which is subordinate to Age Category, which is Subordinate to Site Class, which is subordinate to Report.

Report ^ Site Class ^ Age Category ^ Species ^ Timber Stand

University ^ Department ^ Course ^ Class ^ Section

Library ^ Wing ^ Floor ^ Section ^ Row ^ Shelf ^ Book

The hierarchy symbol can also be used for recursive data relations. The example below specifies that a parent organization unit cannot have the same identifier as the subordinate organization unit. In other words, an organization unit cannot report to itself.

Organization Unit. Identifier ^ <> Organization Unit. Identifier

The example below specifies that any organization unit in the hierarchy cannot have the same identifier as the subordinate organization unit. In other words, no parent, grandparent, great grandparent, and so on, can have the same identifier as the subordinate organization unit.

Organization Unit. Identifier ^^ <> Organization Unit. Identifier

Concatenation

Concatenations use the double parallel symbol. The example below shows that a person's complete name in the normal sequence is obtained from the person's individual name concatenated with a blank, concatenated with the person's middle name, concatenated with a blank, concatenated with a person's family name.

Person. Name Complete, Normal = Person. Individual Name || ' '
|| Person. Middle Name || ' ' || Person. Family Name

Person. Name Complete, Inverted = Person. Family Name || ', '

|| Person. Individual Name || ' ' || Person. Middle Name

Sub-stringing

Sub-stringing uses the back slashes with the ranges of the sub-stringing outside the back slashes and the data attribute inside the back slashes. In the example below, the vehicle's manufactured date is obtained by sub-stringing fields 5 through 8 from the vehicle comment data attribute.

Vehicle. Year Manufactured = 5 \ Vehicle. Comment \ 8

Valid For

The valid for symbol specifies a constraint for a data value. The example below specifies that student type code contained in the student data entity must equal one of the type codes in the student type data reference set that is valid for the student's registration date.

Student: Student. Type Code ><
Student Type. Code :: Student. Registration Date

Move To

The move to symbol specifies that data are moved from one location to another location. The example below specifies that the violation action for a data integrity rule failure of trailer data results in the trailer data record begin moved to the trailer suspense data entity.

Violation! Trailer >> Trailer Suspense

Data Reconstruction Rules

Student
   Reconstruct! Current back through January 1984
      STDNT_NME
      STDNT_BRTH_DT
      STDNT_WGHT
      STDNT_CHNG_DT
   And so on.

Data Recast Rules

Recast! 1970 through 1999 to 1970 using Recast Algorithm 6
   BDG:OBJ
   BDG:SOB
   BDG:PRG
   BDG:SPRG
And so on.

Appendix B

DATA HIERARCHY NOTATION

The data on screens, reports, and forms are documented in a data hierarchy for better understanding and inventorying. The traditional data hierarchy, using set theory notation, is shown in Figure B.1. The data hierarchy represents a simple report for an organization showing departments, divisions, sections, and units within the organization. The nested data sets show a parent – subordinate relationship

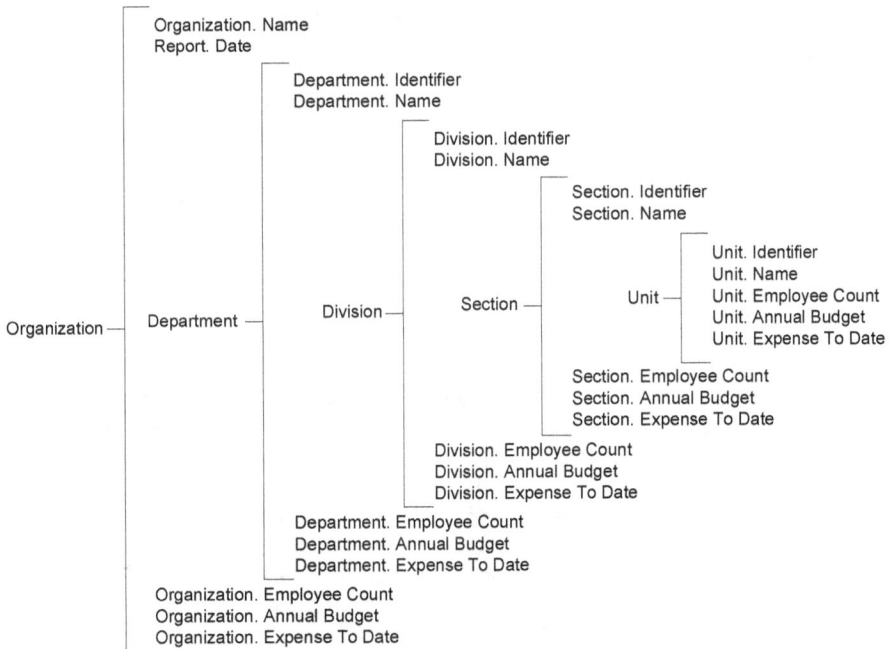

Figure B.1. Data hierarchy using traditional notation.

The name of each data set in the hierarchy is shown on the left of the data set symbol and the contents of each data set are shown on the right. The contents at the top of the data set are identifying data items and the contents at the bottom of each data set are the summary data items.

The traditional data hierarchy notation can become quite wide and difficult to print on a single page. The data hierarchy notation can be adjusted to a narrower notation by moving the data set name to the top, right of the data set symbol, as shown in Figure B.2. The data hierarchy is identical to the data hierarchy shown in Figure B.1, except that it has a narrower and longer format.

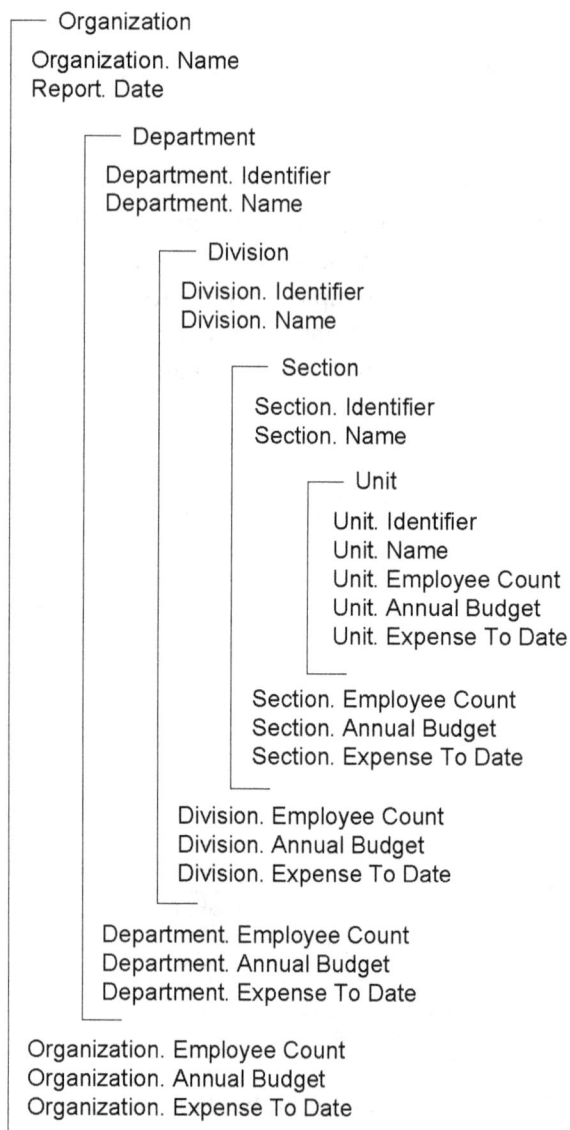

```
┌─ Organization
│  Organization. Name
│  Report. Date
│     ┌─ Department
│     │  Department. Identifier
│     │  Department. Name
│     │     ┌─ Division
│     │     │  Division. Identifier
│     │     │  Division. Name
│     │     │     ┌─ Section
│     │     │     │  Section. Identifier
│     │     │     │  Section. Name
│     │     │     │     ┌─ Unit
│     │     │     │     │  Unit. Identifier
│     │     │     │     │  Unit. Name
│     │     │     │     │  Unit. Employee Count
│     │     │     │     │  Unit. Annual Budget
│     │     │     │     └  Unit. Expense To Date
│     │     │     │
│     │     │     │  Section. Employee Count
│     │     │     │  Section. Annual Budget
│     │     │     └  Section. Expense To Date
│     │     │
│     │     │  Division. Employee Count
│     │     │  Division. Annual Budget
│     │     └  Division. Expense To Date
│     │
│     │  Department. Employee Count
│     │  Department. Annual Budget
│     └  Department. Expense To Date
│
│  Organization. Employee Count
│  Organization. Annual Budget
└  Organization. Expense To Date
```

Figure B.2. Data hierarchy using adjusted notation.

The choice of a data hierarchy notation is up to the organization, or to individuals in the organization who are developing the data hierarchy. The choice may depend on the tools available, the method of documentation, and how well people understand the data hierarchy. A consistent data hierarchy notation may be used throughout the organization, or both data hierarchy notations may be used.

The highest level in the data hierarchy represents the screen, report, or form. The organization name and date of the report are shown at the top of the data set. The nested data sets in the data hierarchy represent subordinate organizational units.

The data hierarchy shown in Figures B.1 and B.2 is commonly referred to as a fixed data hierarchy. The parent – subordinate relations are fixed and cannot change. For example, sections cannot belong to units, and departments cannot belong to sections.

The totals in a fixed data hierarchy are commonly referred to as summary data. For example, the totals for employee count, annual budget, and expense to date are accumulated from individual units, through sections, divisions, and departments, to a total for the organization. These summary data are named according to their place in the hierarchy, such as Unit. Employee Count, Section. Employee Count, Division. Employee Count, Department. Employee Count, and Organization. Employee Count.

The data hierarchies may show either the formal data names according to the data naming taxonomy, or common data names that may appear on the screen, report, or form. Some people prefer to see the formal data names so that they can relate the data to a common data architecture. Other people prefer to see the common data names. Either way is acceptable.

Appendix C

AGGREGATED DATA

Data sets in a variable data hierarchy have no fixed sequence as they do in a fixed data hierarchy. The data sets in a variable data hierarchy can be rearranged in many different ways that change the parent – subordinate relationships. The aggregated data in variable data hierarchies change according to the hierarchy of data.

Unlike summary data, aggregated data in variable data hierarchies are not named according to the data set in which they appear. They are named according to the parent data sets above the data set where they are located. The name of the data set where aggregated data appears must represent the parent data sets.

For example, a variable data hierarchy for Student Analytics contains data sets for school district, school, academic year, race, and grade level. Those data sets could be arranged in many different ways, such as:

State ^ School District ^ School ^ Academic Year ^ Race ^ Grade Level

State ^ Academic Year ^ School District ^ School ^ Grade Level ^ Race

State ^ School District ^ School ^ Race ^ Grade Level ^ Academic Year

State ^ Academic Year ^ Race ^ Grade Level ^ School

And so on.

Clearly, the aggregated data by race would be different in these three data hierarchies, for the same basic set of data. Therefore, aggregated data need to be named according to the parent data sets.

A sample report for school enrolment data is shown in Figure C.1. The report is relatively simple, but it shows the types of reports that are typically encountered. The report is also typical of the screens and forms that may be encountered.

The report has a title and date at the top, and is broken down into students with disabilities and students with no disabilities. Within each disability grouping are four grade levels for preschool, elementary school, middle school, and senior high school. On the left are funding types for public schools and private schools. Individual schools are listed within each funding type. An X indicates detail values, an S indicates first level summaries, an SS indicates second level summaries, a T indicates first level totals, a TT indicates second level totals, and a TTT indicates a grand total for the report.

STUDENT ENROLLMENT SUMMARY

JANUARY 1997

		Disability					No Disability					Total
		Pre	Elem	Jr	Sr	Sum	Pre	Elem	Jr	Sr	Sum	
Public Schools												
	A	X	X	X	X	S	X	X	X	X	S	T
	B	X	X	X	X	S	X	X	X	X	S	T
	C	X	X	X	X	S	X	X	X	X	S	T
	D	X	X	X	X	S	X	X	X	X	S	T
	Sum	S	S	S	S	SS	S	S	S	S	SS	TT
Private Schools												
	P	X	X	X	X	S	X	X	X	X	S	T
	Q	X	X	X	X	S	X	X	X	X	S	T
	R	X	X	X	X	S	X	X	X	X	S	T
	S	X	X	X	X	S	X	X	X	X	S	T
	Sum	S	S	S	S	SS	S	S	S	S	SS	TT
Total		T	T	T	T	TT	T	T	T	T	TT	TTT

Figure C.1. Sample school enrollment report.

The traditional data hierarchy for the School Enrollment Summary report is shown in Figure C.2. The name of each data set is shown on the left of the set symbol, and the contents of the set are on the right. The contents at the top of the set are identifying data attributes and the contents at the bottom of the set are the summary data. Nested sets show a subordinate relationship. The aggregated data names are the physical data names according to the report.

The highest level in the report shows the report name and date at the top and the report total at the bottom. Funding is subordinate to the report, school is subordinate to funding, disability is subordinate to school, and grade level is subordinate to disability. Each of these sets has the identifying data attributes and the summary data. Additional nested sets are shown for disability subordinate to funding and grade level subordinate to disability, and for grade level subordinate to disability.

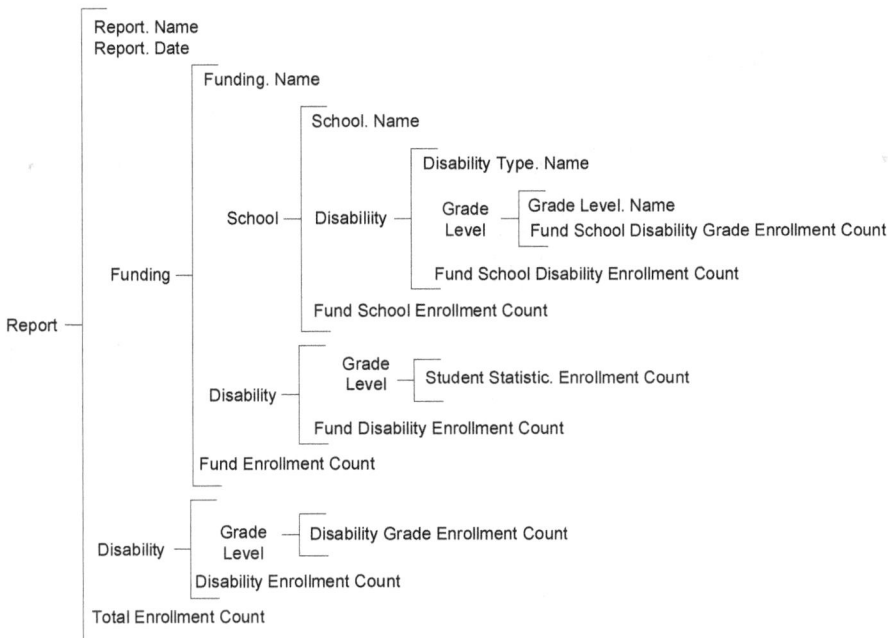

Figure C.2. Traditional report data hierarchy.

The adjusted data hierarchy notation for the same data structure is shown in Figure C.3. The data hierarchy is the same as that shown in Figure C.2, except that it has a narrower and longer format.

These two data hierarchies show the data subject portion of the aggregated data names as Student Analytics. However, as described above, the Enrollment Count for each of the data sets has a different data value. Therefore, they are not the same data values, even though they have the same data names.

The data naming taxonomy provides a way to name aggregated data based on the parent data subjects. The data subject name is formed by using the data focus name, such as Student Analytics, and adding a sequential number for each new collection of parent data subjects, such as Student Analytics 1, Student Analytics 2, and so on. Student Analytics Focus identifies the data focus, and the sequential numbers identify manifestations of that data focus. The manifestations of a data focus are numbered in the order that they are identified. The sequence of the numbers has no meaning other than unique identification.

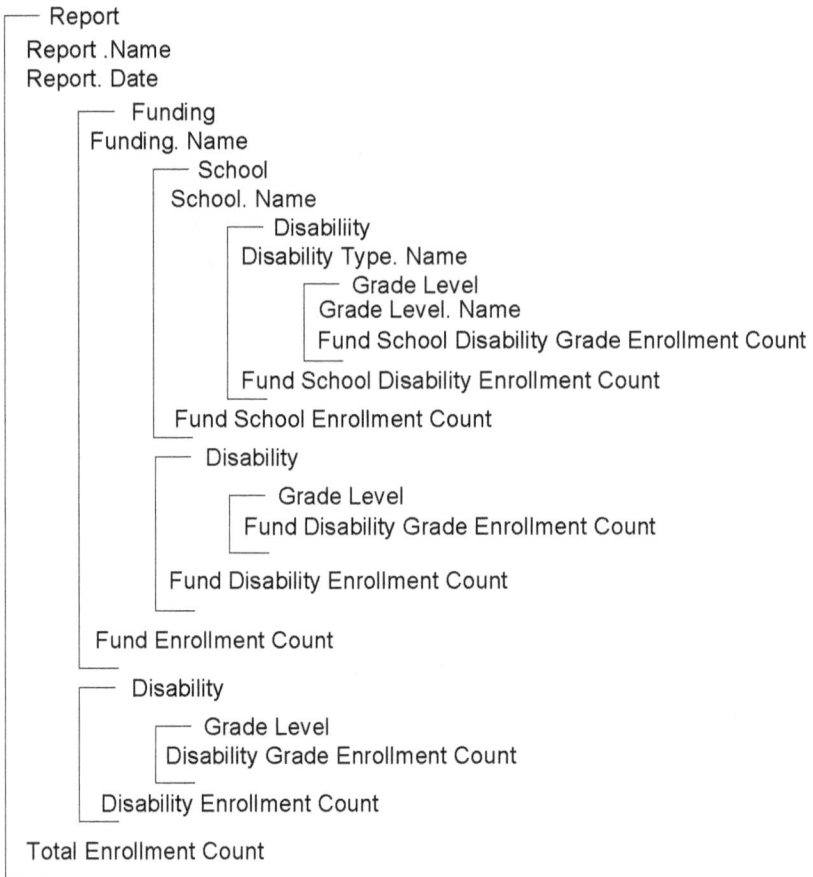

Figure C.3. Adjusted report data hierarchy.

Each collection of parent data sets results in a new manifestation of the data focus. The sequence of the parent data sets is not important. Only the collection of parent data sets is important.   For example, Grade Level Enrollment Count has the same value for :

Funding ^ School ^ Disability ^ Grade Level

School ^ Disability ^ Funding ^ Grade Level

Disability ^ School ^ Funding ^ Grade Level

And so on.

Therefore, a difference in the collection of parent data sets indicates a new manifestation of the data focus. Note that the data set containing the aggregated data is included in the collection of data sets that identifies a manifestation of the data focus.

The collection of parent data subjects is listed in alphabetical order for convenience and ease of identifying different manifestations of the data focus. Using the example above, the data subjects would be listed as:

Disability
Funding
Grade Level
School

The primary keys for the data focus manifestations are shown below. The formal data names are used in the example. Note that the names are in alphabetical order, not in order according to the data hierarchy. The highest level aggregation for the state has a primary key of the report name and date. Those data characteristics do not appear for the other data sets in the data hierarchy.

Fund School Disability Grade
    Disability Type. Name
    Funding. Name
    Grade Level. Name
    School. Name

Fund School Disability
    Disability Type. Name
    Funding. Name
    School. Name

Fund School
    Funding. Name
    School. Name

Fund Disability Grade
    Disability Type. Name
    Funding. Name
    Grade Level. Name

Fund Disability
    Funding. Name
    Disability Type. Code

Fund
    Funding. Name

Disability Grade
    Disability Type. Name
    Grade Level. Name

Disability
    Disability Type. Name

Total
    Report. Name
    Report. Date

A revised data hierarchy diagram for the Student Enrollment Summary Report containing the formal data focus manifestation names is shown in Figure C.4. Both the data hierarchy in Figure C.3 and the data hierarchy in Figure C.4 are acceptable. Some people prefer to see the data hierarchy with the physical data names, while others prefer to see the data hierarchy with the common data architecture names.

If the data from multiple states were combined, then the primary key for the highest level would include State. Identifier as the primary key, rather than the report name and date. In addition, State. Identifier would be added to each of the other manifestations of the data focus.

```
─── Report
Report .Name
Report. Date
        ─── Funding
   Funding. Name
           ─── School
      School. Name
              ─── Disabiliity
         Disability Type. Name
                 ─── Grade Level
            Grade Level. Name
            Student Analytics 1.  Enrollment Count
         Student Analytics 2.  Enrollment Count
      Student Analytics 3.  Enrollment Count
         ─── Disability
             ─── Grade Level
            Student Analytics 4. Enrollment Count
      Student Analytics 5. Enrollment Count
   Student Analytics 6.  Enrollment Count
     ─── Disability
         ─── Grade Level
        Student Analytics 7.  Enrollment Count
   Student Analytics 8.  Enrollment Count
Student Analytics 9.  Enrollment Count
```

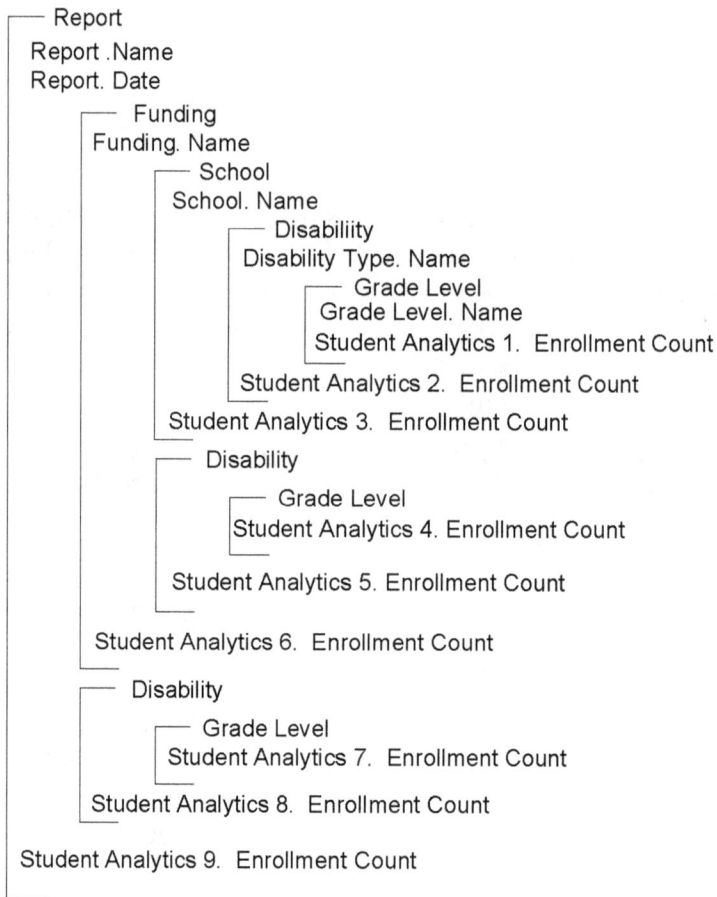

Figure C.4. Revised data hierarchy for student analytics.

Data hierarchies can become extensive, and identifying all of the data focus manifestations can be difficult. The best approach is to develop a matrix of the data focus manifestations and the data sets that qualify that manifestation. The data focus manifestation matrix for the student analytics data is shown in Figure C.5. The letter B shows the base of a specific hierarchy and an X shows the parents in that specific hierarchy.

Aggregated data are often developed from a subset of the data, such as a date range or particular data values. For example, the student analytics data might have been developed for only one county in the state, for only the years 2000 through 2009, or for grade levels 9 through 12. Selection criteria are specified by data selection rules for and apply to the report. They do not apply to manifestations of the data focus.

	Disability	Funding	Grade Level	School	State
Student Analytics 1	X	X	B	X	X
Student Analytics 2	B	X		X	X
Student Analytics 3		X		B	X
Student Analytics 4	X	X	B		X
Student Analytics 5	B	X			X
Student Analytics 6		B			X
Student Analytics 7	X		B		X
Student Analytics 8	B				X
Student Analytics 9					B

Figure C.5. Matrix for student analytics.

GLOSSARY

The Glossary contains terms that are formally defined and consistently used throughout the current book. Where possible, the terms align with traditional terms used in data resource management. However, in situations where the traditional terms are confusing, contradictory, redundant, overlapping, and so on, those terms have been specifically defined and consistently used in the current book. In addition, terms unique to the Common Data Architecture have been defined, In situations where the terms are a direct quote, the reference is given.

The Glossary builds on the Glossary provided in *Data Resource Simplexity* to create an all-inclusive Glossary. The terms from *Data Resource Simplexity* have (Brackett 2011) after them and are unchanged. The terms that appeared in *Data Resource Simplexity* and have been modified in the current book have (Brackett 2011, 2012) after them. Terms new to *Data Resource Integration* have (Brackett 2012) after them. Terms in bold italics are defined terms, and terms in italics only are references to defined terms.

You may use these terms and definitions in your material as long as you give due credit to the source. The intent is to provide a common and consistent terminology for data resource management and resolve the lexical challenge. These terms and definitions have been offered to DAMA for inclusion in their Dictionary of Data Management.

Acceptable means capable or worthy of being accepted. (Brackett 2012)

Acceptable data availability is the situation where data are readily available to meet the business information demand while those data are properly protected and secured. (Brackett 2011)

Acceptable data characteristic variation is any data characteristic variation that is not preferred, but is acceptable to use for an interim period until appropriate changes can be made to databases or application programs. (Brackett 2012)

Acceptable data culture variability is the acceptable level of variability in management of the data resource. (Brackett 2012)

Acceptable data reference set variation is any data reference set variation that is not preferred, but is acceptable to use for an interim period until appropriate changes can be made to databases or application programs. (Brackett 2012)

Acceptable data resource variability is the acceptable level of variability for an organization's data resource. (Brackett 2012)

Acceptable variability is the situation where a normal range of variability is acceptable. Variability exists in all aspects of a business and a normal level of variability must be accepted to perform business successfully. (Brackett 2012)

Accuracy is freedom from mistakes or errors, conformity to truth or to a standard, exactness, the degree of conformity of a measure to a standard or true value. (Brackett 2011)

Accurate data definition principle states that a comprehensive data definition must accurately represent the business. The data definition could be meaningful, and it could be thorough, but it may not be accurate.(Brackett 2011, 2012)

Active data contributors are data attributes that still exist and can change, and are used to create active derived data. (Brackett 2011)

Active derived data are derived data based on active data contributors. (Brackett 2011)

Actual data redundancy is the existence of the same business fact in multiple data files that contain non-redundant data occurrences. It's the redundancy of a business fact based on the data characteristic name and a determination of the redundancy in data occurrences. (Brackett 2012)

Actual data resource scope is the portion of the data resource that is actually formally managed. (Brackett 2011)

Adequate means sufficient for a specific requirement; sufficient or satisfactory; lawfully and legally sufficient. (Brackett 2011)

Adequate data accessibility principle states that access to the data resource must be sufficient to allow people to perform their business activities, and for citizens and customers to obtain the data they need regarding services and products. (Brackett 2011)

Adequate data protection principle states that the data resource must be protected from unauthorized access, alteration, or destruction. (Brackett 2011)

Adequate data recovery principle states that the data resource must have reasonable protection against reasonable failures, and must be recoverable as quickly as possible when the data are altered or destroyed by human or natural disasters. (Brackett 2011)

Adequate data responsibility is the situation where the responsibility, as defined, meets the need for properly managing a comparate data resource. The responsibility is formal, consistent, coordinated, and suitable for a shared data environment. (Brackett 2011)

Aggregation data derivation is where two or more values of the same data attribute in different data occurrences contribute to the derived data. (Brackett 2011)

Alias data name is any data name, other than the primary data name, for a fact or group of related facts in the data resource. (Brackett 2011)

All-inclusive data inventory principle states that all existing data, or references to data, will be inventoried and cross-referenced to a common data architecture so they can be thoroughly understood in a common context. No existing data or references to data, such as data files, reports, screens, documents, dictionaries, data flows, and so on, will be exempt from the data inventory and data cross-reference processes, although priorities may be designated. (Brackett 2012)

Alternate foreign key is a foreign key that matches an alternate primary key in a parent data subject. (Brackett 2012)

Alternate primary key is a primary key that is valid and acceptable, but is not the preferred primary key. (Brackett 2011)

Analysis is separation of the whole into its parts; an examination of a complex, its elements, and their relations; the separation of the ingredients of a substance; a statement of the constituents of a mixture. (Brackett 2011)

Analytical data normalization is the process of re-normalizing the operational logical schema to an analytical logical schema for the purpose of analytical processing. (Brackett 2011)

Analytical tier represents the data in true data warehouses. The data are used to verify or disprove known or suspected trends and patterns. Mathematically the analytical tier is in the aggregation space. (Brackett 2011)

Anthropic principle is the law of human existence. Our existence in the universe depends on numerous constants and parameters whose values fall within a very narrow range. If a single variable was slightly different, we would not exist. (Brackett 2011)

Apparent data redundancy is the apparent existence of the same business fact in multiple data files, regardless of whether those data files contain redundant data occurrences. It's the redundancy of a business fact based on the data characteristic name. (Brackett 2012)

Application alignment principle states that purchased applications must be selected that align with the business and prevent or minimize warping the business into the application. (Brackett 2011)

Application data transformation is the process of transforming disparate data applications from reading and storing disparate data to reading and storing comparate data. The entire application may not be changed, but the data read and data store routines of the application can be changed from disparate data to comparate data. (Brackett 2012)

Appropriate means especially suitable or compatible; fitting. (Brackett 2011)

Appropriate data recognition is the situation where the organization recognizes that data are a critical resource of the organization, the data resource is disparate, and an initiative to develop a comparate data resource is needed. The recognition is organization-wide and the data resource is managed with the same intensity as the financial resource, the human resource, and real property. (Brackett 2011)

Appropriate data use principle states that an organization must constantly review the use of data to ensure the use is appropriate and ethical. (Brackett 2011)

Appropriate detail principle states that a proper data structure must contain all the detail needed for all audiences, but only provide the detail desired by a specific audience. (Brackett 2011)

Agility is the quality or state of being agile; marked by ready ability to move with quick easy grace; mentally quick and resourceful. (Brackett 2012)

Arc from set theory. See *Edge*. (Brackett 2011)

Architected data are any data that are formally understood and managed within a common data architecture, including both disparate and comparate data. (Brackett 2011)

Architecture (general) is the art, science, or profession of designing and building structures. It's the structure or structures as a whole, such as the frame, heating, plumbing, wiring, and so on, in a building. It's the style of structures and method of design and construction, such a Roman or Colonial architecture. It's the design or system perceived by people, such as the architecture of the Solar system. (Brackett 2011)

Architecture (data) is the art, science, or profession of designing and building a data resource. It's the structure of the data resource as a whole. It's the style or type of design and construction of the data resource. It's a system, conceived by people, that represents the business world. (Brackett 2011)

Attribute is an inherent characteristic, an accidental quality, an object closely associated with or belonging to a specific person, place, or office; a word ascribing a quality. (Brackett 2011)

Availability heuristic states that the better you can imagine a dangerous event, the likelier you are to be afraid of that event. (Brackett 2012)

Base data type is a specific type or form of data within a data megatype, based on format. (Brackett 2011)

Borgesian nightmare is a labyrinth that is impossible to navigate, which causes people to have nightmares. (Brackett 2011)

Broker is one who acts as an intermediary; an agent who makes arrangements. (Brackett 2012)

Brute-force-physical approach goes directly to the task of developing the physical database. It skips all the formal analysis and modeling activities, and often skips involvement of the business professionals and domain experts.

People taking such an approach consider that developing the physical database is the real task at hand. (Brackett 2011)

Business activity data are any data documenting the business activities. (Brackett 2011)

Business data architecture is the architecture of the business schema—the data as used by the business. It represents the data in the three business schemas. (Brackett 2011)

Business data domain specifies the data values allowed with respect to the business, and the conditions under which those data values are allowed. It represents what is reasonable for the business and results in the highest quality data. (Brackett 2011)

Business data optionality is a specific statement about the presence of a data value, including the conditions under which it will be present. (Brackett 2011)

Business driven data resource is a data resource where the design, development, and maintenance are driven by business needs, as defined by the business information demand. The data resource is about the business, by the business, and for the business. (Brackett 2011, 2012)

Business event is a happening in the real world, such as a sale, purchase, fire, flood, accident, and so on. (Brackett 2011)

Business event group is a subset of business events based on specific selection criteria. (Brackett 2012)

Business event happening is the actual happening of a business event, such as a specific sale, a purchase, a fire, a flood, an accident, and so on. (Brackett 2011)

Business feature is a trait or characteristic of a business object or business event, such as a customer's name, a city's population, a fire date, and so on. (Brackett 2011)

Business inclusion principle states that business professionals must be directly involved in the development of a comparate data resource. The understanding and knowledge that business professionals have about the business must be included to ensure development of a comparate data resource that supports the current and future business information demand. (Brackett 2011, 2012)

Business information demand is an organization's continuously increasing, constantly changing need for current, accurate, integrated information, often on short notice or very short notice, to support its business activities. It is a very dynamic demand for information to support the business that constantly changes. (Brackett 2011)

Business intelligence is a set of concepts, methods, and processes to improve business decision making using any information from multiple sources that could affect the business, and applying experiences and assumptions to deliver accurate perspectives of business dynamics. (Brackett 2011)

Business Intelligence Value Chain is a sequence of events where value is added from the data resource, through each step, to the support of business goals. The data resource is the foundation that supports the development of information. Information supports the knowledge worker in a knowledge environment. The knowledge worker provides business intelligence to an intelligent, learning organization. Business intelligence supports the business strategies, which support the business goals of the organization. (Brackett 2011, 2012)

Business key is a primary key consisting of a fact or facts whose values have meaning to the business. A business key is sometimes referred to as an *intelligent key*, however that term is not used because a primary key cannot possess intelligence. (Brackett 2011, 2012)

Business object is a person, place, thing, or concept in the real world, such as a customer, river, city, account, and so on. (Brackett 2011)

Business object existence is the actual existence of a business object, such as a specific person, river, vehicle, account, and so on. (Brackett 2012)

Business object group is a subset of business objects based on specific selection criteria. (Brackett 2012)

Business orientation principle states that the data resource must be oriented toward business objects and events that are of interest to the organization and are either tracked or managed by the organization. Those business objects and events become data subjects in a subject-oriented comparate data resource. (Brackett 2011)

Business schema represents the structure of data as used by the business. (Brackett 2011)

Business term glossary is a list of terms and abbreviations used in the business, and a definition of each of those terms. (Brackett 2011)

Candidate data integrity rule is a data integrity rule that was documented during the data inventory and brought over to a common data architecture. (Brackett 2012)

Candidate foreign key is a foreign key that has been documented during the data inventory and placed in a common data architecture, but has not been reviewed and given a specific designation.

Candidate primary key is a primary key that has been identified and considered as a primary key, but has not been verified. (Brackett 2011)

Canon is an accepted principle or role; a body of principles, rules, standards, or norms. (Brackett 2011)

Canonical is conforming to a general rule or acceptable procedure reduced to the simplest and cleanest scheme possible. (Brackett 2011)

Canonical synthesis is the concept that if everyone followed the canons (rules) for developing a data model, then those independent data models could be readily plugged together, just like a picture puzzle, to provide a single, comprehensive, organization-wide data architecture. (Brackett 2011)

Centralized control principle states that centralized control of a comparate data resource within a common data architecture evolves from the assignment of data stewards and the development of reasonable data management procedures. (Brackett 2011)

Change documentation principle states that all changes to the data resource that occur over time must be identified and documented, no matter how slight or major those changes may be. (Brackett 2012)

Clarity is the quality or state of being clear, easily understood, free from doubt, free from obscurity or ambiguity, and capable of being readily understood and used Clarity means clear and understandable. (Brackett 2011)

Class word is a word that has a consistent meaning wherever it is used in a data attribute name. (Brackett 2011)

Coded data codes is the situation where single property data codes are combined into a multiple property data code. (Brackett 2012)

Coded data value is any data value that has been encoded or shortened in some manner. (Brackett 2011)

Cognitive dissonance is the disharmony that is created when an individual's personal reality does not fit with the actual reality of a situation. (Brackett 2011)

Cohesive is sticking together tightly, a union between similar parts. (Brackett 2012)

Cohesive data culture is a data culture composed of business processes that are integrated to effectively and efficiently manage an organization's data resource. The business processes are seamless, consistent, and work together in a coordinated manner to develop and maintain a comparate data resource. (Brackett 2012)

Cohesive data culture state is the desired state where the fragmented data culture has been substantially and permanently transformed to a cohesive data culture. It's a persistent integration according to the preferred data culture prescription. A single set of processes has been established across the organization. It's the ideal, mature state for management of the organization's data resource. (Brackett 2012)

Collection frequency states how often data are collected. (Brackett 2011)

Combined data are a concatenation of individual facts. (Brackett 2012)

Combined data characteristic is the combination of two or more closely related elemental data characteristics into a group that is managed as a single unit. Note the qualification for *related facts*. (Brackett 2011, 2012)

Common Data Architecture (capitalized) is a single, formal, comprehensive, organization-wide, data architecture that provides a common context within which all data are understood, documented, integrated, and managed. It transcends all data at the organization's disposal, includes primitive and derived data; elemental and combined data; fundamental and specific data; structured and super-structured data; automated and non-automated (manual) data; current and historical data; data within and without the organization; high level and low level data; and disparate and comparate data. It includes data in purchased software, custom-built application databases, programs, screens, reports, and documents. It includes all data used by traditional information systems, expert systems, executive information systems, geographic information systems, data warehouses, object oriented systems, and so on. It includes centralized and decentralized data regardless of where they reside, who uses them, or how they are used. (Brackett 2011)

Common data architecture (not capitalized) represents the actual common data architecture built by an organization for their data resource, based on the concepts, principles, and techniques of the Common Data Architecture. The common data architecture contains all of the data used by the organization. (Brackett 2011, 2012)

Common data architecture adjustment principle states that a common data architecture should be periodically reviewed and adjusted during data cross-referencing to ensure that it adequately represents the organization perception of the business world. (Brackett 2012)

Common data architecture reference principle states that the thorough understanding and resolution of a disparate data resource, and the development of a comparate data resource, are done within the construct of a Common Data Architecture. The Common Data Architecture is the common construct for understanding and resolving a disparate data resource and developing a comparate data resource that fully supports the business information demand. (Brackett 2012)

Common data architecture variation is a language variation in a common data architecture. The same common data architecture exists in a different language. (Brackett 2012)

Common Data Culture is a single, formal, comprehensive, organization-wide data culture that provides a common context within which the organization's data culture is understood, documented, and integrated. It includes all components in the Data Culture Segment of the Data Resource Management Framework for a reasonable data orientation, acceptable data availability, adequate data responsibility, expanded data vision, and appropriate data recognition. (Brackett 2012)

Common data culture (lower case) is the actual data culture built by an organization for the proper management of their data resource It's based on the concepts, principles, and techniques of the Common Data Culture. It provides the overarching construct for a common view of the organization's data culture. All variations in the data culture are understood within the context of a common data culture. The preferred data culture is defined within the context of a common data culture. Data culture integration is done within the context of a common data culture. (Brackett 2012)

Common-to-common cross-reference is a data cross-reference between an interim common data architecture that is treated as a data product, and the final common data architecture. (Brackett 2012)

Common-to-common data translations are data translations between the preferred and non-preferred data designations within a common data architecture, and applied as needed to physical data translation. (Brackett 2012)

Common-to-physical data translations are data translations between a common data architecture and the disparate data documented as data products. (Brackett 2012)

Common word is a word that has consistent meaning whenever it is used in a data name. (Brackett 2011)

Communication theory states that information is the opposite of entropy, where entropy is disorderliness or noise. A message contains information that must be relevant and timely to the recipient. If the message does not contain relevant and timely information, it is simply noise (non-information). (Brackett 2011, 2012)

Comparate is the opposite of disparate and means fundamentally similar in kind. (Brackett 2011)

Comparate data are data that are alike in kind, quality, and character, and are without defect. They are concordant, homogeneous, nearly flawless, nearly perfect, high-quality data that are easily understood and can be readily integrated. (Brackett 2011)

Comparate data application is any application that reads and stores comparate data. (Brackett 2012)

Comparate data cycle is a self-perpetuating cycle where the use of comparate data is continually reinforced because people understand and trust the data. It is the flip side of the disparate data cycle. When people come to the data resource, they can usually find the data they need, can trust those data, and can readily access those data. The result is a shared data resource. Similarly, people that can't find the data they need, they formally add their data to the data resource, and the enhanced data resource is readily available to anyone looking for data to meet their business need. ()Brackett 2011, 2012)

Complete data documentation principle states that data documentation must cover the entire scope of the data resource, and must include both the technical and the semantic aspects of the data resource. (Brackett 2011)

Comparate data resource is a data resource composed of comparate data that adequately support the current and future business information demand. The data are easily identified and understood, readily accessed and shared, and utilized to their fullest potential. A comparate data resource is an integrated, subject oriented, business driven data resource that is the official record of reference for the organization's business. (Brackett 2011)

Comparate data resource state is the desired state where disparate data have been substantially and permanently transformed to comparate data and the disparate data are substantially gone from the organization's data resource. It's a persistent data transformation where the data are subject oriented according to the organization's perception of the business world and are integrated within the common data architecture. The disparate data cycle is broken and the natural drift of the data resource is toward comparate data. (Brackett 2012)

Comparate data resource vision is the disparate data resource thoroughly understood and integrated into a comparate data resource, supported by a Data Resource Guide, to fully support the current and future business information demand. (Brackett 2012)

Complete historical data instance contains a complete set of data items in the data occurrence, whether or not the data values changed. (Brackett 2012)

Complete occurrence data record is a data record that contains all of the data items for a data occurrence. (Brackett 2012)

Complete set of data codes contains all of the data properties for a single data subject. (Brackett 2012)

Complete subject data file is a data file that contains all of the data items representing all of the data characteristics for a single data subject or for multiple data subjects. (Brackett 2012)

Complex means composed of two or more parts; having a bound form; hard to separate, analyze, or solve; a whole made up of complicated or interrelated parts; a composite made up of distinct parts; intricate as having many complexly interrelating parts or elements. (Brackett 2011, 2012)

Complex fact data attribute contains any combination of multiple values, multiple facts, and variable facts, and might be formatted in several different ways. (Brackett 2011)

Complex primary key contains multiple data attributes from both the home data entity and a foreign data entity. (Brackett 2011)

Complex structured data are any data that are composed of two or more intricate, complicated, and interrelated parts that cannot be easily interpreted by structured query languages and tools. The complex structure needs to be broken down into the individual component structures to be more easily analyzed. Complex structured data include text, voice, video, images, spatial data, and so on. (Brackett 2012)

Complexity is to become complex or the state of being complex. (Brackett 2011)

Compound primary key contains multiple home data attributes in their home data entity. (Brackett 2011)

Comprehensive means covering completely or broadly. (Brackett 2011)

Comprehensive data definition is a data definition that provides a complete, meaningful, easily read, readily understood definition that thoroughly explains the content and meaning of the data with respect to the business. It helps people thoroughly understand the data and use the data resource efficiently and effectively to meet the current and future business information demand.(Brackett 2011, 2012)

Concept is something conceived in the mind, a thought, or notion; an abstract or generic idea generalized from particular instances; a generic or generalized ideal from specific instances. A concept can be basic, applying to data resource management in general, or it can be specific, applying to one aspect of data resource management. (Brackett 2011)

Conceptual schema was defined as the common link between the internal schema and the external schema. From the database perspective, it was a common translation between the two schemas. (Brackett 2011)

Concordant means agreeing; in a state of agreement; a harmonious combination. (Brackett 2012)

Concordant data resource management is the situation where the overall management of an organization's data resource, including the data resource itself and the data culture, is in agreement and harmony. (Brackett 2012)

Conditional data source rule is a data source rule that specifies multiple locations as the preferred data source and the conditions for selecting one of those locations. (Brackett 2012)

Conditional data sourcing is the process of selecting preferred data from a variety of different locations based on which location has the most current and most accurate data. (Brackett 2012)

Conditional data structure rule is a data integrity rule that specifies the conditional data cardinality for a data relation between two data entities when conditions or exceptions apply. It specifies both the conditions and exceptions with respect to the business, not with respect to the database management system. (Brackett 2011)

Conditional data value rule is a data integrity rule that specifies the domain of allowable values for a data attribute when conditions or exceptions apply. It specifies both the conditions for optionality and the condition for a relationship between data values in other data attributes. It specifies the rule with respect to the business, not with respect to the database management system. (Brackett 2011)

Connotative meaning is the idea or notion suggested by the data definition, that a person interprets in addition to what is explicitly stated. (Brackett 2011)

Consistent characteristic data item is a data item that always contains an elemental or combined data characteristic. (Brackett 2012)

Continuous enhancement principle states that documentation of disparate data should be continuously enhanced as additional insight is gained. Documenting and understanding disparate data is not a one-time process—it's an ongoing process through all phases of data resource integration. Any time that additional insight is gained about disparate data, that insight must be documented. (Brackett 2012)

Contrarian thinking is not following the herd and thinking outside the box. Current wisdom is not simply accepted without question. Current practices are always scrutinized for better ways. The questions *Why?* or *Why not?* are frequently asked. Wanting to know what others are doing, and why, is persistent. Multiple voices are encouraged to speak on issues. Risk taking and innovations are valued, and leveraged for maximum benefit. Thinking gray is common, without group think or crowd mentality. Synergy and teamwork are encouraged. (Brackett 2012)

Cooperative development principle states that the stakeholders of the data resource must be involved in developing the vision for a comparate data resource. (Brackett 2011)

Critical business principle states that a comparate data resource must be developed by beginning with the critical areas of the business. The general approach is to identify critical business areas where the data resource needs to provide strong support, and may not be providing that support. (Brackett 2011)

Critical mass principle states that when the understanding of disparate data appears insurmountable, a critical mass of information is reached and collapses into a meaningful understanding of the disparate data. (Brackett 2012)

Cross-system reporting is the collection of operational data from various, often disparate sources, and merging those for reporting or operational decision making. Many data integration approaches are simply cross-system reporting, not true integration of the data resource. (Brackett 2011)

Crowd psychology is the situation where people individually are objective, but when they get together in a crowd regarding a critical issue, that objectivity is lost. (Brackett 2011)

Cultural variability is the normal differences due to culture, geography, politics, and so on, such as different names, addresses, monetary units, and so on. The data resource must reflect these cultural differences. (Brackett 2012)

Culture is the act of developing the intellectual and moral faculties; expert care and training; enlightenment and excellence of taste acquired by intellectual and aesthetic training; acquaintance with and taste in fine arts, humanities, and broad aspects of science; the integrated pattern of human knowledge, belief, and behavior that depends upon man's capacity for learning and transmitting knowledge to succeeding generations; the customary beliefs, social forms, and material traits of a racial, religious, or social group. (Brackett 2012)

Current budget principle states that any first initiative to improve data resource quality should begin within the current budget. (Brackett 2011)

Current data definition principle states that a comprehensive data definition must be kept current with the business. (Brackett 2011)

Current data documentation principle states that the data resource data must be kept current with the business. They must represent the current state of the data resource for both business and data management professionals. (Brackett 2011)

Current data instance is the most recent data instance that represents the current values of the data items in the data occurrence. (Brackett 2012)

Data are the individual facts that are out of context, have no meaning, and are difficult to understand. They are often referred to as *raw data*, such as 123.45. Data have historically been defined as plural. (Brackett 2011)

Data accuracy is a measure of how well the data values represent the business world at a point in time or for a period of time. Data accuracy includes the method used to identify objects in the business world and the method of collecting data about those objects. It describes how an object was identified and the means by which the data were collected. (Brackett 2011)

Data accuracy assurance is a proactive process of ensuring that data represent the business world as closely as the organization desires, to meet the business information demand. (Brackett 2011)

Data accuracy control is a reactive process of determining how well data already captured represent the business world. It determines the data accuracy after the data are acquired. (Brackett 2011)

Data anomaly is any data value that does not follow a pattern that matches a reasonable expectation of the business. It could be a correct data value, or it could be an error. If it's a correct data value, it could be acceptable or unacceptable for the business. (Brackett 2012)

Data architectnology is the technology for producing comparate data within a common data architecture. It's the formal technology for building a common data architecture within an organization and managing data within that architecture. It consists of specific concepts, principles, and techniques for developing a comparate data resource. It's very formal and detailed, yet results are very elegant and simple. (Brackett 2011, 2012)

Data architecture (1) is the method of design and construction of an integrated data resource that is business driven, based on real-world subjects as perceived by the organization, and implemented into appropriate operating environments. It consists of components that provide a consistent foundation across organizational boundaries to provide easily identifiable, readily available, high-quality data to support the current and future business information demand. (Brackett 2011)

Data architecture (2) is the component of the Data Resource Management Framework that contains all the activities, and the products of those activities, related to the identification, naming, definition, structuring, integrity, accuracy, effectiveness, and documentation of the data resource. (Brackett 2011)

Data architecture quality is how well the data architecture components contribute to overall data management quality. (Brackett 2012)

Data attribute is the variation of an individual fact that describes or characterizes a data entity. It represents a data characteristic variation in a logical data model. (Brackett 2011, 2012)

Data attribute denormalization is the technique of implementing data attributes for optimum performance without compromising the normalized data structure. (Brackett 2011)

Data attribute history is when only the data attribute whose data value changed is retained. (Brackett 2011)

Data attribute normalization, commonly referred to as *fact normalization*, is the technique for ensuring that each data attribute represents one business fact or a set of closely related business facts. (Brackett 2011)

Data attribute partitioning places data attributes in different data sites. (Brackett 2011)

Data attribute retention rule is a data integrity rule that specifies the retention for individual data attribute values. (Brackett 2011)

Data attribute structure is a list showing the data attributes contained within each data entity and the roles played by those data attributes. It shows the primary keys, foreign keys to parent data entities, and all the data attributes contained in a data entity. (Brackett 2011)

Data availability is the process of ensuring that the data are available to meet the business information demand, while properly protecting and securing those data. (Brackett 2011)

Data awareness is the knowledge about all of the data that are available to the organization and where those data are located. (Brackett 2012)

Data bridge is an application that moves data from one disparate data file to another disparate data file to keep the two data files in synch. The primary purpose is to maintain redundant data in a disparate data resource. (Brackett 2012)

Data broker is an application that acts as an intermediary between disparate data and comparate data in databases or applications. It performs formal data transformations in both directions between disparate data and comparate data. (Brackett 2012)

Data brokering is the process of using data brokers to perform formal data transformation. (Brackett 2012)

Data cardinality is a specification of the number of data occurrences that are allowed or required in each data subject or data entity that are involved in a data relation, or the number of data records that are allowed or required for each data file that are involved in the data relation. (Brackett 2011)

Data category is a data entity that represents a *can also be* situation. Each data category contains data attributes that characterize that particular data category, as well as the parent data entity. Separate data categories may be defined that are peers of each other and further define the parent data entity. (Brackett 2011)

Data characteristic is an individual fact that describes or characterizes a data subject. It represents a business feature and contains a single fact, or related facts, about a data subject. (Brackett 2011)

Data characteristic source list is a list of all of the data sources for each data characteristic. The data characteristics are listed for each data subject, and the data sources are listed for each data characteristic. (Brackett 2012)

Data characteristic structure is a list showing the data characteristics contained within each data subject and the roles played by those data characteristics. It shows the primary keys, foreign keys to parent data subjects, and all the data characteristics contained in a data subject. (Brackett 2011)

Data characteristic substitution indicates that any data characteristic variation can be used for a data characteristic, such as (Date) can mean any form of a date. (Brackett 2011)

Data characteristic translation rule is a data translation rule that translates data values between non-preferred and preferred variations of a data characteristic. (Brackett 2012)

Data characteristic variation is a variation in the content or format of a data characteristic. It represents a variant of a data characteristic, such as different units of measurement, different monetary units, different sequences as in a person's name, and so on. (Brackett 2011, 2012)

Data characteristic variation list is a list of all of the data characteristic variations within a data characteristic. (Brackett 2012)

Data code is any data item whose data value has been encoded or shortened in some manner. (Brackett 2012)

Data code set is a complete group of data codes that represent all of the data properties for a single data subject. (Brackett 2012)

Data code variability is the variability in the coded data values, names, definitions, and domain of codes in a set of data codes. It's a measure of how many variations exist for a particular set of data codes across data files. (Brackett 2012)

Data completeness is a measure of how well the scope of the data resource meets the scope of the business information demand. It ensures that all the data necessary to meet the current and future business information demand are available in the organization's data resource. (Brackett 2011)

Data completeness assurance is the proactive process of analyzing the business information demand and ensuring that the data needed are available when needed. (Brackett 2011)

Data completeness control is the reactive process of determining what data are available and how completely those data support the business information demand. It's an inventory process to determine the data available and how often those data are being used. (Brackett 2011)

Data consolidation is the process of merging existing data from different sources into one location. The data may be restructured slightly, but nothing is done to thoroughly understand the data or to resolve data disparity. (Brackett 2012)

Data conversion is the process of changing the same physical data schema from one database management system to another database management system. The data values are not altered in any way. They are simply moved from one database management system to another. (Brackett 2012)

Data conversion rule is a data integrity rule that defines the conversion of a data value from one unit to another unit. It represents the conversion of the values of a single fact to different units, and is not considered to be a data derivation rule. (Brackett 2011)

Data converter is an application that changes the data between heterogeneous databases. It does not transform the data in any way. It only changes the physical form of the data from one database environment to another database environment. (Brackett 2012)

Data cross-reference is a logical mapping between disparate data names and common data names. It's a link between components of the inventoried disparate data and components in a common data architecture. (Brackett 2012)

Data cross-reference concept is the inventoried disparate data are cross-referenced to a common data architecture to further increase the understanding of those disparate data within a common context. An initial understanding of disparate data was gained during the data inventory process. That initial understanding is increased through a cross-referencing of the inventoried disparate data to a common data architecture. (Brackett 2012)

Data cross-reference objective is to thoroughly understand the content, meaning, structure, and integrity of all data at the organization's disposal within the context of a common data architecture so that a comparate data resource can be developed that fully supports the current and future business information demand. The objective is to take the initial understanding of disparate data that was documented at an elemental level during the data inventory and increase that understanding within the context of a common data architecture at the organization level. (Brackett 2012)

Data cross-walk is the physical movement of data from one data file to another data file without any formal data transformation or the application of data integrity rules The analogy is like using a cross-walk at an intersection where people cross, but are not altered in the process. The term is not used with data resource transformation because it implies an easy task of moving the disparate data to a comparate data resource without any transformation. (Brackett 2012)

Data culture (1) is the function of managing the data resource as a critical resource of the organization equivalent to managing the financial resource, the human resource, and real property. It consists of directing and controlling the development, administering policies and procedures, influencing the actions and conduct of anyone maintaining or using the data resource, and exerting a guiding influence over the data resource to support the current and future business information demand. (Brackett 2011)

Data culture (2) is the component of the Data Resource Management Framework that contains all the activities, and the products of those activities, related to orientation, availability, responsibility, vision, and recognition of the data resource. (Brackett 2011)

Data culture insights are any insights necessary for thoroughly understanding the organization's existing fragmented data culture and developing a cohesive data culture for properly managing data as a critical resource of the organization. (Brackett 2012)

Data culture integration is the thorough understanding of the existing fragmented data culture within a common data culture, the designation of a preferred data culture, and the transition toward that preferred data culture. It's the act or process of integrating and coordinating the organization's data management function and processes into a cohesive data culture. (Brackett 2012)

Data culture integration concept is to resolve the fragmented data culture and create a cohesive data culture for the management of a critical data resource. A thorough understanding of the current fragmented data culture leads to its resolution and the creation of a cohesive data culture. (Brackett 2012)

Data culture quality is how well the data culture components contribute to the overall data management quality. (Brackett 2011)

Data culture survey is the act of surveying the current data management practices in an organization and documenting the results of that survey. (Brackett 2012)

Data culture survey concept is that the existing fragmented data culture in an organization is leading to the creation of increasing quantities of a disparate data resource that are impacting business activities. (Brackett 2012)

Data culture survey objective is to survey and document all of the fragmented data management practices that are explicitly and implicitly being performed by people within and without the organization. (Brackett 2012)

Data culture transformation is the formal process of transforming a fragmented data culture to a cohesive data culture, within the context of a common data culture, according to the preferred data culture. It's a subset of overall data culture transition that includes transforming the data orientation, data availability, data responsibility, data vision, and data recognition. (Brackett 2012)

Data culture transformation concept is that all data culture transformation will be done within the context of a common data culture using the preferred data culture. The best existing data culture practices are combined with new data culture practices to provide a cohesive data culture. (Brackett 2012)

Data culture transformation objective is to transform the existing fragmented data culture to a cohesive data culture to support management of data as a critical resource of the organization. The objective is more than just documenting the exiting fragmented data culture. It's a precise, detailed process that creates a cohesive data culture. (Brackett 2012)

Data culture transition is the transition of an organization's data culture from a fragmented data culture state, through a formal data culture state, to a cohesive data culture state. It's a pathway that is followed from a fragmented data culture to a cohesive data culture. It's unique to each organization depending on their existing data culture and desired data culture. (Brackett 2012)

Data culture variability is a state where all aspects of data management are inconsistent, characterized by variations, and are not true to the concepts and principles for managing data as a critical resource. The management procedures are highly variable and that variability is pervasive throughout the organization. (Brackett 2012)

D*ata culture variability principle* states that every organization has a level of variability that must be accepted and clarified, and that any variability above that acceptable level must be resolved. (Brackett 2012)

Data currentness is a measure of how well the data values remain current with the business. (Brackett 2011)

Data currentness assurance is the proactive process of analyzing the business information demand and ensuring that the data collected meet the currentness requirements of the business. (Brackett 2011)

Data currentness control is the reactive process of determining the data currentness and how well that currentness supports the business information demand. It's a review process that documents the currentness of the existing data. (Brackett 2011)

Data de-coherence is an interference in the coherent understanding of the true meaning of data with respect to the business. It is due to the variability in the meaning, structure, and integrity of the data. The variability is large in a disparate data resource leading to a large data de-coherence. (Brackett 2012)

Data definition inheritance principle states that specific data definitions can inherit fundamental data definitions or other specific data definitions to minimize the size and increase the consistency of specific data definitions. (Brackett 2011)

Data definition variability is the situation where data definitions are vague and have a wide range of variability that contributes little to understanding the data resource. (Brackett 2012)

Data deluge is the situation where massive quantities of data are being captured and stored at an alarming rate. These data are being captured by traditional means, by scanning, by imaging, by remote sensing, by machine generation, and by derivation. Those data are being stored on personal computers, networks, departmental computers, and mainframe computers. The quantity of data in many organizations is increasing exponentially. (Brackett 2011, 2012)

Data denormalization is the process that adjusts the normalized data structure for optimum performance in a specific operating environment, without compromising the normalized data structure. (Brackett 2011)

Data de-optimization is the technique that transforms the logical data structure into the deployment data structure for the data sites where the databases will be implemented. It deals with the specific data that will be maintained in different data sites. (Brackett 2011)

Data deployment rule specifies how the data are deployed from the primary data site to secondary data sites, and how those deployed data are kept in synch with the primary data site. (Brackett 2012)

Data depot is a place for storing data for formal data transformation. It's a staging area or work area for transforming data independent of the data source or data target. (Brackett 2012)

Data derivation – See **Derive data**.

Data derivation rule is a data integrity rule that specifies the contributors to a derived data value, the algorithm for deriving the data value, and the conditions for deriving a data value. (Brackett 2011)

Data dilemma is the situation where the ability to meet the business information demand is being compromised by the continued development of large quantities of disparate data. (Brackett 2011)

Data dimensions are the surrounding data entities that qualify the data focus. (Brackett 2011)

Data discovery is the process of identifying all the data that are at the organization's disposal, and learning the content and meaning of those data. It's the process of finding all the data, understanding those data, and using those data to meet the business information demand. (Brackett 2011)

Data documentation design principle states that all data resource data must be formally designed the same as business data. Data resource data are part of the data resource, the same as business data, and need to be designed the same as business data. (Brackett 2011)

Data documentation variability is the variability that exists with the documentation about a disparate data resource. Ideally, all components of the organization's data resource are formally documented and readily available. (Brackett 2012)

Data domain is a set of allowable values for a data attribute. (Brackett 2011)

Data domain profiling analyzes the existing domain of data values for data items in a database. The existing data values, their frequency of distribution, variability, missing values, existence of multiple values, possibility of redundancy, and so on, are analyzed and documented. The analysis can identify the variability in data values, both within a data file and across data files. (Brackett 2012)

Data editing – See ***Edit data***.

Data engineering is he discipline that designs, builds, and maintains the organization's data resource and makes the data available to information engineering. It's a formal process for developing a comparate data resource. Data engineering is also responsible for maintaining the disparate data resource and for transforming that disparate data resource to a comparate data resource. (Brackett 2011, 2012)

Data entity is a person, place, thing, event, or concept about which an organization collects and manages data. It represents a data subject in the logical data model. The name of a data entity is singular, since it represents a collection of data occurrences. (Brackett 2011)

Data entity fragmentation is the situation where data entities are created when data attributes are removed, but those data entities are not merged when they represent the same data entity. (Brackett 2011)

Data entity hierarchy is a hierarchical structure of data entities with branched one-to-one data relations between the parent data entity and the subordinate data entities. It represents a mutually exclusive, or *can-only-be*, situation between the subordinate data entity and the parent data entity. (Brackett 2011)

Data entity normalization, commonly referred to as just *data normalization*, deals with the normalization of data attributes within and between data entities. (Brackett 2011)

Data entity optimization, commonly referred to as *data optimization*, is the technique of making sure that data attributes removed from a data entity as a result of data normalization are optimized into the appropriate data entity. (Brackett 2011)

Data entity partitioning places data entities in different data sites. If a data entity appears in the data deployment schema, then that data entity is maintained at the data site. (Brackett 2011)

Data entity-relation diagram shows the arrangement and relationships between data entities. It contains only data entities and the data relations between those data entities. It does not contain any of the data attributes in those data entities, nor does it contain any roles played by the data attributes. (Brackett 2011)

Data error is a data value that provides incorrect or false knowledge about the business, or about business objects and events that are important to the business. (Brackett 2011)

Data extract is the formal process of identifying and extracting the preferred disparate data and loading those data into a data depot for data transformation. (Brackett 2012)

Data file is a physical file of data that exists in a database management system, such as a computer file, or outside a database management system, such as a manual file. It is referred to as a table in a relational database. A data file generally represents a data entity, subject to adjustments made during formal data denormalization. (Brackett 2011)

Data file-relation diagram shows the arrangement and relationships between data files. It contains only the data files and the data relations between those data files. It does not contain any of the data items in those data files. (Brackett 2011, 2012)

Data file variability is the variability that exists within and across data files in a disparate data resource. Data file variability can exist at the data file level, the data record level, and the data instance level. (Brackett 2012)

Data focus is the central data entity that is being analyzed by the data warehouse. (Brackett 2011)

Data governance is a term that is not used because it represents a hype-cycle. See ***Data resource management***, ***Data culture***. (Brackett 2011)

Data heritage is documentation of the source of the data and their original meaning at the time of data capture. It's the content and meaning of the data at the time of their origination and as they move from their origin to their current data location. It describes the original content and meaning of the data when initially captured. (Brackett 2011, 2012)

Data hierarchy aggregation identifies the level of aggregation of a hierarchy, such as the product hierarchy in a data warehouse. (Brackett 2011)

Data in context are individual facts that have meaning and can be readily understood. They raw facts wrapped with meaning. (Brackett 2011)

Data-information-knowledge cycle is the cycle from data, to data in context, to specific or general information, to knowledge, and back to data when stored. (Brackett 2012)

Data inheritance is the process of using fundamental data to support consistent definitions of specific data. (Brackett 2011)

Data instance is a specific set of data values for the characteristics in a data occurrence that are valid at a point in time or for a period of time. Many data instances can exist for each data occurrence, particularly when historical data are maintained. One data instance is the current instance and the others are historical instances. (Brackett 2011)

Data instant is the point in time or the timeframe the data represent in the business world. (Brackett 2011)

Data integration is the merging of data from multiple, often disparate, sources, usually based on some record of reference, to provide a single output, such as an interim database or report. It does not resolve any existing data disparity, and may further increase data disparity. It is seldom done within the context of a common data architecture. (Brackett 2011, 2012)

Data integration key is a set of data characteristics that could identify possible redundant physical data occurrences in a disparate data resource. It's not a primary key because it does not uniquely identify each data occurrence. It's not a foreign key because no corresponding primary key exists. (Brackett 2012)

Data integration key index is a table showing the values of a data integration key for each data occurrence, in all data files, within a data subject. (Brackett 2012)

Data integration quality is a measure of how well the data resource integration process is performed, based on how well the resulting comparate data resource supports the current and future business information demand. (Brackett 2012)

Data integrity is a measure of how well the data are maintained in the data resource after they are captured or created. It indicates the degree to which the data are unimpaired and complete according to a precise set of rules. (Brackett 2011)

Data integrity failure principle states that a violation action and a notification action must be taken on any data that fail precise data integrity rules The violation and notification actions to be taken must be specified and followed. (Brackett 2012)

Data integrity notification action specifies the action to be taken for notifying someone that data have failed the data integrity rules and a violation action was taken. The action may alert someone who is responsible for taking action, or place an appropriate entry in an error log that will be reviewed by someone at a later date. The notification action includes the implementation of an algorithm to correct the data.(Brackett 2011, 2012)

Data integrity rule definition principle states that each data integrity rule must be comprehensively defined, just like data entities and data attributes are comprehensively defined. The definition must explain the purpose of the data integrity rule and the action that is taken. (Brackett 2011)

Data integrity rule edit principle states that precise data integrity rules must be denormalized as the proper data structure is denormalized and be implemented as data edits. Data integrity rules are the logical specification and must match the logical data structure, while data edits are the physical specification and must match the physical data structure. (Brackett 2011, 2012)

Data integrity rule lockout principle states that the precise data integrity rules must be reviewed to ensure that the rules do not result in a lockout, where data are prevented from entering the data resource. (Brackett 2011)

Data integrity rule management principle states that the management of data integrity rules must be proactive to make optimum use of resources and minimize impacts to the business. (Brackett 2011)

Data integrity rule name principle states that every data integrity rule must be formally and uniquely named according to the data naming taxonomy and supporting vocabulary. (Brackett 2011)

Data integrity rule normalization principle states that data integrity rules are normalized to the data resource component which they represent or on which they take action. (Brackett 2011)

Data integrity rule notation principle states that each data integrity rule must be specified in a notation that is acceptable and understandable to business and data management professionals, must be based on mathematical and logic notation where practical, and must use symbols readily available on a standard keyboard. (Brackett 2011)

Data integrity rule type principle states that seven different types of data integrity rules must be identified and defined. (Brackett 2011)

Data integrity rules specify the criteria that need to be met to insure that the data resource contains the highest quality necessary to support the current and future business information demand. (Brackett 2011)

Data integrity variability is the variability that exists with data edits in a disparate data resource. Ideally, data integrity rules are defined during logical data modeling and are transformed to data edits during physical data modeling. (Brackett 2012)

Data integrity violation action specifies the action to be taken with the data when the data violate a data integrity rule. That action may be to override the error with meaningful data, to suspend the data pending further correction, to apply a default data value, to accept the data, or to delete the data. Overriding the error could include implementing an algorithm to correct the data. (Brackett 2011, 2012)

Data inventory is the process of identifying and documenting all of the data at an organization's disposal so those data can be readily understood and used to develop and maintain a comparate data resource that supports the business information demand. It begins the process of understanding disparate data and

461

developing a comparate data resource within a common data architecture. (Brackett 2012)

Data inventory concept is that all data at the organization's disposal will be completely and comprehensively inventoried, and documented in one location that is readily available to anyone in the organization, so that the organization at large understands the content, meaning, and quality of those data. (Brackett 2012)

Data inventory objective is to identify, inventory, and document all data that currently exist in the organization's data resource or are readily available to the organization so that those data can be readily understood and used to support the current and future business information demand. It raises the awareness of the data that exist and solves the first problem with disparate data. (Brackett 2012)

Data inventory process identifies the existing data, collects the existing documentation, and enhances that documentation with additional insights.

Data item is an individual field in a data record and is referred to as a column in a relational database. A data item represents a data attribute, subject to adjustments made during formal data denormalization. (Brackett 2011)

Data item content is the physical variation in the data values contained in a data item. (Brackett 2012)

Data item format is the physical format of the data value contained in the data item. (Brackett 2012)

Data item length is the physical length of the data value contained in the data item. (Brackett 2012)

Data item structure is a list showing the data items contained in each data file and the roles played by those data items. It shows the primary keys, foreign keys to data files, and all the data items contained in a data file. (Brackett 2011)

Data item variability is the variability in the format or content of data items representing the same business fact. It's a measure of how many different formats or contents exist for a particular data item across data files, and on screens, reports, and forms. (Brackett 2012)

Data key is any data attribute or set of data attributes used to identify a data occurrence within a data entity. (Brackett 2011)

Data key denormalization is the process of implementing data keys in the physical database without compromising the logical data structure. (Brackett 2011)

Data lineage is a description of the pathway from the data source to their current location and the alterations made to the data along that pathway. It is a process to track the descent of data values from their origins to their current data sites. It includes determining where the data values originated, where they were stored, and how they were altered or modified. It's a history of how the content and meaning of the data were altered from their origin to their present location. (Brackett 2011, 2012)

Data load is the formal process of loading the target database after the data transformation has been completed. The transformed data are edited according to the preferred data integrity rules, loaded into the target database, and reviewed to ensure the load was successful before the data are released for use. (Brackett 2012)

Data loading – See ***Load data***.

Data management optionality principle states that organizations have the opportunity to manage data as a critical resource of the organization. Each organization can choose whether or not to take that opportunity and develop a comparate data resource. (Brackett 2011)

Data management quality is how well the data management components contribute to overall data resource quality. (Brackett 2011)

Data megatype is a broad grouping of data based on their structure and physical management. (Brackett 2011)

Data migration is the movement of data to change location periodically from one database or platform to another depending on the physical environment and the needs of the organization. The migration seldom includes a thorough understanding of the data and is usually done outside of any context. The term *migration* is acceptable because periodic movements can be made depending on the conditions. (Brackett 2012)

Data mining is the analysis of evaluational data to find unknown and unsuspected trends and patterns, using techniques such as artificial intelligence and fuzzy logic.

Data model includes formal data names, comprehensive data definitions, proper data structures, and precise data integrity rules. A complete data model must include all four of these components. (Brackett 2011)

Data model concept is the development of a data model, for a specific audience, representing a particular business activity, using appropriate data modeling techniques, based on data contained in the Data Resource Guide. The data model is an expression of knowledge about the data resource that is presented in an appropriate form for a specific audience. (Brackett 2011)

Data name is a label for a fact or a set of related facts contained in the data resource, appearing on a data model, or displayed on screens, reports, or documents. (Brackett 2011)

Data name abbreviation is the shortening of a primary data name to meet some length restriction. (Brackett 2011)

Data name abbreviation algorithm is a formal procedure for abbreviating the primary data name using an established set of data name word abbreviations.

(Brackett 2011)

Data name abbreviation scheme is a combination of a set of data name word abbreviations and a data name abbreviation algorithm. (Brackett 2011)

Data name - definition synchronization principle states that a comprehensive data definition and a formal data name must be kept in synch with each other. Formal data names help guide development of comprehensive data definitions, and comprehensive data definitions help verify formal data names. Synchronization is a two-way, value-added approach ensuring that formal data names match comprehensive data definitions. (Brackett 2011, 2012)

Data name homonym is different business facts with the same data name. (Brackett 2011, 2012)

Data name synonym is the same business fact with different data names. (Brackett 2011)

Data name variability is the situation where data names are informal and have a wide range of variability that contributes little to understanding the data resource. (Brackett 2012)

Data name vocabulary is the collection of all twelve sets of common words representing the twelve components of the data naming taxonomy. (Brackett 2011)

Data name word abbreviation is the formal abbreviation for each word used in a data name. The abbreviation must be unique for the root word and for all manifestations of the root word, and it must not create another word. (Brackett 2011)

Data naming taxonomy provides a primary name for all existing and new data, and all components of the data resource. It provides a way to uniquely identify all components of the data resource as well as all of the disparate data. It meets all of the data naming criteria and complies with the three components of semiotic theory. (Brackett 2011, 2012)

Data normalization is the process that brings data into a normal form that minimizes redundancies and keeps anomalies from entering the data resource. It provides a subject-oriented data resource based on business objects and events. (Brackett 2011)

Data occurrence is a logical record that represents the existence of a business object or the happening of a business event in the business world, such as an employee, a vehicle, and so on. It represents a business object existence or a business event happening.(Brackett 2011, 2012)

Data occurrence denormalization is the process of splitting the data occurrences in a data entity into two or more data files for processing efficiency or for database limitations. (Brackett 2011)

Data occurrence group is a subset of data occurrences within a specific data subject that meet specific selection criteria. A data occurrence group represents a business object group or a business event group. (Brackett 2011, 2012)

Data occurrence history is when the entire data occurrence is retained when one or more data values in that data occurrence change. (Brackett 2011)

Data occurrence partitioning places data occurrences in different data sites. (Brackett 2011)

Data occurrence redundancy is the existence of multiple data occurrences for the same existence of a business object or happening of a business event. (Brackett 2012)

Data occurrence role is a role that could be played by a specific data occurrence, such as a maintenance vendor or a lease vendor. (Brackett 2011)

Data optimization: See ***Data entity optimization***.

Data optionality indicates whether a data value is required or is optional. Most of these labels are not specific. (Brackett 2011)

Data orientation is the orientation of data resource management in response to business information needs which allows the business to operate effectively and efficiently in the business world. (Brackett 2012)

Data origin is the location where a data value originated, whether those data were collected, created, measured, generated, derived, or aggregated. (Brackett 2012)

Data overload is a deluge of data or data in context coming at a recipient that is not relevant and timely. It's a deluge of non-information that is not wanted by the recipient. (Brackett 2011, 2012)

Data ownership is not used because people don't own the data. See ***Data steward***. (Brackett 2011)

Data perspective is the subject area represented by the data entity-relation diagram, and includes a data focus and data dimensions. (Brackett 2011)

Data precision is how precisely a measurement was made and how many significant digits are in the measurement. (Brackett 2011)

Data product is a major independent set of documentation of any type that contains the names, definitions, structure, integrity, and so on, of disparate data. It's anything about the data resource, electronic or manual, that is a product of some development effort. A data product can be an information system, a database, a data dictionary, a major project, a major data model, or anything else that provides insight into the existing disparate data. It is the highest level in the data product model. (Brackett 2012)

Data product code is any coded data value that exists in a data product unit or data product unit variation. It represents a specific property of the subject of interest. (Brackett 2012)

Data product code cross-reference is a cross-reference between a data product code or variation and a data reference set variation. Each data product code or variation is cross-referenced to a data reference set variation to which it belongs. (Brackett 2012)

Data product code variation is a recursion of a data product code to document multiple variations contained in a data product code. However, only one level of recursion is allowed. The data product code variation is not intended to document a hierarchy of data product codes. (Brackett 2012)

Data product concept is that the existing data resource, any documentation about the existing data resource, and any insights people have about the existing data resource are a product of some development effort. It's those products that need to be identified and documented to fully understand the existing disparate data. (Brackett 2012)

Data product model is a subset of data resource data architecture pertaining to documentation of an organization's disparate data resource. The input for the documentation comes from the data inventory process. (Brackett 2012)

Data product set is a major grouping of data within a data product. It may represent a data file, a data record, a data record type, a screen, a report, a form, a data entity, an application program, and so on. (Brackett 2012)

Data product set cross-reference is a cross-reference between a data product set or variation and a data subject variation solely for the purpose of designating data   selections, subsets of data, and data roles, or for designating the manifestations of a data focus. (Brackett 2012)

Data product set variation is a recursion of a data product set to document multiple variations contained in a data product set. However, only one level of recursion is allowed. The data product set variation is not intended to document a hierarchy of data product sets. A data product set variation could be a data record type, a data entity type, changes over time, or any other breakdown of a data product set. (Brackett 2012)

Data product unit is any unit of data within a data product set, such as data attribute in a data model, a data item in a data record, a data field on a screen or report, a data item in a program, and so on. (Brackett 2012)

Data product unit cross-reference is a cross-reference between a data product unit or variation and a corresponding data characteristic variation. Each data product unit or variation is cross-referenced to a data characteristic variation. (Brackett 2012)

Data product unit cross-reference list is a list of the data product units or variations and the corresponding data characteristic variation. (Brackett 2012)

Data product unit variation is a recursion of a data product unit to document multiple variations contained in a data product unit. However, only one level of recursion is allowed.   The data product unit variation is not intended to

466

document a hierarchy of data product units. (Brackett 2012)

Data profiling, in the context, of data resource integration is the process of analyzing the data values in databases to determine possible data meaning, data structure, and data integrity rules in preparation for data resource integration. These determinations must be verified before they can be accepted as fact and used for data resource integration. (Brackett 2012)

Data property is a single feature, trait, or quality within a grouping or classification of features, traits, or qualities belonging to a data characteristic. (Brackett 2012)

Data provenance is provenance applied to the organization's data resource. (Brackett 2011)

Data provenance principle states that the source of data, how the data were captured, the meaning of the data when they were first captured, where the data were stored, the path of those data to the current location, how the data were moved along that path, and how those data were altered along that path must be documented to ensure the authenticity of those data and their appropriateness for supporting the business. (Brackett 2011)

Data quality is a subset of data resource quality dealing with data values. (Brackett 2011)

Data quality assurance is the proactive process of ensuring that data adequately support the business information demand. It determines the data accuracy, data completeness, and data currentness required by the business information demand and ensures that the data meet that demand. (Brackett 2011)

Data quality control is the reactive process of determining how well the data support the business information demand. It determines the existing data accuracy, data completeness, and data currentness and evaluates how well each supports the business information demand. (Brackett 2011)

Data recasting – See ***Recast data***.

Data recasting rule is a data rule that specifies the adjustment of data values to a specific time period, such as adjusting financial data values to a specific time period for a comparison of trends independent of monetary inflation. (Brackett 2012)

Data recognition is the situation where management of the data resource is recognized as professional and directly supporting the business activities of the organization. (Brackett 2012)

Data Reconstruction – See ***Reconstruct data***.

Data reconstruction rule is a data rule that specifies the reconstruction of historical data into full historical data instances in preparation for data transformation. The data reconstruction rule shows the conditions for data reconstruction and the data reconstruction that is performed. (Brackett 2012)

Data record is a physical grouping of data items that are stored in or retrieved from a data file. It is referred to as a row or tuple in a relational database. A data record represents a data instance. (Brackett 2011)

Data record group is a subset of data records based on specific selection criteria. A data record group represents a data occurrence group in a data file. (Brackett 2012)

Data rederivation rule is a data integrity rule that specifies when any rederivation is done after the initial derivation. A derived data value may be rederived when the conditions change or the contributors change, which often occurs in a dynamic business environment. The derivation algorithm and the contributors are usually the same, but timing of the rederivation needs to be specified. (Brackett 2011, 2012)

Data redundancy is the unknown and unmanaged duplication of business facts in a disparate data resource. It's the same facts, for the same data occurrence, for the same time period. It's the situation where a single business fact is stored in more than one location, and the locations may not be in synch. It's the unnecessary duplication of data that is a major contributor to data disparity. (Brackett 2011, 2012)

Data redundancy factor is the number of sources for a single business fact in an organization's data resource. (Brackett 2011)

Data reference item is single set of coded data values, data names, and data definitions representing a single data property in a data reference set variation.

Data reference item list is a listing of all of the data reference items in a data reference set variation, including the data reference item codes, data reference item names, and data reference item definitions. (Brackett 2012)

Data reference item matrix is a matrix of all of the data reference items, for all of the data reference set variations, for a single data subject, including the coded data values, data reference item names, and data reference item definitions. (Brackett 2012)

Data reference item translation rule is a data translation rule that translates coded data values and names between data reference items in preferred and non-preferred data reference set variations within a data subject. (Brackett 2012)

Data reference set is a specific set of data codes for a general topic, such as a set of management level codes in an organization. (Brackett 2011)

Data reference set variation is a variation of a data reference set that has a difference in the domain of data reference items, their coded data values, their names, or substantial difference in the data definitions. Any difference, however slight, constitutes a different data reference set variation. (Brackett 2012)

Data refining is no longer used. See *data resource transition*. (Brackett 2012)

Data relation is an association between data occurrences in different data subjects or data entities, or within a data subject or data entity, or between data records in different data files or within a data file. It provides the connections between data subjects for building the proper data structure and between data files for navigating in the database. (Brackett 2011, 2012)

Data relation variability is the variability that exists with the data relations, the names and cardinalities for those data relations, primary keys, and foreign keys. Ideally, data relations with their names and cardinalities, primary keys, and foreign keys are formally designed. However, that is far from the norm in a disparate data resource. (Brackett 2012)

Data replication is the consistent copying of data from one primary data site to one or more secondary data sites. The copied data are kept in synch with the primary data on a regular basis. (Brackett 2011)

Data resource is a collection of data (facts), within a specific scope, that are of importance to the organization. It is one of the four critical resources in an organization, equivalent to the financial resource, the human resource, and real property. The term is singular, such as the *organization data resource*, the *student data resource*, or the *environmental data resource*. (Brackett 2011, 2012)

Data resource agility principle states that an organization's data resource must be agile enough to change in a manner that supports the business change needed to remain successful in a dynamic business world. The data resource must change so that it provides one version of truth about the business world where the organization operated. (Brackett 2012)

Data resource clarity is the state of being clear and understandable. The data resource must be free from doubt, obscurity, and ambiguity. (Brackett 2011)

Data resource comparity principle states that if the data resource management rules are followed, a comparate data resource will be developed. The rules create the right conditions for development of a comparate data resource. If the rules are not followed, a disparate data resource will be developed. (Brackett 2011, 2012)

Data resource data are any data necessary for thoroughly understanding, formally managing, and fully utilizing the data resource to support the business information demand. (Brackett 2011)

Data resource data aspect principle states that data documentation must include both the technical aspect and the semantic aspect of the data resource. Both are needed for all audiences to fully understand, manage, and utilize the organization's data resource. (Brackett 2011)

Data resource data model is a complete data model of the data resource data contained in the Data Resource Guide. (Brackett 2011)

Data resource direction is the course of data resource development toward a particular goal or objective. (Brackett 2011)

Data resource discovery principle states that data resource integration is a discovery process where any insights about the data resource are captured, understood, and documented. The process is performed by people, who may be supported by automated tools. (Brackett 2012)

Data resource drift is the natural, steady drift of a data resource towards disparity if its development is not properly managed and controlled. The natural drift is toward a disparate, low quality, complex data resource. The longer the drift is allowed to continue, the more difficult it will be to achieve a comparate data resource. The natural drift is continuing unchecked in most public and private sector organizations today, and will continue until organizations consciously alter that natural drift. (Brackett 2011, 22012)

Data resource elegance is the state of being beautiful, graceful, and dignified. It's high grade, and has desirable characteristics and qualities. (Brackett 2011)

Data resource excellence is the quality or state of a data resource being excellent, having outstanding or valuable data quality, being superior in supporting the business information demand. (Brackett 2011)

Data Resource Guide provides a complete, comprehensive, integrated index to the organization's data resource. It provides a thorough understanding of the data resource, and is readily available to everyone in the organization so they can use the data resource to meet their business needs. It provides one version of truth about the data resource. (Brackett 2011, 2012)

Data Resource Guide principle states that the data resource data must be placed in a comprehensive Data Resource Guide which serves as the primary repository for all data resource data. It contains data resource data about disparate data, comparate data, and the transformation of disparate data to comparate data. The Data Resource Guide contains the single version of truth about the data resource. (Brackett 2011)

Data resource hazard is the existence of disparate data. A greater volume and a greater degree of disparity make the hazard greater. (Brackett 2011)

Data resource horizon is the distance into the future that an organization is interested in planning for its data resource development. (Brackett 2011)

Data resource iatrogenesis principle states that the disparate data resource was caused by or resulted from the actions of the data management professionals and/or business professionals in an effort to create data to meet the business information demand. Unlike medicine, the actions may have been intentional or unintentional. (Brackett 2011, 2012)

Data resource information is any set of data resource data in context, with relevance to one or more people at a point in time or for a period of time. (Brackett 2011)

Data resource information demand is the organization's continuously increasing, constantly changing need for current, accurate, integrated information about the data resource that is necessary for formally managing the data resource. (Brackett 2011)

Data resource integration is the thorough understanding of existing disparate data within a common data architecture, the designation of preferred data, and the development of a comparate data resource based on those preferred data. It is the act or process to form, coordinate, or blend disparate data into a comparate data resource. It resolves the existing data disparity. (Brackett 2011, 2012)

Data resource integration concept is to resolve the disparate data and produce a comparate data resource that meets the current and future business information demand. The awareness of the data resource and a thorough understanding of that data resource lead to the resolution of the disparate data. (Brackett 2012)

Data resource management is the formal management of the entire data resource at an organization's disposal, as a critical resource of the organization equivalent to the human resource, financial resource, and real property, based on established concepts, principles, and techniques, leading to a comparate data resource, that supports the current and future business information demand. (Brackett 2011)

Data Resource Management Framework is a framework that represents the discipline for complete management of a comparate data resource. It represents the cooperative management of an organization-wide data resource that supports the current and future business information demand. (Brackett 2011)

Data resource management integration is the overall integration of the management of an organization's data resource, including integration of the data resource itself and integration of the data culture. It is the process of moving from discordant data resource management to concordant data resource management. (Brackett 2012)

Data resource management transition is the transition from a state of discordant data resource management to a state of concordant data resource management. It includes both data resource transition and data culture transition. The transition has a direction and purpose, and permanence to the extent that a return is not made to discordant data resource management. (Brackett 2012)

Data resource perfection is the state of a data resource being perfect, being free of defective data, having an unsurpassable degree of accuracy to support the business information demand. (Brackett 2011)

Data resource precautionary principle states that if an action or policy has a suspected risk of causing harm to the data resource, in the absence of scientific consensus that the action or policy is not harmful, the burden of proof that it is not harmful falls on those who advocate taking the action. (Brackett 2011)

Data resource probability neglect is overestimating the odds of not meeting the current business information demand and underestimating the odds of not meeting the future business information demand. (Brackett 2012)

Data resource quality is a measure of how well the data resource supports the current and future business information demand. Ideally, the data resource should fully support all the current and future business information demands of the organization to be considered a high quality data resource. (Brackett 2011)

Data resource quality tolerance is the degree of acceptable variation from perfection that is allowed in the data resource. It's the acceptable level of quality that is adequate for supporting the business information demand. (Brackett 2011)

Data resource risk is the chance that use of the disparate data will adversely impact the business. (Brackett 2011)

Data resource scope is the total data resource available to an organization. (Brackett 2011)

Data resource simplicity is the state of being simple, uncomplicated, and maintainable. It's free from pretense and subtlety. (Brackett 2011)

Data resource transformation is the formal process of formally transforming a disparate data resource to a comparate data resource within the context of a common data architecture according to the preferred data architecture designations. It's a subset of overall data resource transition that is based on the preferred physical data architecture. It's a metamorphosis of the physical disparate data to form physical comparate data. (Brackett 2012)

Data resource transformation concept states that all data transformation, whether disparate data to comparate data or comparate data to disparate data, will be done within the context of a common data architecture, using the preferred data architecture designations, according to formal data transformation rules. The best existing disparate data are extracted and transformed to comparate data to create a single, high quality version of truth about the business. (Brackett 2012)

Data resource transformation objective is to transform the best of the existing disparate data to a high quality comparate data resource so it can support the current and future business information demand. The objective is more than just connecting a few database and merging the data, building bridges between databases, or sending electronic messages over a network. It's a precise, detailed, and very rigorous process that creates a high quality comparate data resource. (Brackett 2012)

Data resource transition is the transition of an organization's data resource from a disparate data resource state, through an interim data resource state and a virtual data resource state, to a comparate data resource state. It's the pathway that is followed from a disparate data resource to a comparate data resource. It's unique to each organization depending on their current situation and future needs. (Brackett 2012)

Data resource value is the worth and importance of the data resource. Its value is in its usefulness and its reusability. (Brackett 2011)

Data resource variability principle states that every data resource has a level of variability that must be accepted and clarified, and that any variability above that acceptable level must be resolved. (Brackett 2012)

Data responsibility is the assignment of appropriate responsibility for development and maintenance of the data resource to specific individuals. (Brackett 2011)

Data restructuring – See *Restructure data*.

Data retention rule is a data integrity rule that specifies how long data values are retained and what is done with those data values when their usefulness is over. It specifies the criteria for preventing the loss of critical data through updates or deletion, such as when the operational usefulness is over, but the evaluational usefulness is not over. (Brackett 2011)

Data reviewing – See *Review data*.

Data rule is a subset of business rules that deals with the data column of the Zachman Framework. They specify the criteria for maintaining the quality of the data resource. (Brackett 2011, 2012)

Data rule domain specifies the data domain in the form of a rule. (Brackett 2011)

Data rule version principle states that data rule versions are designated by the version notation in the data naming taxonomy. (Brackett 2011)

Data scanning in the context of data resource integration is the process of electronically or manually scanning databases or application programs to identify the data stored by databases, or the data used or produced by applications. Data scanning can capture technical insight into the data, but cannot capture semantic insight into the data. (Brackett 2012)

Data selection rule is a data integrity rule that specifies the selection of data occurrences based on selection criteria. (Brackett 2011)

Data sharing concept states that shared data are transmitted over the data sharing medium as preferred data. Any organization, whether source or target, that does not have or use data in the preferred form is responsible for translating the data. (Brackett 2011, 2012)

Data sharing cycle is an ongoing cycle where people understand the data get involved in sharing data, improving data quality, and promoting data resource integration. (Brackett 2011)

Data site is any location where data are stored, such as a database, a server, a filing cabinet, and so on. (Brackett 2011)

Data source rule specifies the preferred source from which a particular business fact is obtained and the conditions that determine the preferred source. (Brackett 2012)

Data steward is a person who watches over the data and is responsible for the welfare of the data resource and its support of the business information demand, particularly when the risks are high. (Brackett 2011)

Data stewardship principle states that data stewards will be assigned at all levels of an organization with appropriate responsibilities for developing and maintaining a comparate data resource. (Brackett 2011)

Data structure is a representation of the arrangement, relationships, and contents of data subjects, data entities, and data files in the organization's data resource. (Brackett 2011)

Data structure components principle states that a proper data structure must integrate data entity-relation diagrams, data relations, semantic statements, data cardinalities, and data attribute structures. All of these components must be developed to have a complete proper data structure. (Brackett 2011)

Data structure integration principle states that each component of proper data structures must be stored once and only once within the organization's data resource, and then integrated as necessary when data structures are presented to specific audiences. (Brackett 2012

Data structure rule is a data integrity rule that specifies the data cardinality for a data relation between two data entities that applies under all conditions. No exceptions are allowed to a data structure rule. (Brackett 2011)

Data structure uniformity principle states that all proper data structures in an organization must have a uniform format. (Brackett 2011)

Data structure variability is the variability that exists in the improper structure of data in a disparate data resource. Data structure variability can occur with data files, data records, data items, data codes, and data relations, and usually occurs with all five. (Brackett 2012)

Data subject is a person, place, thing, concept, or event that is of interest to the organization and about which data are captured and maintained in the organization's data resource. Data subjects are defined from business objects and business events, making the data resource subject oriented toward the business. (Brackett 2011)

Data subject-relation diagram represents data subjects and the relations between those data subjects. (Brackett 2011)

Data subject thesaurus is a list of synonyms and related business terms that help people find data subjects that support their business information needs. It's a list of business terms and alias data entity names that point to the formal data subject name. (Brackett 2011)

Data subject variation is a variation of a data subject to support data selections, subsets of data, and data roles, and to support evaluational data subjects. (Brackett 2012)

Data suitability is how suitable the data are for a specific purpose. The suitability varies with the use of data. The same data may be suitable for one use and unsuitable for another use. (Brackett 2011)

Data tracking is the process of tracking data from the data origin to their current location. It documents any alterations or modifications to the data, the addition of new data, and the creation of derived or aggregated data. It's a process to help understand and manage the movement of data within and between organizations. (Brackett 2011, 2012)

Data transform is the formal process of transforming disparate data into comparate data, in the data depot, using formal data transformation rules. (Brackett 2012)

Data transformation is the process of transforming disparate data to comparate data, or comparate data to disparate data, within the context of a common data architecture. (Brackett 2012)

Data transformation rule is a data rule that specifies how the data will be transformed within the context of a common data architecture based on the existing disparate data and the preferred physical data architecture. (Brackett 2012)

Data translation – See **Translate data**.

Data translation principle states that data translation rules are prepared between preferred data designations and non-preferred data designations to assist in the transformation between disparate data to comparate data. (Brackett 2012)

Data translation rule is a data rule that defines the translation of a data value from one unit to another unit. It represents the translation of the values of a single fact to different units, and is not considered to be a data derivation rule. (Brackett 2012)

Data translation scheme was the former name for data translation rule and is no longer used so that all translations could be stated as rules. (Brackett 2012)

Data type hierarchy provides the construct for understanding and managing all data that are currently defined or may be defined in the future. It consists of a hierarchy for data megatypes, base data types, and distinct data types. (Brackett 2011)

Data value is any data value, such as a date, a name, a code, or a description. (Brackett 2011)

Data value domain specifies the data domain as a set of allowable values. (Brackett 2011)

Data value rule is a data integrity rule that specifies the unconditional data domain for a data attribute that applies under all conditions. It specifies the rule with respect to the business, not with respect to the database management system. No exceptions are allowed to a data value rule. (Brackett 2011, 2012)

Data variability is the variation in format and content of a redundant fact stored in a disparate data resource. (Brackett 2011)

Data variability factor is the number of variations in format or content for a single business fact. (Brackett 2011)

Data variation is the variation in the data meaning, data structure, data integrity, data domain, data content and format, and so on. (Brackett 2012)

Data version identifies the specific version of data, such as a date or time frame. Two to four words are usually sufficient to uniquely designate a data version. (Brackett 2011)

Data view schema represents the structure of data as normalized from the business schema. (Brackett 2011)

Data vision is the power of imagining, seeing, or conceiving the development and maintenance of a comparate data resource the meets the current and future business information demand. (Brackett 2012)

Data volatility is a measure of how quickly data in the business world changes. (Brackett 2011)

Data volume breadth is how many data entities and data attributes are in the data resource and data models, and how many data files and data items are in the databases. It depends on the number of business facts and how those business facts are grouped into data entities and stored in data files. (Brackett 2012)

Data volume depth is how many data occurrences exist for the data entities and how many data records are stored in the data files. (Brackett 2012)

Data warehousing is the storage of evaluational data for the analysis of trends and patterns in the business. (Brackett 2011)

Database conversion is the process of changing a database management system from one operating environment to another operating environment. The data are not altered in any way. The database management system is simply moved from one operating platform to another. (Brackett 2012)

Database data domain specifies the values allowed in a data attribute with respect to the database management system. (Brackett 2011)

Database data optionality is a general statement about the requirements of a data value with respect to the database management system. The possibilities are usually Required or Optional because that's all database management systems can handle. (Brackett 2011)

Database merge is the process of merging separate compatible databases together into one single database. The data are not altered in any way. Data records are simply merged into one database. (Brackett 2012)

Datum has historically been defined as the singular form of data related to one fact. (Brackett 2011)

Default data value is a data value that is automatically entered when no other data values are available. (Brackett 2011)

Definition is a statement conveying a fundamental character or the meaning of a word, phrase, or term. It is a clear, distinct, detailed statement of the precise meaning or significance of something. (Brackett 2011)

Deniability is the ability to deny, a valuable but often deceptive ability to deny. (Brackett 2011)

Denotative meaning is the direct, explicit meaning provided by a data definition. (Brackett 2011)

Denotative meaning principle states that a comprehensive data definition must have a strong denotative meaning that limits any individual connotative meanings. (Brackett 2011)

Deployment data architecture is the architecture of the deployment data as they are deployed over a network. It represents the data in the deployment schema. (Brackett 2011)

Deployment schema represents the structure of the logical schema as de-optimized and distributed over several physical databases. (Brackett 2011)

Depot is a place for storing goods; a store or cache; a place for storing and forwarding supplies; a building for railroad or bus passengers or freight. (Brackett 2012)

Derive data is the formal process of deriving target data from source data according to formal data derivation rules. It applies to deriving individual data values, to summarizing operational data, and to aggregating evaluational data to the lowest level of detail desired. (Brackett 2012)

Derived data are data that are obtained from other data, not by the measurement or observation of an object or event. (Brackett 2012)

Derived data – See *Fourth normal form*.

Descriptive is to describe; referring to, consulting, or grounded in matters of observation or experience; expressing the quality, kind, or condition of what is denoted by a modified term. It is finding out what currently exists and describing it. (Brackett 2012)

Detail data steward is a person who is knowledgeable about the data by reason of having been intimately involved with the data. That person is usually a knowledge worker who has been directly involved with the data for a considerable length of time. (Brackett 2011)

Deterministic is the quality or state of being determined; every event, act, and decision is the consequence of some previous event, act, and decision. (Brackett 2012)

Diagram segmentation principle states that a data entity-relation diagram must be segmented in a manner that is readily understandable by the intended audience. (Brackett 2011)

Dimensional data modeling is used for modeling evaluational data in the analytical tier using analytical data normalization. (Brackett 2011)

Dimensional data structure shows the detail necessary for implementing data entities in a data warehouse. (Brackett 2011)

Discordance is the state of disagreement, a lack of agreement among persons and groups, dissension. It's tension or strife resulting from a lack of agreement. (Brackett 2011)

Discordant is being at variance; disagreeing; quarrelsome; relating to disagreement or clashing. (Brackett 2012)

Discordant data management is the situation where disagreement exists in the organization about how the data resource should be managed and whether an initiative should be started to formally manage the data resource. (Brackett 2011) No longer used. See *Discordant data resource management*.

Discordant data resource management is the situation where the overall management of an organization's data resource, including the data resource itself and the data culture, has a high variance and disagreement. (Brackett 2012)

Disparate means fundamentally distinct or different in kind; entirely dissimilar. (Brackett 2102)

Disparate data are data that are essentially not alike, or are distinctly different in kind, quality, or character. They are unequal and cannot be readily integrated to meet the business information demand. They are low quality, defective, discordant, ambiguous, heterogeneous data. (Brackett 2011)

Disparate data application is any application that reads and stores disparate data. (Brackett 2012)

Disparate data codes is the situation where data codes can represent single, multiple, or partial data properties; where data codes can represent single or multiple data subjects; where sets of data codes can represent single or multiple data subjects; and where sets of data codes can be complete or partial. (Brackett 2012)

Disparate data cycle is a self-perpetuating cycle where disparate data continue to be produced at an ever-increasing rate because people do not know about existing data or do not want to use existing data. People come to the data resource, but can't find the data they need, don't trust the data, or can't access the data. These people create their own data, which perpetuates the disparate data cycle. The next people that come to the data resource find the same situation, and the cycle keeps going. (Brackett 2011, 2012)

Disparate data definition is any vague definition about the data in the existing data resource. (Brackett 2012)

Disparate data file is a data file that did not go through formal data normalization and data denormalization, and does not represent a single, complete data subject, or related data subjects resulting from formal data denormalization. Disparate data files often represent multiple data subjects, partial data subjects, or a combination of multiple and partial data subjects. (Brackett 2012)

Disparate data instances is the situation where the retention of historical data instances across disparate data files and disparate data records can easily result in large quantities of disparate data. (Brackett 2012)

Disparate data integrity rule is any data integrity rule that exists in the data resource. (Brackett 2012)

Disparate data item is a data item that contains other than an elemental or combined data characteristic. Disparate data items may contain multiple data characteristics, partial data characteristics, or complex data characteristics. (Brackett 2012)

Disparate data name is any informal data name in the disparate data resource. (Brackett 2012)

Disparate data record is data record that did not go through formal data normalization and denormalization, and does not represent a single data occurrence, or multiple data occurrences resulting from formal data denormalization. (Brackett 2012)

Disparate data resource is a data resource that is substantially composed of disparate data that are dis-integrated and not subject oriented. It is in a state of disarray, where the low quality does not, and cannot, adequately support an organization's business information demand. (Brackett 2011)

Disparate data resource state is the current state of a disparate data resource in an organization and is outside the context of a common data architecture. The data exhibit the four characteristics of disparate data: unknown existence, unknown meaning, high redundancy, and high variability. The disparate data cycle is in full swing and the natural drift of the data resource is toward disparity. It's the least desirable state of the data resource and is the initial state for data resource transition process. (Brackett 2012)

Disparate data resource variability is a state where all aspects of a disparate data resource are inconsistent, characterized by data variations, and are not true to the concepts and principles of a comparate data resource. The data are highly variable in their names, definitions, structure, integrity, and documentation. The variability is pervasive throughout the disparate data resource. (Brackett 2012)

Disparate data shock is the sudden realization that a data dilemma exists in an organization and that it is severely impacting an organization's ability to be responsive to changes in the business environment. It's the panic that an organization has about the poor state of its data resource. It's the realization that disparate data are not adequately supporting the current and future business information demand. It's the panic that sets in about the low quality of the data resource, that the quality is deteriorating, and very little is being done to improve the situation. (Brackett 2011, 2012)

Disparate data spiral is the spiraling increase in data disparity from existing technologies into new technologies. Both the volume of disparate data and the complexity of that disparity are increasing. (Brackett 2011)

Disparate data structure is any improper data structure that exists in the data resource. (Brackett 2012)

Disparate data understanding principle states that all disparate data variability, including data names, definitions, structure, integrity, and existing documentation will be understood and formally documented at a detailed level within the context of a common data architecture. (Brackett 2012)

Disparate foreign key is any foreign key defined in a disparate data resource that does not meet the formal criteria for a true foreign key. (Brackett 2012)

Disparate information is any information that is disparate with respect to the recipient. It could result from information acquired from different sources that are organized differently, or it could result from information created from disparate data that provides conflicting information. (Brackett 2012)

Disparate primary key is any primary key defined in a disparate data resource that does not meet the formal criteria for a true primary key. The specific situations are described below. (Brackett 2012)

Distinct data type is a unit style within a base data type, based on variations in content or format. (Brackett 2011)

Documentation known to exist principle states that the data resource data must be known to exist so data management and business professionals can take advantage of those data. (Brackett 2011)

Dormant means inactive or a suppression of activity, but having the capability of becoming active again. (Brackett 2011)

Dormant data are data that exist in the data resource but are never used or are seldom used. Data can be dormant because they are hidden, out of date and don't represent the real world, or useless for any business activity. (Brackett 2011)

Dynamic data conversion is where the data conversion is based on changing conversion criteria, such as monetary units with varying exchange rates. (Brackett 2011)

Dysfunction is a behavior caused by uncertainty and lack of understanding. (Brackett 2011)

Dysfunctional organization exhibits dysfunctional behavior; it is not a learning organization. A lack of knowledge about the business environment limits understanding and results in uncertainty, which perpetuates a dysfunctional organization. (Brackett 2011)

Edit data is the formal process of applying the preferred data edits to the transformed data to ensure the quality of the data before they are loaded into the target database. (Brackett 2012)

Effective data cross-referencing principle states that thoroughly understanding existing disparate data is only effective when those data are inventoried and documented at a detailed level and are cross-referenced to a common data architecture. (Brackett 2012)

Elegance is refined grace, dignified propriety, tasteful richness of design or ornamentation, dignified gracefulness or restrained beauty of style, high grade or quality. Elegance is beautiful and graceful. (Brackett 2011)

Electronic database data includes data located in databases and database management systems. They can be searched and analyzed relatively easily.

Electronic non-database data includes data in word processing documents, spreadsheets, electronic presentations, e-mails, and so on. These data can be searched and analyzed electronically, but with some difficulty. (Brackett 2011)

Elemental data are individual facts that cannot be subdivided and retain any meaning. (Brackett 2012)

Elemental data characteristic is a single elemental fact that cannot be further divided and retain their meaning, such as a month number or a day number within a month. (Brackett 2011, Brackett 2012)

Enhanced disparate data definition is a disparate data definition that is enhanced in some way based on insight gained from another source, such as a person's memory. (Brackett 2012)

Enterprise – See *Organization.*

Enterprise architecture is an initiative to comprehensively describe the architectures in an organization. It describes the terminology, composition, and relationships of each architecture, the relationships between architectures, and the relationships with external organizations. It includes business goals, business processes, hardware, software, data, and information systems. (Brackett 2011)

Entity is a being, existence; independent, separate, or self-informed existence; the existence of a thing compared with its attributes; something that has separate and distinct existence and objective or conceptual reality. (Brackett 2011)

Entity in mathematics is a single existent, such as an employee John J. Smith. (Brackett 2011)

Entity in the data resource is really an *entity set* in mathematics. The term is often made plural, such as Employees, to hide the fact that it has a different meaning from mathematics. (Brackett 2011)

Entity-relation diagram, often referred to as an *E-R diagram* or a *data structure diagram*, is a (Brackett 2011)

Entity set in mathematics is a group of like entities, such as Employee. (Brackett

2011)

Entropy is the state or degree of disorderliness. It is a loss of order, which is increasing disorderliness. Entropy increases over time, meaning that things become more disorderly over time. (Brackett 2011)

E-R diagram: See *Entity-relation diagram.*

Evaluational data are subject oriented, integrated, time variant, non-volatile collections of data in support of management's decision making process. They are used to evaluate the business and usually contain summary data with some capability to drill down to detail data. (Brackett 2011)

Excellence is the quality or state of being excellent, having outstanding or valuable quality, being superior, distinguishable by superiority, first class, very good of its kind. (Brackett 2011)

Existing disparate data definition is a disparate data definition that currently exists in a data dictionary, database management software, or some other form of documentation. (Brackett 2012)

Expanded means to increase the extent, number, volume, or scope of something; to enlarge; to express fully or in detail; to write out in full; to increase the extent, number, volume, or scope. (Brackett 2011)

Expanded data vision is an intelligent foresight about the data resource that includes the scope of the data resource, the development direction, and the planning horizon. It's the situation where the scope of the data resource includes the entire data resource, the development direction is aligned with the business and technology, and the planning horizon is realistic. (Brackett 2011, 2012)

Expect anything principle states that when seeking to understand and resolve disparate data, anything should be expected. One should expect any situation, even if it seems irrational. (Brackett 2012)

Explicit data culture variability is the variability that can be readily visible, or identified in documented procedures and data management actions pertaining to data orientation, data availability, data responsibility, data vision, and data recognition. (Brackett 2012)

Explicit data error is a data error that is readily visible and known. Explicit data errors are routinely identified and made apparent through data edits. (Brackett 2011)

Explicit data integrity rule principle states that any implicit data integrity rule shown on a proper data structure must be shown explicitly in a precise data integrity rule. All data integrity rules must be stated explicitly so they can be enforced. (Brackett 2011)

Explicit data transformation rules are stated as a formal data rule using specific notations. (Brackett 2012)

Extract source data is the formal process of extracting the source data from the preferred data source based on the specifications, performing any database conversions necessary between the data source and the data depot, and placing the source data into a data depot for data transformation. (Brackett 2012)

Explicit disparate data integrity rule is a disparate data integrity rule that is explicitly stated in the data documentation or in a data model. (Brackett 2012)

Explicit disparate data name is a disparate data name that exists in the data resource, such as a data file name. (Brackett 2012)

Explicit disparate data resource variability is the variability that can be readily seen or identified in the data names, definitions, structure, integrity, and documentation of a disparate data resource. (Brackett 2012)

Explicit disparate data structure is a disparate data structure that is explicitly defined in the documentation or in a data model. (Brackett 2012)

Explicit knowledge, also known as formal knowledge, is knowledge that has been codified and stored in various media, such as books, magazines, tapes, presentations, and so on, and is held for mankind, such as in a reference library or on the web. It is readily transferable to other media and capable of being disseminated. (Brackett 2011, Brackett 2012)

External data tracking is data tracking in an environment where the organization does not have control of the data. It usually deals with data tracking between organizations, where changes to the data may not be known. (Brackett 2011, 2012)

External schema is the structure of the data used by programs. (Brackett 2011)

Fact normalization: See *Data attribute normalization*.

Farsighted horizon is the situation where an organization's data resource horizon is very long term. The vision is too far over the horizon to be of interest to most people. (Brackett 2011, 2012)

Federated database is a set of databases that are documented and then interconnected to operate as one database, even when those databases are on different platforms. A person desiring data goes to the *federation* and gets the data they need without knowing where those data reside. (Brackett 2011)

Fifth normal form, commonly known as *inter-entity dependencies*, is a technique to find dependencies between entities and document those dependencies as additional data entities. (Brackett 2011)

Final common data architecture is a common data architecture that includes all data in the organization's data resource and is used to designate a preferred data architecture. (Brackett 2012)

First dimension of data variability is the variability in data names, definitions, structure, integrity, and documentation that exists at any point in time with the operational data in a disparate data resource. (Brackett 2012)

First level of data redundancy is created when disparate data files and disparate

483

data records contain redundant data. The data redundancy can be quite large, particularly in organizations that have been in business for many years and have a large data resource. (Brackett 2012)

First normal form, commonly known as *repeating groups*, is a technique to find repeating groups and move them to a separate data entity. (Brackett 2011)

Five-Tier Five-Schema concept represents all the schema involved in data resource management within the context of a common data architecture. The five tiers are strategic logical, tactical logical, operational, analytical, and predictive. The five schema in the operational, analytical, and predictive tiers are business schema, data view schema, logical schema, deployment schema, and physical schema. (Brackett 2011, 2012)

Five-Tier Five-Schema orientation principle states that development of a comparate data resource within a common data architecture must be done according to the Five-Tier Five-Schema Concept. (Brackett 2011)

Fixed format data item is a data item whose data value is always in the same format. (Brackett 2012)

Fixed length data item is a data item whose length is fixed. (Brackett 2012)

Foreign data attribute is any data attribute that does not have the same data entity name as the data entity in which is appears. (Brackett 2011)

Foreign data entity is a data which is foreign to a data attribute and which is not characterized by that data attribute. (Brackett 2011)

Foreign key in logical data models is the primary key of a data occurrence in a parent data entity that is placed in each data occurrence of a subordinate data entity to identify the parent data occurrence in that parent data entity. In data files, a foreign key is the primary key of a data record in a parent data file that is placed in each data record of a subordinate data file to identify the parent data record in that parent data file. (Brackett 2011, 2012)

Foreign key list is a list of the foreign keys for a data subject that exists in the disparate data. Only the data characteristic is listed for each foreign key, not the data characteristic variation. (Brackett 2012)

Formal means having an outward form or structure, being in accord with accepted conventions, consistent and methodical, or being done in a regular form. (Brackett 2011)

Formal data culture integration is any data culture integration done within the context of a common data culture. (Brackett 2012)

Formal data culture state is a necessary state where the data culture is readily understood within the context of a common data culture. The variability of the fragmented data culture is understood and documented, the preferred data culture is designated, and the data culture integration is prescribed. No changes to the data culture have yet been made, pending review and approval by the organization. (Brackett 2012)

Formal data name readily and uniquely identifies a fact or group of related facts in the data resource, based on the business, and using formal data naming criteria. (Brackett 2011)

Formal data name abbreviation is the formal shortening of a primary data name to meet a length restriction according to formal data name word abbreviations and a formal data name abbreviation algorithm. (Brackett 2011)

Formal data resource integration is any data resource integration done within the context of a common data architecture. (Brackett 2012)

Formal data resource state is a necessary state where the disparate data are readily understood within the context of a common data architecture. It's the first step in the data resource transition process where disparate data are put in context using a common data architecture. It's not a separate data resource since the data are only understood within a formal context. (Brackett 2012)

Formal data transformation is done within the context of a common data architecture and follows all of the concepts, principles, and techniques for formal data resource integration. (Brackett 2012)

Formal data transformation principle states that formal data transformation will be used to create a comparate data resource. Informal data transformation will not be considered or used. (Brackett 2012)

Formal design techniques principle states that proper data structures must be developed according to formal, recognized data design techniques. (Brackett 2011)

Formal knowledge – See **Explicit knowledge**.

Forward data transformation is the formal transformation of disparate data to comparate data. Data are extracted from the preferred data source, transformed, and loaded into the data target. (Brackett 2012)

Forward data translation rule is a data value translation rule from a non-preferred data designation to a preferred data designation. (Brackett 2012)

Fourth normal form, commonly known as *derived data*, is a technique to identify data attributes that are derived and remove them from the data entity. (Brackett 2011)

Fragmented is broken apart, detached, or incomplete; consisting of separate pieces. (Brackett 2012)

Fragmented data culture is a data culture that is broken apart into separate pieces that are unrelated, incomplete, and inconsistent. It is similar to a disparate data resource, and leads to the creation of a disparate data resource. A fragmented data culture cannot effectively or efficiently manage an organization's data resource. (Brackett 2012)

Fragmented data culture state is the situation where every organizational unit,

485

and possibly every person, is managing data in their own way, with their own orientation, vision, processes, and software tools. The data culture is highly variable and exhibits all of the characteristics of a fragmented data culture. The management is informal and seldom documented, and the fragmentation is not known. It is the least desirable state and is the initial state for data culture integration. (Brackett 2012)

Functional dependency profiling analyzes the data values for possible data relations between sets of data. If the same domain of data values is identified in different data files, a presumption can be made that those two data files might be related through a primary key – foreign key relationship. (Brackett 2012)

Fundamental data are data that are not stored in databases and are not used in applications, but support the definition of specific data. (Brackett 2011)

Fundamental data definitions are the comprehensive data definitions for fundamental data. (Brackett 2011)

Fundamental data definition inheritance is the process of comprehensively defining fundamental data and allowing specific data definitions to inherit those fundamental data definitions. It's a technique that implements the data inheritance principle. (Brackett 2011)

Fundamental data integrity rule is a data integrity rule that can be developed for and used by many specific data attributes. The data integrity rule is defined once and is applied to many different situations. (Brackett 2011)

Fundamental data translation rule is a basic data translation rule that can be applied to many specific data translations. The data translation rule is specified once and can be inherited for many specific data translations. (Brackett 2012)

General data cardinality is a data cardinality specified by the data relation or by a semantic statement. (Brackett 2011)

General information is a set of data in context that could be relevant to one or more people at a point in time or for a period of time. (Brackett 2012)

General primary key is a primary key that uniquely identifies every data occurrence in a data entity. (Brackett 2011)

Generation data derivation is where the data derivation algorithm generates the derived data values without the input of any other data attributes. (Brackett 2011)

Generic data structure principle states that universal data models and generic data architectures can be used to guide an understanding of the organization's data, but should not be used in lieu of thoroughly understanding the organization's business. (Brackett 2011)

Graph theory is a branch of discrete mathematics that deals with the study graphs as mathematical structures used to model relations between objects from a certain collection. A graph consists of a collection of vertices (or nodes), and a collection of edges that connect pairs of vertices. The edges may be directed from one vertex to another, or undirected meaning no distinction between the two vertices. (Brackett 2012)

Group think is the situation where a group of people under stress tend to find a solution, but have lost their objectivity. (Brackett 2011)

Hazard is a possible source of danger or a circumstance that creates a dangerous situation. (Brackett 2011)

Heritage is property that descends from an heir, something transmitted by or acquired from a predecessor, or something possessed as a result of one's natural selection or birth. Heritage usually applies to biological or cultural descendants, but can be applied to data. (Brackett 2012)

Hidden data code hierarchy is the situation where a single set of data codes represents a hierarchy of data codes. (Brackett 2012)

Hidden data resource is the large quantities of data that are maintained by the organization, but are largely unknown, unavailable, and unused because people are not aware that those data exist, or do not understand the data well enough for appropriate use. The data just sit in databases, on hard drives, in filing cabinets and desk drawers, and in archive boxes just waiting to be useful if only their existence and meaning were known and understood. (Brackett 2011)

Hidden information is the information that could be available from the hidden data if those hidden data were known to exist. (Brackett 2011)

Hidden knowledge is the knowledge that could be gained through the understanding of the hidden information. (Brackett 2011)

Historical data instance is any data instance, other than the current data instance, that represents previous data values of the data items in the data occurrence. (Brackett 2012)

Home data attribute is any data attribute that has the same data entity name as the data entity in which it appears. For example, Employee. Name is a home data attribute within the Employee data entity. (Brackett 2011)

Home data entity is the data entity which is the home to a data attribute and which is characterized by a data attribute. (Brackett 2011)

Homeostasis is the property of an open or closed system that regulates its internal environment and tends to remain in a stable, constant condition. (Brackett 2011)

Horizon is the distance into the future which a person is interested in for planning. (Brackett 2011)

> A *horizon* is the distance into the future which a person is interested in for planning.

Horizontal partitioning is denormalizing data occurrences into two or more data files when the number of data records exceeds the capability of the database.

(Brackett 2011)

Human data profiling identifies the pattern of actions different people exhibit when entering or editing data. Patterns about how people collect data, enter data, and edit data can be helpful for understanding disparate data. The patterns can also be useful for identifying data integrity rules that are not documented anywhere. (Brackett 2012)

Hype-cycle is a major initiative that is promoted in an attempt to properly manage an organization's data resource, but often ends up making the data resource more disparate and impacting the business. (Brackett 2011)

Iatrogenesis refers to the inadvertent adverse effects or complications caused by or resulting from medical treatment or advise. The term originated in medicine and is generally referred to as harm caused by the healer. The medical profession strives to do no harm, hence iatrogenesis is a result of inadvertent actions. (Brackett 2011)

Identify source data is the formal process of determining the source data that will be needed to prepare the target data. The source data are specified as a physical data structure of the disparate data as documented during data inventorying. (Brackett 2012)

Identify target data is the formal process of determining the desired target data. The desired target data are specified as the preferred physical data structure and will be used throughout the data transformation process. (Brackett 2012)

Imagination is the power of uncertainty, the ability to spark intrigue to keep the imagination going, a suspense about what's next. It's a way to spark innovation and engage people in an activity. (Brackett 2011)

Implicit data culture variability is the variability that is not readily visible, or identified in documented procedures and data management actions. (Brackett 2012)

Implicit data error is a data error that is hidden and is only known through discovery during business processing, rather than through data edits. (Brackett 2011)

Implicit data integrity rule is a data integrity rule that is implied in a proper data structure. (Brackett 2011)

Implicit data transformation rules are stated in the form of a table or matrix for data value translations. (Brackett 2012)

Implicit disparate data integrity rule is a disparate data integrity rule that is not explicitly stated in the documentation or in a data model, but exists in database management systems or applications. (Brackett 2012)

Implicit disparate data name is a disparate data name that is implied through a definition, contents, or use of the data. (Brackett 2012)

Implicit disparate data resource variability is the variability that is not readily seen or identified in the data names, definitions, structure, integrity, and documentation of a disparate data resource. Implicit disparate data resource variability is either implied by existing documentation or exists in people's minds. (Brackett 2012)

Implicit disparate data structure is a disparate data structure that is not explicitly defined and is implied through the use of foreign keys. (Brackett 2012)

Implicit knowledge – See *Tacit knowledge*.

Imprecise means not precise, not clearly expressed, indefinite, inaccurate, incorrect, or not conforming to a proper form. (Brackett 2011)

Imprecise data integrity rules are data integrity rules that do not provide adequate criteria to ensure high quality data. (Brackett 2011)

Improper means not suited to the circumstances or needs. (Brackett 2011)

Improper data structure is a data structure that does not provide an adequate representation of the data supporting the business for the intended audience. (Brackett 2011)

Inadequate means insufficient, or not adequate to fulfill a need or meet a requirement. (Brackett 2011)

Inadequate data responsibility is the situation where the responsibility, as defined, does not fulfill the need for properly managing a comparate data resource. The responsibility is casual, lax, inconsistent, uncoordinated, and not suitable for the current environment of a shared data resource. (Brackett 2011)

Inappropriate means not appropriate. (Brackett 2011)

Inappropriate data recognition is the situation where the organization at large does not recognize data as a critical resource of the organization, the fact that the data resource is disparate, or the need to develop a comparate data resource. (Brackett 2011)

Incorrect data definitions are data definitions that are incorrect or inaccurate with respect to the business. The definitions are not in synch with the data name, the data structure, the data integrity rules, or the business. (Brackett 2011)

Incorrect data name is any data name that does not correctly represent the contents of the data component. Incorrect data names are just flat wrong. (Brackett 2011, 2012)

Incrementally cost effective principle states that any data management initiative to resolve disparate data and create a comparate data resource should begin small, produce meaningful results, and continue to grow to a fully recognized initiative. (Brackett 2011)

Informal means casual, not in accord with prescribed form, unofficial, or inappropriate for the intended use. (Brackett 2011)

Informal data culture integration is any data culture integration done outside the context of a common data culture. It usually does not resolve variability in the data culture and seldom leads to development and maintenance of a comparate data resource. (Brackett 2012)

Informal data name is any data name that is casual and inappropriate for the intended purpose of readily and uniquely identifying each fact, or set of related facts, in an organization's data resource. It has no formality, structure, nomenclature, or taxonomy. (Brackett 2012)

Informal data name abbreviation is any abbreviated data name that has no formality to the abbreviation. (Brackett 2011)

Informal data resource integration is any data resource integration done outside the context of a common data architecture. It usually does not result in a comparate data resource or any substantial resolution to the disparate data. (Brackett 2012)

Informal data transformation is done outside the context of a common data architecture, seldom follows formal concepts, principles, and techniques, and seldom resolves data disparity. (Brackett 2012)

Information is a set of data in context, with relevance to one or more people at a point in time or for a period of time. Information is more than data in context— it must have relevance and a time frame. Information has historically been defined as singular. (Brackett 2011, 2012)

Information architecture is not used because it's difficult to place relevance to one or more people and a time into an architecture. (Brackett 2011)

Information assimilation overload occurs when information is coming too fast for a person to assimilate. (Brackett 2011)

Information engineering is the discipline for identifying information needs and developing information systems to meet those needs. It's a manufacturing process that uses data from the data resource as the raw material to construct and transmit information. (Brackett 2011)

Information engineering objective is to get the right data, to the right people, in the right place, at the right time, in the right form, at the right cost, so they can make the right decisions, and take the right actions. The operative term is *the right data*. (Brackett 2011)

Information excellence is the state of fully meeting the business information demand. Information perfection is the state of information being perfect, free from defect, and having an unsurpassable degree of accuracy in meeting the business information demand. (Brackett 2011)

Information frustration is a situation where needed information exists, but the information is so fragmented that the time to locate and relate the information causes frustration. (Brackett 2011)

Information integration is the integration of information, using the formal definition of information, from multiple sources into an understandable set of information for a specific use. It's the process of taking disparate information and developing comparate information for some business activity. (Brackett 2012)

Information management is coordinating the need for information across the organization to ensure adequate support for the current and future business information demand. It should not be confused with data resource management. (Brackett 2012)

Information paranoia is the fear of not knowing everything that is relevant or could be relevant at some point in time. It's a situation where a person is obsessed with gaining information for information's sake. (Brackett 2011)

Information perfection is the state of information being perfect, free from defect, and having an unsurpassable degree of accuracy in meeting the business information demand. (Brackett 2011)

Information quality is how well the business information demand is met. It includes both the data used to produce the information and the information engineering process. (Brackett 2011)

Information sharing is the sharing of information between people and organizations according to the definition of information. (Brackett 2012)

Information system data are any data documenting the information system. (Brackett 2011)

Information technology infrastructure provides the resources necessary for an organization to meet its current and future business information demand. (Brackett 2011)

Infrastructure is the underlying foundation or framework for a system or an organization.

Integrate means to form or blend into a whole; to unite with something else; to incorporate into a larger unit; to bring into common organization. (Brackett 2011)

Integrated data culture is a data culture where all of the data management functions and processes in an organization are integrated within a common context, and are oriented toward developing and maintaining a comparate data resource. Data culture variability has been resolved and data resource management is performed consistently across the organization. (Brackett 2012)

Integrated data resource is a data resource where all data are integrated within a common context and are appropriately deployed for maximum use supporting the current and future business information demand. Data awareness and data understanding are increased. Data variability is at a minimum and data redundancy is reduced to a known and manageable level. Data integrity is known and at the desired level. The data are as current as the organization needs to conduct its business. (Brackett 2011, 2012)

Integration is the act or process of integrating. (Brackett 2012)

Integrity is the state of being unimpaired, the condition of being whole or complete, or the steadfast adherence to strict rules. (Brackett 2011)

Intelligence is the ability to learn or understand or to deal with new or trying situations; the skilled use of reason; the ability to apply knowledge to manipulate one's environment or to think abstractly. (Brackett 2011)

Intelligent key is a term that is not used because data keys cannot possess intelligence. See Business key. (Brackett 2011)

Inter-attribute dependencies: See *Third normal form*.

Inter-entity dependencies: See *Fifth normal form*.

Inter-entity derived data attribute is one that is derived from data attributes in another subordinate data entity. (Brackett 2011)

Interim common data architecture is a common data architecture that is developed for cross-referencing one major segment of the data resource for a very large organization. (Brackett 2012)

Interim common data architecture principle states that interim common data architectures may be developed in very large organizations where it is not possible to achieve a final common data architecture in one step because of the size of the task. Data products are cross-referenced to interim common data architectures, and those interim data architectures are cross-referenced to a final common data architecture. (Brackett 2012)

Internal data tracking is data tracking in an environment where the organization has control of the data. It usually deals with data tracking within an organization, where changes to the data may be known. (Brackett 2011, 2012)

Internal schema was the structure of the data in the database. (Brackett 2011)

Intra-entity derived data attribute is one that is derived from other data attributes within that same data entity. (Brackett 2011)

Inventory is an itemized list of assets; a catalog of the property of an individual or estate; a list of goods on hand; a survey of natural resources; a list of traits, preferences, attitudes, interest, or abilities; the quality of goods or materials on hand. It is also the act or process of taking an inventory. (Brackett 2012)

Knowledge is cognizance, cognition, the fact or condition of knowing something with familiarity gained through experience or association. It's the acquaintance with or the understanding of something, the fact or condition of being aware of something, of apprehending truth or fact. Knowledge is information that has been retained with an understanding about the significance of that information. Knowledge includes something gained by experience, study, familiarity, association, awareness, or comprehension. (Brackett 2011)

Knowledge base principle states that the existing, often hidden, base of knowledge about the data resource must be tapped to ensure a complete and thorough understanding of the data. (Brackett 2011)

Knowledge management is the management of an environment where people generate tacit knowledge, render it into explicit knowledge, and feed it back to the organization. The cycle forms a base for more tacit knowledge, which keeps the cycle going in an intelligent learning organization. It's an emerging set of policies, organizational structures, procedures, applications, and technology aimed toward increased innovation and improved decisions. It's an integrated approach to identifying, sharing, and evaluating an organization's information. It's a culture for learning where people are encouraged to share information and best practices to solve business problems.(Brackett 2011, 2012)

Law of increasing entropy states that a system reaches a state of maximum entropy—an equilibrium. The law is inevitable and irreversible for a closed system. In an open system, entropy continues to increase and an equilibrium is not reached. (Brackett 2011)

Learning means to gain knowledge or understanding, to come to realize, to be informed of something, to acquire knowledge, skill, or behavior, to discover. (Brackett 2011)

Learning organization is an organization where critical knowledge is leveraged to understand the business environment and meet business initiatives. It's an organization where the employees are well informed, well trained, knowledge workers empowered to take action. (Brackett 2011)

Lessons learned principle states that every initiative has some failures and some successes, and the lessons learned can be included in the next initiative. (Brackett 2011)

Limited data documentation is any documentation about the data resource that is sparse, incomplete, out of date, incorrect, inaccessible, unknown, poorly presented, poorly understood, and so on. (Brackett 2011)

Limited foreign key is a foreign key that matches a limited primary key in a parent data subject. (Brackett 2012)

Limited primary key is a primary key that is available for all data occurrences, but has a limited range of uniqueness for data occurrences. (Brackett 2011, 2012)

Lineage is the direct descent from an ancestor or common progenitor to the descendants of a common ancestor that is regarded as the founder of the line. Lineage is commonly used for biological or cultural descendants, but can be applied to data. (Brackett 2012)

Load data is the formal process of loading the data from the data depot into the target database. Any database conversion that is necessary is done during the data load process. (Brackett 2012)

Logical data architecture is the architecture of the logical data represented by the logical schema. It represents the data in the logical schema from the strategic tier down to the predictive tier. (Brackett 2011)

Logical data relation is an association between data occurrences in different data subjects or data entities, or within a data subject or data entity. It is defined during data normalization and has a name or short phrase describing the data relation. (Brackett 2012)

Logical schema represents the structure of the logical data, independent of the physical operating environment, that are optimized from the data view schema. (Brackett 2011)

Lost productivity cycle is the situation where disparate data grows, more time is spent resolving the impacts, and less time is spent on value-added business activities. More time is spent resolving problems and less time is spent on preventing problems. (Brackett 2011)

Malthusian Principle deals with the power of populations to overwhelm their means of subsistence, causing misery, suffering, and eventually leading to extinction of that population if no corrective action is taken. Populations tend to grow geometrically, and their means of subsistence tend to grow arithmetically. At some point in time, the population growth exceeds the means of subsistence. (Brackett 2011)

Many-to-many data relation occurs when a data occurrence in one data entity is related to more than one subordinate data occurrences in the second data entity, and each data occurrence in that second data entity is related to more than one data occurrence in the first data entity. A many-to-many data relation is shown by a dashed line with an arrowhead on each end. (Brackett 2011)

Many-to-many recursive data relation is where a data occurrence in a data entity is related to more than one data occurrences in that same data entity, and each of those data occurrences are related to more than one other data occurrences. (Brackett 2011)

Many-to-one data reference item translation rule translates the coded data value and/or the name from many different data reference items in the source to one data reference item in the target. (Brackett 2012)

Massively disparate data is the existence of large quantities of disparate data within a large organization, or across many organizations involved in similar business activities. (Brackett 2011)

Master data management is a term that is not used because it represents a hype-cycle. See *Data resource management*. (Brackett 2011)

Mathematical data domain specifies the data values that are mathematically possible. Usually, it's a maximum range allowed and is applied to all values in that data attribute. (Brackett 2011)

Meaningful data definition principle states that a comprehensive data definition must define the real content and meaning of the data with respect to the business. It is not based on the use of the data, how or where the data are used, how they were captured or processed, the privacy or security issues, or where they were stored. (Brackett 2011)

Meaningless data definitions are data definitions that are meaningless to the business. The English and grammar may be acceptable, but the explanation of the content and meaning of the data with respect to the business is useless. (Brackett 2011)

Meaningless data name is any data name that has no formal meaning with respect to the business. (Brackett 2011)

Merge means to blend or combine together, to become combined or united. (Brackett 2011)

Meta-data is a term that is no longer used because its meaning has become so confused that it is meaningless. See *Data resource data*, *Para-data*. (Brackett 2011)

Migration is a movement to change location periodically, especially by moving seasonally from one region or country to another. It's wandering without a long term purpose, or wandering with only current objectives in mind, like nomadic wandering or bird migration. It's a lack of a permanent settlement, especially resulting from seasonal or periodic movement. (Brackett)

Multiple characteristic data item is a data item that contains more than one data characteristic. (Brackett 2012)

Multiple contributor data derivation is where many data attributes from the same data entity or from different data entities contribute to the derived data. (Brackett 2011)

Multiple data characteristic is two or more single or combined data characteristics that are not closely related and should not be stored together or managed as a single unit. The data characteristics may be from the same data subject or from different data subjects. (Brackett 2012)

Multiple fact data attribute is where multiple facts appear in the same data attribute. (Brackett 2011)

Multiple fact data field is any data field that contains multiple, unrelated business facts. (Brackett 2011)

Multiple file data subject is a data subject that exists in multiple data files. The situation is common in a disparate data resource. (Brackett 2012)

Multiple occurrence data record is a data record that represents multiple data occurrences in a single data record. A multiple occurrence data record may contain subordinate data occurrences or parallel data occurrences. (Brackett 2012)

Multiple preferred data designations is the situation where multiple data characteristic variations or multiple data reference set variations are designated as preferred due to culture, geography, or politics. (Brackett 2012)

Multiple property data code is a data code that represents two or more data properties of the same data subject. (Brackett 2012)

Multiple subject data code is a data code that represents two or more different data subjects. (Brackett 2012)

Multiple subject data file is a data file that contains all of the data items, or a subset of the data items, representing the data characteristics for multiple data subjects. (Brackett 2012)

Multiple subject set of data codes is a set of data codes that represent more than one data subject. (Brackett 2012)

Multiple value data attribute is where multiple values of a fact appear in the same data attribute. (Brackett 2011)

Nearsighted planning horizon is the situation where an organization's data resource horizon is very short term. Data resource development is focused on short term objectives to the detriment of long term goals. (Brackett 2011, 2012)

New technology syndrome is a repeating cycle of events that occurs with new technology. New technology appears as a new way of doing things. People play with the new technology, in a physical sense, to see what it can do or is capable of doing, like a child plays with a new toy. (Brackett 2011, 2012)

No blame – no whitewash principle states that the disparate data situations exists, that laying blame for that situation only polarizes and alienates people, and whitewashing the situation only allows it to continue. (Brackett 2011)

Non-architected data are any data that are not formally managed within a common data architecture. (Brackett 2011)

Non-business key is a primary key consisting of a fact or facts whose values have no meaning to the business. (Brackett 2012)

Non-correcting principle states that the data resource cannot correct itself when it encounters complexity. (Brackett 2011)

Non-electronic data includes all data located in filing cabinets, archive boxes, desk drawers, and so on. These data cannot be searched or analyzed electronically without some form of data entry. (Brackett 2011)

Non-existent data definitions have never been developed, or were developed at one time and have since been misplaced or lost. Whatever the reason, there exists considerable data in the data resource that have no data definition. (Brackett 2011, 2012)

Non-information is a set of data in context that is not relevant or timely to the recipient. It is neither specific information or general information. (Brackett 2011, 2012)

Non-integrating principle states that the data resource cannot integrate itself when it encounters disparity. (Brackett 2011)

Non-preferred data characteristic variation is a data characteristic variation within a data characteristic that has not been designated as preferred. A non-preferred data characteristic variation may be either acceptable or obsolete. (Brackett 2012)

Non-preferred data designation is a data variation that has not been accepted as preferred. (Brackett 2012)

Non-preferred data name abbreviation algorithm is any data name abbreviation algorithm that is not the official data name abbreviation algorithm for the organization. (Brackett 2011)

Non-preferred data name abbreviation scheme is any data name abbreviation scheme that does not contain the preferred data name word abbreviations and the preferred data name abbreviation algorithm. (Brackett 2011)

Non-preferred data name word abbreviations are any sets of data name word abbreviations that are not the official set of data name word abbreviations for the organization. (Brackett 2011)

Non-preferred data reference set variation is a data reference set variation within a data subject that has not been designated as preferred. (Brackett 2012)

Non-preferred data translation rule is a data translation rule between different non-preferred data designations. (Brackett 2012)

Non-redundant data documentation principle states that the data resource data must represent a single version of truth about the data resource. (Brackett 2011)

Non-unique data name is any data name, whether abbreviated or unabbreviated, that is not unique across the organization or across multiple organizations engaged in the same business activities. (Brackett 2011)

Objective data resource quality is based on facts or metrics without any distortion by personal experience. It's a technical quality based on reality and is not impacted by perception or experience. It tends to remain constant as long as the data resource is unchanged. (Brackett 2011)

Obsolete data characteristic variation is any data characteristic variation that is obsolete and can no longer be used. (Brackett 2012)

Obsolete data reference set variation is any data reference set variation that is obsolete and can no longer be used. (Brackett 2012)

Obsolete foreign key is a foreign key that matches an obsolete primary key in a parent data subject. (Brackett 2012)

Obsolete primary key is a primary key that has no further use and should not be used. (Brackett 2011)

Occurrence in the data resource is really an *entity* in mathematics. (Brackett

2011)

Occurrence group or *group of occurrences* in the data resource is really a set of entities in mathematics. (Brackett 2011)

One-to-many data reference item translation rule translates one coded data value and/or name from the source to many data reference items in the target. These translations are difficult and require additional input to make the split from one source value to many target values. (Brackett 2012)

One-to-many data relation occurs when a parent data occurrence in one data entity is related to more than one subordinate data occurrences in a second data entity, and each subordinate data occurrence in the second data entity is related to the parent data occurrence in the first data entity. A one-to-many data relation is shown by a dashed line with an arrow on one end pointing to the data entity with many occurrences. (Brackett 2011)

One-to-many recursive data relation is where a parent data occurrence in a data entity is related to more than one subordinate data occurrences in the same data entity, and each of those subordinate data occurrences is related to the parent data occurrence. (Brackett 2011)

One-to-one data reference item translation rule translates the coded data value and/or the name from one data reference item in the source to one data reference item in the target. (Brackett 2012)

One-to-one data relation occurs when a data occurrence in one data entity is related to only one data occurrence in a second data entity, and that data occurrence in the second data entity is related to the same data occurrence in the first data entity. A one-to-one data relation is shown by a dashed line with no arrowheads. (Brackett 2011)

One-to-one recursive data relation is where a data occurrence in a data entity is related to one other data occurrence, and that other data occurrence is related to the first data occurrence. It is shown by a dashed line with no arrowhead leaving and returning to the same data entity. (Brackett 2011)

Operational data are subject oriented, integrated, time current, volatile collections of data in support of day to day operations and operational decision making. (Brackett 2011)

Operational data modeling is used for the operational data using operational data normalization. (Brackett 2011)

Operational data normalization is the process of normalizing the operational data according to the formal rules of data normalization. (Brackett 2011)

Operational data stores is often used to represent the collection of operational data. (Brackett 2011)

Operational processing is the day-to-day transactional processing using operational data to support business operations and operational decisions.

Operational tier represents data used for data to day operations of the business and operational business decisions. The data are usually detailed with some summary data, and may be on any platform or in any software product. (Brackett 2011)

Opportunistic principle states that every opportunity should be taken to promote the initiative in the organization, regardless of the size of the opportunity. (Brackett 2011)

Opt for detail principle states that when in doubt about the level of detail to document during the data inventory, always opt for greater detail. Experience has shown that more detail is needed to fully understand and integrate the data resource. (Brackett 2012)

Organization represents any administrative and functional structure for conducting some form of business, such as a public sector organization, quasi-public sector organization, private sector organization, association, society, foundation, and so on, however large or small, whether for profit or not for profit, and for however long it has been operating. (Brackett 2012)

Organization agility principle states that an organization must be agile to remain successful in their business endeavor. Agility depends on how the organization perceives the business world and how well it adjusts to changes in that business world. It depends on how well the organization understands the business world, how quick the organization perceives changes in that business world, and how quick they can respond to those changes. (Brackett 2012)

Organization perception principle states that the comparate data resource developed to support an organization's business must be based on the organization's perception of the business world. If a comparate data resource is to support an organization's business activities, that comparate data resource must be based primarily on the organization's perception of the business world and how the organization chooses to operate in that business world. (Brackett 2012)

Organization umwelt principle states that each organization has a particular perception of the business world in which they operate based on previous experiences that are unique to that organization. Those experiences affect the organization's behavior in the business world, and determines how the organization adapts to a changing business world and operates in that business world. (Brackett 2012)

Organizational knowledge is information that is of significance to the organization, is combined with experience and understanding, and is retained by the organization. It is information in context with respect to understanding what is relevant and significant to a business issue or business topic—what is meaningful to the business. It's analysis, reflection, and synthesis about what information means to the business and how it can be used. It's a rational interpretation of information that leads to business intelligence.(Brackett 2011, 2012)

Orientation means the act or process of orienting or being oriented; the state of being oriented; the general or lasting direction of thought, inclination, or interest; the change of position in response to external stimulus. (Brackett 2012)

Outdated data definitions are data definitions that are not current with the business. (Brackett 2011)

Overly optimistic horizon is the situation where the data resource horizon is the best, and can be easily and quickly achieved. The vision may be valid and realistic, but the horizon is too optimistic. (Brackett 2011, 2012)

Para-data are any data that are ancillary to or support core business data. Para-data are a perception by the observer based on their role in the business world. (Brackett 2011)

Parallel data occurrence is a data occurrence from the same data subject represented by the data file. (Brackett 2012)

Paralysis-by-analysis is a process of ongoing analysis and modeling to make sure everything is complete and correct. Data analysts and data modelers are well known for analyzing a situation and working the problem forever before moving ahead. They often want to build more into the data resource than the organization really wants or needs. The worst, and most prevalent, complaint about data resource management is its tendency to paralyze the development process by exacerbating the analysis process. (Brackett 2011, 2012)

Partial characteristic data item is a data item that contains part of a data characteristic. Other parts of the data characteristic are contained in one or more other data items. (Brackett 2012)

Partial historical data instance contains a subset of data items in the data occurrence, usually the data items whose data values changed and appropriate identifiers. (Brackett 2012)

Partial key dependencies: See *Second normal form*.

Partial occurrence data record is a data record that contains only part of the data items for a data occurrence. The complete data occurrence is split across multiple data records, usually due to some length limitation. (Brackett 2012)

Partial set of data codes contains a subset of the data properties for a single data subject. (Brackett 2012)

Partial subject data file is a data file that contains a subset of the data items representing the data characteristics for a single data subject or for multiple data subjects. (Brackett 2012)

Partially architected data is the situation where some data are managed within a common data architecture and some data are not managed within a common data architecture. (Brackett 2011)

Passive data contributors are data attributes that no longer exist or whose value will never change. (Brackett 2011)

Passive derived data are derived data based on passive data contributors. (Brackett 2011)

Pattern of failure is a sequence of events which lead toward a disparate data resource and its failure to fully support the current and future business information demand. (Brackett 2011)

Pattern of success is a sequence of events which lead toward a comparate data resource and full support for the current and future business information demand. (Brackett 2011)

Perceived data resource scope is the portion of the data resource that is perceived to be formally managed. (Brackett 2011)

Perfection is the quality or state of being perfect, freedom from fault or defect, an unsurpassable degree of accuracy or excellent. Perfection is the ultimate state of excellence. (Brackett 2011)

Physical data architecture is the architecture of the data in the physical databases. It represents the data in the physical schema. Moving the data to a different physical database means going back to the deployment schema and denormalizing the data for the new database. (Brackett 2011)

Physical data relation is an association between data records in different data files or within a data file. It is typically defined during formal data denormalization and has now name. (Brackett 2012)

Physical key is a preferred or alternate primary key that may or may not be meaningful to the business, but is useful for physical navigation in the database. (Brackett 2011, 2012)

Physical schema represents the structure of data in physical databases as denormalized from the deployment schema. (Brackett 2011)

Physical-to-physical data translations are data translations between the disparate data documented as data products and the comparate data resource. (Brackett 2012)

Platform resource data are any data documenting the platform resource. (Brackett 2011)

Plausible means reasonable, superficially fair, valuable but often having deceptive attraction or allure, superficially pleasing or persuasive. (Brackett 2011)

Plausible deniability is the ability of an organization to deny the fact that their data resource is disparate and live with the illusion of high quality data. (Brackett 2011)

Pragmatics deals with the relation between signs and symbols, and their users. Specifically it deals with their usefulness. (Brackett 2011)

Precautionary principle states that if an action or policy has a suspected risk of causing harm to the public or the environment, in the absence of scientific consensus that the action or policy is not harmful, the burden of proof that it is not harmful falls on those who advocate taking the action. (Brackett 2011)

Precise means clearly expressed, definite, accurate, correct, and conforming to proper form. (Brackett 2012)

Precise data integrity rule is a data integrity rule that precisely specifies the criteria for high quality data values and reduces or eliminates data errors. (Brackett 2011)

Precision is the quality or state of being precise, exactness, the degree of refinement with which a measurement is stated. (Brackett 2011)

Predictive data normalization is the process of re-normalizing the analytical logical schema to predictive logical schema for the purpose of predictive processing. (Brackett 2011)

Predictive tier represents true data mining, which is the search for unknown and unsuspected trends and patterns. Mathematically, it is in the variation and influence space. (Brackett 2011)

Preferred means to put before; to promote or advance to a rank or position; to like better or best; to give priority; to put or set forward for consideration. (Brackett 2012)

Preferred data are data that have the preferred names, definitions, structure, integrity rules, format, and content acceptable for data sharing. (Brackett 2011, 2012)

Preferred data architecture is a subset of the common data architecture that contains preferred data. It's the desired data architecture that provides a pattern for designing a comparate data resource and for transforming a disparate data resource to a comparate data resource. (Brackett 2011, 2012)

Preferred data architecture concept is that the redundancy and variability of disparate data will be resolved through the designation of a preferred data architecture and the transformation of disparate data to comparate data according to that preferred data architecture. The data redundancy and variability may not be eliminated, but will be reduced to a known and manageable level. (Brackett 2012)

Preferred data architecture objective is to designate the preferred representation of all data at the organization's disposal so those data can be readily understood and shared within and without the organization. The objective is to take a common data architecture that was enhanced to cover the data cross-references and designate preferred components that will become a pattern or template for designing and building a comparate data resource and transforming disparate data to comparate data. (Bracket 2012)

Preferred data characteristic variation is a data characteristic variation within a data characteristic that has been designated as the one preferred for data sharing and development of a comparate data resource. (Brackett 2012)

Preferred data culture is a subset of a common data culture that contains the preferred practices for managing data as a critical resource. It's the desired data culture that provides the pattern for building a cohesive data culture and transforming the fragmented data culture to that cohesive data culture. It's how the organization chooses to manage their data as a critical resource. (Brackett 2012)

Preferred data culture concept is that the variability of the existing fragmented data culture will be resolved through the designation of a preferred data culture and the transformation of the fragmented data culture to a cohesive data culture. The variability may not be eliminated, but will be reduced to a known and manageable level. (Brackett 2012)

Preferred data culture objective is to designate the preferred practices for managing data as a critical resource, so that those practices are readily understood and consistently performed throughout the organization. (Brackett 2012)

Preferred data definition is a comprehensive and denotative data definition developed from all of the insights documented during data inventory and cross-referencing that fully explains the data with respect to the business. (Brackett 2012)

Preferred data designation is a data variation that has been accepted by the consensus of knowledgeable people as being preferred for data sharing and development of a comparate data resource. (Brackett 2012)

Preferred data designation principle states that all preferred designations that comprise the preferred data architecture will be made within a common data architecture, after data cross-referencing has been completed, according to the organization's perception of the business world, by knowledgeable detail data stewards. (Brackett 2012)

Preferred data designation process is the process of designating and finalizing preferred data names, data definitions, data integrity rules, primary and foreign keys, data characteristic variations, data reference set variations, and data sources. Data translation rules between data characteristic variations and data reference items are based on the preferred data designations. (Brackett 2012)

Preferred data integrity rule is a data integrity rule that has either been confirmed or created to ensure the integrity of a common data architecture. (Brackett 2012)

Preferred data name abbreviation algorithm is the data name abbreviation algorithm that is the official data name abbreviation algorithm for the organization. (Brackett 2011)

Preferred data name abbreviation scheme uses the preferred data name word abbreviation set and the preferred data name abbreviation algorithm. (Brackett 2011)

Preferred data name word abbreviations is a set of data name word abbreviations that is the official set of data name word abbreviations for the organization. (Brackett 2011)

Preferred data source is the data product unit or variation within a data product set or variation representing a data file that will be the source for a business fact. It's the location where an individual business fact can be obtained that is the most current and most accurate. It's the location for the highest quality data that is sometimes referred to as the best-of-breed data. (Brackett 2012)

Preferred data template is a subset of the preferred logical data architecture for a specific subject area that promotes data sharing within or between organizations, and helps organizations develop applications and databases using preferred data. (Brackett 2012)

Preferred data translation rule is a data translation rule between a preferred data designation and a non-preferred data designations. (Brackett 2012)

Preferred foreign key is a foreign key that matches the preferred primary key in a parent data subject. (Brackett 2012)

Preferred foreign key principle states that each subordinate data subject in a common data architecture will have one and only one preferred foreign key designated that uniquely identifies the parent data occurrence in a parent data subject. (Brackett 2012)

Preferred logical data architecture is the common, desired, to-be logical data architecture for the organization. It's a subset of a common data architecture developed from a thorough understanding gained through data inventorying and cross-referencing. (Brackett 2012)

Preferred logical data name is the data name developed according to the data naming taxonomy and approved by the business as the preferred name for the data. The preferred logical data names are the data names developed for an initial common data architecture and for enhancements to that common data architecture. (Brackett 2012)

Preferred physical data architecture is the common, desired, to-be, physical data architecture for the organization. It's developed from a formal denormalization of the logical preferred data architecture. (Brackett 2012)

Preferred physical data name is the data name developed from the preferred logical data name during formal data denormalization according to a set of data name word abbreviations and a formal data name abbreviation algorithm. (Brackett 2012)

Preferred primary key is a primary key that has been designated as preferred for use in a comparate data resource. (Brackett 2011, 2012)

Preferred primary key principle states that each data subject in a common data architecture will have one and only one preferred primary key designated that uniquely identifies all data occurrences within that data subject in the organization's common data architecture. (Brackett 2012)

Preferred data reference set variation is a data reference set variation within a data subject that has been designated as preferred for data sharing and development of a comparate data resource. (Brackett 2012)

Prescriptive is serving to prescribe; acquired by, founded on, or determined by prescription or long-standing custom. It's describing how to get from an existing situation to a desired situation. (Brackett 2012)

Presumed data culture variability principle states that an existing fragmented data culture is highly variable and should be considered as the norm in most public and private sector organizations. Seldom is any organization free from some degree of data culture variability. (Brackett 2012)

Presumed data resource variability principle states that disparate data are highly variable in their names, definitions, structure, integrity, and documentation. Data resource variability should be considered as the norm in most public and private sector organizations. (Brackett 2012)

Primary data name is the formal data name that is the fully spelled out, real world, unabbreviated, un-truncated, business name of the data that has no special characters or length limitations. (Brackett 2011)

Primary data name abbreviation principle states that data name word abbreviations, data name abbreviation algorithms, and data name abbreviation schemes be developed to consistently provide formal data name abbreviations. (Brackett 2011)

Primary data name principle states that each business fact, or set of closely related business facts, in the data resource must have one and only one primary data name. All other data names become aliases of the primary data name. (Brackett 2011)

Primary key is a set of one or more data attributes whose values uniquely identify each data occurrence in a data entity in a logical data model. In a database, a primary key is a set of one or more data items whose values uniquely identify each data record in a data file. (Brackett 2011, 2012)

Primary key composition indicates the number and nature of the data attributes forming the primary key. (Brackett 2011)

Primary key list is list of the primary keys for a data subject that exists in the disparate data. Only the data characteristic is listed for each primary key, not the data characteristic variation. (Brackett 2012)

Primary key matrix is a matrix of the primary keys that shows all of the disparate primary keys for a data subject and across related data subjects. (Brackett 2012)

Primary key range of uniqueness is the range of data occurrences for which the primary key provides a unique identification. The primary keys in disparate data may have different ranges of uniqueness that must be identified before a preferred primary key can be designated. (Brackett 2012)

Primary key scope indicates the range of data occurrences covered by the primary key. (Brackett 2011)

Primary key status indicates the status of the primary key. (Brackett 2011)

Primary key type indicates whether or not the primary key is meaningful or meaningless to the business.

Primary productivity loss is the loss related to understanding and using the data.

Primitive data are data that are obtained by measurement or observation of an object or event in the business world. (Brackett 2012)

Principle is a comprehensive and fundamental law, doctrine, or assumption; a rule of conduct. A principle can be basic, applying to data resource management in general, or it can be specific, applying to one aspect of data resource management. (Brackett 2011, 2012)

Principle of delayed change states that nothing will change to prevent a situation from getting worse until it's too late. When the situation is finally discovered, such as a disparate data resource, it becomes a monumental task to resolve the problem. (Brackett 2011)

Principle of gradual change states that the disparate data resource evolved slowly and almost unnoticed until it was too late to correct. (Brackett 2011)

Principle of independent architectures states that each primary component of the information technology architecture has its own architecture independent of the other architectures. (Brackett 2011)

Principle of intended consequences states that any intervention in a complex system, such as a data resource, should be guaranteed to have the intended result. If that guarantee cannot be made, then the intervention should not be taken. (Brackett 2011, 2012)

Principle of unintended consequences states that any intervention in a complex system may or may not have the intended result, but will inevitably create unintended and often undesirable outcomes. (Brackett 2011)

Privacy and confidentiality principle states that the data resource must be protected from any disclosure that violates a person's or organization's right to privacy and confidentiality. (Brackett 2011)

Proactive data resource quality is the process of establishing the desired quality criteria and ensuring that the data resource meets those criteria from this point forward. It's oriented toward preventing defects from entering the data resource. (Brackett 2011)

Probabilistic is of, referring to, based on, or affected by probability, randomness, or chance. (Brackett 2012)

Probability neglect is overestimating the odds of things we most dread and underestimating the odds of things we least dread. Probability neglect for the data resource is happening in most public and private sector organizations. (Brackett 2012)

Product-to-common cross-reference is a data cross-reference between data products and a common data architecture. (Brackett 2012)

Product-to-product cross-reference is a data cross-reference between data products without the benefit of a common data architecture. Product-to-product cross-references are between sets of disparate data, usually databases, bridges, or feeds between information systems. (Brackett 2012)

Proof positive principle states that when you go to executives for approval with proof of positive results, you are more likely to gain their support than if you ask for support based on a promise to deliver. (Brackett 2011)

Proper means marked by suitability, rightness, or appropriateness; very good, excellent; strictly accurate, correct; complete. (Brackett 2011)

Proper balance principle states that a proper balance needs to be maintained between allowing enough access for people to perform their business activities and limiting access to protect the data from unauthorized alteration or deletion. (Brackett 2011)

Proper data structure is a data structure that provides a suitable representation of the business, and the data supporting the business, that is relevant to the intended audience. (Brackett 2011)

Proper sequence principle states that proper design proceeds from development of logical data structures that represent the business and how the data support the business, to the development of physical data structures for implementing databases. (Brackett 2011)

Prospective is likely to come about; likely to be or become; expected to happen; looking to the future. It is looking ahead at what's needed. (Brackett 2012)

Provenance comes from the French *provenir,* meaning *to come from.* It represents the origin or source of something, the history of ownership, or the current location of an object. The term is used mostly for art work, but is now used in a wide range of fields, including science and computing. (Brackett 2011, 2012)

Psychological denial is the situation where people are inherently aware of a dangerous situation, but choose not to recognize that situation or deny that the situation exists.

Quality is a peculiar and essential character, the degree of excellence, being superior in kind. Quality is defined through four virtues -- clarity, elegance, simplicity, and value. (Brackett 2011)

Raw Data – See **Data.**

Readily available data documentation principle states that all data resource data must be readily available to all audiences. Both technical and semantic data must be available. (Brackett 2011)

Realistic planning horizons principle states that realistic planning horizons must be challenging, yet achievable, and must be developed to cover all audiences in the organization. The horizons must stretch the imagination slightly, but not unrealistically. It must be understandable and achievable, but not too close or too distant. (Brackett 2011, 2012)

Reasonable means agreeable to reason, not extreme or excessive, having the faculty of reason, and possessing sound judgment. (Brackett 2011)

Reasonable data orientation is an orientation toward the business and support of the current and future business information demand. It depends on the architectural concepts, principles, and techniques, but more importantly depends on the culture of the organization.(Brackett 2011, 2012)

Reasonable development direction principle states that the direction of data resource development must focus primarily on the business direction and secondarily on the database technology direction. (Brackett 2011)

Reasonable management procedures principle states that reasonable procedures for development and maintenance of a comparate data resource must be established. (Brackett 2011)

Recast data is the formal process of adjusting data values for historical continuity. It aligns data values for a common historical perspective using data recast rules. (Brackett 2012)

Recognition means the action of recognizing; the state of being recognized; acknowledgement; special notice and attention. (Brackett 2012)

Reconstruct data is the formal process of rebuilding complete historical data that are not stored as full data records. (Brackett 2012)

Recursive data relation is a data relation between two data occurrences within the same data entity. (Brackett 2011)

Redundant means exceeding what is necessary or normal; superfluous; characterized by or containing an excess; characterized by similarity or repetition; profuse; or lavish. (Brackett 2012)

Redundant data are inconsistently maintained on different data sites, by different methods, and are seldom kept in synch. (Brackett 2011)

Redundant data items is the situation where a data item representing the same data characteristic exists in different data files or different data records, whether that data item has the same data name or a different data name. (Brackett 2012)

Redundant historical data instances is the situation where redundant physical data occurrences may have corresponding physical historical data instances. (Brackett 2012)

Redundant physical data occurrences is the situation where the same logical data occurrence exists multiple times in different data files in a disparate data resource. (Brackett 2012)

Relational theory was developed by Dr. Edgar F. (Ted) Codd to describe how data are designed and managed. The theory represents data and their interrelations through a set of rules for structuring and manipulating data, while maintaining their integrity. It is based on mathematical principles and is the base for design and use of relational database management system. (Brackett 2012)

Repeating groups: See *First normal form*.

Replication is a copy or reproduction; the action or process of replicating or reproducing; or creating a replica. (Brackett 2012)

Resistance to change principle states that everyone has some resistance to change. The resistance exists because most people are unsure of new approaches, particularly with new techniques. The uncertainty causes anxiety and apprehension about the outcome. (Brackett 2011)

Resolution is the degree of granularity of the data, indicating how small an object can be represented with the current scale and precision. (Brackett 2011)

Resource is a source of supply or support; an available means; a natural source of wealth or revenue; a source of information or expertise; something to which one has recourse in difficulty; a possibility of relief or recovery; or an ability to meet and handle a situation. (Brackett 2012)

Responsibility is the quality or state of being responsible; moral, legal, or mental accountability; reliability and trustworthiness; something for which one is responsible. (Brackett 2011)

Restricted means to confine within bounds; subjected to some restriction; not general; available to particular groups and excluding others; not intended for general circulation or use. (Brackett 2011)

Restricted data vision is the situation where the scope of the data resource is limited, the development direction is unreasonable, or the planning horizon is unrealistic. (Brackett 2011)

Restructure data is the formal process of changing the structure of the disparate source data to the structure of the comparate target data. It takes physical disparate data structures that have existed in the past and changes them to a preferred physical data structure. (Brackett 2012)

Retroactive data resource quality is the process of understanding the existing quality of the data resource and improving the quality to the extent that is reasonably possible. It's oriented toward correcting the existing low quality data resource by removing defects. (Brackett 2011)

Retrospective is the act or process of surveying the past; based on memory;

affecting things past; looking back, contemplating, or directing to the past. It is looking at what has happened in the past to reach what currently exists. (Brackett 2012)

Reverse data transformation is the formal transformation of comparate data to disparate data. It's necessary to maintain disparate data that supports disparate applications until they can be converted to comparate data. (Brackett 2012)

Reverse data translation rule is a data translation rule from a preferred data designation to a non-preferred data designation. (Brackett 2012)

Review data is the formal process of reviewing the data that have been transformed and loaded into the target database to ensure they are appropriate for production use. (Brackett 2012)

Risk is the possibility of suffering harm or loss from some event; a chance that something will happen. (Brackett 2011)

Robust means having or exhibiting strength or vigorous health; firm in purpose or outlook; strongly formed or constructed; sturdy. (Brackett 2011)

Robust data documentation is documentation about the data resource that is complete, current, understandable, non-redundant, readily available, and known to exist. (Brackett 2011)

Rotational data structure shows the detail necessary for implementing data mining. It is developed from a renormalization of the logical dimensional data structure, but is independent of the physical operating environment. (Brackett 2011)

Rule is an authoritative, prescribed direction for conduct, or a usual, customary, or generalized course of action or behavior; a statement that describes what is true in most or all cases; a standard method or procedure for solving problems. (Brackett 2011)

Scale is the ratio of a real world distance to a map distance. (Brackett 2011)

Schema is simply a data structure. (Brackett 2011)

Scope pertains to the range of a person's perceptions, the breadth or opportunity to function, or the area covered by a given activity. (Brackett 2012)

Second dimension of data variability is the variability in data names, definitions, structure, integrity, and documentation that occurs over time with the operational data in a disparate data resource. (Brackett 2012)

Second level of data redundancy is created when disparate data instances contain redundant data. The data redundancy greatly magnifies the data redundancy created in the first level of data redundancy, leading to massive quantities of redundant data. (Brackett 2012)

Second normal form, commonly known as *partial key dependencies*, is a technique to find data attributes that are dependent on only part of the primary key, and move them to a data entity where they are dependent on the complete primary key. (Brackett 2011)

Secondary productivity loss, which includes unnecessary business activities, such as legal appeals, suits, returned merchandise, protests, vandalism, and other actions against the organization that take resources to resolve. (Brackett 2011)

Seduction relates to being creative, engaging people in the task at hand, captivating people's attention, and activating their imagination. It's how you draw people into the process of creating a comparate data resource that meets the business information demand. (Brackett 2011)

Self-contained historical data is the situation where historical data instances are retained in the same data file along with the current data instance. (Brackett 2012)

Self-defeating fallacy states that no matter how much you believe that something can happen, if it is not possible, it will not happen. (Brackett 2011)

Self-fulfilling prophecy states that if you really believe in something that can happen, and it is possible, it will happen. It's the flip side of the self-fulfilling fallacy. (Brackett 2011)

Semantic data resource data are the data that help business professionals understand the content and meaning of the data and use them to support business activities. (Brackett 2011)

Semantic heterogeneity is a general lack of understanding about the data that makes it very difficult to fully utilize those data to support the business information demand. (Brackett 2011)

Semantic homogeneity is a formal understanding about the data that makes it easy to fully utilize those data to support the business information demand. (Brackett 2011)

Semantic information has context and meaning. It is relevant and timely. It is also arranged according to certain rules. (Brackett 2011)

Semantic statement is a textual statement of the relationship between data entities. (Brackett 2011)

Semantics deals with the relation between signs and symbols, and what they represent. Specifically, it deals with their meaning. (Brackett 2011)

Semiotic theory deals with the relation between signs and symbols, and their interpretation. It consists of syntax, semantics, and pragmatics. (Brackett 2011)

Semiotics is a general theory of signs and symbols and their use in expression and communication. (Brackett 2011)

Separate historical data is the situation where historical data instances are retained in a separate data file. (Brackett 2012)

Set of data codes is a subset of a data codes representing only part of the data properties for a complete data code set, or a mixture of properties from different data code sets. (Brackett 2012)

Set of entities in mathematics is a subgroup of an entity set, such as Retirement Eligible Employees. (Brackett 2011)

Set theory is a branch of mathematics or of symbolic logic that deals with the nature and relations of sets. (Brackett 2011)

Short data definitions are data definitions that are short, truncated phrases, or incomplete sentences that provide little meaning. (Brackett 2011)

Silver bullet is an attempt to achieve some gain without any pain. The result of seeking a silver bullet is usually considerable pain with minimal gain, and maybe considerable loss. (Brackett 2011)

Silver bullet syndrome is the on-going syndrome that organizations go through searching for quick fixes to the data problems. (Brackett 2011)

Simple primary key contains one home data attribute in its home data entity, such as Employee. Social Security Number in the Employee data entity. (Brackett 2011)

Simplicity is the state of being simple or uncompounded, having a lack of subtlety or penetration, freedom from pretense or guile, directness of expression, and maintainable. Simplicity is plain and uncomplicated.

Simplicity principle that states everything should be a simple as possible ... but not simpler. Albert Einstein. (Brackett 2011)

Single architecture orientation principle states that the entire data resource of an organization must be developed and managed within a single, organization-wide, common data architecture. (Brackett 2011)

Single characteristic data item is a data item that contains only one elemental or combined data characteristic. (Brackett 2012)

Single contributor data derivation is where one data attribute is the contributor to an algorithm that generates the derived data. (Brackett 2011)

Single data architecture principle states that the entire data resource of an organization must be developed and managed within a single, organization-wide, common data architecture. (Brackett 2012)

Single file data subject is a complete data subject that is contained in a single data file. (Brackett 2012)

Single occurrence data record is a data record that represents a single data occurrence. (Brackett 2012)

Single property data code is a data code that represents one specific data property of a single data subject. (Brackett 2012)

Single subject data code is a data code that represents a single data subject, such as the ones shown above for gender, management level, and hair color. (Brackett 2012)

Single subject data file is a data file that contains all of the data items, or a subset of the data items, representing the data characteristics for a single data subject. (Brackett 2012)

Single subject set of data codes is a set of data codes that represent one data subject. Single subject sets of data codes are relatively common in a disparate data resource. (Brackett 2012)

Source data extraction – See *Extract source data*.

Source data identification – See *Identify source data*.

Specific data are data that are stored in databases and are used in applications. (Brackett 2011)

Specific data cardinality is the data cardinality specified by a notation at the end of a data relation and is more specific than the general data cardinality. (Brackett 2011, 2012)

Specific data definitions are the comprehensive data definitions for specific data. (Brackett 2011)

Specific data definition inheritance is the process of specific data definitions inheriting other specific data definitions. It's a technique that implements the data inheritance principle. (Brackett 2011)

Specific data integrity rule is a data integrity rule that is developed and applied to the data. (Brackett 2011)

Specific data translation rule is a data translation rule that applies directly to the data translations. It may inherit a fundamental data translation rule, or it may specify a unique data translation rule. (Brackett 2012)

Specific information is a set of data in context that is relevant to a person at a point in time or for a period of time. (Brackett 2012)

Specific primary key is a primary key that is not available for all data occurrences. (Brackett 2011)

Static data conversion is where the data conversion is always done by the same conversion criteria, such as changing miles to kilometers. (Brackett 2011)

Steward came from the old English term *sty ward*; a person who was the ward of the sty. These people watched over the stock and were responsible for the welfare of the stock, particularly at night when the risks to the welfare of the stock were high. (Brackett 2011)

Strategic data steward is a person who has legal and financial responsibility for a major segment of the data resource. That person has decision-making authority for setting directions, establishing policy, and committing resources for that segment of the data resource. (Brackett 2011)

Strategic schema represents the structure of data as perceived by executives. It is relatively general in nature and includes only major data subjects and a few relations. (Brackett 2011)

Strong data resource comparity principle states that rules were designed for the development of a comparate data resource. (Brackett 2011)

Strong anthropic principle states that the constants and parameters were designed for our existence. (Brackett 2011)

Strong application data transformation is the complete transformation of an application to read and store comparate data as well as operate with comparate data. (Brackett 2012)

Structurally stable – business flexible principle states that a proper data structure must remain structurally stable across changing technology and changing business needs, yet adequately represent the current and future business as it changes. (Brackett 2011)

Structured means something arranged in a definite pattern of organization; manner of construction; the arrangement of particles or parts in a substrate or body, arrangement or interrelation of parts as dominated by the general character of the whole; the aggregate of elements of an entity in their relationships to each other, the composition of conscious experience with its elements and their combination. (Brackett 2011)

Structured data are data that are structured according to traditional database management systems with tables, rows, and columns that are readily accessible with a structured query language. Structured data are considered tabular data. (Brackett 2012)

Structureless data name is any data name that has no formal structure to the words composing the data name. (Brackett 2011)

Subject-oriented data resource is a data resource that is built from data subjects that represent business objects and events in the business world that are of interest to the organization. The basic structure of a comparate data resource is based on data subjects and the relations between those data subjects. All characteristics of a data subject are stored with that data subject. (Brackett 2011, 2012)

Subjective data resource quality is a perception of the quality of the data resource based on an individual's experience. It's a cultural oriented quality based on an individual's reality and varies from person to person, and from time to time. It's like beauty—it's in the eyes of the beholder. (Brackett 2011)

Subordinate data occurrence is a data occurrence from a data subject that is subordinate to the data subject represented by the data file. (Brackett 2012)

Subtraction is economy, doing less, and conserving. It's about finding what to eliminate and how to eliminate what's unnecessary. (Brackett 2011)

Success motivation cycle is a cycle where success encourages people to continue their effort, which leads to more success. Success begets success.

(Brackett 2011)

Suck-and-squirt approach is the process of finding the single record of reference, or system of reference, for operational data, sucking the operational data out of that reference, performing superficial cleansing, and squirting the data into the data warehouse. (Brackett 2011)

Super means over and above, higher in quantity, quality, or degree; exceeding a norm, in excessive degree or intensity, surpassing all or most others of its kind; situated or placed above, on, or at the top of, situated on the dorsal side; having the ingredient present in a large or unusual large proportion; constituting a more inclusive category than that specified; superior in status, title, or position. (Brackett 2011)

Super-structured data are any data that are structured in a manner more intricate than tabular data and, therefore, cannot be interpreted by structured query languages and tools. (Brackett 2011)

Surrogate key is a physical key contained within the database that is not visible to the business, and is seldom identified on any logical data structures. It is solely for database management purposes. (Brackett 2011)

Survey is the act or instance of surveying; something that is surveyed; the examination of a condition, situation, or value; appraise, inspect, scrutinize. (Brackett 2012)

Sustainability is a repeatable and lasting process. It is symmetry, seduction, and subtraction applied over and over. It's the ability to maintain something at a creative level indefinitely. (Brackett 2011)

Symmetry includes structure, order, and esthetics. It is something that is pleasing to people. Symmetry does not mean symmetrical, but is more about the dynamic properties of ordering, organizing, and operating than about the static proportions of objects. (Brackett 2011)

Syntactic information is raw data. It is arranged according to certain rules. Syntactic information alone is meaningless—it's just raw data. (Brackett 2011)

Syntax deals with the relation between signs and symbols, and their interpretation. Specifically it deals with the rules of syntax for using signs and symbols. (Brackett 2011)

Synthesis is to put together; the combination of parts or elements to form a whole; the production of a substance by the union of elements, or groups to form a whole. (Brackett 2011)

Tacit knowledge, also known as *implicit knowledge*, is the knowledge that a person retains in their mind. It's relatively hard to transfer to others and to disseminate widely. (Brackett 2011)

Tactical data steward is a person who acts as liaison between the strategic data stewards and the detail data stewards to ensure that all business and data concerns are addressed. (Brackett 2011)

Tactical schema represents the structure of data as perceived by managers. It is more specific, but is not a fully detailed operational schema. (Brackett 2011)

Target data identification – See ***Identify target data***.

Tarnished silver bullet is the result of attempting to find a silver bullet—considerable pain with minimal gain, and maybe considerable loss. (Brackett 2011)

Taxonomy is the science of classification, a system for arranging things into natural, related groups based on common features. (Brackett 2011)

Teamwork synergy principle states that the appropriate business and data management professionals must be involved at the appropriate time in any project to ensure that development or enhancement of a comparate data resource supports the business information demand. (Brackett 2011)

Technical data resource data are the data that technicians need to build, manage, and maintain databases and make the data available to the business. (Brackett 2011)

Technically correct – culturally acceptable principle states that a proper data structure must be both technically correct in representing the data and culturally acceptable for the intended audience. A proper data structure must integrate all of the technical detail about the data resource and present it in a manner that is acceptable to the recipients.(Brackett 2011, 2012)

Technique is a body of technical methods; a method of accomplishing a desired aim. Technique as used here represents how to accomplish a principle; the principle is the what and the technique is the how. (Brackett 2011)

Temporal variability is the normal change in the data resource due to changes in the business over time. Organizations add or drop lines of business, reorient their focus, establish new initiatives, and so on. The data resource must reflect these changes. (Brackett 2012)

Tertiary productivity loss is the loss of customers and sales in the private sector and the avoidance of regulations in the public sector. (Brackett 2011)

Theory is a plausible or scientifically acceptable general principle or body of principles offered to explain phenomena; a body of theorems presenting a concise systematic view of a subject. (Brackett 2011)

Thesaurus is a list of synonyms and related terms that help people find a specific term that meets their needs. (Brackett 2011)

Think globally – act locally principle provides a broad orientation for developing a comparate data resource. People need to think globally about the comparate data resource, but act locally to ensure that data resource contains their data and those data are readily available. (Brackett 2011, 2012)

Third dimension of data variability is the variability in data names, definitions, structure, integrity, and documentation that occurs with evaluational data in a disparate data resource. (Brackett 2012)

Third normal form, commonly known as *inter-attribute dependencies*, is a technique to find data attributes in a data entity that are dependent on another data attribute in that same data entity and move them to another data entity. (Brackett 2011)

Thorough data definition principle states that a comprehensive data definition must be thorough to be fully meaningful to the business. To be thorough, a data definition must not have any length limitation. The data definition must be long enough to fully explain the data in business terms. (Brackett 2011)

Thorough understanding principle states that a thorough understanding of the data with respect to the business resolves uncertainty and puts the brakes on data disparity. It's the understanding of data with respect to the business that's important. (Brackett 2012)

Transforming data – See ***Data transform***.

Transition is the passage from one state, stage, or place to another; a movement, development, or evolution from one form, stage, or style to another. It is moving in a consistent direction toward a desired goal. It implies a permanence of the passage or evolution without a return to the former state. (Brackett 2012)

Translate data is the formal process of translating the extracted data values to the preferred data values, if they are not already in the preferred format or content, using appropriate data translation rules. (Brackett 2012)

Ultimate data resource quality is a data resource that is stable across changing business and changing technology so it continues to support the current and future business information demand. (Brackett 2011)

Umwelt is a German word meaning the environment or the world around. It's the world as perceived by an organism based on its cognitive and sensory powers. It's the environmental factors collectively that are capable of affecting an organism's behavior. It's a self-centered world where organisms can have different umwelten, even though they share the same environment. It's an organism's perception of the current surroundings and previous experiences which are unique to that organism. It's the world as experienced by a particular organism. (Brackett 2012)

Unacceptable means not acceptable, not pleasing or unwelcome. (Brackett 2012)

Unacceptable data availability is the situation where the data are not readily available to meet the business information demand or are not properly protected or secured. (Brackett 2011)

Unacceptable data culture variability is any unacceptable level of variability in management of the data resource. (Brackett 2012)

Unacceptable data resource variability is any temporal or cultural variability in the data resource that is beyond the acceptable level. Any data resource variability that is unacceptable and impacts the business must be resolved. (Brackett 2012)

Unacceptable variability is the situation where the variability exceeds the normal range and becomes unacceptable. Most organizations seek to resolve the unacceptable variability. (Brackett 2012)

Unavailable data definitions are data definitions that are not readily available. The best data definitions may have been written, but if they are not readily available, it's the same as being non-existent. (Brackett 2011)

Uncertainty resolution principle states that when people thoroughly understand the situation, most of the uncertainty about that situation is resolved. (Brackett 2011)

Unconditional data source rule is a data source rule that specifies only one location as the preferred data source. (Brackett 2012)

Understandable data documentation principle states that the data resource data must be understandable to all audiences. The appropriate data resource data must be selected and presented to the intended audience in a manner appropriate for that audience. (Brackett 2011)

Understanding principle states that a thorough understanding of the data with respect to the business resolves uncertainty and puts the brakes on data disparity. (Brackett 2011)

Unnecessary justification principle states that an extensive justification is not needed to begin an initiative for developing a comparate data resource. An extensive justification is *not* needed to improve data resource quality.(Brackett 2011, 2012)

Unrealistic planning horizon is the situation where the data resource horizon is too nearsighted, too farsighted, or overly optimistic. (Brackett 2011)

Unreasonable means not acting according to reason, not conforming to reason, or exceeding the bounds of reason or moderation. (Brackett 2011)

Unreasonable data orientation is an unreasonable attitude about developing the data resource that is physically oriented, short term, and narrowly focused. (Brackett 2011)

Unrelated data definitions are data definitions that are unrelated to the content and meaning of the data with respect to the business. The data definition may be useful in another context, but it is not useful for understanding the data with respect to the business.

Unstructured means not structured, having few formal requirements, or not having a patterned organization without structure, having no structure, or structureless. (Brackett 2011, 2012)

Unstructured data are data that are not structured, have few formal requirements, or do not have a patterned organization. See *Complex structured data*. (Brackett 2011)

Vague means not clearly expressed; stated in indefinite terms; not having a precise meaning; not clearly grasped, defined, or understood. (Brackett 2011)

Vague data definition is any data definition that does not thoroughly explain in simple, understandable terms, the real content and meaning of the data with respect to the business. (Brackett 2011)

Value is the monetary worth of something, its relative utility or importance, its usefulness and reusability, or its degree of excellence. It's having desirable or esteemed characteristics or qualities. (Brackett 2011)

Variability is the quality, state, or degree of being variable or changeable; apt or liable to vary or change; changeable; inconsistent; characterized by variations; having much diversity; or not true to type. (Brackett 2012)

Variable characteristic data item is a data item that could contain several different data characteristics, but only one of those data characteristics appears in any data record. (Brackett 2012)

Variable fact data attribute is where different facts may appear in the same data attribute depending on the situation. (Brackett 2011)

Variable format data item is a data item whose data value could be in one of a variety of different format. (Brackett 2012)

Variable sequence data item is the situation where the data items can be in any sequence in a data record. The specific data item is identified by a keyword or mnemonic, followed by the data value. (Brackett 2012)

Variation is the act or process of varying; the state or fact of being varied; the existent to which a thing varies; or an instance of varying. (Brackett 2012)

Vertical partitioning is denormalizing data occurrences into two or more data files when the length of the data record exceeds the capability of the database.

Vertices from set theory. See *Nodes*.

Vested interest principle states that the audience with a vested interest in managing data as a critical resource of the organization should be targeted for supporting any quality improvement initiative. (Brackett 2011)

Virtual data resource state is an interim state between the formal data resource and a comparate data resource where real-time data transformation is performed to produce interim comparate data. The data are transformed in real time, according to formal data transformation rules, in either direction between disparate data and comparate data. Disparate data may be transformed to comparate data to support new applications or databases. Comparate data may be transformed to disparate data to support disparate applications or databases. (Brackett 2012)

Virtue is a beneficial quality or power of something, a commendable quality or trait, a merit. (Brackett 2011)

Vision is the act or power of imagination, a mode of seeing or conceiving, discernment or foresight. (Brackett 2011)

Weak anthropic principle states that the constants and parameters just happen to be right for our existence. (Brackett 2011)

Weak application data transformation is the use of routines to read and store comparate data while the application still operates with the disparate data. (Brackett 2012)

Weak data resource comparity principle states that a comparate data resource will be developed if people just happen to do it right, which is unlikely to happen. (Brackett 2011)

Wider scope principle states that data resource management must ultimately include all data at the organization's disposal. It includes non-critical data, super-structured data, historical data, and non-automated data. (Brackett 2011)

Willingness to change principle states that most people are willing to change if they understand the need to change. Most people want to change the current disparate data situation. They see the need for change and would willingly participate in the change. (Brackett 2011)

BIBLIOGRAPHY

Bauval, Robert. *The Egypt Code*. New York: Disinformation, 2008.

Berns, Gregory. *Iconoclast: A Neuroscientist Reveals How to Think Differently*. Boston, Massachusetts: Harvard Business Press, 2010.

Brackett, Michael H. *Developing Data Structured Information Systems*. Topeka, KS: Ken Orr and Associates, Inc., 1983.

_____. *Developing Data Structured Databases*. Englewood Cliffs, NJ: Prentice Hall, 1987.

_____. *Practical Data Design*. Englewood Cliffs, NJ: Prentice Hall, 1990.

_____. *Data Sharing Using a Common Data Architecture*. New York: John Wiley & Sons, Inc., 1994.

_____. *The Data Warehouse Challenge: Taming Data Chaos*. New York: John Wiley & Sons, Inc., 1996.

_____. *Data Resource Quality: Turning Bad Habits Into Good Practices*. New York: Addison-Wesley, 2000.

_____. *Data Resource Simplexity: How Organizations Choose Data Resource Success Or Failure*. New Jersey: Technics Publications, LLC, 2011.

Brockman, John. *The Next Fifty Years: Science in the First Half of the Twenty-First century*. New York: Vantage Books, 2003.

_____. *Intelligent Thought: Science Versus the Intelligent Design Movement*. New York: Vantage Books, 2006.

Calvin, William H. *The Cerebral Code: Thinking a Thought in the Mosaics of the Mind*. London: Bradford Book, 1996.

Cole, K. C. *The Hole in the Universe: How Scientists Peered Over the Edge of Emptiness and Found Everything*. New York: Harvest Book, 2001.

Cook, Nick. *The Hunt for Zero Point: Inside the Classified World of Antigravity Technology*. New York: Broadway Books, 2001.

Davies, Paul. The 5th Miracle: *The Search for the Origin and Meaning of Life*. New York: Simon and Schuster, 1999.

_____. *The Goldilocks Enigma: Why Is the Universe Just right for Life?*

Boston: Mariner Book, 2006.

Deutsch, David. *The Fabric of Reality*. New York: Penguin Books, 1997.

Doidge, Norman. *The Brain That Changes Itself: Stories of Personal Triumph from the Frontiers of Science*. New York: Penguin Books, 2007.

Dunn, Christopher. *Lost Technologies of Ancient Egypt*. Rochester, NY: Bear & Company, 2010.

Dyer, Wayne W. *The Power of Intention: Learning to Co-create Your World Your Way*. Carlsbad, California: Hay House, Inc., 2004.

_____. *Inspiration: Your Ultimate Calling*. Carlsbad, California: Hay House, Inc., 2006.

Feynman, Richard P. *The Meaning of It All: Thoughts of a Citizen-Scientist*. New York: Basic Books, 1998.

Filkin, David. Stephen Hawking's Universe: The Cosmos Explained. New York: Basic Books, 1997.

Frazier, Kendrick. *Science Under Siege: Defending Science, Exposing Pseudoscience*. New York: Prometheus Books, 2009.

Gilbert, Adrian. *Signs in the Sky: The Astrological & Archaeological Evidence for the Birth of a New Age*. New York: Three Rivers Press, 2000.

Gleick, James. *Genius: The Life and Science of Richard Feynman*. New York: Vintage Books, 1992.

_____. *Isaac Newton*. New York: Vintage Books, 2003.

Goswami, Amit, Reed, Richard E., and Goswami, Maggie. *The Self-Aware Universe: How Consciousness Creates the Material World*. New York: Penguin Putnam, Inc., 1995.

Gribbin, John. *Unveiling the Edge of Time: Black Holes, White Holes, Wormholes*. New York: Three Rivers Press, 1992.

Hammer, Michael, and Campy, James. *Reengineering the Corporation: A Manifesto for Business Revolution*. New York: Harper Business, 1993.

Hawking, Stephen. *A Brief History of Time: From the Big Bang to Black Holes*. New York: Bantam Books, 1988.

_____. *Black Holes and Baby Universes and Other Essays*. New York: Bantam Books, 1994.

Hoagland, Richard C., and Bara, Mike. *Dark Mission: The Secret History of NASA*. Pt. Townsend, Washington: Feral House, 2009.

Johnsonbaugh, Richard. *Discrete Mathematics*. New York: Macmillan Publishing Company, 1984.

Kaku, Machio. *Hyperspace: A Scientific Odyssey through Parallel Universes,*

Time Warps, and the 10th Dimension. New York: Anchor Books, 1995.

_____. *Physics of the Impossible: A Scientific Exploration into the World of Phasers, Force Fields, Teleportation, and Time Travel*. New York: Anchor Books, 2009.

Knight, Christopher, and Butler, Alan. *Who Built the Moon?* London: Watkins Publishing, 2005.

Maran, Stephen P., and Marschall, Laurence A. *Galileo's New Universe: The Revolution in Our Understanding of the Cosmos*. Dallas, TX: Benbella Books, Inc., 2009.

Meyer, Anna. *The DNA Detectives. How the Double Helix is Solving Puzzles of the Past*. New York: Thunder's Mouth Press, 2005.

Minsky, Marvin. *The Society of Mind*. New York: Simon and Schuster,1986.

Moore, Wendy. *The Knife Man: Blood, Body Snatching, and the Birth of Modern Surgery*. New York: Broadway Books, 2005.

McCormick, Joseph B., and Fisher-Hoch, Susan. *Level 4: Virus Hunters of the CDC*. New York: Barnes and Noble Books, 1999.

Nasar, Sylvia. *A Beautiful Mind: The Life of Mathematical Genius and Nobel Laureate John Nash*. New York: Touchstone Book, 1994.

Netz, Reviel, and Noel, William. *The Archimedes Codex: How a Midieval Prayer Book is Revealing the True Genius of Antiquity's Greatest Scientist*. Philadelphia, Pennsylvania: Da Capo Press, 2007.

Osborne, David, and Gaebler, Ted. *Reinventing Government: How the Entrepreneurial Spirit is Transforming the Public Sector*. New York: Plume Book, 1993.

Petrie, Charles J. Jr. *Enterprise Integration Modeling: Proceedings of the First International Conference*. MIT, 1992.

Picknett, Lynn, and Prince, Clive. *The Stargate Conspiracy: The Truth About Extraterrestrial Life and the Mysteries of Ancient Egypt*. New York: Berkley Books, 1999.

Preston, Richard. *The Hot Zone: A Terrifying True Story*. New York: Random House, 1994.

_____. *The Demon in the Freezer*. New York: Ballentine Books, 2002.

_____. *Panic In Level 4*. New York: Random House, 2008.

Quammen, David. *The Reluctant Mr. Darwin*. New York: W.W. Norton and Company, 2006.

Rogers, Everett M. *Diffusion of Innovations. 5th Edition*. NY: Free Press, 2003.

Sagan, Carl, and Druyan, Ann. *Shawdows of Forgotten Ancestors*. New York: Ballantine Books, 1992.

Sagan, Carl. *Pale Blue Dot: A Vision of the Human Future in Space.* New York: Random House, 1994.

_____. *Billions & Billions: Thought on Life and Death at the Brink of the Millennium.* New York: Ballantine Books, 1997.

_____. *The Demon-Haunted World: Science as a Candle in the Dark.* New York: Ballantine Books, 1997.

_____, and Druyan, Ann. *Comet.* New York: Ballantine Books, 1997.

Schulze-Makuch, Dirk, and Darling, David. *We Are Not Alone: Why We Have Already Found Extraterrestrial Life.* Oxford: Oneworld, 2010.

Scott, Christopher Thomas. *Stem Cell Now: A Brief Introduction to the Coming Medical Revolution.* New York: Plume Book, 2006.

Shreeve, James. *The Genome War.* New York: Ballantine Books, 2004.

Sitchen, Zecharia. *There Were Giants Upon The Earth.* Rochester, NY: Bear & Company, 2010.

Sobel, Dava. *Longitude: The True story of a Lone Genius Who Solved the Greatest Scientific Problem of His Time.* New York: Penguin Books, 1995.

Spewak, Steven H, and Hill, Steven C. *Enterprise Architecture Planning: Developing a Blueprint for Data, Applications and Technology.* Boston: QED Publishing Group, 1992.

Suskind, Leonard. *The Black Hole War.* New York: Back Bay Books, 2008.

Sykes, Bryan. *The Seven Daughters of Eve: The Science That Reveals Our Genetic Ancestry.* New York: W. W. Norton & Company, 2001.

Talbot, Michael. *The Holographic Universe.* New York: Harper Perennial,1991.

Temple, Robert. *The Sirius Mystery: New Scientific Evidence of Alien Contact 5,000 Years Ago.* Rochester, Vermont: Destiny Books, 1998.

Tierno, Philip M. *The Secret Life of Germs: hat They Are, Why We Need Them, and How We Can Protect Ourselves Against Them.* New York: Atria Books, 2001.

Turner, Gillian. *North Pole, South Pole:The Epic Quest to Solve the Great Mysteries of Earth's Magnetism.* New York: The Experiment, 2011.

Ward, Peter D., and Brownless, Donald. *Rare Earth:Why Complex Life is Uncommon in the Universe.* New York: Copernicus Books, 2004.

Wilber, Ken. *Quantum Questions: Mystical Writings of the World's Greatest Physicists.* Boston: Shambhala, 2001.

Wood, Lawrence. *Evolution and the Future of Mankind.* New York: iUniverse, Inc., 2010

INDEX